Teaching
Gifted
Children

Teaching Gifted Children

Success Strategies for Teaching High-Ability Learners

Edited by
**Jeff Danielian, C. Matthew Fugate, Ph.D.,
and Elizabeth Fogarty, Ph.D.**

Service Publication

NATIONAL ASSOCIATION FOR
Gifted Children

PRUFROCK PRESS INC.
WACO, TEXAS

Library of Congress Cataloging-in-Publication Data

Names: Danielian, Jeff, editor.
Title: Teaching gifted children : success strategies for teaching
  high-ability learners / edited by Jeff Danielian, C. Matthew Fugate,
  Ph.D., and Elizabeth Fogarty, Ph.D.
Description: Waco, Texas : Prufrock Press : National Association For Gifted
  Children, [2018] | "Copublished With the National Association for Gifted
  Children."
Identifiers: LCCN 2017032969 (print) | LCCN 2017034329 (ebook) | ISBN
  9781618216731 (pdf) | ISBN 9781618216748 (epub) | ISBN 9781618216724 (pbk.)
Subjects: LCSH: Gifted children--Education--United States.
Classification: LCC LC3993.9 (ebook) | LCC LC3993.9 .T438 2018 (print) | DDC
  371.95--dc23
LC record available at https://lccn.loc.gov/2017032969

Prufrock Press Inc.
P.O. Box 8813
Waco, TX 76714-8813
Phone: (800) 998-2208
Fax: (800) 240-0333
http://www.prufrock.com

Table of Contents

Acknowledgements

Ariel Baska, Jaime A. Castellano, Steve V. Coxon, Ruth Lyons, Connie Phelps, Jennifer Ritchotte, and Sarah Sumners, for their careful review of the entire catalog of *Teaching for High Potential* (*THP*) issues. Without them, the process would not have been able to move forward.

Jane Clarenbach, for her keen eye and everlasting involvement with the publication of each and every issue of *THP*. Her work has been invaluable.

Richard M. Cash, Joy Lawson Davis, Rebecca D. Eckert, and Thomas P. Hébert, for their willingness to read through sections of the book and write a thoughtful introduction to an assigned section. In addition, we thank Rebecca for her work as the first editor of *THP* for the inaugural issue in 2006. She opened the door for what was to come.

Joseph S. Renzulli, for his initial inspiration, which led to the creation of *THP*. His continued support and encouragement moves the field and our individual ideas forward.

Stacy Frankel, *THP*'s designer, whose expert layout and attention to detail is noticed in each and every issue.

Katy McDowall, our editor, who has made the process as smooth and enjoyable as possible. It has been an honor to work with her.

Foreword: Where the Rubber Meets the Road

A How-to Guide For Promoting
the Goals of Gifted Education

by Joseph S. Renzulli

> The test of all beliefs is their practical effect in life.
>
> —Helen Keller

The field of gifted education has benefitted from many years of high-quality research, theory development, and commentary about issues related to our field. This material has served as a solid foundation that gives any and all fields of study their unique identity. The real payoff of all this research and development, however, has no value until it can be translated into effective classroom practices. In order to make changes in the lives of the young people we serve, these practices must be easy for teachers to learn and to use and reasonable to integrate within the complexities of the industrial education establishment. Variations in financial support, local and state regulations, and administrative and parental expectations must be addressed by people who have "been there" and understand teachers' ways of knowing and doing. The editors of *Teaching for High Potential* have purposefully selected these practitioner-friendly writers because they have the know-how and the how-to for addressing the kinds of action that can bring about the brand of learning so necessary to challenge the hearts and minds of our most able learners.

Whether the focus of your program is on acceleration and improved achievement test scores, general enrichment activities, more depth and complexity in curriculum, creative productivity, or combinations of all of these special programming options, the payoff for teachers is how they can make these things happen in their classrooms. Equally important, and what is captured so effectively in this book, is the practical advice about classroom practices provided by persons who are or have been directly involved in classrooms. Notable advantages of this book are concerns for factors beyond instruction—factors that contribute to effective program organization, learner characteristics, classroom environments, social-emotional development, the role of technology in learning, and issues related to special populations and underrepresented students. These issues, together with the instructional guidance provided in this book, encompass the real world of the classroom, which teachers of the gifted deal with on a daily basis. The classroom is where "the rubber meets the road," and this book is as good as it gets for the wisdom provided in the above quotation by Helen Keller.

Editors' Note

The efforts of educators never cease to amaze me. From the bottom up or top down, the trials and tribulations faced on every level, and over time, the issues they address and overcome are enough to frazzle even the strongest of resolves. The kindergartner with the oversized backpack becomes the hopeful college freshman. A first-year teacher, lesson plans in hand, blooms into a mentor, guide, and expert educator. Administrators, glassy-eyed and tired amidst mountains of paperwork and decision making, find a way to manage and lead. Advocates press on amidst pushback and resistance, and writers and researchers alike offer the products of years of thought and study. Each situation presents a continuous journey, for all involved play a part in this giant perpetual educational engine. The key to a successful expedition lies in continual commitment, understanding, communication, and an endless pursuit of knowledge.

As educators, we need to be supported in our endeavors to create environments that take into account the immense variations present in our schools. The students that make up our classrooms are different in so many ways. Each requires numerous instructional strategies and responses to ensure that classrooms are places where discovery and experience are at the forefront, and where each student is treated and respected as an individual learner, with potential to succeed in any area. The outcome—students who possess a love for learning and appreciation for the education they receive. In this way, we can truly make education better for each student. Talent, whether latent, emergent, or manifest, should be understood, nurtured, and encouraged.

As often happens when routines become commonplace, expectations and assumptions become part of the fabric of our lives. Statements such as "that's the way it's always been," or "that's how we've always done things" are often the last words of a conversation. If we fail to stay abreast of new developments in our field—about best practice, definitions of giftedness, and student identification, among other important topics—how can we possibly expect our students to develop a keen interest for themselves in the importance and value of investigation as a path to greater understanding? How many students have become complacent in stagnant classrooms, expecting nothing above the ordinary, for they have never known what it means to be challenged? How many teachers are satisfied with textbook questions and definitions at the end of each chapter, relying on multiple choice questions, letter grades, and standardized tests as motivating factors in their classroom? How many twice-exceptional students have been diagnosed with syndromes and disorders before their talents were recognized, and how many of them were identified with talents, assuming everything else would fall into place?

We have the power to change our schools, our students, and our educational system. We have the power to recognize talent, serve the students identified, and pass on our understanding to other educators. We have the power to advocate—for ourselves, our students, and our vocation.

I'm hopeful for the field of gifted and talented! I really am. Despite the grunts and groans in reaction to an education system that seems to dismiss what our field stands for, I am hopeful for the future—for new opportunities to learn from experts in gifted education and to share what I've learned with interested colleagues. I have to be. We have to be. Our students are depending on us.

It has been 11 years since the first publication of the National Association for Gifted Children's *Teaching for High Potential* (*THP*), and in that time, *THP* has found a great niche in the field and a collective group of voices to carry it. Throughout that time the mission has remained the same: to provide practical guidance and classroom-based materials for educators striving to understand and challenge their high-potential students. This collection highlights the most highly rated articles and columns from a catalog of more than 500 published works. It is our hope that it will become a new and valued resource for you.

—Jeff

As educators who work with the gifted, we know that there is no such thing as "the ideal gifted student." The image of the student who sits, intently hanging on our every word is a myth. These students challenge us every day. They come from a variety of backgrounds and experiences. They ask questions. They seek out new ways to look at problems, usually in a manner that contradicts what we have just taught. In short, *they teach us*! Working in a teacher preparation program, I often tell the preservice teachers in my courses that if you walk out of your classroom at the end of the day and your students have not taught *you* something, then it has been a bad day.

When I worked as a classroom teacher and gifted coordinator, I was always on the lookout for resources and tools that would benefit my students' growth and development. All too often, what I would find sounded "cute" but seemed to have little evidence of being anything more than that. When I would turn to research journals, the results described in the articles would often sound interesting, but more times than not I would find myself asking, "So what? How does this help my students?" Since moving to a research focus, I have made it a priority to answer those questions in my own work. That is what I love about *THP*. It builds a bridge between the practices and theories identified through research and connects them to the work being done every day by "the boots on the ground"—the teachers, paraprofessionals, and administrators in the schools throughout our country who have dedicated themselves to their students.

When Jeff first approached me with the idea of creating this anthology, I knew that it had the potential to be a valuable resource for teachers. Personally, I know that over the years I have read many articles from the journal that have inspired me and provided a road map for strategies focused on increasing student achievement. With the best of intentions, I have saved these articles to refer to as situations arose so that I could put them to good use—some saved with success, and others that ended up buried under a stack on my desk only to be found sometime later, after the moment had passed. This book represents the very best of the articles from the first 11 years of *THP* all in one place. We have been blessed to have some of the very best minds—at the university, state, district, and school levels—as contributors to this journal. These are people who are passionate about gifted education and want to share that passion with others. It has been one of the highest honors of my career to be a part of this journal and I hope that you find this book to be a valuable resource.

—Matt

I had *that* conversation again with a colleague just last week. You know the one, right? You've had this conversation at least 10 times yourself. It's the one where you justify the need for gifted education. Again. And the trouble is that I'm having the conversation with people whose work I respect, people who are excellent teachers. And I wonder to myself, "How do they not understand that gifted kids also need rigor and challenge and deserve to learn something new every day?" The problem is that we are *still* justifying the need for gifted education all these years later.

Thinking about my own career in teaching, I've come to realize that justifying what we know to be true and right for kids can be one of the hardest parts about our job. When we feel as if we have to work so hard to justify what we know is right for kids, it can be exhausting and leave little time for the real work of teaching. This might be the conversation you had last week when you convinced a colleague that the gifted student should not have to sit through the multiplication chapter because she's already demonstrated that she can multiply . . . and do long division . . . and algebra. . . . Or it could be that conversation when your principal mentioned he didn't believe your school had ever enrolled a gifted student; and you realized he'd been the principal there for 10 years. In times like these, when you must don your armor and go once more into the breach to defend your students, try to remember that you are not alone. There are many like you who are also working to create space for gifted students in systems where that space does not exist.

When I came on board as associate editor for *THP* many years ago, I realized that *Teaching for High Potential* is the resource that I needed when I was in the classroom. Back then I used to wonder, "Doesn't anyone else see these students? Doesn't anyone recognize how different their learning needs are from their peers'?" If *THP* had been in publication, I would have been able to hear from educators around the country and the world who share their solutions to the questions with which I'd been grappling. And I might have felt a little less like an island, and a little more like a fisherwoman casting her nets wide for the best ideas for her little school.

Because you now have this little treasure, this edited *THP* volume, you have access to knowledge and insight from people who understand the needs of gifted students. You can utilize their solutions for some of those stay-awake-at-night kinds of challenges you've been facing. And I know that this book will help you with those. It's all in here. But I'm wondering if this book can also help us with what's *out there*. You know, those conversations with others about why gifted education is necessary and defensible. I think it can help us with those challenges as well. It's up to us to share the information provided in this volume with those who don't think they've ever met a gifted student, or have never heard of curriculum compacting. It's up to us to share this information with those who don't have it. After all, isn't that what we do?

—Liz

PART / I

Classroom Practices
by Richard M. Cash

Like many teachers of the gifted, my first experiences with gifted students were like being thrown into the deep end of a volcano. I had no knowledge of who gifted students where, what they needed, or how to teach them. My credentials, along with an education degree, included a degree in theater; therefore, it was believed I would be fine with gifted and *talented* students. *Not so*!

What I learned very quickly as a teacher of gifted students is the curricular and instructional practices learned during "teacher school" were insufficient to meet the needs of my students. Most of my students were already proficient or knowledgeable about the general curriculum. I was not provided recourse to take my students into deeper levels of age-appropriate materials. My students would often ask questions well beyond the levels of the general curriculum—leaving me to try and answer those questions. Plus, my students craved to go further with topics of interest than I had materials. This truly was baptism by lava!

This part of the book contains a wealth of information regarding effective classroom practices for gifted students. The first part provides an overview of gifted education. To be able to apply effective practice for gifted students, teachers must have a comprehensive knowledge of the whole gifted child and the needs for a quality gifted program. Therefore, the first two chapters cover both the need for identification, as well as ideas for developing talent.

The classroom environment has a significant impact on how students learn. All classrooms should be safe for risk-taking and welcoming of diversity. In a gifted classroom the space becomes a place for exploring new ideas, discussing controversial issues, building an understanding of different points of view and of scholarly dispositions and each author brings a dimension to consider.

Another way to look at changing up the space in the classroom for gifted students is through the use of Socratic seminars. The authors in this section aptly show how the Socratic process actually enhances student learning and benefits argumentative writing and provide the logistical nuts and bolts and methodology to use Socratic Circles in your classroom to increase critical, evaluative, and synthetic thinking.

The next group of chapters offers insight into creativity in the classroom for gifted students. In my experience as a classroom teacher, I found many of my gifted students reticent to attempt creativity, whether in actions or production. Additionally, some of my students controlled a fixed mindset—they were only as smart as their last right answer—where fear of failure possessed them. Creativity has no sure "right" answer. This section is helpful in understanding the critical nature of creativity in the gifted classroom and authors explore the barriers to and concerns over teaching creativity in the gifted classroom, offering solid arguments for the inclusion of this essential tool.

The final chapters provide varying methods and perspectives on planning curriculum and teaching thinking skills and lay the foundation for best practices in teaching gifted students. Far beyond the curriculum design offered in my teacher training, the strategies here offer best practices in differentiation. Several authors offer advice on examining students' depth of thinking, especially in relation to examining essential questions and the use of Bloom's taxonomy in curriculum development. Authors in this section encourage us to really delve into looking at curriculum with fresh eyes, one encouraging the teaching of current events, another advocating that we examine the epistemology behind the learning we impart, and the third encouraging us to plan with a more conceptual lens. One chapter in this section focuses entirely on the process of compacting curriculum so that we may provide greater challenge to those students demonstrating previous mastery of content. This section concludes with a self-assessment we can use to check up on our progress in utilizing best practices for teaching gifted students.

I hope that you will find these chapters as valuable as I have and I only wish I might have utilized these in my own days teaching gifted and talented students. Moving beyond trial by fire, these strategies offer ways for us to teach in a manner that is engaging and gets students "fired up" about learning.

Section I: General Gifted Education

Chapter 1

A Guide to Teaching the Gifted

What We Need to Know . . . and
Why We Need to Know It

by Rachel Levinson

As a teacher, I am constantly bombarded with questions when it comes to educating my most advanced students. Such questions come from every side, but the most pressing ones come from my own conscience. In striving to be the best teacher I can be, I am constantly asking myself whether I am meeting the needs of *all* of my students.

The population known as "gifted" is often the most overlooked. People often assume these students are just fine on their own. After all, they would probably pass the state test even if they didn't show up for school all year! Others think that calling some kids "gifted" fosters elitism and makes other children feel inferior. Given these opinions about gifted students, I asked myself whether it is even necessary to have such a label. Why do we care who is "gifted" and who is "not gifted"? Should we lose the label altogether and just look for what Renzulli (2005) calls "gifted behaviors"? Using "gifted" as an adjective rather than a noun is certainly appealing. Borland (2005) suggests that we dispense with the idea of gifted children altogether. He proposes that we instead focus on providing appropriate modifications to curriculum and instruction for all children, because every child is different on an individual (and not categorical) level. In this way, there would be no need for labeling or classifying children, as their differing needs and readiness levels at any given time would be recognized and addressed.

"Why isn't my child in the accelerated math program?"—parent
"What do I do with a student who already knows everything I'm supposed to teach?"—teacher
"How come I'm the only one in the class who goes to TAG?"—student

---

I wish it were that simple. Unfortunately, there can be no aid for meeting students' needs if there is no identification, and there can be no identification without a definition. However, given the controversy over the "g" word, it would be prudent to use it only when doing so will serve a greater purpose. To that end, I suggest a definition of giftedness that is needs based. Teachers need to be able to identify children who are gifted only when it is a necessary step toward meeting an individual student's needs. A good teacher should almost always be able to provide developmentally appropriate learning experiences for students who fall within two standard deviations from the norm. Labels only become necessary when the teacher needs to provide something more than what can typically be provided through differentiation within the regular classroom. Being able to identify the gifted students will help guide a teacher's actions both within the regular classroom and in reaching out to other resources when necessary.

Identification and Education: Why and How?

There are three basic reasons a "gifted" student may need to be identified, whether formally or informally (see Figure 1.1):

1. to better understand some of the social-emotional issues that may accompany advanced cognitive abilities;
2. to qualify students for specific preexisting special programs for the gifted, such as school-sponsored afterschool programs, a pull-out program, or special summer camps; and
3. to be aware of a greater need for differentiation in the classroom, and in some cases, to validate a drastically modified curriculum.

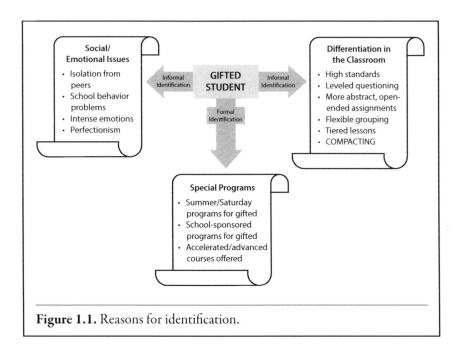

Figure 1.1. Reasons for identification.

Social-Emotional Issues

Due to their advanced cognitive abilities, gifted students may experience certain issues more intensely than their peers. This leads to certain social and emotional problems that are often misunderstood or ignored (Davis & Rimm, 2004). Here are a few examples of the most common of these issues:

▸ isolation—difficulty interacting/connecting with peers;

▸ behavior—frustration and boredom may lead to school behavior problems;

▸ intense emotions—depression, anxiety about world problems (e.g., hunger, war, and death); and

▸ perfectionism—intense fear of failure; unrealistic, self-imposed standards.

Many experts in the field have recommended that counseling be an integral part of any program for the gifted (Davis & Rimm, 2004). Although this would be extremely beneficial, the fact remains that school counselors are often overburdened with students. Additionally, many regular school counselors are not trained to understand and counsel gifted students. These students' social-emotional issues are numerous and serious, but who can help them in their time of need? With the ideal situation in the back of our minds, we need to think about what we as teachers can do now to help gifted students cope with such issues.

Identification. The identification process rooted in social and emotional behaviors is usually quite informal and relies upon observation. Just like a physician, teachers must be able to observe certain behaviors and provide a timely and accurate assessment. Identifying a problem early may make all the difference in a child's development. To do this, teachers and others in the school building need to have some basic knowledge of these issues.

Simply being aware that there are social-emotional issues connected to giftedness may help teachers and others connect the dots. This minimal goal can be met through a one-time professional development session for the entire school, with the possibility for additional follow-up training for those who express more interest.

Intervention. An understanding and supportive teacher presents the greatest variable in the education of a gifted child. Behavior problems caused by boredom can be remedied through more challenging class work, once a teacher recognizes that there is a need. Students who have difficulty connecting with their peers may benefit from a class or program for the gifted where they will be able to interact with students more like themselves. Teachers can also make parents aware of the issues, recommending that they learn more about their child's particular issues. Once the problem is identified, the adults in a child's life will be able to react more appropriately to each situation, and thus ease the often-misunderstood relationship between the adult and the child. Table 1.1 shows how identification can alter the way a teacher reacts to a student's social and emotional needs.

Special Programs

Special programs for gifted students are varied in design, intensity, frequency, and purpose. Part of a teacher's job may be to recommend a student for a school-sponsored gifted program. This could be anything from an afterschool enrichment session that occurs once a week to a full-time, self-contained gifted class.

Identification. Schools usually use a combination of criteria to select students for gifted programs (VanTassel-Baska, 2005). The tools of identification should match the program, of course. For example, a student would not take a

TABLE 1.1

Identification and Social-Emotional Needs

Situation	Without Identification	With Identification
Max is disruptive in class. He frequently interrupts lessons to call out ideas or make a joke.	Max is disciplined with increasing severity. Trips to the vice principal become frequent. Max begins to see himself as the "bad kid" and, fed up with the system, ends up dropping out of high school.	Max's teacher recognizes that he is bored and frustrated. The teacher begins to provide more challenging work for him and also recommends him for accelerated learning in an advanced course. Max finds renewed interest in school, and by the end of the year, his behavior problems are less evident.
Max is very upset every time he receives any grade below 100.	Max's teacher tells him that his grades are very good and he should be proud of himself. Max is never satisfied by a brief remark, and eventually this fear of failure causes him to underachieve, first by not turning in assignments, and later expresses itself as an unwillingness to participate in any extracurricular activities.	Max's teacher recognizes aspects of perfectionism, speaks to his parents about it, and together, through suggested resources and strategies, they try to help Max understand and deal with his perfectionism, recognizing it as a characteristic of his giftedness to be overcome.

written test to get into advanced band. Similarly, a 500-word essay may not help determine whether to place a student into an accelerated math class. Because each program has specific qualifications and objectives, the identification process must be formal. Teachers must follow whatever formal identification process the school requires.

When teacher recommendations are used, the teacher must be able to answer questions about the student being considered. Objectives of the program must be made clear, in order that the teacher will be better equipped to answer the questions and identify students who would be a good match for the program.

1. Is this domain in the student's strength and/or interest area?
2. Does the student possess the prerequisite knowledge?
3. Does the student have the ability and/or motivation to keep pace?
4. Would the student benefit from this program? How?

Carefully considering these questions should help any teacher decide whether to recommend a student for a given program.

Intervention. Matching a specific student, or keeping an eye out for other underidentified students suited for the program, presents the largest role for the regular classroom teacher. To avoid elitism and conflict, teachers are also responsible for cultivating an accepting environment to support differences in students' learning needs. When necessary, teachers should articulate that special school programs and services exist because students learn differently, and learning experiences that these students require are often not provided in the regular classroom. Students should come to understand that they are being given learning opportunities that are best for them, regardless of what other students in the class may be doing.

Differentiation in the Classroom

The first essential component to helping gifted students in the regular classroom is to have consistently high expectations. In my experience, children will only work as hard and perform as well as we expect them to perform. Therefore, try to keep the bar as high as possible to encourage growth, good work habits, and self-efficacy. Teaching to the middle or low end of the class is not only frustrating for the gifted kids, but will actually be counterproductive for the majority of students. According to Vygotsky's (1978) Zone of Proximal Development, children learn best when they are reaching just outside their comfort zone. A challenging environment with plenty of support from the teacher is an ideal way to reach a larger pool of students, keeping them all engaged.

Although maintaining high expectations is a helpful way to keep students challenged and engaged most of the time, there are times when teachers must alter the content, process, or product in some way to meet individual needs. There are many and varied ways to differentiate, from leveled questioning to tiered activities. Carol Ann Tomlinson (2001) offers a comprehensive guide for teachers to the why, what, and how of differentiating at all readiness levels. Incorporating some of these differentiation strategies will help classroom teachers challenge an even greater range of students.

There sometimes comes a point when the curriculum itself is the problem, and teachers must make more drastic adjustments. The most effective way to do this is through curriculum compacting (Reis, Burns, & Renzulli, 1992). This strategy allows the most advanced students to prove what they know and move on to more developmentally appropriate activities, projects, skills, and/or curriculum concepts.

Identification. The identification process for classroom differentiation is largely informal, but teachers must be able to support their decisions. Much of the identification process rests on knowing students very well. In the beginning of the year, teachers should administer a learning styles inventory, an interest inventory, and a placement test in each subject. It is beneficial to keep records, so that at any time, recommendations can be made.

Intervention. Once the students have been identified, the process becomes a bit more formal, but extremely flexible. Tomlinson (2001) presents a number of differentiation strategies that can be utilized as interventions. Curriculum compacting, mentioned previously, is also a flexible strategy for advanced differentiation that all teachers may implement in their own way. Once intervention strategies have been targeted for a specific student population, professional development is necessary to give teachers the background knowledge needed to understand how to go about using them and the confidence to succeed. It is also essential that there be an individual available for support should anyone have questions and concerns.

Conclusion

There is much to be done to improve the educational experiences of gifted children in regular classrooms throughout the country. Teachers are the front line. Theorists in the field of gifted education have produced volumes of research, articulated lofty conceptions, and designed some excellent systems and models. However, it is up to the *teachers* to implement these ideas effectively. All regular classroom teachers, and those being trained to teach at present, should be educated about the characteristics and needs of the gifted and talented children. They should also have access to the resources, services, and programs available to schools and districts. Identifying a child as gifted is only useful if some action results from it. Teachers need help understanding when and how to identify gifted students, but most importantly, they need to understand *why* they are identifying students.

References

Borland, J. H. (2005). Gifted education without gifted children: The case for no conception of giftedness. In R. J. Sternberg & J. Davidson (Eds.), *Conceptions of giftedness* (2nd ed., pp. 1–19). New York, NY: Cambridge University Press.

Davis, G. A., & Rimm, S. B. (2004). *Education of the gifted and talented* (5th ed.). Boston, MA: Pearson.

Reis, S. M., Burns, D. E., & Renzulli, J. S. (1992). *Curriculum compacting: The complete guide to modifying the regular curriculum for high-ability students.* Mansfield Center, CT: Creative Learning Press.

Renzulli, J. S. (2005). The three-ring conception of giftedness: A developmental model for promoting creative productivity. In R. J. Sternberg & J. Davidson (Eds.), *Conceptions of giftedness* (2nd ed., pp. 246–279). New York, NY: Cambridge University Press.

Tomlinson, C. A. (2001). *How to differentiate instruction in mixed-ability classrooms* (2nd ed.). Alexandria, VA: Association for Supervision and Curriculum Development.

VanTassel-Baska, J. (2005). Domain-specific giftedness: Applications in school and life. In R. J. Sternberg & J. Davidson (Eds.), *Conceptions of giftedness* (2nd ed., pp. 358–376). New York, NY: Cambridge University Press.

Vygotsky, L. S. (1978). *Mind in society: The development of higher psychological processes.* Cambridge, MA: Harvard University Press.

Chapter 2

Bridging the Divide

Building on the Best of Gifted Education With Programming for Talent Development

by Paula Olszewski-Kubilius,
Rena F. Subotnik, and Frank C. Worrell

In our monograph, *Rethinking Giftedness and Gifted Education: A Proposed Direction Forward Based on Psychological Science* (2011), which was the basis for our Fall 2012 article in *Gifted Child Quarterly*, we argued for a framework for gifted education that emphasizes several critical components. The identification of exceptional ability in children, especially domain-specific abilities, is important and should be early and continuous. Different talent areas (e.g., music, mathematics) have unique developmental trajectories, including different starting points, peaks, and endpoints, and because of these trajectories, different kinds of opportunities should be provided at every stage of development, specifically, ones that match the domain and students' level of developed talent within the domain. Gifted students must take advantage of opportunities and demonstrate commitment through sustained effort at some point along these developmental trajectories. Psychosocial skills, such as mindsets and persistence, are vitally important and should be systematically developed in talented students and not left to chance. Finally, the outcome of gifted education should be to help more gifted individuals find meaningful ways to contribute creatively to society.

What are the implications for K–12 education?

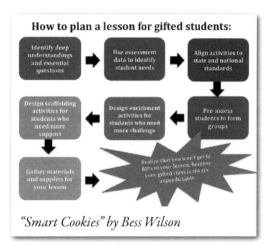

How to plan a lesson for gifted students:

Identify deep understandings and essential questions ➡ Use assessment data to identify student needs ➡ Align activities to state and national standards

Design scaffolding activities for students who need more support ⬅ Design enrichment activities for students who need more challenge ⬅ Pre-assess students to form groups

Gather materials and supplies for your lesson ➡ Realize that you won't get to 80% of your lesson, because your gifted class is always unpredictable.

"Smart Cookies" by Bess Wilson

Identification procedures should assess exceptional ability in domains of talent. This is especially needed in the upper grades, in addition to identifying high general ability.

Teachers should use advanced curriculum with children who already manifest giftedness. In order to spot burgeoning creative writers, budding scientists, and nascent mathematicians, advanced curriculum can be used to bring out talent, especially in children who have had fewer early opportunities to learn.

Provide opportunities for growth to children at different levels of developed talent. For example, begin to offer enrichment opportunities in mathematics for children with developing interests (e.g., afterschool clubs or within-class enrichment) and emerging talents as well as opportunities for acceleration and very advanced work for children who are making rapid growth through the content area. (See Treffinger's work on levels of service, http://www.creativelearning.com.)

Assess for talent early but provide opportunities to capture late bloomers. Keep the doors to opportunities open to students who may not demonstrate interest or ability or commitment to achievement until they are older.

Specify and implement an articulated series of talent development opportunities within each core subject area. Work continuously with students to increase higher levels of competence, which incorporates "critical" experiences specific to each domain (e.g., research experience in science, opportunities for critique of work by professionals in performance domains).

Remove any barriers that hold students and their individual pacing back. These include obstacles to dual enrollment or credit for outside-of-school coursework, policies against any form of acceleration, or policies linking credit solely to seat time.

Place more emphasis on the development of psychosocial skills supportive of giftedness and high achievement. Attempt to integrate these into programming and day-to-day classroom activities. Skills include intellectual risk-taking, coping, and resiliency needed to deal with choosing a less traveled path and being different, appropriate attitudes toward effort and study, and mindsets supportive of doing advanced and challenging work.

Be clear about expectations for demonstrated achievement. Clearly specify the indicators that a student is making sufficient progress to be able to continue onto more challenging learning activities within a particular domain.

Make sure that programs and services acknowledge and support a variety of gifted learners. These include underrepresented students, underachieving students, twice-exceptional students, and highly gifted students.

Make sure that all teachers are trained to be "talent spotters." Recognizing the signs of giftedness and talent within students from diverse socioeconomic, geographical, cultural, and linguistic backgrounds and within various domains of talent is a key element of identification.

Make sure that all teachers are trained in and use gifted education best practices in their classrooms. Acceleration, ability cluster grouping, problem-based learning, inquiry-based learning, curriculum compacting, and differentiation are just a few of the many strategies available.

There is great diversity among gifted students in terms of their talent areas, their levels of achievement, and their psychological and social characteristics. Our goal with the ideas we presented in Subotnik et al. (2011) is to generate discussion and thinking in the field about additional ways to envision programs and services that will provide opportunities and contexts to enable all gifted students, those with demonstrated ability and those with potential, to find meaningful outlets for their talents and abilities, gain competencies in their talent areas, and acquire the psychological and social skills and receive the social and emotional support needed to become creative contributors to our society.

Reference

Subotnik, R. F., Olszewski-Kubilius, P., & Worrell, F. C. (2011). Rethinking giftedness and gifted education: A proposed direction forward based on psychological science. *Psychological Science in the Public Interest, 12,* 3–54.

Editor's Note: In order to connect current research and theory with quality classroom practice, issues of *THP* periodically contain a complementary article to one found in the pages of *Gifted Child Quarterly*. It presents a brief look at an issue and associated educational implications. A more expanded version of this column is originally published in *TEMPO*, published by the Texas Association for the Gifted and Talented, http://www.txgifted.org/tempo, as well as in the NAGC Professional Development newsletter, http://www.nagc.org/get-involved/nagc-networks-and-special-interest-groups/networks-professional-development.

Section II: Changing Classroom Spaces

Three Reasons to Plan an Advocacy Field Trip

by Kathryn Fishman-Weaver

A young man in a black suit and red tie raises the heavy gavel. As it strikes, the sound reverberates across the Senate. Instinctively everyone looks up. No, the young man is not the speaker pro tem, at least not yet. For now, he is still one of my high school students.

I recently took a group of eight high school students to our state capital to advocate for gifted education. Student advocacy provided us with several powerful learning opportunities including: personal affective growth, authentic learning, and civic action.

I believe this field trip could be replicated in any secondary program, in any district within driving distance of its state's capital. I planned our field trip in conjunction with the state gifted association's education day. There are many such educational associations to partner with for a similar field trip although you could also create your own advocacy day. For more information about what your state is doing, visit NAGC's "Gifted By State" webpage.

Preparation

My students and I spent 2 months preparing for advocacy day. We held regular before-school practices to perfect our education "elevator" speeches—very brief statements explaining our purpose in being at the capitol building. At one of our practices we met with a lobbyist for additional coaching. I began trying to schedule meetings with legislators 7 weeks before our visits and received a great response. Our preparation was rewarded with an empowering field experience at the state capitol building. There are at least three key advantages that this type of advocacy experience provides students. They learn that their voice matters, they see the political process in action, and they learn that they can be powerful advocates for education.

Students Learn Their Voice Matters

A poised young woman speaks passionately (and concisely) about the role service learning has played in her own experiences and development as a learner. The representative she is speaking with is fully engaged, nodding as my student makes her key points. After my student's short speech, the representative affirms her with a genuine "well said" and a follow-up question on service learning.

Researchers have found that a majority of teachers of the gifted ranked the teaching of processing skills such as problem solving, critical thinking, and research as a priority in their classrooms. However, fewer of these teachers placed a priority on communication skills and personal growth and human relations (Rash & Miller, 2000). As an educator, teaching my students that their voices matter may be the most important benefit of student advocacy. As with all authentic learning opportunities, on advocacy day my students saw that their preparation and efforts mattered. Students were in real legislative meetings, sharing and defending their opinions. In the classroom, I teach public speaking, critical thinking, and synthesis. However, when my students can apply those skills in real-world environments, these lessons take on a significance I can't replicate in the traditional classroom. On advocacy day my students were asked tough questions by their legislators about current events and educational issues. My students took pride in wanting to be heard. Because their voices were valued, they were thoughtful and articulate in their responses. Formulating and defending tight arguments is a skill that cuts across content areas and it is one my students had to employ several times throughout our advocacy field trip. One representative shared that our students were the most eloquent speakers he had heard all day, including while he was in session. This compliment was visibly empowering to our team.

Students Can See the Political Process in Action

The students are seated at a long bench behind the senate research team. Senators are debating a bill on proactive planning for school districts that are unable to fiscally complete the school year. My students are literally on the edge of their seats straining to read the books and notes that researchers pass to senators while in the midst of debate.

McNall (2011) stated that, "service learning, as opposed to just service, deepens disciplinary knowledge" (p. 62). Many of my students had toured the capitol building in elementary school, but they hadn't seen a legislative session in action. On advocacy day we spent time in both the Senate and the House. We were fortunate to have a relationship with a senator who has championed gifted education. He offered to introduce my students on the floor. In addition to the pomp and circumstance of yet again being validated as important guests, my students enjoyed a front row seat to the political process.

The contrast between the civil debate in the Senate and the flurry of activity in the House of Representatives was stark. In the House, my students' eyes darted back and forth trying to make sense of the scene before them. Several representatives came off the floor to visit with us. A representative from our district talked to my group for a long time, patiently answering my students' questions about the real-time political activity going on behind us.

As we were walking to lunch afterward, a student shared that a recent AP Government open essay question asked her to describe the differences between the House and the Senate. She told me enthusiastically, "I have so much evidence for this question, now!"

Students Are Powerful
Advocates for Education

A high school freshman shares how in elementary school she was treated like a "done student," meaning she finished her work quickly and teachers didn't have a plan for her once she was done. However, she smiles, in her gifted classes she was never treated as though she was finished learning. The representative we are speaking with starts nodding. He tells us he is from a rural area with no gifted programming. He shares that although he hadn't thought of it that way, he was also a "done student," and he remembers getting into trouble when he finished his work. He asks my students for their ideas for rural gifted programs. He asks for more information about our program. He tells my students this is the first time he feels like he truly understands gifted education and then he promises us his support.

Who better to speak on K–12 education than K–12 students? My students were able to offer their rich and current perspectives on educational programs. Theirs was a fresh perspective in our adult-centered capital. By seeing themselves as agents of change who had the courage to take a stand on gifted education in our state, these students became what Kronick, Cunningham, and Gourley (2011) called "transformational leaders" (p. 121). I am confident that we indeed gained at least one new supporter for gifted programming. This support is the direct result of my students' testimony. Students are inside experts on K–12 education. Their lived experiences speak directly to the effectiveness (and shortcomings) of educational policies, practices, and programs. This firsthand perspective is valuable to our educational leaders and policymakers.

Conclusion

The energy in my car on the drive back to school is charged. Students are buzzing with the things they have learned and seen. On their own, each of the students offers ways they can get involved in public service/policy. One young woman wants to be an attorney general; another shares her ideas about health care policy. A third student asks me to point her to more information about social welfare.

In the 6 hours we spent at the capitol, my students were empowered with the important knowledge that even at a young age they could impact change. They saw how their voices mattered. The confidence to be able to speak to those in power will serve my students indefinitely. They saw firsthand the complexity of the political process and were able to participate actively in that process, including engagement in a debate on health care reform that afternoon. During our legislative meetings students advocated passionately for education in general, and gifted education in particular. Their stories did not fall on deaf ears. All of the learning that occurred on advocacy day was applied, social, and high level.

Check your calendars, form a student team, and try making the state capitol building your classroom for a day. With some work, you will see learning come alive. For more information on advocating for gifted and talented students, visit NAGC's advocacy webpages.

References

Kronick, R. F., Cunningham, R. B., & Gourley, M. (2011). *Experiencing service-learning*. Knoxville, TN: University of Tennessee Press.

McNall, S. G. (2011). What's the matter with American democracy? Responding by embracing civic engagement and sustainability. In T. McDonald (Ed.), *Social responsibility and sustainability: Multidisciplinary perspectives through service learning* (pp. 61–77). Sterling, VA: Stylus.

Rash, P. K., & Miller, A. D. (2000). A survey of practices of teachers of the gifted. *Roeper Review, 22,* 192–194.

Chapter 4

Making a Makerspace

by Steve V. Coxon

With humble beginnings as a means by which adults would rent work-shop space and chip in together to afford expensive tools, Makerspaces are now making their way into schools. I recently toured five Makerspaces in my region geared for kids and am excited by the possibilities they afford for STEM learning. In Makerspaces, technology and engineering are often naturally incorporated, and teachers can provide structure to purposefully incorporate math and science.

The Makerspaces for children that I visited were all quite different: (1) a spare classroom at an elementary school, (2) a section of a middle school library, (3) a dedicated classroom in an inner-city charter high school, (4) a space in a private school showcased behind floor-to-ceiling windows near the school's entryway, and (5) within a children's museum. Some spaces had a dedicated staff member, while others could be used by any teacher in the building with their own planning. Some spaces were very high-tech with 3-D printers, Arduino programming equipment, and wind tunnels. Others focused on recyclables and craft materials. Most had a combination of both high- and low-tech materials. Some things they all had in common: lots of table space for students to work, great organization, and a wealth of age-appropriate tools.

What a Makerspace Is . . . and Isn't

A Makerspace is for open-ended creating, not teacher-led projects. It could be with LEGO robotics, computer hardware, or cardboard, but as an easy test: Student products should not look the same in the end. This doesn't mean that students won't decide to use online resources such as those listed on the following page, but the decisions should be theirs, and the resources, including online instructions, are generally just jumping-off points for unique creations. Teacher-led activities, projects or crafts with single answers, and step-by-step instructions are not the hallmarks of a Makerspace.

Tying in Science

When possible, it is ideal if students come up with their own problems for which they create novel solutions. However, this can be within specific content areas. Makerspace ties in well with many science objectives. Providing a problem statement, as in problem-based learning, is ideal here.

Pose a simple question like: "We need to find good ways to float 20 pennies in this water tub for at least 5 minutes." In this case, young students can learn about sinking and floating through a range of materials, such as notecards, cardboard, plastic wrap, balloons, foil, tape, and more. To appeal to older students, simply bumping it up with a great deal more weight, such as a brick, works well.

Biology can be incorporated by asking students to create a newly discovered animal with behavioral and structural adaptations to capture prey and avoid predators, for example. Students should have access to scissors and tape, pipe cleaners, paper towel rolls, googly eyes, and much more.

The concept of electricity also can be incorporated, such as open and closed circuits, by having students build vehicles with on and off switches run by small motors with wires and batteries. Cardboard, dowels, and various craft materials can be used to construct vehicles.

As a rule, I find it best to use vague language: vehicle instead of car; floatation device instead of boat; airborne object instead of plane or parachute. This helps to skirt around students' preconceived notions of what they'll build, leaning more on creative thought. For example, a car is perceived as having four wheels, but a vehicle is much more open-ended.

What to Stock in Your Makerspace

The most important aspect of a Makerspace is organization. Storage systems are nice, especially when everything is easily visible to students. However, I saw one Makerspace where everything was stored in cardboard boxes. This method worked very well. Keeping things organized is a high priority, but it does not need to be expensive.

Makerspace tools for kids should include scissors, markers, hot glue guns, a sewing machine, LEGO robotics kits, pipe cleaners, batteries, computers, tape, video cameras, Arduino programmers, and Makey Makey electronic kits, to name just a few. Recyclables such as cardboard, wood, and plastic bottles can be very useful in student projects. Many towns have a recycling center where large amounts of these consumable materials, donated by local businesses, can be purchased for minimal cost by teachers. In addition, large tables or work areas are a must. Students should be able to work and move around the area with ease.

Makerspaces offer innovative STEM opportunities for high-ability students. They give students real-world, hands-on learning. Happy making!

Resources

There is a wealth of Makerspace information on the web. Here are some favorites for teachers:

1. Edutopia's "Designing a School Makerspace": http://www.edutopia. org/blog/designing-a-school-makerspace-jennifer-cooper
2. *MAKE* magazine: http://makezine.com
3. *Makerspace Playbook: School Edition*: http://makered.org/wp-content/uploads/2014/09/Makerspace-Playbook-Feb-2013.pdf

Chapter 5

The Enrichment Seminar

A Middle/Secondary Course for Gifted Learners

by Joanna Simpson

As gifted learners move from elementary to middle school and secondary school, traditional gifted pull-out program opportunities typically diminish. Programs and services typical at the middle/secondary level can include independent study courses, honors/advanced courses, and competition courses such as Future Problem Solving, Academic Decathlon, and Speech and Debate. Many of these programs and services target the intellectual needs of gifted learners. This article discusses how an enrichment seminar course offered at the middle/secondary level can be used to meet the social and emotional needs of gifted learners.

Rationale for an Enrichment Seminar

Adolescence is a time when identity development and relationship building are critical. This is just as true for gifted adolescents as it is for their nongifted peers. Gifted learners can find themselves under added stress, however, because of expectations from parents, teachers, administrators, and fellow students that they achieve at high levels in all areas at all times.

Gifted persons may also exhibit certain social and emotional characteristics such as perfectionism, lack of self-confidence, difficulty forming relationships, disorganization, isolation, and narcissism (Pratt, 2009). This becomes problematic because a gifted adolescent may underachieve intentionally or experience stress from trying to overachieve while dealing with social-emotional issues. Many gifted adolescents cope with these issues by allowing members of their various social groups to help form their identity. Personal identity formation is influenced when students are asked to live up to the expectations of those around them, and so it is easier to deal with the social-emotional issues from which they might be suffering when they are around like-minded peers.

Various social situations trigger different social identities, that is, ways of thinking, feeling, and acting, based on the most prominent perceived group membership(s) at the time. Socializing with gifted learners who are like them or who may share the same social-emotional issues could help these adolescents to reconcile the societal expectations and form an identity that is their own.

Gifted adolescents go through a period in which their cognitive development is dynamic, allowing them to understand the world in a more sophisticated manner (Keating, 2004). This rapid cognitive development also allows them to understand that their intellectual ability distinguishes them from their peers. Some gifted learners find that this difference in intellectual ability can be problematic and can be associated with a negative social stigma. Gifted learners who find that negative social consequences are attached to being gifted may deny their giftedness, hide it, or mask it in order to conform (Vialle, Heaven, & Ciarrochi, 2007). Providing these learners with additional coping strategies, in the form of a special course such as an enrichment seminar, may be one way to keep these learners from intentionally or unintentionally underachieving.

Designing a Course that Supports Social-Emotional Needs

An enrichment seminar is a course that is typically offered as an honors elective credit and is facilitated by a teacher who holds a gifted endorsement, if not a degree in gifted education. The teacher constructs a curriculum based on the particular needs of the gifted adolescents in his or her classroom and typically offers projects and special activities that are geared toward gifted and talented youth. Students pursue a topic of their choice and facilitate their own learning. The teacher, acting as guide, provides opportunities for guest speakers and field trips related to the students' individual interests.

The curriculum for the enrichment seminar course, in alignment with the name of the course, also provides curricular enrichment, an instructional strategy intended for students to explore topics of interest in greater detail than is normally feasible with the standard curriculum. For example, rather than learning facts about the author before reading a story, students in the enrichment seminar would research the author, the story, and the time period, and create a story of his or her own. A guest speaker might be brought in who is a published author to talk about the writing process, and a trip to a publishing company might be a part of that curriculum. Student learning is enhanced by in-depth instruction in each topic that is offered, and a focus on the personality characteristics and challenges that one can face in a professional field. Failure, success, and the strategies to deal with those and other social and emotional traits, could be covered during this time.

These seminars can also provide the perfect opportunity for specific curriculum intended for gifted learners who are either dealing with social, behavioral, or emotional issues or require an awareness of them. In addition, the teacher may give lessons on peer leadership and coping skills to help deal with the repercussions of receiving the gifted label.

Attending to the affective needs of gifted and talented students is as important as content and skill knowledge.

Integrating Social-Emotional Coping Strategies

Another unique aspect of the enrichment seminar is that it teaches gifted learners coping strategies to help address the social-emotional issues with which they may be dealing. Rudasill, Foust, and Callahan (2007) conducted a study to assess the social coping strategies of 600 middle and secondary school students. The sample was derived from gifted students who were participating in a 2-week summer enrichment program. The study found that there were six coping strategies that the gifted students had in common: helping others, denial of giftedness, minimizing one's focus on popularity, denying negative impact of giftedness on peer acceptance, conformity to mask giftedness, and hiding giftedness. In the enrichment seminar, a teacher could model coping strategies and share his or her own failures and success experiences that derived from those failures. Sample coping strategies include building confidence to ask questions, breathing exercises, counting, journaling, reflection, learning perseverance, and problem solving.

A curricular aspect of this facet of the course is learning about different types of giftedness. Using books such as *5 Levels of Gifted: School Issues and Educational Options* (Ruf, 2009), the enrichment seminar teacher discusses types of giftedness. Students then categorize their own behaviors and the behaviors of those in their social groups, to help them understand that they are not alone in their actions. An adolescent female who participated in this curricular unit in high school stated,

> I needed the reaffirmation and research-based scientific findings about myself and others gifted like me to realize that it was others' problems with me; there wasn't anything wrong with me. I was no different than anyone else, at least not in a bad way. I grew up always being called crybaby in elementary school. At least now I understand why I was so emotional. (Simpson, 2013)

Other areas for social-emotional development in the enrichment seminar include college and career counseling, culturally responsive relationships, relationship building, and organization skills. Participants in each of these units have found value in them, and have even attributed this curriculum and their gifted teacher to a positive identity formation and increased academic achievement.

It is important to note that the enrichment seminar curriculum is written for gifted learners; however, high-achieving students who have not received the gifted label may suffer the same social stigma as gifted learners and are typically able to take the course with counselor, teacher, or parent recommendation.

Through discussions and activities, adolescents are encouraged to explore their own ways of thinking and those of their peers, and are given strategies to both strengthen their relationships and manage their emotions. In addition, they are provided support with organizing their academics so that they can focus their interests on what would assist them in pursuit of their career or higher education choice. Ultimately, the participation in the enrichment seminar may guide who these gifted adolescents become as adults.

Concluding Thoughts

Secondary schools would be wise to employ a gifted course, such as Enrichment Seminar, that is constructed specifically for gifted adolescents. We have the research and the ability to serve *both* the academic and social-emotional needs of our gifted adolescents. We know what happens when we choose to ignore these needs in favor of the intellectual development. As parents, educators, and advocates of gifted adolescents, we know exactly what it looks like when these students begin suffering from negative behaviors.

There is considerable literature supporting the fact that gifted programming is necessary to reverse or prevent social and emotional problems in gifted adolescents. It is important for educators to write curriculum and create courses, programs, and activities that positively influence the identity formation of these teens.

It is not a question of whether or not we need to meet the needs of the whole child, including their intellectual and social-emotional needs—we know we need to do that. Understanding why we need to do it, and helping others understand why, may help us to advocate for high school gifted programming tailored to more than just the intellectual needs of these students. Having a model that has proven successful, like Enrichment Seminar, may help meet the complete needs of the gifted students we teach.

References

Keating, D. (2004). Cognitive and brain development. In R. M. Lerner & L. Steinberg (Eds.), *Handbook of adolescent psychology* (2nd ed., pp. 45–84). New York, NY: Wiley.

Pratt, M. W. (2009). Looping to meet the needs of gifted children. *Principal, 88*(5), 22–24.

Rudasill, K. M., Foust, R. C., & Callahan, C. M. (2007). The social coping questionnaire: An examination of its structure with an American sample of gifted adolescents. *Journal for the Education of the Gifted, 30,* 353–371.

Ruf, D. (2009). *5 levels of gifted: School issues and educational options.* Tucson, AZ: Great Potential Press.

Simpson, J. (2013). *A case study on enrichment seminar and the social/emotional needs of gifted students.* Grand Canyon University. Phoenix, AZ: ProQuest, UMI Dissertations Publishing.

Vialle, W., Heaven, P. C. L., & Ciarrochi, J. (2007). On being gifted, but sad and misunderstood: Social, emotional, and academic outcomes of gifted students in the Wollongong youth study. *Educational Research and Evaluation, 13,* 569–586.

Chapter 6

Extreme ESP

Meaningful Thematic Activities for High-Ability Middle School Students

by Jennifer Hoffman

Middle school places numerous demands upon students of all ability levels, particularly high-ability learners who are expected to complete assignments in several different advanced classes while expanding their horizons through participation in extracurricular activities. Retention of students in middle school gifted and talented programs may become problematic when so many academic and social demands are exacted upon these students. Mindful of the high expectations placed upon high-ability learners in middle school, I found it necessary to modify the curricula for my seventh-grade Extended Studies Program (ESP), a class designed for these students.

In striving to meet the unique needs of learners in my seventh-grade ESP class, I designed an instructional unit to foster learners' personal and intellectual growth. The program includes challenging activities in math, engineering, social studies, science, language arts, and community service. I conducted extensive research to design meaningful instructional activities learners would find challenging, interesting, and exciting and incorporated high-level thinking activities, interactive and collaborative experiences, and hands-on, inquiry-related lessons into the program. Hoping to motivate students, I named the instructional unit "Extreme Extended Studies Program!" which was subsequently shortened to "Extreme ESP!"

Themes and Curricular Connections

During the first session, learners are introduced to Extreme ESP! by participating in an activity called "Getting to Know You." They answer questions requiring them to name items such as their favorite author, movie, subject, and activity. They are asked if they have ever participated in any extreme sport(s). After answering the questions, students enthusiastically move around the classroom as they compare their responses with every student in the class, recording similarities and differences. The class then discusses its answers, celebrating the shared responses as well as unique interests. This helps establish a collegial, supportive culture where students respect and appreciate each other's opinions and talents, and feel comfortable taking academic risks.

In subsequent sessions, learners conduct research to prepare for a debate about whether or not children and teens should participate in extreme sports. Their arguments include statements such as, "Statistics show that more children are injured while participating in traditional sports than extreme sports" and "Children and teens should not play extreme sports because they lack the maturity, training, and experience needed to play these sports safely." Then, they brainstorm and write legislation they would like to see passed to ensure safety for children.

Interwoven throughout the unit are rigorous math challenges from *Extreme Math* (Tyler & Tyler, 2004) and related interactive, hands-on engineering challenges. Engineering challenges include designing, constructing, and testing parachutes; building gliders; participating in a Barbie bungee-jumping contest (Zordak, 2008); and a cantilever challenge that promotes divergent thinking and innovation.

Type III Enrichment Products (Renzulli & Reis, 1997) were incorporated into the unit. Using data from a survey ESP students administered to fourth graders in the district, Extreme ESP students designed products to promote safety, covering issues such as the importance of wearing helmets when riding bicycles, train track safety, anti-bullying, and Internet safety. One Extreme ESP student created an original video game where players had to navigate their way through various safety hazards encountered along their cyber-journey. Other examples of original products created by learners included an ad campaign, a short movie, a theatrical play, a commercial, a newspaper, poems, skits, posters, and short stories.

What surprised me the most and became the strongest motivating element in this unit was my use of Renzulli's "Artistic Modification Menu" (Davis &

Rimm, 2004), from *The Multiple Menu Model* of instruction, which involves the teacher delivering his or her own creative contribution. For the Artistic Modification Menu, I described an injury I suffered while ice skating with my son at his friend's birthday party. Every student in the class listened wide-eyed with rapt attention as I described the accident, the doctor's responses at the emergency room, and the realization of how I would have had a severe brain injury with long-lasting repercussions had I not been wearing a helmet. Rarely one to share my opinions or talk about myself to my students, the class was incredibly moved by my account. They then began sharing their own experiences. It was after this discussion that students became highly motivated in all aspects of this unit.

Goals of Extreme ESP!

The goals and objectives of Extreme ESP! promote convergent and divergent thinking skills, risk-taking, refinement of thought, and empathy. Learners use convergent thinking skills in math challenges that require finding the solutions to complex math questions and utilize divergent thinking skills by engaging in brainstorming activities during engineering challenges and when developing legislative proposals. Learners are encouraged to take risks while conducting multiple trials to test their models for the engineering challenges and creating their final products. They strengthen their awareness of others and ability to provide assistance to people experiencing hardships by organizing and implementing a service project, raising awareness and funds for victims of natural disasters.

The objectives, specifically the use of convergent and divergent thinking skills, risk-taking, refinement of thought, and empathy, were assessed throughout this unit. Evaluation tools were inspired by methodology and instruments espoused by Davis and Rimm (2004), such as the use of program evaluation questionnaires, collection and analysis of classroom observation data, informal interviews, parent feedback from conferences and surveys, and student self-assessment forms. A teacher reflection journal was used to analyze instructional activities, materials needed, effective practices and areas needing modification. Students wrote that they looked forward to coming to class, being engaged and active, and enjoyed the diverse range of instructional activities.

Meeting Students' Needs

Extreme ESP! is specifically designed to embrace the unique characteristics of high-ability learners. Learners keep a reflection journal in which they gauge the level of difficulty of each math and engineering challenge so that I may adjust these activities to provide additional challenge or support when necessary. The research, debate, and use of evidence to support statements used in the legislative drafting activity satisfy the inquisitiveness, strong desire to learn and ability to form logical, insightful conclusions often demonstrated by advanced learners. Designing a well-communicated, innovative product for their service project suits the advanced vocabulary, strong reading comprehension skills, and adept creative problem-solving skills these students often exhibit. Additionally, ESP! enables students to successfully interact and collaborate with peers with similar needs and strengths, beginning with the very first buddy activity and culminating in the service project expansion.

Conclusion

High-ability middle school students, like their peers, are required to navigate their way through a labyrinth of multiple teachers and classes, extracurricular activities, social norms, and family responsibilities. Amidst these tasks, they often have tremendous amounts of energy, a need to find themselves, and a desire to fit in. Planning instructional units that embrace these students' high energy levels, creativity, and their need for a diverse range of interactive, hands-on learning experiences enables teachers to engage these students and inspire them to think divergently, be innovative, and use their talents to help others. By designing an interdisciplinary program like Extreme ESP, teachers may successfully foster enthusiasm, personal and academic growth, and innovation in their high-ability middle school students.

References

Davis, G, A., & Rimm, S. B. (2004). *Education of the gifted and talented* (5th ed.). Boston, MA: Allyn & Bacon.

Renzulli, J. S., & Reis, S. M. (1997). *The schoolwide enrichment model: A how-to guide for educational excellence* (2nd ed.). Waco, TX: Prufrock Press.

Tyler, K., & Tyler, M. W. (2004). *Extreme math: Real math, real people, real sports*. Waco, TX: Prufrock Press.

Zordak, S. E. (2008). Barbie bungee. *National Council for Teachers of Mathematics*. Retrieved from https://illuminations.nctm.org/Lesson.aspx?id=2157

Chapter 7

Principles and Practices of Socratic Circles in Middle Level Classrooms

A Socratic Conversation

by Scott L. Hunsaker, Christen C. Rose, and Elinda R. Nedreberg

A Socratic Circle is a discussion method that inspires participants to complete deep reading of a text and engage in meaningful discussion of that text. In this article, the authors (a teacher educator and two English Teachers) engage in a Socratic conversation about the rationale, processes, and outcomes of Socratic Circles. The teacher educator acts as the questioner in this conversation, while the teachers serve as experts who have implemented Socratic Circles in their respective seventh- and ninth-grade Honors English Classes. Both teachers serve in a school district in which both these grades are housed in junior high schools.

Questioner: To the best of your understanding, what is the Socratic method?

Experts: We think of the Socratic method as questions used to stimulate critical thinking, which is the ability to analyze ideas in a manner that applies them to students' personal experiences and to other texts and other circumstances. It also opens students' minds to other perspectives, providing the opportunity to understand multiple points of view and clarify their own positions on issues and ideas. We also think it's important, within the Socratic method, to avoid argument and humorous remarks.

Questioner: But aren't you charged to teach argumentative writing?

Experts: Yes, that's true. Argumentative writing is the ability to see at least two sides of an issue and put forth claims and evidence to support one of those sides. However, when middle school students think *argument*, what they often end up with is more heated conflict where one person has to be right and the other person has to be wrong. We don't want that. We want them to be looking at others' perspectives. If they're arguing or maintaining that they're right, they're not open to looking at somebody else's viewpoint.

Questioner: With an already overcrowded curriculum, why would I want to use a method that engenders protracted discussion?

Experts: Oh, we get that! When we first read about Socratic Circles, we were terrified it would be a waste of time. We have so many objectives we can't meet them all; we have so many texts we can't read them all. We had to take the risk that it would be worth it, and it was. We have learned that the method is timeless and goes across age groups.

Many language arts objectives are met through Socratic Circles: speaking and listening skills, reading and writing skills, learning how to respond in discussions, as well as the ability to make connections. Integrating knowledge and skills across content areas is extremely important. In addition, the discussions and questions lay a great foundation for future writing assignments; we can see that Socratic Circles help students write more thoughtful and thorough essays.

The Basics of Socratic Circles

Questioner: So, what are the basics of Socratic Circles, and what resources might I turn to if I want to use this strategy?

Experts: The best source is Copeland's (2005) book *Socratic Circles*. Basically, we teach students how to read closely and annotate with short texts, such as poems, short stories, and nonfiction articles. For example, an opinion piece about the tooth fairy (http://www.cnn.com/2011/LIVING/08/02/tooth.fairy.penny.pincher) has worked really well with our seventh graders. The poem "Kindness" by Naomi Shihab Nye (http://www.poets.org/poetsorg/poem/kindness) has worked well with our ninth graders. The annotation tool we prefer to teach is called "The 'Reading With Your Pen' Palette for Annotating

Texts" (Goble, Fardig, & Davis, 2010). With the text and annotation tool in hand, the students are ready for close reading.

When the students come to class with their annotated texts prepared for the discussion, we organize two circles—an outer circle and an inner circle—each facing into the middle. The circles can be organized by generating a random list using a classroom seating chart program or by dividing the students based on some random element such as a color they are wearing or some individual preference like skiing or snowboarding.

Once we've got the students in the circles, the outer circle members are instructed to listen, take notes, and evaluate the discussion of the inner circle. We then present a question from our list to the inner circle, and students engage in discussion about that question. New questions are posed whenever conversations seem to wane, permitting appropriate wait time, of course, or when prompted by the direction of the conversation. At the end of discussion, the outer circle gives constructive criticism to the inner circle about the discussion, including participation and quality of ideas. We've experienced Socratic Circles as brief as 20 minutes and as long as 60 minutes.

Questioner: What is it about Socratic Circles that makes them Socratic? For example, what are the Socratic functions of each of the circles?

Experts: Well, for the inner circle, it seems obvious that the students are expressing opinions, clarifying ideas, and responding to others. In order to be engaged in a good discussion, you have to be able to listen well. So, the outer circle develops listening skills and the ability to pay attention, to consider ideas. The students in the outer circle have more of an opportunity to actually listen to a discussion and to see a demonstration of a discussion that is functional in comparison to their talking at lunch where they're always interrupting one another.

Questioner: How do you choose the subjects for discussion with deeper meaning and the questions to be asked? What are the cautions a teacher should take in this regard?

Experts: The topics we choose are usually related to an overarching theme drawn from the short stories or larger works we are reading in class. We use nonfiction articles that connect to that theme. So there is groundwork thinking done in advance. Smith, Wilhelm, and Fredricksen (2012) often talk about essential questions that teachers use for a unit, and many English teachers are familiar with the idea of universal themes. For example, from the classic *The*

Odyssey, we could use the theme of heroes, which would generate a number of interesting questions to which students can respond.

The questions must be open-ended. Students need to be able to express multiple viewpoints and a variety of perspectives. If the questions aren't broad enough, the conversation will stall. Students need to care about the question. If they don't care, they're not going to even try to answer the question. They need to be based on concepts they can grasp from their personal life, the general class reading, and the short text—across all three of them. Questions also must be thought-provoking. We intentionally include controversial ideas for which there is, maybe, a majority opinion held that I want students to look at the other side of, or have a person be brave enough to say something that provokes thought in the other people. For example, we have had students express what it's like to be in a minority religion in their school, or how feeling alone and ostracized because of religion might be similar to how someone who is gay or lesbian might feel. They can relate to these different things from the text that they haven't thought of before. It helps them develop greater empathy and see what it's really like to think in a different way and have different life experiences, which they bring with them to class. We give our students a controversial article in which the opinion of the man who wrote the article is that just because you go to war, that doesn't mean you're a hero. It offends a lot of the students, but some students read it and say, "Oh, I see what he's saying. You have to actually go through some sort of ordeal to be a hero." It was a really good discussion, and that goes back to not having a debate or an argument, but being respectful in having a discussion, in having a dialogue. However, even with this emphasis on being thought-provoking, we would not use a controversial issue for the first Circle we held. Students would need to be fairly familiar with the atmosphere of the process before introducing this element. Finally, you should have a sufficient number of questions. Our experience tells us that we should have a minimum of 10 questions prepared, as some questions are more interesting to some groups (or class periods) than others.

Theme: Heroes

- ▸ What is the definition of a hero?
- ▸ What characteristics does a hero possess?
- ▸ What are examples of heroism?
- ▸ Must a hero exhibit perfection? Why or why not?

▸ What flaws and faults are acceptable for heroes to possess?

▸ Which flaws and faults are unacceptable for heroes to possess?

Provide examples of admirable to imperfect heroes (from the literature and from life).

Questioner: When I think about middle school students, what comes to my mind is youngsters who haven't had much experience in or exposure to the world at large, and who are somewhat insecure about putting themselves and their ideas forward for fear of being wrong or being rejected. What preparations do you make to overcome these drawbacks?

Experts: Creating a comfortable classroom climate is a necessity for many risk-taking activities that teachers may want to employ in a classroom. Initially one of our goals was to increase the number of participants who engage in any classroom conversation. This is a problem many teachers encounter; the same three to five hands being raised each time responses are sought. Implementing Socratic Circles helped increase comfort.

Having said that, creating comfortable classrooms where students are willing to take risks always starts at the beginning of the year. So, students learn to share frequently in their informal journal writing and, as teachers, we share some appropriate personal connections to the literature ourselves. Plus, we do laugh with our students. One student wrote in an evaluation, "I love all of the different ways that we are able to learn because everyone learns in different ways. We have Socratic Circles, worksheets, journals, group work, and even videos. This allows a wide variety of learners to all understand through these many activities. Some teachers use the same type of teaching every day, and for those who don't learn very well in that way, they can struggle. Thanks for having a variety of learning methods."

As we've mentioned, carefully scaffold the exercises with prerequisite steps, such as "The 'Reading With Your Pen' Palette for Annotating Texts" (Goble et al., 2010), starting with short texts, short stories, and poetry at the beginning of the year. Modeling a bad conversation or "what not to do" has also worked very well. Elinda wrote a great skit that has worked well in both our classes. Both seventh and ninth graders get a kick out of it!

Finally, during an introductory Socratic Circle, we provide teacher and peer feedback in a gentle and constructive manner. The text by Copeland (2005) has a good feedback and evaluation form in the appendix.

Discussion Roles Skit

(Based on *Willy Wonka and the Chocolate Factory*)

Characters:
- ▸ Charlie Bucket—Quiet; never shares or answers a question
- ▸ Augustus Gloop—Conversation hog; won't stop talking
- ▸ Violet Beauregarde—Interruptor
- ▸ Veruca Salt—Always right
- ▸ Mike Teavee—Distracted; not listening (has an electronic device)

Teacher: Okay, class. Thank you for finishing the poem and annotating it. We will be working on some discussion questions in connection with the article to help you think more about it. Your first question that you need to talk about in your group is: What is this poem about?

(Charlie sits and looks down at the floor; Mike is looking at his phone or tablet a lot.)

Augustus: Well, I think it has to do with the fact that there never seems to be enough food. I mean, look at this poor man. He got beat up 4 weeks ago, and it sounds like he has lost a lot of weight. Hospitals totally have way enough good food for people now. When my mom had surgery last year, she shared some of her food with me. She had—(*Augustus keeps talking even though other people are talking. Lists A LOT of foods.*)

Violet (*interrupting*): I completely disagree. I think this poem is about being free to speak your mind, even if it hurts someone else or someone disagrees with you. This man has said he doesn't want the people who hurt him to suffer the consequences, and I think he's completely batty for saying that, but he has a right to say it.

(Augustus keeps talking about food.)

Veruca Salt: Violet, you are completely wrong, I am afraid. This poor man has been through an ordeal that has challenged him mentally and physically, so THAT is what this poem is about. Discussion over. No need to say any—

Violet (*interrupting again*): How DARE you say that I am WRONG, you NIT! I ought to come over there and SHOW you you're wrong! Augustus, SHUT UP!

(Augustus finally stops talking.)

Veruca: How dare I say that you're wrong? Well, you ARE wrong. You haven't thought it through completely. Mike, Charlie, what you do say?

Mike: What? What's going on? Stop interrupting. You'll make me lose to this boss.

Charlie: (*quietly*) I um ... I don't know who's right. I don't really know what the poem was about, either. (Puts head back down.)

Veruca and Violet: AAAAAARGH!!! MRS. NED!!!!

End Scene

Questioner: Even with this preparation, I anticipate some problems could arise when discussing controversial topics with this age group. Perhaps some will begin to dominate discussion while others withdraw. Some will become impassioned about the topic while others are apathetic. Some will worry that their beliefs and values are being threatened while others will welcome the challenge. How do you encourage informed, reasoned, respectful participation from students?

Experts: Seventh graders are often timid and somewhat reluctant to share. "Bounce Cards" that have a list of sentence starters are required to be on hand during the circles. We pulled this idea from Roake and Varlas (2013). Further, a wheel chart can be used to track the number of times students have contributed to the conversation with a minimum of one share required. A minimum requirement helps them overcome that reluctance we referred to earlier.

Ninth graders can still be shy about participating, although there are more students who are willing to participate, and so with them we focus on a sharing limit. Once a student has reached a maximum of four shares, he or she must remain silent so others can participate. Shy students have expressed appreciation for this because it takes them longer to "work up the courage" to share.

Guiding rules are a good starting point. We developed a list of rules that were suggested by Copeland (2005), such as:

1. Say your name before you speak.
2. Make your comment or ask your question.
3. Comment on what someone else has said if you'd like.
4. Disagree if you choose, but don't be mean.
5. Talk to each other, not to the teacher.
6. Offer evidence, either from the article or from life, to back up what you say.

Note that we give students the opportunity to add to or change the guiding rules. It is also important to learn to tolerate the silences.

If students begin to argue or debate, we remind students that this is not the appropriate time to engage in debate, as we are interested in a variety of viewpoints and perspectives. Many students comment after class that they had never thought a certain way before, and they genuinely appreciate and enjoy hearing what other people think.

Socratic Circles Make a Difference

Questioner: A middle school teacher once remarked to me that she didn't like the gifted program at her school because all the students did was "sit around and talk." It sounds like Socratic Circles could fall into this stereotype. What evidence do you have that these discussions contribute to the attainment of curriculum standards in your academic area in particular? How do you know that Socratic Circles are making a difference in your students' academic achievements in general?

Experts: Socratic Circles are not the only thing we do in class. We read. We do vocabulary. We write essays. We learn reading strategies. We compare and contrast media. Socratic Circles improve essay writing. Students are better able to include different perspectives, which make the writing more thoughtful. We could point to the performance of our students on grade-level criterion reference tests, on which more than 90% met grade-level objectives, but that's not what is most important to us.

Students continue to think, ponder, and discuss ideas from Socratic Circles well beyond the class period. The students are thinking more deeply. On one memorable occasion, a group of boys found a classmate in the hall and, due to confusion with a text they had read for homework, they formed a Socratic Circle right there in the hall to discuss the reading. These kinds of incidents are more meaningful to us than test scores because they show that the students are starting to think for themselves.

The positive benefits of Socratic Circles don't just happen during the discussion, but have effects in the day-to-day functioning of the classroom community. It increases the level of trust, even when not in a circle. We encourage other teachers to just jump in. Join us!

References

Copeland, M. (2005). *Socratic circles: Fostering critical and creative thinking in middle and high school.* Portland, ME: Stenhouse.

Goble, R. R., Fardig, L., & Davis, E. (2010). Handout: The "reading with your pen" palette for annotating texts. *Classroom Notes Plus, 27*(4).

Roake, J., & Varlas, L. (2013). More than words: Developing core speaking and listening skills. *Education Update, 55*(12), 1, 4–5.

Smith, M. W., Wilhelm, J. D., & Fredricksen, J. E. (2012). *Oh yeah?! Putting argument to work both in school and out.* Portsmouth, NH: Heinemann.

Chapter 8

Socratic Circles

Round and Round the Wheels of Thought

by LaVonda Senn

A major concern for our public education today is that teachers appear to be "teaching to the test," and not teaching students how to think critically and how to increase their skills in evaluating and synthesizing information. The dilemma faced when learning higher order thinking skills lies not necessarily in the content of the information, but in the methodology used to teach that skill. Today's multiple-choice tests cannot test critical thinking skills, nor do they allow students to be conversationalists, an important communication skill. Socratic teaching strategies can be used to teach all students, but provide the challenge that gifted students require. Copeland (2005) described Socratic Circles as a method for helping students become participants in the process of learning, not just innocent bystanders of school experiences.

Socratic Circles

In essence, Socratic Circles consist of two concentric circles—a smaller, inner circle of students that discuss and debate a topic, and a larger, outer circle of students who listen to the discussion and provide evaluative feedback following the activity. Socratic questioning used in the Circles revolves around six types of questions (see Table 8.1), which are essential both to the strategy and for student understanding and are embedded in directions given to students when they participate in group discussion. Students should be given the opportunity to participate in both circles over the course of a single or multiple class periods. It is important to keep in mind that the students determine, through teacher observation[1], when they are ready to "join" the inner circle, for the skills necessary for debate and conversation may take time to develop.

The Importance of Questioning

Developing high-quality Socratic questions for a unit and associated daily lessons should include consideration of potential student responses. In creating lists of potential responses and then refining questions, educators become more adept at creating more specific and valuable questions. However, flexibility is required as student responses can be unpredictable and will often veer off topic. It may be necessary to redirect the class discussion, and so having a short list of directed questions is certainly recommended. As Socratic Circles are used more often during class, educators become more adept at the teaching style required for successful student outcomes.

The teacher's role during the initial questioning process is to facilitate the discussion by only asking questions of perspective, elaboration, and understanding. The teacher does not answer any questions, and only students engage each other in conversation. The facilitating questions asked by the teacher during Socratic Circles are thought-provoking and used to lead and guide the students to understand the "big ideas," and to construct knowledge about essential concepts. The teacher is not a referee, nor does he or she participate in the conversation. Socratic Circles are not debate forums for students to argue some abstract point of meaning. Students in the group use prior background knowledge from class research, previous homework assignments, and other notes to add to the discussion.

---

1   *Note.* As the teacher walks around observing the small-group dynamic, he or she creates a list of four to six names of students who have mastered the art of conversation (taking turns, providing input). These students are the first group to enter the inner circle.

TABLE 8.1

Socratic Circles: Six Types of Questions (Theme: WWII)

Questions About Implications and Consequences	What consequences did we face as a result of WWII?	What were the implications for our economy?
Questions About Viewpoint and Perspective	Where did you gain that perspective of Japanese citizens?	Who do you think influences your point of view about Germans?
Questions About Questions	What type of question might you ask about that invasion of Norway during WWII?	What kind of questions might help you to better understand the situation that the U.S. was in during WWII?
Questions That Probe Assumptions	What assumptions have to be made to conclude that the war helped our economy?	Why are you assuming if you make the statement, "We could have stayed out of the war?"
Questions That Clarify	Could you further explain what you mean by, "The war helped our economy?"	Can you provide an example of internal and external conflict for the country during WWII?
Questions About Rationale, Reasons, and Evidence	What evidence do you have from the story to prove what you said is true?	Can you give a reason for your rationale about the refugee camps?

Note. Question types are adapted from Paul & Elder, 1997.

Getting Started

The introduction of Socratic Circles begins when the teacher presents a guiding question related to a curricular topic to the entire class. Through illustrations on the board, the teacher models several possible methods of analysis including: graphic organizers, brainstorming webs, lists, three- to five-word phrases, columns, paragraphs, or shorthand. Students are then placed in small groups (4–6 students) and asked to discuss the topic from a variety of perspectives. Some students may examine the selection for main ideas and key points; others can write down questions they have. One student must be designated as the scribe, or author, who keeps a record of the discussion. Students contribute feedback and input within their respective groups and compile their results through one of the methods listed above.

Establishing the Circles

The teacher pulls desks equal to the number of students chosen, plus two empty ones, to the center of the classroom, and has the students turn all other desks facing the inner circle. Instructions are then given: Students in the outer circle are not allowed to talk until the discussion about the topic is over, and a time limit—generally 5–10 minutes, depending on the grade level, teacher, and students—is specified. The students in the inner circle begin discussing and debating the topic, allowing each member a chance to participate. The teacher acts only as a facilitator, adding direction when necessary. Students in the outer circle watch the inner circle carefully and are encouraged to take notes when they are reminded of anything, or think of something they want to say. Students in the outer circle are also given an evaluation sheet (see Figure 8.1) and are asked for positive feedback to the entire group when the Socratic Circle is complete. The evaluation categories can vary, but generally include such ideas as voice control, tone, discussion ability, transitioning, and others. The two empty desks provide an opportunity for a student from the outer circle to quietly join the inner circle with something substantial he or she would like to add.

Once the students have finished their discussion, the teacher opens a dialogue among all of the students to demonstrate the conversational methods used appropriately by the students in the inner circle. It is important to note that this step is only done on the first day Socratic Circles are introduced in order to model proper conversational techniques that should be used by all students during their inner circle experience. Throughout the students' discussion about conversation techniques, the teacher uses each concern or attribute (e.g., putdowns, positive feedback, and examples of unacceptable comments) to teach students about appropriate corrective feedback. Once students understand their responsibilities as a member of each circle, they begin to share their thoughts and feelings about each student's positive and negative contributions during the discussion.

When the evaluative feedback has been discussed, students trade places and new discussants move to the inner circle. This process continues until the entire class has an opportunity to share and be evaluated. An addition to this stage could include a "self-evaluation" conducted by each student as he or she reflects upon personal experience. Newman (2005) commented on the importance of students' learned ability to self-evaluate. Critical thinking evolves from self-evaluative measures, helping students to become better thinkers, problem solvers, and intrapersonal reflectors.

Names of students	Listens to others	Connects ideas to others comments	Provides original questions	Creates new ideas	Helps others to feel as though their comments are welcome	Compliments others for good ideas	Respectfully disagrees with others' comments	Total score
Sample Student	4	3	4	0	5	2	3	21/28
Amy								
Arnold								
Scott								

Never	Rarely	Sometimes	Frequently	Always
0	1	2	3	4

Figure 8.1. Scoring rubric for inner circle performance.

When the Socratic circle process has been completed, students should reflect on what they felt were positives and negatives about the experience itself. A graphic organizer can be used to help students list their positives and negatives in two columns using a listing form. Also, sticky notes can be used and posted on the board in two separate columns. At the next class meeting, these positive and negative characteristics are reviewed and discussed. It must be noted that once the Socratic Circles become more successful, time and class management may become more difficult as more students want to add to the conversation.

At the end of each class, students should be given additional specific questions to consider as homework. These questions will be used as prompts for future Socratic Circles, a process that continues until the teacher feels that each student has come to understand the importance of the skills being addressed. Students can become astute questioners and responders to topics both abstract and concrete.

An Example Using Socratic Circles

Let's look at an example of the use of Socratic Circles during a fifth-grade unit about World War II (see Table 8.1). The teacher might begin a Socratic Circle situation with the question: "Do you believe that there were any positive results from WWII?" Teachers have to be ready to hear the responses, and know where to guide the conversation, through further questioning in order to meet the curricular goal. The teacher only asks questions but must be able to interject quickly and efficiently so as to maintain an engaging discussion among both the entire class and eventual small-group discussion. The six sample Socratic questions in Table 8.1 illustrate how responses or the information elicited from the students changes, based on the type of question asked.

The use of Socratic Circles can help students learn how to think critically, analyze information, and evaluate others' ideas as well as their own. Students also become well versed at using conceptual background knowledge to understand a topic, helping them become better problem solvers and evaluators of information.

References

Copeland, M. (2005). *Socratic circles: Fostering critical and creative thinking in middle and high school*. Portland, ME: Stenhouse.

Newman, J. L. (2005). Talents and type IIIs: The effects of the talents unlimited model on creative productivity in gifted youngsters. *Roeper Review, 27,* 84–90.

Paul, R., & Elder, L. (1997). *Socratic teaching*. Retrieved from http://www.criticalthinking.org/pages/socratic-teaching/507

Section III: Creativity

Chapter 9

Creative Process Assessment as a Means to Creative Productivity

How to Help Students Make the Most of Their Capabilities

by Elizabeth C. Fairweather

There is little that is more frustrating for a teacher than watching a student with creative potential fail to produce. This article offers suggestions and guidance to teachers seeking to maximize their students' creative output. Applying the following ideas about the creative process opens up a whole new path to facilitating students' creativity.

The Creative Process

Knowledge and understanding of the creative process is the first step in facilitating creativity among students. Creativity is usually defined as that which is novel and appropriate (Sternberg & Lubart, 1999). In the classroom, this definition translates into products that are unusual or uncommon among children and serve their intended purpose. The creative process is the experience of creating such a product. There are many models of the creative process, but most of them contain the components described below in one form or another (Lubart, 2001). Although presented sequentially here, the process does not necessarily move in a particular order, and it can start just about anywhere.

Creative Process Components

The first component of the creative process is usually preparation, the stage at which information for the creative activity is gathered. This happens in two ways. First, is the effortful gathering of specific information related to a creative task (Amabile, 1983; Wallas, 1926). Preparation for creating a website might involve researching the how-tos of website development, examining sample websites, and collecting graphics, text, and other materials intended for the site. A secondary aspect of preparation is the conscious and unconscious gathering of information from the senses, which occurs during a typical day-to-day interaction with the environment and takes place constantly, whether or not a specific creative task is being considered (Taylor, 1959).

Problem development is a second component of the creative process (Treffinger, 1995). This is the point at which individuals look for problems in a given situation and use specifically related information to define and structure the problem so that it can be solved. Here, the website designer identifies the parameters placed on his or her project and defines a structure into which ideas must fit. Generating ideas to solve those problems and realize products is the next step. For the website designer, this means coming up with possible ways to arrange and link text and graphics to fit the general structure proposed earlier.

Implementation, the last component, occurs when ideas are tested or exhibited. When the website designer has an idea he thinks will work, he puts it into practice to get feedback on its effectiveness. At points along the way, some evaluation of the ideas should be made, but it should not be so overwhelming that the individual does not make progress on the product (Torrance, 1979). The website designer might use multiple evaluations and feedback to determine the quality of her ideas during idea generation and to make adjustments to the product.

Assessment

One way to gain this understanding of each student's facility with the creative process is to observe students as they engage in a creative activity. The observing teacher might make a chart tabulating all of the creative process components so that thoughts and comments can be recorded while a student is being observed. Some examples of observations that may be recorded include:

▶ Preparation
  ▷ Selected several books as sources for the project.
  ▷ Read extensively on the topic before beginning.
  ▷ Visited an art museum before beginning to draft artwork.

▶ Problem Development
  ▷ Experimented with chosen media to select the best set up for a piece of art.
  ▷ Asked questions to clarify the parameters of the activity.
  ▷ Made an extensive outline for the paper.

▶ Idea Generation
  ▷ Had multiple solutions for a problem.
  ▷ Came up with numerous possible plots for the short story.
  ▷ Made several sketches before starting the drawing.

▶ Implementation/Verification
  ▷ Proceeded steadily through the final piece of art.
  ▷ Final product was fluently written with minimal editing (erasures, changes).
  ▷ Established personal criteria for self-evaluating product.
  ▷ Sought out constructive criticism on work from peers, teachers, and parents.

In lieu of observations, or to help raise personal awareness, teachers might create a short paper-and-pencil questionnaire (see Figure 9.1 for examples of questions) for students to gather information on their own creative process. The questionnaire can be completed individually by the student or used to prompt discussion while conferring with the student. The items from the survey can be modified to suit a particular need. Alternatively, simply studying the survey may result in better observations when watching students engaged in creative activities.

Using Creative Process Assessments

The assessment information, which will tell you about students' strengths and weaknesses in the various components of the creative process, can be used

Preparation
- ▶ How much time do you spend gathering information about a topic before starting a creative project related to it?
- ▶ When you are assigned a project at school, what kinds of information gathering do you do?

Problem Development
- ▶ When and where do you see problems?
- ▶ Do you tend to be critical of the world around you? Explain.

Idea Generation
- ▶ How easy is it for you to come up with ideas?
- ▶ How likely are you to add details to the things you make, write, draw, etc.?

Implementation/Verification
- ▶ How often do you share your ideas with others?
- ▶ How much time do you spend trying out your ideas to see if they work?

Figure 9.1. Potential questions for a creative process assessment.

to steer students to creative activities in which they can be most successful. Students might be matched to activities suited to their strengths. For example, a student who demonstrates strength in the area of idea generation might be a good candidate for Odyssey of the Mind (http://www.odysseyofthemind.com). Given that the brainstorming portion of this competition is all about numbers of ideas, these students are likely to perform well and continue to develop these skills further. Or, a student who shows relative strengths in problem development might want to participate in the Future Problem Solving Program International (http://www.fpspi.org), which not only asks participants to find problems, but also teaches them how to define problem situations.

Creative process assessments may be useful in directing students toward suitable activities in settings of a more typical nature as well. Students who are strong in preparation might like complex projects that require a great deal of research. This might include making a documentary or writing a research paper. Alternately, students who are weak in preparation but love evaluation might be better suited for writing a film or book review. Finally, students who are strong in problem development might find success in developing and outlining a new genre of film or writing.

Effective diagnosis of creative process component strengths and weaknesses may be helpful in directing students to focus on the appropriate type of research project. Research can be divided into two main types, observational and experimental. Jane Goodall is an observational scientist. The bulk of her work is making observations (preparation), which are later analyzed for the formulation of hypotheses that she confirms with her original observations or further observations. Louis Pasteur, on the other hand, made observations and studied theory, but spent the bulk of his research time on experimenting to test his hypothesis. Students who demonstrate strengths in preparation may be more inclined toward observational research whereas a student high in implementation might be more inclined to experimental research.

Insight into a student's creative process can yield even further benefits. For instance, it can be used as a structure for grouping students. For example, it is often difficult for groups comprised solely of idea generators to implement ideas. Therefore, groups should be composed of students with strengths in different components of the creative process. This helps move the process along more smoothly from preparation to implementation with each child feeling good about contributing from an area of strength.

In order for students to be more aware of their own experiences and draw conclusions about their own personal creativity, it might be helpful to directly teach them about the creative process. Students can begin to match themselves to the right projects, domains, and partners based on what they have learned about their own strengths and weaknesses, increasing their self-efficacy and productivity. Furthermore, it will be useful for advanced students to learn to use the information to become more aware of how to adjust their cognitive resources in order to meet the needs of different creative projects. They can learn when to apply strategies for idea generation when a project calls for better ideas or to extend their information gathering when heavier preparation is what is needed.

The examples given here do rely on generalizations, and each child is different. But, focusing on students' creative process strengths may improve productivity by matching the student and the task. This different approach aids students in facilitating their creative process and making the most of their creative potential.

References

Amabile, T. M. (1983). The social psychology of creativity: A componential conceptualization. *Journal of Personality and Social Psychology, 45,* 357–376.

Lubart, T. I. (2001). Models of the creative process: Past, present and future. *Creativity Research Journal, 13,* 295–308.

Sternberg, R. J., & Lubart, T. I. (1999). The concept of creativity: Prospects and paradigms. In R. J. Sternberg (Ed.), *Handbook of Creativity* (pp. 3–15). New York, NY: Cambridge University Press.

Taylor, C. (1959). The nature of the creative process. In P. Smith (Ed.), *Creativity: An examination of the creative process* (pp. 51–82). New York, NY: Hastings House.

Torrance, E. P. (1979). *The search for Satori and creativity.* Buffalo, NY: Creative Education Foundation.

Treffinger, D. J. (1995). Creative problem solving: Overview and educational implications. *Educational Psychology Review, 7,* 301–312.

Wallas, G. (1926). *The art of thought.* New York, NY: Harcourt, Brace.

Chapter 10

A Pathway for Classroom Creativity

by James Fetterly and Betty Wood

Imagine a classroom of gifted and the talented students. It is full of creative ideas and new processes are developed and old ideas are repurposed to solve meaningful problems. It is a place where teachers and students learn from each other. Creativity is one of the most important topics for the gifted and talented student (Davis, Rimm, & Siegle, 2011). Students with top grades in school and at the university level were found to have not only a high IQ, but also high creativity (Cropley & Urban, 2000). So, how do teachers create a balance between rigid knowledge of intelligence and the fluid craft of unruly ingenuity? Little has been written about balancing the need to meet curricular standards while also addressing the creative needs of gifted students. Here, we attempt to explain, evaluate, and negotiate the dynamics of meeting the needs of the students while creating that all-important balanced classroom.

Creativity Obstacles

There are two barriers to fostering or enhancing classroom creativity. One is intellectual uniformity. This is the classroom with absolute regularity and consistency. The other is intellectual anarchy, which is characterized by irregularity or chaos. In isolation, each is equally harmful to creative productivity, but in different ways: Absolute regularity denies the chance for creativity, while irregularity hampers progress and utility. In other words, uniformity allows for utility but negates novelty, while intellectual anarchy exploits novelty at the expense of utility. In their respective extreme forms, neither is ultimately productive in the creative sense (Sternberg, 2006).

Intellectual Uniformity

With intellectual uniformity, novelty is stifled or eliminated with everyone marching in lockstep. If the classroom is overly rigid, innovation will be eliminated and so will progress. To put it a different way, nothing is created if nothing is creative. Individualization is overshadowed by conformity to the norm. Elitism is a common criticism of gifted education (Sternberg, 1996). As a result, many teachers try to avoid this by teaching all gifted students the same—same content, same process, and same product (Maker, 1982; Mattsson & Bengmark, 2011)—at the expense of individual expression.

Life provides many examples of extreme uniformity (although not always a negative), such as the industrial assembly line, routine procedures in the office, and the repetitive Zumba class. Extreme uniformity is like singing only the melody to a song for an extended period of time, which may eliminate the potential for one to hear and sing the harmony. This uniformity is seen in academic environments with traditional straight-row lecture or in conventional mathematics instruction, such as the monotonous theorem-proof-theorem-proof mantra of the typical geometry class. Lockstep teaching, learning, and thinking, in all likelihood, result in a detrimental influence for creative activity.

Intellectual Anarchy

In contrast, with intellectual anarchy, nonconformity is the norm, with pandemonium the only result. In other words, everything is different for the sole purpose of being different. This is diversity at the expense of unity. Order and structure are abandoned for the sake of the new and unique. The end result of this perpetual and total innovation is that new ideas are firmly planted in midair. One could summarize this classroom as the following: If everything is creative, then nothing is.

Just as life provides examples of extreme uniformity, it also provides instances of extreme anarchy. History is replete with revolutionaries, inventors, and artisans who have broken the mold of traditional thought and challenged classical conventions—Thomas Edison, Albert Einstein, Sir Isaac Newton, and Leonardo da Vinci, just to name a few. Intellectual anarchy does not exclude precocious children with limitless appetites to learn and create. To create what their imaginations envision, these young innovators are constantly repurposing and reinventing the mundane, making it new. As teachers of gifted students, we do not want to repress this type of divergent thought. Yet, in its raw form, intellectual anarchy is not productive for students with exceptional talent.

Extreme anarchy is not like the symphony where different instruments are playing in concert. Rather it is like the noise of every instrument playing without a common beat, meter, measure or melody, or conductor. This is similar to the unruly, nontraditional classroom with purposeless group work and aimless brainstorming without boundaries and responsibilities. In short, chaotic teaching, learning, and thinking may foster diversity of thought, but because it is unharnessed, it may be just as ineffective as extreme uniformity.

Intellectual Irony

In the end, both extremes produce the same result. In the first case, unity of thought was prioritized over diversity of ideas to the point of elimination, and in the second, diversity of ideas replaced any notion of unity. More specifically, in the uniform environment, variation is unachievable, and therefore creativity is unobservable. Everyone is virtually identical. Once again, gifted education becomes the same content, same process, and same product (Maker, 1982). So, when learning is identical for every gifted student, the net gain is limited. Thus, if nothing is creative, nothing is created. Ironically, the same is true for the environment where everything is radically different or irregular. In this scenario, neither an objective nor a subjective standard exists to measure originality. Because everything is uniquely novel, nothing stands out. Thus, nothing is creative if everything is.

Intellectual Ingenuity

Nevertheless, the association of both barriers is not only desirable, it is crucial to embrace and support true creativity. In fact, one may argue that a balance of the two is the key to forging innovative ideas. That is to say, intellectual ingenuity is the productive merger of uniformity and irregularity. But what does this mean? And what is the practical application of this union of intellectual ingenuity that proportionally combines creativity with routine? Simply stated, if one comes from an overly structured and uniform environment, then the introduction of prescribed divergent stimuli is required. The goal of this divergence is to ignite the creative spark. Conversely, adding structure to the chaotic environment counterbalances and streamlines the creative process. This union transforms inaccessible chaos and bland homogeneity into a product that can be valued and embraced by the general public.

Intellectual Reality

In reality, most people are not drowning in a sea of creative chaos. As stated earlier, teaching, learning, and thinking in many classroom environments is monotonously uniform and rigid. This hyper-regularity is often the real obstacle to the curious and the creative. The main objective, therefore, is to enhance creativity by providing both dissonance and harmony to the environment. This allows ambiguity to survive, as well as respect for structure and order. Although potentially painful, it is necessary to evaluate one's position with respect to these two barriers. Generally speaking, teachers are inclined toward one chasm or the other. The solution, however, is not so much navigating our way out of these disproportionate routines, but rather utilizing each in tandem. This paradigm requires counterbalancing dominant and recessive dispositions. Maybe instead of chasms, these extremes can be thought of as stabilizing factors, like the ropes on a hand bridge. Without both, one may fall into the abyss of doldrums or chaos. If these chasms are perceived as ruts, one is stuck. However, if perceived as rails or supports, creative opportunities for students can be optimized. To clear a path for classroom creativity, uniformity and anarchy must be harnessed and utilized in tandem to produce intellectual ingenuity.

References

Cropley, A. J., & Urban, K. K. (2000). Programs and strategies for nurturing creativity. In K. A. Heller, F. J. Monks, R. J. Sternberg, & R. F. Subotnik

(Eds.), *International handbook of research and development of giftedness and talent* (2nd ed., pp. 485–498). Oxford, England: Elsevier.

Davis, G. A., Rimm, S. B., & Siegle, D. (2011). *Education of the gifted and talented* (6th ed.). Boston, MA: Pearson.

Maker, C. J. (1982). *Curriculum development for the gifted.* Rockville, MD: Aspen Systems.

Mattsson, L., & Bengmark, S. (2011). On track to gifted education in mathematics in Sweden. In B. Sriraman & K. H. Lee (Eds.), *The elements of creativity and giftedness in mathematics* (pp. 81–101), Rotterdam, The Netherlands: Sense.

Sternberg, R. J. (1996). Neither elitism nor egalitarianism: Gifted education as a third force in American education. *Roeper Review, 18,* 261–263.

Sternberg, R. J. (2006). The nature of creativity. *Creativity Research Journal, 18,* 87–98.

Chapter 11

Creative Problem Solving Embedded Into Curriculum

by Anna Cassalia

As educators look for strategies and learning models to ensure students are equipped to fully participate and succeed in society in this rapidly changing century, I can recommend the Creative Problem Solving (CPS) model developed by Treffinger and colleagues (Treffinger, Isaksen, & Dorval, 2000), which provides a framework to apply creative thinking processes to solve problems. Embedded in the model are tools and strategies that, when placed in the hands of students, allow them to be engaged in a process for thinking both creatively and critically. When CPS is tied to curriculum, students are learning to think and thinking to learn, rather than being spoon-fed information.

My colleagues and I have found opportunities in our curriculum for students in an academically gifted second-grade classroom to tackle real-world economic problems using the CPS model.

Creative Problem Solving (CPS) is a framework for practical application in problem solving. Groups or individuals define the nature of a problem, generate creative and unique ideas to solve the problem, and use specific tools to focus on solutions. The CPS model is a framework that consists of three process components, six stages, and 10 tools. The actual problem will determine which components of the model will be essential to solve the problem. It is not necessary to do all components, stages, or use all of the tools. The three process components are *Understanding the Challenge*, *Generating Ideas*, and *Preparing for Action*. Within each component are stages for problem solving and an assortment of tools that may be used throughout the model.

Component One: Understanding the Challenge

I began to organize this unit by focusing on economic and class systems, and rather than present prescribed economics lessons, I chose to have the students deal with a problem in their community. When planning for a CPS unit, you must first consider whether the task is complex, important, open-ended, and in need of novelty. If it meets these criteria, CPS may be the right model.

Constructing Opportunities

In the *Constructing Opportunities* stage I posed the headline: Community Needs Are All Around Us. The students then brainstormed various WIBAI (Wouldn't It Be Awful If . . .) statements. Examples of my students' work include: *Wouldn't it be awful if people were left to fend for themselves?* Or, *wouldn't it be awful if no one helped others in need?* With guidance, they reformed these statements into WIBNI (Wouldn't It Be Nice If . . .) statements. Examples from my students include: *Wouldn't it be nice if people helped others in need?* And, *Wouldn't it be nice if everyone had his or her needs met?*

Next, I had the students use the Hits and Hot Spots strategy to help us determine the problem we wanted to explore. To teach Hits and Hot Spots, I gave each of my students two stickers to place on the statements that jumped out at them. They could put both stickers on one idea or spread them out; the statements with stickers were the "Hits." After the students voted we clustered the ideas that were similar into "Hot Spots" to determine the actual problem statement we needed to further explore the data.

Exploring Data

During the second stage, *Exploring Data*, the students identified the key data within the problem, looked at the task from many different angles, and began to frame the challenge on which to work. The students explored data using 5W+H (Who, What, Where, When, Why, and How). These questions helped the students to draw out important information and gain clarity on how to proceed. Then, the students considered many sources of data (newspaper clippings, online articles, periodicals, and television news clippings) that depicted families/community members in need.

At that point in the economics unit, it was apparent that many students were using the language of an economist but had some difficulty fully understanding the terms. I used the Attribute Listing tool to help redefine the language of economics. The students were provided with a graphic organizer displaying economic terms and asked to provide a brief definition and list some attributes of the term. Then they were to read the story *Tight Times* by Barbara Shook Hazen (1983) and identify items or ideas that fit under each category.

Framing Problems

After reviewing the language and identifying the terms in the story, students had a better understanding of economic needs and were ready for the Framing Problems stage. In this stage the students formulated their problem statement. The students were to identify some targeted questions that could be used to stimulate the search for many, varied, and original ideas to solve the problem. I reminded the students to begin their statements with IWWM . . . (In What Ways Might . . .), How Might . . . , or H2 (How to . . .). Some examples of the students' thinking include: *How might we as students help those in need? In what ways might the local government improve its methods of helping those in need?* It is important to remind the students that they will be focusing on looking for the problem/question that they want to ask. This is not the time to look for answers. After the students generated their problem statements, they needed to focus their attention to one statement. The students were able to decide on a problem statement by using the Head and Shoulders test, which simply asks, "Is one of my options head and shoulders above the rest?" They chose to focus on: *In what ways might we help those in need?* After the students *Framed the Problem*, they set out to generate ideas for possible solutions.

Component Two: Generating Ideas

The *Generating Ideas* component has just one stage in which the students generate multiple and varied ideas, then focus their ideas to create a solution.

Creative thinking is often referred to as the divergent process in which we begin with a single thought or question and expand our thinking to create new possibilities. CPS idea-generating tools include: Brainstorming, SCAMPER, Morphological Matrix, Attribute Listing, and Force-Fitting. It is important to stress that during "generating," those involved are not to pass judgment, whether positive or negative. Let the ideas just flow and push for novelty.

Brainstorming is a way to generate multiple and varied options for an open-ended problem. I like to give my students sticky notes to record their ideas first, within a silent work environment, and then the students are encouraged to share their ideas and piggyback off of others. My students began to brainstorm solutions for the problem statement:

In what ways might we help those in need? After the students generated all of their suggestions, we put them on a large sheet of chart paper and used the Hits and Hot Spots tool (see Figure 11.1). The Hot Spots included: take money donations, sell things and donate the profits, donate gently used items, and have a school fundraiser.

Component Three: Preparing for Action

After generating many and varied ideas, the students had to think critically about those ideas to focus them into plausible answers. During this third component, the students were encouraged to put those ideas into action.

Developing Solutions

In this stage the students worked on promising options and refined them to fit our problem statement. At this time, I introduced another focusing tool, ALoU, which stands for: Advantages, Limitations, How to Overcome the Limitations, and Uniqueness. Through this process they determined that making a product and selling it was a good idea and maybe something worth considering.

Based on this new insight, the students needed to further investigate which idea they wanted to pursue. I introduced Force-Fitting, a focusing tool that requires forcing two seemingly dissimilar objects together to create a new or innovative idea. This is a strategy for students to see common objects or ideas in unusual ways. Through the use of the tool, which asked the students to come up

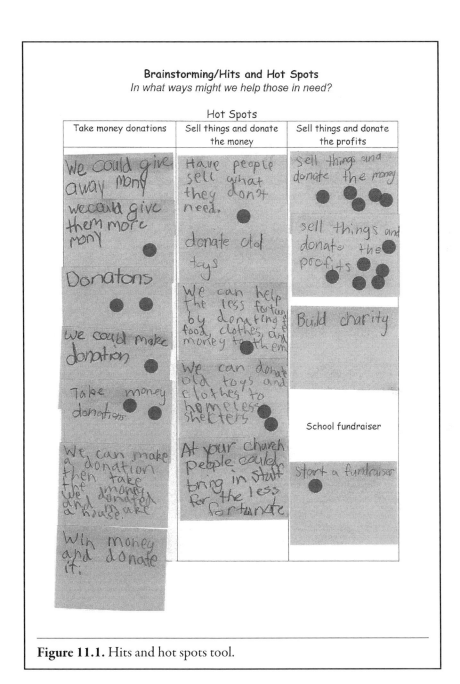

Figure 11.1. Hits and hot spots tool.

with new ideas, the class decided to make Christmas ornaments and sell them to the entire school community, the proceeds going to charity.

Next, the students had to decide which ornaments they were going to sell. The students decided to use the evaluation matrix to determine their product. An Evaluation Matrix is a focusing tool used to rank the options based on pre-determined criteria. For our problem, the students came up with the criteria: (a) most popular, (b) most profitable, (c) least labor intensive, and (d) most novel. There are many ways to use the evaluation matrix; for simplicity, we chose to rank the choices (1 = low; 5 = high) based on each criterion.

Building Acceptance

The students had a plan in mind, but they needed to further prepare how to carry out their solution. At this time we focused on anticipating factors that would possibly hinder successful action and identifying ways to overcome these hindrances. The students considered possible assisters and resisters using the 5W+H. *For example, who will be willing to hear our suggestions and help us with implementation? When can we present this information? Where will we meet obstacles?*

Component Four: Planning Your Approach

Appraising Tasks

As we thought through the possible obstacles, we decided our next course of action would be to create a plan that included action steps. At this time, I introduced the focusing tool, Short-, Medium-, and Long-term goals (or S-M-L), a tool that helps to organize one's options in a logical manner. Students were to decide their time frame and decide what needed to be done at each interval. We determined that in this case, Short-term would be things that needed to be done the same day, Medium-term were things that needed to be done in the next week, and that Long-term would be things that needed to be done in the month before our sale. Under short-term, the students decided they needed to order the ornaments and create a name for the business. In the two weeks that followed they needed to make the ornaments, create advertisements, write a jingle, and divide up into jobs for the actual sale days. Then, in the following month, they would hang posters to advertise, sing jingles on the announcements, set up their storefront, and sell the ornaments. S-M-L is a great focusing tool to use when planning a long-term project.

Designing Process

As we proceeded with our solution it became apparent that the students needed a mini-lesson on product development (in order to make unique ornaments) and creative advertising. I chose to use the tool, SCAMPER for this lesson. SCAMPER is an acronym for Substitute, Combine, Adapt, Modify, Minify, Magnify, Put to other uses, Eliminate, Reverse, or Rearrange. SCAMPER is used to generate new ideas by asking questions such as: *What could I substitute in this item/problem?* Or, *how could I adapt my idea to make a new idea?* We concluded this lesson with the students using the SCAMPER process to determine how to use a $100 donation and to create their advertisements (see Figure 11.2).

Finally, we had to decide to which charity the students would donate the profits from our sale. The kids had four possibilities in mind. To make this decision, we used PCA, Paired Comparison Analysis, a tool for ranking and prioritizing a small number of options. Through this process they decided that they would donate the money to Operation Smile, a charity that raises money for children with facial deformities, namely cleft lips and palates, from all around the globe.

This student-centered unit was based on our citywide curriculum goals: to develop an understanding for systems of knowledge, themes, issues, and problems that frame the external world, to develop metacognitive skills that foster independent and self-directed learning, and to develop creative and critical thinking skills along with problem-solving skills. Through the CPS model the students gained a deep understanding of basic economic principles while solving a real-world problem. This model allowed the students to grapple with difficult subject matter in a friendly and challenging manner.

The Creative Problem Solving model presents a unique and differentiated framework with which to deliver any curricular materials. If you are an educator searching for the tools to create a classroom full of 21st-century learners equipped with tools and strategies to embark upon solving the problems of today's world, look no further.

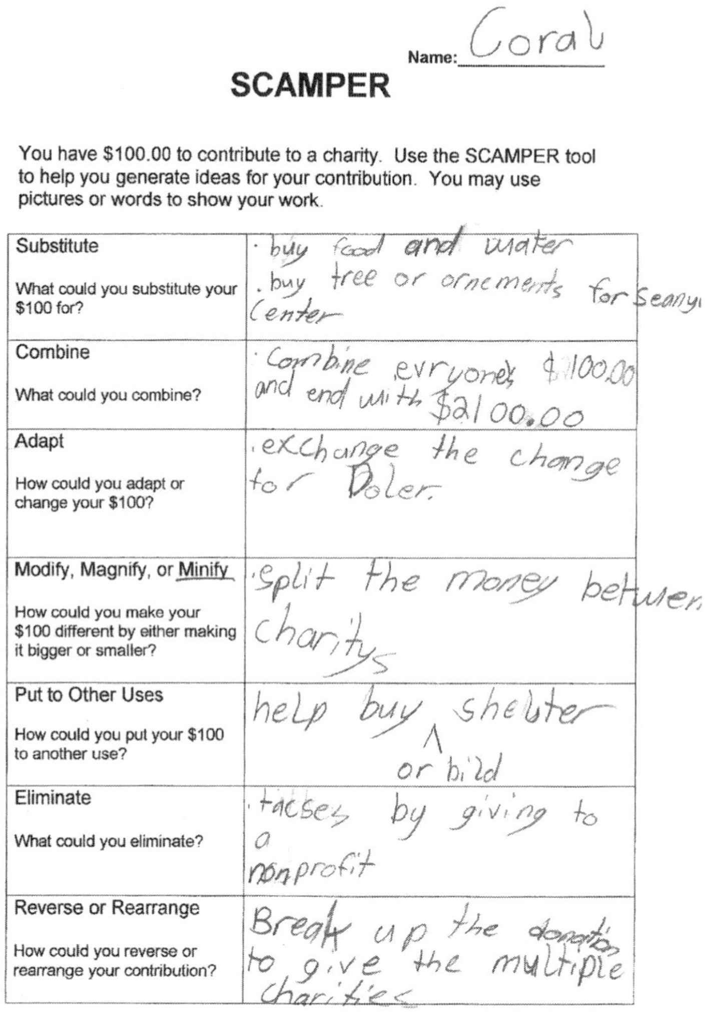

SCAMPER

Name: _Coral_

You have $100.00 to contribute to a charity. Use the SCAMPER tool to help you generate ideas for your contribution. You may use pictures or words to show your work.

Substitute What could you substitute your $100 for?	· buy food and water · buy tree or ornements for Seanyı Center
Combine What could you combine?	· Combine evryones $100.00 and end with $2100.00
Adapt How could you adapt or change your $100?	· exchange the change to r Doler.
Modify, Magnify, or <u>Minify</u> How could you make your $100 different by either making it bigger or smaller?	· split the money between charitys
Put to Other Uses How could you put your $100 to another use?	help buy shelter ∧ or bild
Eliminate What could you eliminate?	· taeses by giving to a nonprofit
Reverse or Rearrange How could you reverse or rearrange your contribution?	Break up the donati to give the multiple charities

Figure 11.2. SCAMPER process.

References

Hazen, B. S. (1983). *Tight times*. New York, NY: Puffin.

Treffinger, D. J., Isaksen, S. G., & Dorval, K. B. (2000). *Creative problem solving: An introduction* (3rd ed.). Waco, TX: Prufrock Press.

Chapter 12

Inspiring Student Creativity From SCRATCH

by Brian C. Housand

Are your students itching to delve into the world of computer programming, but you are not sure how to support them in this creative endeavor? Well, SCRATCH may be the solution.

When I think back to my earliest memories of computers, I was fascinated by the world of programming. Growing up I spoke BASIC and LOGO like they were second languages. The number of hours that I spent typing lines of code on my Commodore 64 was often followed by an even greater number of hours debugging the programs.

In the 21st century, LOGO and BASIC are as archaic as Latin. Seymour Papert (1997), one of the primary developers of LOGO, suggested that Latin is taught in schools because it serves to develop general cognitive skills. Indeed, this is precisely what I learned from programming. I am not suggesting that we teach our students these early computer languages. Instead, I want to introduce you to a programming language designed for today's digital natives.

SCRATCH (http://scratch.mit.edu) was designed to introduce computer programming to ages 8 and up, and it is a free, open-source program available for download on both Mac and PC. Inspired by LOGO, SCRATCH was developed by Mitchell Resnick, director of the Lifelong Kindergarten Group (http://llk.media.mit.edu) at the MIT Media Lab (http://www.media.mit.

edu). SCRATCH is a graphical programming language that allows the users to manipulate different bits of media, called sprites, using a simple interface that eliminates the need for complicated program coding. Users create a series of scripts or "blocks" to create motion and sound. Blocks of code are snapped together, like puzzle pieces, to create a larger structure. Interaction can be programmed so that when certain keystrokes are entered, a reaction takes place. Sprites can even be programmed to respond to one another. Users are able to create interactive stories, animation, games, and music.

SCRATCH allows students to imagine, program, and share their own creative ideas. One of the most interesting features of SCRATCH is the online community of users. Students are encouraged to share their completed projects in the online project gallery; approximately 170,000 projects have been uploaded to the site. Rather than being limited to viewing only the final project, SCRATCH users are able to see all of the programming that was involved in the creation of the process. This transparency allows students to closely examine how the process was designed.

SCRATCH is intended to be accessible to a wide audience with a range of abilities. The designers describe it as having a "low floor," meaning that it is easy to learn the basics. Although SCRATCH was created for ages 8 and up, do not be fooled by the simplicity of its design. SCRATCH also enables users to create complex projects and is used as part of many college-level computer science courses as an introduction to programming. Perhaps most meaningful for gifted educators, SCRATCH has wide walls, or the ability to support a wide variety of diverse projects related to any interest area via its online community.

The SCRATCH website provides resources for educators (https://scratch.mit.edu/educators), including tips on getting started and videos to guide teachers through the introduction to their students. There are also a series of "SCRATCH Cards" that provide mini-lessons on specific programming ideas. The cards may be used as scaffolding for the students to improve on or add new elements to their program. Discussion forums (https://scratch.mit.edu/discuss) are a good source of ideas for using SCRATCH. By visiting the educators' forum you can learn how others are using SCRATCH with their students and post your questions, ideas, and experiences.

When using SCRATCH, the best advice that I can offer to teachers is to get out of the way and see what the students create. After your students have acquired the basic skills of programming with SCRATCH, you could further develop their programming skills and creativity by creating specific challenge problems for your students to solve. Our students are itching to learn by creating, why not let them "SCRATCH" that itch and develop critical thinking and problem-solving skills at the same time by using this technology tool?

Reference

Papert, S. (1997). Why school reform is impossible. *The Journal of the Learning Sciences, 6,* 417–427.

Chapter 13

Creativity and the Common Core

Shining Light Into a Dark Space

by Chea Parton

Creativity is a nebulous concept with an array of definitions and ways of attempting to measure it. No matter which definition people accept as their own, it is easy to agree that creativity is important to students in schools. In his seminal work, "What Makes Giftedness? Reexamining a Definition," Renzulli (1978) outlines his three-ring conception of giftedness, emphasizing the importance of creativity. According to Renzulli, gifted behaviors occur at the intersection and overlap of above-average ability, task commitment, and creativity. The fact that creativity has its own ring indicates its importance in educating gifted students. With the advent of Common Core State Standards (CCSS) in states across the nation, educators—grades kindergarten through high school—must not forget the importance of creativity in gifted classes and programs, easy though it may be to get caught up in teaching the standards. Using finger painting as a catalyst for thought and emotive expression is one way to approach teaching poetry in middle and high school gifted English language arts (ELA) classes.

In today's world of high-stakes testing, teachers may feel forced to limit their students' educational experiences to those that will foster high scores on the standardized state test. This myopic focus on testing and the concept of the inherently right or wrong answers that it instills in both teachers and students stifles creative expression in classrooms and convinces teachers that preparing for the test and creativity are mutually exclusive. This is not true, and within the CCSS there is content that lends itself well to creative expression. Combining the use of those standards with activities that foster creativity is a great way to meet the standards and nurture creative thinking. Poetry is just one example. The CCSS include poetry (see Figure 13.1), and students are tested on their ability to read poetry and interpret what the poem conveys. Writing poetry is undoubtedly a creative act, and reading it in a way that yields understanding is just as creative a process. Clearly, though not necessarily explicitly stated in the standards, creativity is part of the Common Core.

Designing a lesson plan that teaches students to read creatively can be difficult because poetry is highly interpretive, with each reader viewing the ideas and emotions presented through his or her own set of experiences. Introducing this highly emotive and interpretive art form through a different art form like finger painting can open students up to the concept of multiple interpretations, easing them into something that seems overwhelming and foreboding (like reading and interpreting poetry) with something that is reminiscent of childhood. Once students are able to make connections to their own emotions and ideas, further reading and interpreting the work of other poets and meeting the standards are much less daunting tasks.

A Sample Lesson Plan

Sometimes it is difficult to design lessons that appeal to students' creativity while meeting the standards. Approaching poetry through song lyrics is something that has been done often, to the point that teachers and students now find it a bit cliché. Using finger painting to inspire students' own poetry and using that experience to inform their reading of other poetry is not as widely used and reaches students on a unique level. The following section outlines a week of 50-minute lessons that introduces students to ekphrastic poetry (poetry written about/inspired by artwork; see Figure 13.2) via reading, analysis, and finger painting. Students will:

- ▸ Gain awareness of ambiguity and multiple interpretations.
- ▸ Create finger paintings of abstract scenes.
- ▸ Write poetry inspired by paintings.
- ▸ Share and peer review poetry with trusted peers.
- ▸ Read and analyze ekphrastic poetry.
- ▸ Write reflections of experiences.

A Selection of Common Core Standards Concerning Poetry	
Elementary	**Middle/High School**
CCSS.ELA-Literacy.RL.K.5 Recognize common types of texts (e.g., storybooks, poems).	CCSS.ELA-Literacy.W.6.3d Use precise words and phrases, relevant descriptive details, and sensory language to convey experiences and events.
CCSS.ELA-Literacy.RL.2.4 Describe how words and phrases (e.g., regular beats, alliteration, rhymes, repeated lines) supply rhythm and meaning in a story, poem, or song.	CCSS.ELA-Literacy.W.7.5 With some guidance and support from peers and adults, develop and strengthen writing as needed by planning, revising, editing, rewriting, or trying a new approach, focusing on how well purpose and audience have been addressed.
CCSS.ELA-Literacy.RL.4.2 Determine a theme of a story, drama, or poem from details in the text; summarize the text.	CCSS.ELA-Literacy.RL.8.10 By the end of the year, read and comprehend literature, including stories, dramas, and poems, at the high end of grades 6–8 text complexity band independently and proficiently.
CCSS.ELA-Literacy.RL.5.7 Analyze how visual and multimedia elements contribute to the meaning, tone, or beauty of a text (e.g., graphic novel, multimedia presentation of fiction, folktale, myth, poem).	CCSS.ELA-Literacy.RL.9-10.7 Analyze the representation of a subject or a key scene in two different artistic mediums, including what is emphasized or absent in each treatment (e.g., Auden's "Musée des Beaux Arts" and Breughel's Landscape with the Fall of Icarus).

Figure 13.1. Selected poetry standards under the CCSS.

In order to complete the activity teachers will need the following materials: finger paints—red, blue, yellow, black; small paper plates to be used as palettes; newspaper to cover desks; white paper for canvases; paper, pencils, or pens; selected ekphrastic poems; and the artwork to go with those poems.

Day 1: Introduction

1. Review types of figurative language (e.g., metaphor, simile, imagery, idiom) and generate examples with students.
2. Ask students to write responses to the question, "What is good poetry?" Share and discuss—many students will have difficulty defining good poetry or hold inaccurate opinions of what good poetry is (e.g., good poetry rhymes). This discussion needs to set the foundation for how

Restless Mind

Thoughts fly,
Like fireworks burning in the sky.
Thoughts connect,
And become lines that intersect.
Dots of sadness,
Soon turn to blackness
But never overtake
The colors that happiness
makes.
Yellows and blues,
 And other bright hues,
Fill the never-ending canvas.
—Sophomore girl

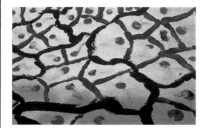

Cells

The building blocks of life
The puzzle of our being
Fitting together in perfect harmony
If one goes wrong
The result is complete catastrophe
Multiplying and dividing at an
enormous rate
As the doctors give you your death date
The power to give, the power to take
But the greatest power of all
Is the power to create.

Figure 13.2. Examples of ekphrastic poetry.

their poetry will be evaluated as well as how they will be evaluating the poetry of others. Having a framework ready beforehand and leading students toward defining that framework is important here.

3. Ask students to fill in the blanks of the following statement, "I think poetry is _____ because _____ ." (Remind them these should be school appropriate.) Share and discuss—being open to their opinions and validating their feelings about poetry is important here, but equally important is to encourage them to be open to new experiences.

4. Ultimately, students should leave the class with the understanding that good poetry is that which moves the reader and that is often ambiguous and subjective.

Day 2: Painting

1. Have students write a journal entry about how their day, week, month, etc., has been thus far. What has gone right? What has gone wrong? How are they feeling overall?
2. Review the definition of "good" poetry, emphasizing the importance of emotion.
3. Distribute newspaper, canvases, palettes, and paint.
4. Instruct students that these paintings must be abstract (no smileys or hearts), should reflect how they are feeling in that moment, and that they can experiment with technique.
5. Allow time for painting and clean up.

Day 3: Sharing/Writing

1. Have students collect their dried paintings.
2. Allowing them to share/brainstorm with classmates and revisit their journals, ask them to decide what is going on in their painting/what emotion it conveys.
3. Remind students to look at their notes from Day 1 and try to include figurative language that was reviewed to write poems based on their paintings.
4. Have an example of ekphrastic poetry ready and, together, read through the poem and analyze its figurative language use, and discuss the emotional message it conveys ("Musée des Beaux Arts" and "Ode on a Grecian Urn" are good examples). This is helpful for students who are reluctant or have difficulty getting started.

Day 4: Peer Revising

1. Because poetry can be very personal, allow students to work together in self-selected groups of 2–3 as they peer review the poetry. Students should be looking for the use of figurative language, clarity of content, originality of voice, correct spelling, and conclude with a comment about the overall feeling conveyed in the poem. (Reminder: This will be subjective.)
2. Once students are finished, have them regroup, and assign final drafts to be finished for homework.

Day 5: Reading and Reflecting

1. Allow interested students time to read their poetry aloud to the class before they turn in their final drafts.
2. If time permits, present another example of ekphrastic poetry to the class. This will help solidify their understandings of the medium now that they have completed their own.
3. Allow students to work in small groups while reading and analyzing the poetry and the painting.
4. Give them a prompt and have them write short analyses together (e.g., How does the poet use figurative language to capture the emotion of the painting?).
5. Have an entire class discussion in a large group once all groups are finished.
6. Allow time at the end of class for students to write reflections on their experiences with this medium.

Assessment Criteria

Many students may be apprehensive about their poetic abilities and the evaluation they receive on their poetry. Quite often, students' opinions of their writing capabilities are much lower than what their work reveals. It is important to stress to students that grading will be holistic and low-risk (e.g., their work on the poems will not ruin their grade in the course). Giving students the criteria with which they will be assessed is important so that they have some guidance, but the use of rubrics to grade creative works often detracts from individual creativity and freedom of the assignment, leading students to produce exactly what is "required." Instead, it is recommended that the following criteria be used to grade students' paintings and poetry: (1) abstractness of the painting, (2) connection between the poem and painting, and (3) use of figurative language and poetic devices.

As for assessing their reflections, the following criteria can be used: (1) Reflection covers the assigned topic and is thoughtful/insightful; (2) writing is clear, focused, and direct; and (3) spelling and grammar errors are infrequent. It is important to remember the power of positive feedback when assessing students' work, so encouraging comments that focus on what they have done well is crucial. If teachers openly encourage and congratulate students through the process, students will gain confidence and produce good work.

Notes and Conclusion

Not every student is a future poet laureate, but all students have feelings and emotions. Teaching them to recognize and channel those feelings into artistic expression in this way allows them creative and artistic expression and prepares them for high-stakes testing in a more enjoyable way. Becoming writers of poetry makes students more aware of the use of figurative language and generic conventions, which in turn makes them better readers of poetry. Although they might not be required to write a poem on a standardized test, they likely will be required to read and interpret one. The lessons presented here can be easily altered to suit any classroom's needs, and are intended to serve as a springboard for more lessons like it. There is nothing better than students who are excited to take part in an activity, happy to produce work, and proud of what is produced. Enriching their individual creativity and understanding for an often-confusing topic is an added plus!

References

National Governors Association Center for Best Practices, & Council of Chief State School Officers. (2010). *Common Core State Standards for English language arts*. Washington, DC: Author.

Renzulli, J. S. (1978). What makes giftedness? Reexamining a definition. *Phi Delta Kappan, 60,* 180–184, 261.

Chapter 14

Standard Deviations

Creative Writers Take
Standardized Writing Tests

by Michael H. Miller

Students at the Thomas Jefferson High School for Science and Technology produce the highest SAT and ACT scores in the nation. All of the students take at least one Advanced Placement exam, with 97% of them scoring well enough to receive college credit.

But those high scores are not always without intellectual cost. In taking test-prep courses for the SAT and ACT, or in preparing for the myriad AP and state tests, students often default to formulaic writing. In doing so, there is an inevitable closing down of the mind, where the traditional essay is the only acceptable mode of response, and oversimplified, superficial, and binary answers are the result.

The good news is that creative writing and standardized testing are not mutually exclusive. By encouraging students to consider multiple genre possibilities in responding to writing prompts, teachers can lead students toward more complex and creative thinking.

An Early Autumn Harvest of Five-Paragraph Nonfiction

In September, our English department gave each 11th-grade student in the school 60 minutes to respond to the following Virginia End-of-Course (EOC) Writing Test prompt:

> Thomas Jefferson wrote, "Determine never to be idle . . . It is wonderful how much may be done if we are always doing." Do we accomplish more if we are always doing something, or does inactivity also serve a purpose?

The writing that came back had been the sort of water torture only the steady drip of five-paragraph essays can inflict upon an English teacher. An introduction that ends in an obvious thesis statement. A paragraph on Thomas Jefferson. A paragraph on Bill Gates. A paragraph on high-achieving high school students. Basically a carefully organized piece that had the writer staying very safe and demonstrating little thought.

Only one student, Dana[2], had written something other than a traditional essay. She chose a screenplay format to express her response. With her permission, I shared what she had written with the rest of the class. Dana's writing featured an unhappily married couple: a workaholic husband who routinely clocked 60 or more hours a week at the office, and his wife at home, alone, with nothing to do. The husband eventually committed a white-collar crime, and the final scene found him in a jail cell alone—with nothing to do. Although Dana hadn't written an explicit thesis statement, she had answered the question about whether we should always be doing something; her screenplay argued that we should opt for a balance between action and inaction. Most of the class had never considered writing creatively in response to a standardized writing prompt, but Dana's example had inspired them—it gave them permission and encouragement to explore other possibilities beyond the traditional essay.

---

2   *Note.* All student names in this article are pseudonyms.

A Christmas Miracle of Creative Writing

In December, our English department again gave each 11th-grade student in the school 60 minutes to respond to another EOC Writing Test prompt:

> Author Ralph Waldo Emerson wrote, "To be yourself in a world that is constantly trying to make you something else is the greatest accomplishment." Do you agree or disagree with Emerson's statement about individuality?

The majority of responses were not traditional essays; there were interviews, plays, short stories, poems, narratives, and satires. This time, the responses were more focused, more willing to challenge the prompt: Is the world constantly trying to make you something else? Is individuality the greatest accomplishment? How do we measure accomplishment? Most students didn't fully agree or disagree with Emerson. Some were very candid about their lack of surety. They were displaying the best aspects of Neil Postman and Charles Weingartner's (1970) "good learners," who

> do not need to have an absolute, final, irrevocable resolution to every problem. The sentence, "I don't know," does not depress them, and they certainly prefer it to the various forms of semantic nonsense that pass for "answers" to questions that do not as yet have any solution—or may never have one. (pp. 32–33)

Heather responded with a fictional short story about a girl who is on her way to her first day at a new school. Her father is driving her to school, and he tries to mitigate her nervousness by telling her to "Just be yourself."

> *Be yourself?* I think. *Who's "myself" and how can I even be her?* Perhaps in order to "be yourself" you should know who you are in the first place.... I try to think of things I know I am.
> —I'm Stephanie.
> —I'm 16.
> —I'm in a car.

—I'm from Iowa.

—Wait, scratch that; I'm from Kansas. I was just born in Iowa.

—I'm . . . nice?

By that last point I'm stuck. Am I even nice? I am sure as hell not confident about these answers, at least that's for sure. Every time I think of something else "I am" I shoot it down with a counter example. After wrestling with myself for a good 5 minutes, I come up with a much better list.

—I am named Stephanie.

—I am 16 years old.

—I am in a car.

—I am confused about who I am.

Heather engaged in deep thinking and questioning here, comfortable with complexity and uncertainty; before she could answer the prompt, she had to consider some more fundamental questions: Who am I? What does it mean to be myself? Is it even possible to be anything but myself?

Michelle, who had written a forgettable five-paragraph essay in September, wrote a heartfelt story about a girl whose passion and purpose reside in rowing, but whose father is obsessed with getting her into Harvard. The climax occurs when her report card comes home:

My heart was racing, and I squeezed my mother's hand. "B-?" he roared. "How could you get a B- in physics? I give you everything you need, and you get a B-. Do you think you'll get into Harvard with these grades?" He picked up the nearest magazines on the coffee table and slung them in my direction. "No more crew," he continued. "No more friends. No more church. You can say goodbye to your weekends. You will not leave this house until your grades are up. How are you supposed to become a doctor like this?"

He motioned for me to go upstairs and study. I crawled into bed and stared at the ceiling, wondering how I could be myself when my dad was set on shaping the rest of my life.

Michelle's response challenged the simplicity of the prompt, pushing back with an implicit question of its own.

Justin wrote a narrative poem about being torn between the love of music and the pressure to pursue a career in science. Midway through the poem, the narrator reflects on his decision to abandon music:

That was my dream—the life I wanted for myself
To study the way notes dance on paper
And how drums sing
But my father still thinks the saxophone is a brass instrument
What's the difference between a trombone and a tuba?
He never saw the colors of music

Was there a connection between the creative writing and complex thinking my students produced? In writing a free-verse poem, Justin was already a far distance from the rigid thinking of a five-paragraph essay, a "preset format" that "lulls students into a non-thinking automaticity" (Rorschach, 2004, p. 19). By focusing on a central protagonist, Michelle was able to achieve thoughtful depth over superficial breadth. Heather, by turning her story over to a frightened, confused, 16-year-old narrator, was able to ask a series of hard questions, of both the prompt and herself. In giving their characters and narrators voices, my students put their individual fingerprints on each paragraph. Students who wrote fiction were able to develop and address counterarguments through dialogue between foils. Many of the fictionalized pieces were reflections of their writers' lives, and real life often defies ready-made templates, generalizations, and easy answers. Ironically, the fiction from the second round seemed to reflect the real world more accurately than the essays from the first, even when those essays were about real people.

My students and I began to wonder if they might replicate these successes on the actual EOC Writing Test. Would they be required to write essays? What constitutes an essay, anyway? Together we looked up the definition of essay. It is "a short literary composition . . . usually in prose." That last phrase, "Usually in prose," meant that some essays aren't written in prose. Short stories, plays, and poems all qualify as short literary compositions.

We started looking more closely at actual EOC Writing prompts. All of them asked for a "response," not an essay. Even though all of the online anchor papers were traditional essays, did that mean it wasn't possible or permissible to write one?

As a class, we weighed potential consequences. If students were to fail the test for writing creatively, they would be placed in remediation and would have to take the test again. At that point, they could either write an essay or continue to write creatively, failing the test a second time. All students felt that they would have an argument if they failed, for they were following the directions given to them and satisfied all of the requirements of the scoring rubric.

The Rites of Spring and Beyond

Of the 68 students who took the actual 2014 Virginia EOC Writing Test, 33 of them chose to write creative pieces: plays, short stories, diary entries, letters, interviews, and personal narratives. All 33 of those students passed at the advanced level, some with perfect scores.

Several students have gone on to write creative pieces on the SAT Writing section. Angela chose to write in the voice of Holden Caulfield from *The Catcher in the Rye*. Jiyoon wrote a short story about himself taking the SAT—a metaresponse. David crafted a story about a husband who reconfigures his work-life balance in the wake of his wife's death. All of them achieved nearly perfect scores.

Deconstructing the Norm

These results should begin to dispel the myth that creativity, questioning, and deep thinking in K–12 education—especially on standardized tests—are more likely to be punished than rewarded. And yet the myth persists. Heather recently showed me her response to a practice ACT essay. She had written a short story, and her teacher had awarded her a 2 out of 6: "Creative and entertaining! However, standardized tests (unfortunately) require a more formal argument." Gifted students can be particularly vulnerable to this mythology. They are naturally thoughtful and creative, but many of them are also high achievers, with their sights set on Ivy League schools that require tests they feel they must succeed on in order to gain admittance. They perceive that their teachers want a certain type of writing, or that a certain formula will yield a perfect—or at least safe—score. College writing instructors, meanwhile, "spend the first half of their semester unteaching the skills and traits students acquired during high school, encouraging initiative, autonomy, and invention" (Fanetti, Bushrow, & DeWeese, 2010, p. 82). In trying to please teachers, testmakers, and admissions officers, gifted students can become very adept at "the game of school."

As teachers of the gifted, we bear a particular responsibility to "reject a focus on right answers and conventional methods, in other words, not only because it promotes shallow learning but because it promotes passive acceptance" (Kohn, 2004, p. 190). We can begin by supporting creativity in responding to writing prompts, but we can also ask our students to reconsider what a presentation might look like, or how a research paper could be written. Our students' test scores—whether high or low—do not matter as much as their willingness to take reasonable risks when writing, speaking, and thinking in complex and creative terms. Some skills, after all, are more important than the ability to write a good essay.

Suggestions for Further Reading

Allen, C. A. (2001). *The multigenre research paper: Voice, passion, and discovery in grades 4–6.* Portsmouth, NH: Heinemann.

Campbell, K. H., & Latimer, K. (2012). *Beyond the five-paragraph essay.* Portland, ME: Stenhouse.

Moss, G. (2002). The five-paragraph theme: Does it prepare students for college? *The Quarterly, 24*(3), 23–38.

Romano, T. (2000). *Blending genre, altering style: Writing multigenre papers.* Portsmouth, NH: Heinemann.

References

Fanetti, S., Bushrow, K. M., & DeWeese, D. L. (2010). Closing the gap between high school writing instruction and college writing expectations. *English Journal, 99,* 77–83.

Kohn, A. (2004). Challenging students . . . And how to have more of them. *Phi Delta Kappan, 86,* 184–194.

Postman, N., & Weingartner, C. (1970). *Teaching as a subversive activity: A no-holds-barred assault on outdated teaching methods—with dramatic and practical proposals on how education can be made relevant to today's world.* New York, NY: Delacourte.

Rorschach, E. (2004). The five-paragraph theme redux. *The Quarterly, 26,* 16–19, 25.

Section IV:
Curriculum Planning and Thinking Skills

Chapter 15

Looking at Information Differently

The Importance of Understanding Epistemology

by Felicia A. Dixon

In her recent book, *The Geeks Shall Inherit the Earth* (2011), Robbins presents several different case studies of students (and, in one case, a teacher) who collectively represent adolescent differences. One student, called "Blue," describes his way of knowing as "I guess I tend to look at things a lot differently than other people. I can always look at both sides . . . the big picture, and draw my own conclusions." (p. 238). Later in the book, after returning home from a national competition, he reflected on what a team member had said to him, "You're an intellectual . . . You have a one-in-a-million kind of mind" (p. 354). Blue had been able to present issues to the judges in ways they had not considered before. His unique understandings were noted by his fellow students and experts alike.

The questions, What do we do with the "Blues" of the world? How do we educate them adequately? And, what strategies work best with these "global thinkers?" are worthy issues to explore when we work with high-ability adolescents. Not everyone in our classes designed for high ability fit this mold. Indeed, only a very few are truly dialectic thinkers, who are able to see both sides of an issue and arrive at a well-thought-out synthesis of the two.

When I began writing this column (Winter, 2011), I presented a top 10 list of issues I have found to be worthy of consideration when working with high-ability adolescents. On that list, presented in ascending order, my No. 2 issue was as follows:

> Never forget that these students are not all the same. They have different epistemologies and different learning styles as well. Learn how to plan your classes by using a variety of approaches, but always consider their affective needs when you plan for them. When I learned to focus on these areas, my classes became more interesting and high powered.

Often, the "Blues" of the world get passed over because, frankly, they do not shout out answers or even speak up to be noticed. Many teachers simply do not know what to do with them, so they do nothing with them. Such a global thinker, a "diamond in the rough" is left alone because he or she does not demand attention. How can the best thinker in the class be so marginalized? The fact of the matter is that many educators simply do not understand this unique epistemology and thus, do not know how to teach to it. But if we believe that each student deserves to learn something new each day, then we must teach to it, and understanding epistemology is one way to begin.

Perry (1970) defined epistemology as one's belief about the nature of knowledge.

He presented a developmental scheme that made direct and pragmatic application of the value of epistemology to the classroom, for it described both how students' views of knowledge change over time and also the powerful effect differing views have in the classroom. Perry's nine-stage theory can be broken down into four manageable chunks, which Gallagher (2008) also summarized. These four stages present a clear sequence of "knowing."

1. **Dualism:** This way of knowing is marked by a black-and-white perspective of understanding issues. Students at this stage believe all legitimate questions have certain answers and they characterize questions without answers as just nonsense questions that are pointless to discuss. Students at this level of understanding love unambiguous factual tests and appreciate lectures that lay out the facts clearly, in a "right or wrong" fashion.

2. **Multiplicity:** In this second way of knowing, students acknowledge that there are multiple unanswered questions, but they only believe this in the absence of a clear definitive answer. Consider the students in your class who will not discard any idea, thinking that all ideas are equally valid. Comparing issues to come up with the best solution, if it is not presented to them, is a difficult task. Discussion, in general,

causes discomfort because they allow all ideas without rejecting them if there is ambiguity.

3. **Contextual Relativism:** In this third way of knowing, students investigate unanswered questions using the tools provided by each discipline. Because each discipline approaches questions in a different way, one must revise her or his thinking for each class. In this way of knowing, absolutely certain answers are unlikely, but a "best answer" can be achieved using the proper tools. Hence, a student thinks as a professional would, with each skill perceived as a discrete methodology. But, students do arrive at consensus with a "best answer." Discussions are often quite productive to these students. Many high-ability students have this epistemology.

4. **Dialectic:** In this final way of knowing, theories are used to set directions for important questions, most of which have no "right" or "wrong" answers. Students seek to gain a clear understanding of an issue by building upon the possibilities presented by data as interpreted by a consciously selected point of view. Teaching to the dialectical epistemology requires teachers to present issues with contradictory sides that must be examined. Problem-based-learning, debate, and essays that present a consideration of differing points that arrive at a synthesis, and science projects that seek to find a solution through experimental design are all curricular ways to teach to the dialectical epistemology.

These different ways of knowing are important to understand in the classroom context. A very routine-oriented class with predictable events each day may work well for some (e.g., Dualistic and Multiplicity students), but may not be the best way to teach to students with Contextual Relativism or Dialectic epistemologies. Consider "Blue" once again. An adequate education for him would be one in which a very skillful and wise teacher trusted his or her students' abilities and designed a curriculum—AP or other—that offered high-level content through examination of issues. Class activities should be designed to include both individual and collaborative work. Class discussions must be designed to allow for the "other side" of the issue to be presented.

We are in the business of fostering cognitive growth; designing experiences in which our students can grow is paramount. So, never forget the "one-in-a-million mind," and provide activities that allow this student to engage and not tune out for lack of challenge.

References

Gallagher, S. A. (2008). Designed to fit: Educational implications of gifted adolescents' cognitive development. In F. A. Dixon (Ed.), *Programs and services for gifted secondary students: A guide to recommended practices* (pp. 3–21). Waco, TX: Prufrock Press.

Perry, W. G. (1970). *Forms of intellectual and ethical development in the college years: A scheme.* New York, NY: Holt, Rinehart &Winston.

Robbins, A. (2011). *The geeks shall inherit the Earth: Popularity, quirk theory, and why outsiders thrive after high school.* New York, NY: Hyperion.

Chapter 16

Becoming a Genuine Bloomarian

by Jason S. McIntosh

Of all of the tools and strategies teachers use to differentiate, none is more legendary than Bloom's taxonomy (see Figure 16.1). We are taught how to use it in our teacher prep courses, hear it mentioned during every workshop and conference we attend, and even preach it to our students. The question I would ask is this: Are we truly applying our knowledge of Bloom's taxonomy to our own learning and professional development?

The answer for many of us is no. This revelation came to me while conducting classroom walkthroughs of gifted cluster teachers throughout my district. Being responsible for providing the professional development they receive on differentiating for gifted learners, I have firsthand knowledge of the training that occurs. For instance, I am confident that each gifted cluster teacher can explain the meaning of all 11 Depth and Complexity icons. I have watched them practice conducting Socratic Seminars with each other; I have helped them collaborate to create choice menus; and I know that they can easily list three or more ways to preassess their students and know how to determine if compacting is needed. So, how is it possible for me to conduct dozens of walkthroughs and see very little application of these concepts? How can there be such a disconnect between the theory and its practice?

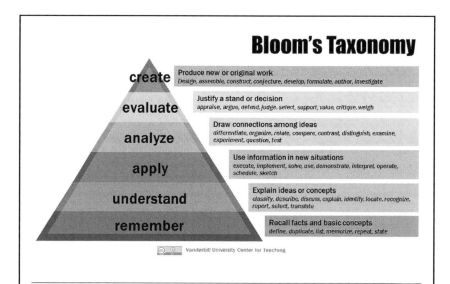

Figure 16.1. Bloom's Taxonomy. From "Bloom's Taxonomy" by Vanderbilt Center for Teaching, 2016, retrieved from https://cft.vanderbilt.edu/guides-sub-pages/blooms-taxonomy. Used under Creative Commons Attribution 2.0 Generic.

When I posed this question to the teachers themselves, the answers I received were not surprising. Understandably, lack of time and large class sizes were explanations that made the top of the list. For just a moment, however, let's shift the focus to the educator. Would we allow our students to make excuses for why they were not applying, analyzing, synthesizing, or evaluating if we knew they were more than capable of doing so? Of course not.

The skills required for higher level thinking take time and effort to develop. Making differentiation a daily practice in the classroom is not an easy task. It takes creative problem solving, risk-taking, and a certain amount of courage to make it work.

Putting Bloom's Taxonomy Into Action

We need to be living examples of Bloom's taxonomy in action. Our students need to see us grapple with new teaching strategies to work our way up from the knowledge level to the synthesis level. They need to see us practice what we preach by struggling with a new concept or skill until we have mastered it. We must find a solution for the barriers we face instead of falling victim to them. Not only will the students' respect for us grow, but each time they are faced with a difficult task they will think of it as a summit they have the ability to climb. Why? Because they once had someone show them how.

A genuine "Bloomarian" seeks to develop expertise by reflecting on his or her own teaching practices in order to identify where improvement is needed. It involves practice, persistence, and patience, but has a great payoff. In addition to increased student achievement, there is deep pride in persistence. True master teachers forgo excuses in exchange for excellence. Are you a genuine Bloomarian or have you let a lack of time, resources, or support stand in your way?

As Victor Frankl said, "When we are no longer able to change a situation, we are challenged to change ourselves." Here are a few ideas for doing just that.

- ▶ Begin by posting a sign in your classroom that reads, "This is a risk-taking, mistake-making classroom." Refer to it often with your students, and let it serve as a personal reminder to try something new and take a chance.
- ▶ Start off small and choose one new strategy to implement. Then persist until you "own it."
- ▶ Quality differentiation does not happen spontaneously so consider planning collaboratively with a friend. Arrange time to observe each other using new strategies, and provide feedback on improvements that can be made.
- ▶ Keep a reflection journal, and remember to celebrate the small victories along the way.

Using Your Resources

Professional learning communities among the staff are vital, but a truly brave teacher will be open to involving students in his or her learning opportunities as well. Consider giving your students a simple form to evaluate you periodically, just as we so often do at the conclusion of a conference or workshop. If a group of students has tested out of a particular concept, consider asking them to create a learning center or choice menu during the time they bought back that you can then use with the rest of the class. Not only will this be a time saver for you, but it will serve as a higher level thinking activity for those students ready for the challenge.

There are many wonderful professionally created materials available to make differentiating easier, but if money is an issue, consider using the free resources right at your fingertips. Basal reading programs and other series have long been criticized for being low level and one-size-fits-all. Curriculum developers have made great strides in recent years in addressing all levels of learners. Revisit your teachers' manuals and you might be surprised at what you find. In addition, there are many free Web 2.0 applications just waiting to be used by creative teachers. Prezi, Glogster, Jing, and GoAnimate are just a few worth mentioning.

Webster's Dictionary defines synthesis as "the combination of ideas into a complex whole." Strive to reach the synthesis level in your own professional development. The combination of courage, collaboration, and dedication create the perfect recipe for a teacher who there are no better words to describe than . . . is a genuine Bloomarian. I don't know about you, but I wouldn't mind having that on my résumé someday!

Reference

Vanderbilt University Center for Teaching. (2016). *Bloom's taxonomy*. Retrieved from https://cft.vanderbilt.edu/guides-sub-pages/blooms-taxonomy

Chapter 17

Teaching What Is Essential

Asking the Essential Questions

by Bronwyn MacFarlane

Determining what is essential for high-ability students to learn in a gifted program curriculum is one of the most important aspects of curriculum design work. If curriculum is a set of written decisions for what students will learn, know, and be able to do, then the use of *Essential Questions* in curricular planning and delivery can help students learn independently and also provide the connective tissue between what matters at the heart of the curriculum and assessment of what students have learned.

Curricular Planning With EQs

Essential Questions (EQs) are written by teachers as an overarching articulation of what is important in the curriculum content. When planning curriculum, carefully developed Essential Questions can increase the quality of a unit of study because EQs not only provide organization and a clear conceptual commitment, they also provide opportunities for creative choice and an articulation of skills to be encouraged in students. Essential Questions should be written to be complex and abstract and can lend themselves to making connections and understanding about universal truths.

Related to *Essential Understandings* (EU), which are broad, abstract, timeless, and universal statements that show the relationships between concepts, Essential Questions provide a question form of an EU statement. EQs should also tie to the unit's universal concept or theme but differ from general scaffolded questions, which are more basic for purposes of defining terminology, making abstract ideas concrete, or bringing concepts to a personal level. EQs provide both teachers and students with information about what is essential to understand in the unit of study and when embedded into delivering the curriculum, students can learn to recognize, appreciate, and generate EQs of their own for further inquiry.

In a graduate course that I teach focused on differentiated curriculum and instruction for gifted learners, teacher candidates begin designing curriculum units by first determining "what is essential" related to their selected curricular topic. Prior to writing lessons and unit assessments, every curriculum writer must first determine the Goals, Outcomes, and Essential Questions to guide the curriculum unit design. When drafting and revising robust EQs, educators should reference the following criteria:

1. EQs should be written at the appropriate grade level and/or cognitive level for students to understand.
2. The language of the questions should be written in broad, organizational terms.
3. The questions should reflect conceptual priorities.
4. Each question should be distinct and substantial.
5. Questions should not be repetitive.
6. The questions should be realistic given the amount of time allocated for the unit or course.
7. There should be a logical sequence to a set of essential questions.
8. The questions should be posted in the classroom.

EQs in Classroom Instruction and Assessment

EQs should not be isolated in the written curriculum but should be actively integrated into the classroom during instructional and assessment activities. In general, 5–8 EQs are adequate to stimulate formative and summative assessment checks for student understanding at different points of the unit. Teachers should post the EQs for students to reference throughout the unit of study. By integrating references to EQs during discussions and lesson activities, the EQs can be referenced as a guide for students to independently discover related topics of study and to make additional connections.

When assessing student learning, Essential Questions should be used to demonstrate what students know, understand, and are able to do. The questioning process is the cornerstone of inquiry and assessment and EQs can be used to lead students through predictive discussions, problem-finding group activities, as well as formative and summative assessment activities in which the EQs provide a cornerstone to measuring student understanding.

Determining what is essential and what is the essence of a subject is critically important for gifted curriculum. Carefully planned Essential Questions support students with opportunities for differentiated learning experiences by examining essential understandings and developing the thinking and project-based skills that are the foundation for advanced learning. By integrating EQs throughout the curriculum plan, instructional delivery process, and assessment activities, students can explore a well-articulated set of essential understandings through a series of questions in a specific unit of study.

Resource

For more information about Essential Questions, access Carol Fertig's article at https://www.goodreads.com/author_blog_posts/1359107-universal-themes-and-essential-questions-for-the-gifted.

Chapter 18

Differentiating Content Using a Conceptual Lens

by Todd Jeffrey

Ask a group of parents what their goals are for their gifted children after going through the K–12 experience. What do parents want them to become? The answers are typically: "Thinkers," "Problem Solvers," "Self-Evaluators," "Lifelong Learners."

Ask a group of teachers the same question and you will get many of the same answers. Our hopes for our children are truly lofty goals, which provide an educational compass for me as both a public school teacher and a private school principal. With this in mind, the question becomes, "How do we assist students in becoming thinkers, problem solvers, self-evaluators, and lifelong learners?"

Strengthening the curriculum through the use of conceptual learning methodologies is one way that teachers and administrators can develop the aforementioned desirable student traits. In my former school settings, the use of both depth and complexity concepts as well as universal concepts brought a greater degree of rigor to the material being studied. These concepts allowed students to gain a deeper understanding of a topic or issue, and to tie previous learning together with current topics. Additionally, the use of conceptual learning methodologies proved beneficial to students of all grade levels. Innovative school districts have embedded these concepts in comprehensive curriculum frameworks, seeking to develop holistic learners. For example, the Round Rock

Independent School District (n.d.) uses concept and generalizations to develop students who seek knowledge and understanding, think critically and engage in problem solving. In a second-grade classroom this manifests itself with students identifying, describing, and extending addition and subtraction patterns; a ninth-grade biology class discusses how changes in matter affect everyday life.

Depth and Complexity Concepts

Depth and complexity is a form of differentiated learning that modifies curricular content. Infusing depth and complexity in the curriculum, concepts are posed as words or prompts and stimulate higher levels of knowing (Kaplan, 1996). They help a student decode meaning and gain increased knowledge in a domain. Depth and complexity concepts can be thought of as the tools that practitioners in a field or discipline use to gain knowledge. Archaeologists, for example, use specific language of the discipline, find patterns, and uncover big ideas in order to gain understanding. Universal concepts, although similar to depth and complexity concepts, provide the academic glue that binds the unearthed knowledge together. They connect learning across and within disciplines.

Rules are an example of a depth and complexity concept. Using the concept of rules, students are instructed to define how a topic is structured. Rules are laws, norms, formulas, or orders to be followed. It is easy to see how working with the concept of rules is important when discussing forms of government; however, the investigation of rules reveals knowledge in other disciplines as well. Literature contains several instances of rules. If students are studying fairy tales, for example, one common rule is that the story has a happy ending. Another rule might be that fairy tales contain some form of magic. Studying fairy tales through the lens of rules allows students to make connections among stories from various times and cultures.

Another often-used depth and complexity concept is big ideas. Students are instructed to determine the overarching statement that best summarizes what is being studied. A big idea can be a generalization, principle, or theory. Inductive learning is at the heart of big ideas. Students gather an assortment of information from numerous sources and then put a label on it. At its basic level, first- and second-grade teachers can start introducing big idea concepts by having students identify the "golden sentence" in a story. The students then provide support, textual or experiential, for why the sentence is the most important within the story.

Discussion and dialogue using a Socratic seminar method is an authentic way for students to investigate the depth of an idea (Copeland, 2005). There are certain ideas that are essential to the study of a discipline or field. Sovereignty is an example of a core idea that students in a high school history class need to understand. For example, Jefferson and Madison had very different beliefs on sovereignty in regard to secession, the former espousing that within a union of states, one party may withdraw from the agreement and remain sovereign. Lincoln had opposing views on this subject. A comparative reading and dialogue of the Federalist Papers and Lincoln's First Inaugural Address could generate a thorough understanding of the big idea—sovereignty.

Details, patterns, language of the discipline, changes over time, trends, unanswered questions, and points of view are all depth and complexity concepts. These concepts are nothing new to teachers. They are tried-and-true ways of gaining deeper understanding. However, by using these specific terms to characterize concepts, both teachers and students share a common terminology for the connections they make. Doing so enables them to make such conceptual connections more frequently and consistently. Many schools have created posters with the concept and its associated icon or picture to help ensure that these concepts are continually being investigated and discussed. The commitment to a common conceptual vocabulary is apparent to parents, teachers, and students throughout the school building.

Universal Concepts

The second aspect of the conceptual learning model we used was universal concepts. Traditionally, education's primary focus was on memorizing and regurgitating key facts, figures, and events. However, due to the exponential increase of data and the need for students to be problem solvers and thinkers, this accumulation model is outdated. In programs where universal concepts are emphasized, students categorize facts into representative groups, rather than memorize facts. The use of universal concepts, then, is a way to teach students how to think about, then cluster information (Wiggins & McTighe, 1998). According to H. Lynn Erickson (2002), universal concepts are timeless, abstract, and typically can be represented by as few as two words. Universal concepts are interdisciplinary; they strengthen and weave learning together across subject and grade-level lines.

The universal concept of change can be found throughout U.S. history, but is exemplified by the fact that America went from an agrarian to an industrial economy. In biology, change can be studied by examining the metamorphosis of a butterfly. In literature, change occurs in the character arc of a protagonist.

A simple way to infuse universal concepts into your classroom is to use them at the conclusion of a lesson to summarize the content. A science teacher could ask her students, "What have we learned about electricity, and how does it relate to our new understanding of systems?" Another way to embed this kind of teaching in the culture of a school is to assign each grade level a universal concept to examine over the course of the year. Examples of common universal concepts are power, systems, conflict, order, structure, patterns, and interdependence.

The conceptual learning methodologies described above allow students to examine ideas in complex ways. They also illuminate the connectedness of information. Information presented without a framework is like a random assortment of puzzle pieces. Shape and color can be defined easily. However, until placed together, they hold no meaning. Through the use of conceptual teaching methods, students learn how those puzzle pieces fit together (Taba, 1962). All students, and gifted students in particular, have the ability to make connections and see complex relationships. Conceptual learning builds on that ability and strengthens it.

Not all aspects of curricular differentiation are accomplished with equal effort. Even teachers new to differentiation can provide multiple options for differentiating the products that students produce to demonstrate their learning. The differentiation of process often involves varying instructional strategies learned in teacher preparation courses. However, differentiating content is much more elusive. Although the importance of differentiating content is widely agreed upon, the methods for differentiating content are not and often take a great degree of skill and preparation to execute successfully. Assessing student learning of ideas is difficult using traditional multiple-choice standardized tests. Using universal as well as depth and complexity concepts assists teachers in modifying curricular content. The sample lesson framework on the next page is an example of how depth and complexity concepts modify rigor and relevance of a typical famous person report.

Applying the concepts of depth and complexity to traditional grade-level reports raises the level of academic rigor and understanding.

Famous Person Depth and Complexity Report:
1. **Details:**
   a. Date of birth
   b. Education
   c. Profession
   d. Death
   e. Four other important details

2. **Language of the Discipline:** Any unknown vocabulary related to their profession or life.
3. **Big Idea:** Why is this person famous? What did he or she contribute?
4. **Patterns/Over time:** Because of his or her contributions, what can we predict will happen next in America or the world?
5. **Ethics/Perspectives:** What dilemmas or controversies was your person involved in or did his or her contribution create?
6. **Unanswered Question:** Based on your research, compose two questions about the person.
7. **Trends:** Did this person's contribution lead to any trends?

Dr. Sandra Kaplan mentioned in a workshop that successful people recognize connections between knowledge. Therefore, the intelligent plumber and the intelligent heart surgeon can hold a conversation on valves and clamps. Conceptual learning provides teachers with a framework to teach students how to make authentic connections. They achieve the ultimate educational goal of parents and teachers to develop students who are more than just great test takers and consumers of knowledge but rather thinkers, problem solvers, and producers of knowledge.

References

Copeland, M. (2005). *Socratic circles: Fostering critical and creative thinking in middle and high school.* Portland, MN: Stenhouse.

Erickson, H. L. (2002). *Concept-based curriculum and instruction: Teaching beyond the facts*. Thousand Oaks, CA: Corwin Press.

Kaplan, S. (1996). *Definitions of dimensions of depth and complexity. Differentiating the core curriculum and instruction to provide advanced learning opportunities*. Sacramento, CA: California Department of Education and California Association for the Gifted.

Round Rock Independent School District. (n.d.). *Teaching and learning*. Retrieved from https://teachlearn.roundrockisd.org/teaching-and-learning

Taba, H. (1962). *Curriculum development: Theory and practice*. New York, NY: Harcourt, Brace & World.

Chapter 19

Teaching Current Events as a Feature of a Differentiated Curriculum

by Sandra N. Kaplan

Picture a student standing in front of the class nervously fondling an excerpt from a newspaper and hesitatingly presenting a 2- to 5-minute overview of the news. In the same room there is a bulletin board in the classroom labeled "WHAT'S NEW" with several articles posted under the title. These are two of the traditional strategies used to incorporate current events in the curriculum. Now picture a group of gifted fourth-grade students studying the Gold Rush whose teacher asks them about the current gold standard and why it is presently calculated at such a high rate. One student asks if there is still a gold standard. Another student queries why a specific mass of gold has such an influence on the contemporary monetary system. Incidents such as these have aroused an effort to justify the importance of current events as a valued feature of a "well-designed differentiated curriculum" to respond to the needs, interests, and abilities of gifted learners.

There are myriad arguments beyond adding relevance to a curriculum that can be posed to substantiate the integration of current events in a differentiated curriculum for the gifted. One view could be their alignment to the development of a well-educated individual: the individual who can recognize the bridge between "in-school studies" and the real world. Another point of view is that current events provide access to another type of genre and therefore can extend students' experiences in reading, critical analysis, and problem solving. The presence of current events also invites students to study the discipline of journalism: its purpose, significance, language, skills, and methodology. Most significantly, current events can spark students' curiosity, awe, and appreciation for the topical possibilities that will be the history, science, art, and mathematics to be studied as subjects within and over time. A common misconception of today's education is that what is valued and tested is what is known; there is scant emphasis attributed to what is currently happening that illustrates what is not known.

News as a Predictor

Students should be made aware of the various sections or areas of news presentations in print and in online media and the purpose underlying each: feature stories, business, entertainment, op-ed, advertisements, and local news. The distinct qualities of each of these sections can be correlated to the different styles of reading each demands, the type of information each yields, and the different styles of writing each requires. The idea of perceiving the news as a predictor allows teachers to teach and students to purposefully practice critical thinking and problem-solving skills: state and test assumptions, hypothesize, prove or validate with evidence, determine the relevance, and differentiate fact from opinion. Figure 19.1 presents a worksheet for students to document the information found through media research as they ponder a variety of predictions. More importantly, these predictions demand that students learn how to make connections, establish links, and define relationships that "weave" new understandings and underscore students as independent thinkers.

Another strategy to reinforce the concept of news as a predictor is one that asks students to identify a trend of the past and study the events of the present in order to identify and verify today's trends. The learning experience, "Current Events Over Time Identify Trends" (see Figure 19.2), facilitates the students' ability to recognize that trends do not merely occur by chance but instead could be a result of understanding the connections between the past and present. This learning experience also reinforces the concepts of becoming an intellectual: a person who can access and use information analytically and critically. The act of understanding trends is a skill that can be used across multiple disciplines. Training students to identify trends in any cultural milieu reinforces the "prediction" activity discussed earlier while at the same time offering students a

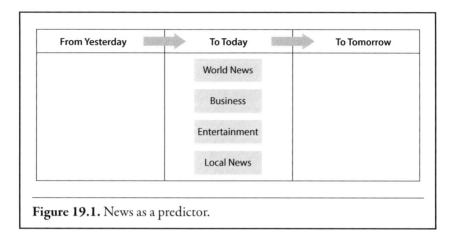

Figure 19.1. News as a predictor.

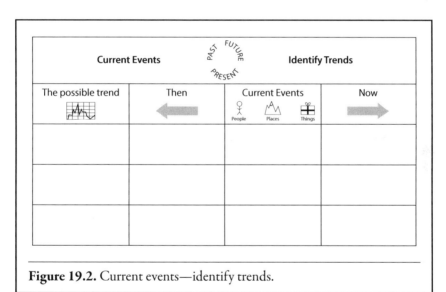

Figure 19.2. Current events—identify trends.

chance to make connections between different issues in society. Information consumption is often seen as a necessity rather than a chore.

Classics and Current
Event Relationships

Students need to understand that the process of reporting and disseminating the news has occurred in societies and cultures throughout time and has included a variety of mediums: writing on caves, smoke signals, quilts hanging on tree limbs, and semaphores. A concomitant understanding to the historic transmission of the news or current events is the realization that artifacts also have been the source of communication. For a generation of iPod, iPad, laptop, Twitter, and blog users, an understanding that news writing and delivery has occurred throughout the ages in various forms is an important realization. The following learning experience illustrates how classical ideas can be linked or associated to present forms of media or sources of current events. Two basic guiding questions can facilitate these connections along with sample worksheets (Figures 19.3 and 19.4) that could be replicated easily for the educator in any subject area.

Q1: What are the relationships between contemporary forms of developing social networks and the uses of historical documents and artifacts?

Q2: What are the similarities and differences between events of the past and the same type of event that is occurring currently?

Conclusion

The importance of teaching information literacy is defined in the 21st Century Skills, as well as other documents articulating the pressing academic needs of today's students. Although the emphasis on information literacy often reinforces developing students' awareness of the benefits of digital media, the true nature lies in the analysis and critique of the information uncovered. Accessing and reporting information are crucial skills for gifted students to acquire and these skills can be realized as gifted students also recognize the impact and influence of current events on people, places, problems, and issues. The emphasis on teaching and learning about globalization and the evolution of students as "members of the world" are contingent on many factors including the study of current events.

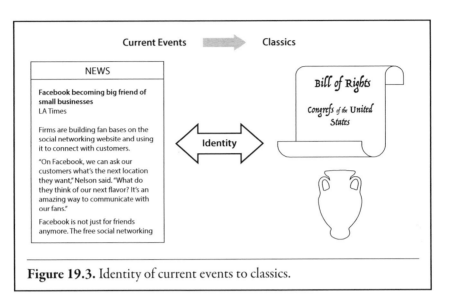

Figure 19.3. Identity of current events to classics.

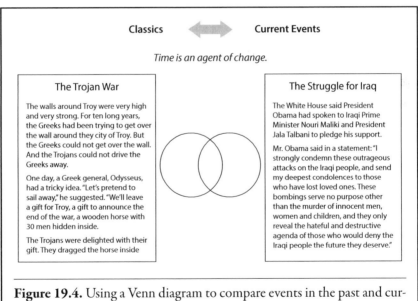

Figure 19.4. Using a Venn diagram to compare events in the past and current events.

Chapter 20

Knowing Is a Process, Not a Product

by Jennifer Beasley

> We teach a subject not to produce little living libraries on that subject, but rather to get a student to think mathematically for himself, to consider matters as an historian does, to take part in the process of knowledge-getting. Knowing is a process, not a product. (Bruner, 1966, p. 72)

Jerome Bruner wrote *Toward a Theory of Instruction* more than 4 decades ago and yet his words remain as powerful today as they did then. At the time his book was written, the nation was in the midst of an educational crisis. Many countries were outperforming the U.S. in the areas of math and science. The launch of Sputnik in 1957 triggered an educational movement, one result being increased research and spending in the area of curriculum development. The government wanted to better prepare children for the future. Bruner's words were a warning to us then—of what was important in education.

Today's educational climate is not too different than what it was 4 decades ago. Our students are again finding themselves falling behind other developing countries in the areas of math and science. The education departments in state and local governments have responded by increasing control over curriculum. State standards are now the guide for curriculum development as well as the end goal. Bruner's words again prove to be a reminder and a warning to us today—of what is important in education.

For high-potential students, emphasis on high-stakes testing has resulted in what I can only think of as "low-stakes learning." Many students arrive in classrooms able to pass the year-end test before the year even begins and are given few opportunities to experience rigor. In this setting, how do we help all children to realize that "knowing is a process, not a product"? How do we get students to think mathematically for themselves, to consider matters as an historian does? Can we help each student to, as Dr. Sandra Kaplan says, "think like a disciplinarian"?

I was confronted with this dilemma when it came time to prepare a unit on state history. In school, this unit in social studies has always been laden with facts and skills that seem to make no real connection to authentic learning. Students need to locate state resources on a map, identify famous people in our state history, and so on. I searched for a way to connect the unit with powerful learning experiences where all students would be challenged. Turning again to Jerome Bruner (1966), who believed that the major responsibility of the teacher is to help the student understand the structure and meaning of his or her subject, I started by asking myself "Why is studying state history important?" and "Who is the practicing professional that is concerned about the history of a state?"

As a teacher, I wanted to help my students find meaning in what we were learning. For my own social studies unit, I arrived at the understanding that state history is important because each of us identifies with the place that we live and through it we can make connections with our own identity. In my unit, I wanted students to delve into the "famous faces and facts" of our state using the methods and practices of someone who really does work with this information—a public historian. The journey I took when planning this unit was not always the shortest path between two points. It involved asking myself questions that I did not necessarily have answers to at the time:

- ▶ How do practitioners organize their knowledge and skill in this field?
- ▶ What tools does a practitioner use in his or her work?
- ▶ What are the methods used by practitioners and contributors in the field to generate new questions, to generate new knowledge, and to solve problems (Tomlinson et al., 2002, pp. 29–30)?

In the course of the unit on state history, I had students take on the role of a practicing public historian. They examined primary source documents and began to realize that the perspective of a historian impacts the interpretation of historical events. Students learned how to examine artifacts and spoke with experts in their state government. I saw students excited to talk, even argue, about events that helped form the identity of their state. Through this journey, I realized that my students and I were experiencing the joy of the knowledge-getting process. It is this process that helps us find meaning in what we are learning and how it connects to our own lives.

We seem to be at yet another turning point in the story of education. It is becoming harder to create curriculum that both challenges and motivates our students, but the opportunity is still there. I found my own journey through the creation of curriculum to be as important as my students'. I hope to keep listening to the wisdom of the past to help direct the road to the future:

> A curriculum is more for teachers than it is for pupils. If it cannot change, move, perturb, inform teachers, it will have no effect on those whom they teach. It must be first and foremost a curriculum for teachers. If it has any effect on pupils, it will have it by virtue of having had an effect on teachers. (Bruner, 1960, p. xv)

References

Bruner, J. S. (1960). *The process of education*. Cambridge, MA: Harvard University Press.

Bruner, J. S. (1966). *Toward a theory of instruction*. Cambridge, MA: Harvard University Press.

Tomlinson, C. A., Kaplan, S. N., Renzulli, J. S., Purcell, J., Leppien, J., & Burns, D. (2002). *The parallel curriculum: A design to develop high potential and challenge high-ability learners*. Thousand Oaks, CA: Corwin Press.

Chapter 21

Curriculum Compacting

How and Why to Differentiate Beyond Proficiency

by Chris A. Caram and Patsy B. Davis

When our brightest students are asked about their main obstacle, they almost always say it is their school. (Davidson, Davidson, & Vanderkam, 2004)

Consider Jack's Story

Jack sat in the principal's office of his middle school with his head in his hands. He knew he was in trouble and, frankly, he didn't care. So what if he had been rude and disruptive? He didn't want to be there, and he had told his parents over and over again that the teachers in his new school obviously didn't know how to teach. He was just wasting his time being there every day. If he were only allowed to stay at home with his grandparents, he could work on the project that meant the most to him . . . space!

He dreamed of the day when he would be a great scientist for NASA. At night he researched the designs of spacecraft that had been used in space exploration and created drawings of his own. What would he need to know? What would a journey to outer space be like? Would he ever have the chance to travel to the moon?

Jack unhappily went through the motions of school, waiting anxiously for the last bell of the day. That was until today. He decided he was not going to spend one more day doing the work that he already knew how to do! As far as he was concerned he was wasting his time, and he had a plan. One of his classmates had gotten angry, hit a girl in his class, and was suspended for 3 days! If he behaved badly, maybe he, too, would be sent home for punishment.

When his parents arrived, they asked for a private conference with the teacher and principal. They shared the concerns Jack had with his new school environment. His parents explained that at his previous school the students' learning styles, interests, and developmental readiness were evaluated, and students who proved mastery in certain curricular areas were given opportunities to pursue other avenues of interest. Here, Jack felt stifled. He felt he was on a journey to nowhere.

The principal and teacher were embarrassed for not recognizing Jack's abilities and were surprised at how much his parents knew about the optimal learning environment for Jack. Because of Jack's inattentiveness to tasks and behavioral challenges, this teacher assumed he was not a very bright student and was disinterested in learning. Upon hearing the parents' perspective, a specialist assisted the teacher in planning strategies to maximize the learning opportunities for Jack. He and other interested classmates were given preassessments to determine mastery of specific objectives. When mastery was validated, Jack and the other students were given alternate assignments that were relevant, purposeful, and appropriate. School, once again, became not a prison but rather a place of liberation and learning.

Are We Capping Student Potential?

Since the one-room classroom, where children worked on instruction planned just for them, whole-class instruction, lecture, recall, and rote skill and drill have characterized classroom instruction as the dominant approach to teaching and learning. Despite frequent and perpetual demands for reform by parents of special needs and advanced children, teachers have continued to design instruction focusing on content rather than on *students*. Like Jack, many students have lost their identity as individuals to whole-class instruction.

The current call for heightened accountability in educational practice led policymakers to design reforms that require a look at individual performance. School districts nationwide have indicated a commitment to serving students' individual needs while at the same time focusing funding and professional development on increasing the achievement of only the low-performing students in an effort to meet the proficiency requirements of No Child Left Behind (NCLB)[3]. Expectations are too low for those already proficient, leaving our brightest students little opportunity for real learning gains.

The greatest challenge for the classroom teacher is to provide appropriate and challenging academic experiences, differentiating for students who have mastered the basic curriculum (Betts, 2004). Although there is no universal blueprint for differentiating to adjust or modify the regular curriculum for proficient students, teachers should be expected to design instruction that advances children beyond their current performance level. Using a *one-size-fits-all* approach in the classroom may yield scenarios where repetitious work for the whole leads not only to boredom but also to discipline problems, inattentiveness, and failure to develop creativity, curiosity, ownership for learning, and organized and rigorous study patterns.

Unleashing Student Potential

Although not a new concept, implementing the strategy of curriculum compacting is more important than ever. Compacting is a method of differentiation, an instructional strategy designed to condense, modify, or streamline the state-mandated curriculum by reducing repetition of previously mastered material for those who are capable of proficiency at a faster pace. This differentiation technique allows time for acceleration or enrichment beyond the basic curriculum for students who would otherwise be simply practicing what they already know (Reis, Burns, & Renzulli, 1992; Renzulli & Reis, 1997; Renzulli & Smith, 1978; Winebrenner, 2001).

When planning for curriculum compacting, the teacher first identifies the relevant learning objectives in a subject area or grade level. Most states have a state-mandated curriculum with identified minimum competencies. Students must master and demonstrate competence of the objectives at each grade level. State gateway competencies also clearly delineate the baseline or minimum that students are responsible for learning. An overarching expectation is that teachers take capable students beyond minimum competency.

---

3   *Note.* In December 2015, Congress passed the Every Student Succeeds Act (ESSA), which replaced NCLB. Unlike previous reauthorizations of the Elementary and Secondary Education Act of 1965, ESSA includes several provisions that support gifted and talented students.

Planning for Compacting

In order to determine students' levels of knowledge and mastery, teachers must first identify an appropriate preassessment on one or more objectives prior to instruction. Critical to compacting is determining the objectives students have already mastered and those still needed to master the required curriculum (see example in Figure 21.1). Teachers must take time to locate preassessments or create their own based on desired learning outcomes. Teacher-made assessments used frequently and designed to evaluate specific performance skills have a far greater chance of measuring competency on relevant learning objectives.

A list of students and the required learning objectives, with mastery indicated, illustrates which students should be considered for compacting. Those demonstrating mastery of any objective should be given the opportunity to compact out—to work on an acceleration or enrichment project during the time that a specific skill is being taught to students not yet showing mastery. Making productive use of every student's instructional time is critical to raising student achievement. Figure 21.1 illustrates a class profile matrix that identifies which students would benefit from curriculum compacting (indicated by a + for demonstrating mastery), and therefore should receive compacting options. The + is then circled to indicate that the student has begun some form of compacting.

As evidenced by the class profile in Figure 21.1, all students evidenced mastery on the first objective. The second objective has been mastered by all but four students; focused instruction is needed for them. Whole-class instruction should be focused on objectives 3, 4, and 5 for all but student A, C, D, and K. Although students A and C show mastery of the majority of the objectives, they still need instruction on one or more objectives. Acceleration or enrichment options should be developed for students D and K as they show complete mastery of preassessed skills.

Appropriate strategies for the students who have demonstrated mastery of required objectives should be identified and planned. Nonmastered objectives cannot be disregarded, nor can it be assumed that the students will master them without planned instruction, practice, and assessment. Accomplishing this may require students to participate in designed instruction for the whole class or streamlining individualized instruction for the specific objectives. Additionally, a class profile may be used to identify objectives on which students need focused instruction.

FRACTIONS / Objectives	Student A	Student B	Student C	Student D	Student E	Student F	Student G	Student H	Student I	Student J	Student K	Student L	Student M	Student N	Student O	Student P	# Focused Instruction
Recognize common/uncommon denominators	⊕	⊕	⊕	⊕	⊕	⊕	⊕	⊕	⊕	⊕	⊕	⊕	⊕	⊕	⊕	⊕	
Find least common denominator	⊕	⊕	⊕	⊕		⊕		⊕	⊕		⊕	⊕	⊕	⊕	⊕		E, G, J, P
Recognize equivalent fractions	⊕		⊕	⊕							⊕						
Convert fractions to have common denominators			⊕	⊕							⊕						
Add and subtract fractions				⊕							⊕						

⊕ = Mastered objective and receiving Curriculum Compacting

Figure 21.1. Fractions pretest: Class profile.

Teachers and students should collaboratively design purposeful acceleration or enrichment activities for students who are eligible for compacting (Douglas, 2004). This phase of compacting is the most rewarding aspect because it is based on cooperative decision making and creativity on the part of teachers and students. The compacting process allows reflection that engages students and teachers in the planning of extended learning experiences, which can also prove to be the most challenging aspect of compacting. Careful consideration must be given to the curriculum alternatives that will best address the needs, interests, and developmental readiness of the students while at the same time offering inquiry-based learning experiences that foster the development of critical, creative, and problem-solving skills.

Planning for Acceleration or Enrichment

Teachers should organize and plan instruction centered on a set of questions that create a learning plan for each child (see Figure 21.2).

- ▶ Assess what the student knows of the standard curriculum.
- ▶ Assess what the student doesn't know of the standard curriculum.
- ▶ With the student, plan strategies for the student to gain proficiency in what she or he needs to know.
- ▶ With the student, identify which acceleration or enrichment activities will be appropriate and be of interest to the student.

Clearly, the student in Figure 21.2 would benefit from compacting out of mastered objectives in order to provide time to extend his learning experiences.

An acceleration/enrichment plan can become a curriculum compacting plan that allows students opportunities that maintain motivation and enhance achievement. An acceleration plan, whether it's modeled after "The Compactor" (Renzulli & Smith, 1978) or is a matrix adapted by the teacher, should be developed for each student or group of students with similar curricular strengths.

Classroom management of students involved in compacting is another area for attention. Teachers who compact successfully know that compacting does not mean assigning more of the same work. Although compacting requires initial planning for individuals or groups who have similar proficiency levels and/or interests, it actually saves time in the long run after they have learned to implement it effectively. For example, preassessment analysis often results in not having to correct homework and tests that students have done unnecessarily,

Student Name(s): *Mark Adams*	Age/Grade: *6 yrs/1st grade*		Subject: *Reading*
What objectives have been mastered?	What objectives still need to be mastered?	Strategies to complete mastery of required objectives	Acceleration or enrichment activities

▲ Pre-Test Assessment
▲ Reading Level 30 DRA
▲ Mastery of most objectives
   a. . .
   b. . .
   c. . .
   d. . .
	▲ Alphabetical order
	▲ Unconventional vowel sounds
		▲ Individual instruction in alphabetical order- phonics workbook
		▲ Group instruction for vowel sounds
		▲ Skill sheets # 23, 26, 31, at own pace
			▲ Language expressive narrative stories- Writers' Workshop
			▲ Research interest group on solar system in library with library aide
			▲ Scholastic Reading Assessments
			▲ Participate in Junior Great Books

Figure 21.2. Same acceleration/enrichment plan.

practicing concepts they have already mastered. It might be important to note that for a teacher new to compacting, math and spelling often are the easiest curricular areas to address (Reis et al., 1992).

Reflection

A large number of the nation's high school dropouts are high-achieving students who have become disinterested in school because they are not challenged and have not been offered appropriate differentiation of instruction for their ability. In this era of high-stakes testing and defined curriculum, there is little hope that our most promising students will maximize their potential if districts fail to recognize that their abilities and interests require modified classroom instruction. It is not ethical practice to limit the learning experiences of our above proficient students to the curriculum designed and paced for standard grade levels.

Unfortunately, for many teachers, the regular curriculum is seen as a prescribed set of standards and objectives; instructional pacing is a race against a clock to "cover" the standards. Most importantly, the sole goal of teaching is now reduced to raising test scores on a single test, the value of which has rarely been challenged in the public forum (Tomlinson, 2000).

Curriculum compacting is a strategy with a philosophical heart about how we allow students to use learning time. For far too long, students have been going through the motions of learning without really ever being part of the decision-making process. When students are consulted about the direction of their learning and asked about their interests, they often accept responsibility and seek a breadth and depth that would not ordinarily be observed in a teacher-directed assignment.

Yang and Siegle (2006) assert that between the means and the goal there should be a bridge—curriculum compacting. The positive effects of this learning philosophy and practice are prophetic. Students who were once unmotivated and bored experience a resurgence of interest. Many students who were once careless and disengaged now take pride in their work and reach new depths and heights of creative productivity. Teachers become motivated by the eagerness and enthusiasm these students exhibit as they work cooperatively with the teacher during the initial development of their compacting plan. Parents also are satisfied that their children's academic abilities are being recognized and supported.

In order to produce students who are engaged throughout school, see relevancy in their learning, and can apply their competencies for the workforce of this country, a drastic change in the education of proficient students is required. Teachers and administrators must feel an obligation to take students beyond proficiency. It is all about how we maximize the use of time for those too often left behind because of our acceptance of a national minimal competence level, defined by NCLB as "proficiency."

References

Betts, G. (2004). Fostering autonomous learners through levels of differentiation. *Roeper Review, 26,* 190–191.

Davidson, J., Davidson, B., & Vanderkam, L. (2004). *Genius denied: How to stop wasting our brightest minds.* New York, NY: Simon & Schuster.

Douglas, D. (2004). Self-advocacy: Encouraging students to become partners in differentiation. *Roeper Review, 26,* 223–228.

Reis, S. M., Burns, D. E., & Renzulli, J. S. (1992). *Curriculum compacting: The complete guide to modifying the regular curriculum for high-ability students.* Waco, TX: Prufrock Press.

Renzulli, J. S., & Reis, S. M. (1997). *The schoolwide enrichment model: A how-to guide for educational excellence.* Mansfield Center, CT: Creative Learning Press.

Renzulli, J. S., & Smith, L. H. (1978). *The compactor.* Mansfield Center, CT: Creative Learning Press.

Tomlinson, C. A. (2000). Reconcilable differences? Standards-based teaching and differentiation. *Educational Leadership, 58,* 6–11.

Winebrenner, S. (2001). *Teaching gifted kids in the regular classroom.* Minneapolis, MN: Free Spirit.

Yang, W., & Siegle, D. (2006). Curriculum compacting: The best way to bridge the education of school-house giftedness and creative/productive giftedness in China. *Gifted Education International, 22,* 101–107.

Chapter 22

Self-Assessment

Are You Including the Best Practices for Teaching Gifted and Advanced Learners

by Willard L. White

More forces are affecting instruction in American classrooms today than at any time in modern history. Regulations and mandates for what must be taught, including state curriculum standards as well as local requirements, have added to the pressure classroom teachers are experiencing.

Gifted Students Left Behind

The national movement stemming from the No Child Left Behind Act focuses on the lowest performing students in our classes; thus both the curriculum and instruction in America's public schools are aimed primarily at remediation. What about the advanced learners and gifted students? Where are the directions for instructing our highest performing students? Curriculum based only on the chronological age of the students offers little opportunity for the appropriately challenging instruction gifted students require. Advanced learners are being left behind, and in many schools there is little administrative support for subject- or grade-level acceleration for these students (Colangelo, Assouline, & Gross, 2004).

"Smart Cookies" by Bess Wilson

It is clear that teachers across the country, especially those with general education backgrounds, are asking for assistance in not only identifying but in serving gifted and talented students. "When will I have time to teach, given the diverse nature of my students?" and "How is it possible to accomplish all that is expected now that I am aware of what can be done?" are questions that are commonly asked, and the answers to these questions are certainly not simple. Oftentimes, accomplishing the mammoth task of linking standards to advanced curriculum seems far out of reach, for even the most seasoned educator. Sometimes all that may be needed is a small step back, a moment for reflection, a chance to assess what is known about the best practices for teaching gifted and talented learners.

Time for Self-Assessment

The list of questions in Table 22.1 may be helpful in guiding teachers through the maze of best practices, including ways to enrich and accelerate instruction for the benefit of all students. Teachers should reflect on these practices when planning curriculum for use with gifted students, and revisit them on a regular basis. Self-assessment is an important skill to instill in students and to utilize for ourselves.

NAGC has posted guiding questions for each of the new Pre-K–Grade 12 Gifted Programming Standards that serve a similar purpose. These questions can be viewed at http://www.nagc.org/resources-publications/resources/national-standards-gifted-and-talented-education/pre-k-grade-12. Self-assessment tools provide a host of opportunities to stimulate discussion. Whether teachers bring some of the questions up in the lunchroom, during a conversation in the hall, offer to organize professional development around the topic areas, or focus specifically on their own style and methods of teaching, I am confident that the self-assessment exercise will help improve their teaching practice.

TABLE 22.1

*20 Questions: Self-Assessment of Best Practices for
Teaching Gifted and Advanced Learners*

1. In what ways do I incorporate higher order thinking skills (analysis, synthesis and evaluation) in my classroom?

2. In what ways do I include the benchmarks of creativity (fluency, flexibility, elaboration, and originality) in my classroom?

3. In what ways do I provide opportunities for independent study in my classroom?

4. Do I use preassessment before teaching major concepts or units of study?

5. How do I ensure that my students understand what is expected in each assignment?

6. How do my students demonstrate that they have the basic skills necessary to complete assignments?

7. In what ways do I assess my students' strengths and weaknesses?

8. In what ways do I provide for accelerated instruction or enrichment when a student is academically advanced in a skill or problem area, or keenly interested in a particular topic, issue, or problem?

9. In what ways do I communicate the successes of my students to parents?

10. How do both curriculum and instruction in my classes differ from that which is offered in regular classrooms at the same grade level in my school?

11. In what ways do I group students for instruction in my classroom?

12. How do I incorporate students' interests in my teaching?

13. How often do I review the educational plans for each of my students?

14. In what ways do I pursue my own professional growth in the field of gifted education?

15. In what ways do I provide for the social and emotional development of students?

16. What evidence is there that I have high expectations for my students?

17. How do I model creativity in my classroom management, in-class activities, long-term assignments, interaction with students, and homework assignments?

18. To what extent do I share my own creative productivity with my students?

19. How can I share what I observe about specific students with their other teachers?

20. Could I or anyone I know provide a more detailed presentation to the faculty and administration in the form of an in-service?

Reference

Colangelo, N., Assouline, S. G., & Gross, M. U. M. (2004). *A nation deceived: How schools hold back America's brightest students.* Iowa City: University of Iowa.

PART / II

Curriculum Content

by Rebecca D. Eckert

> Educators must possess a repertoire of evidence-based instructional strategies in delivering the curriculum (a) to develop talent, enhance learning, and provide students with the knowledge and skills to become independent, self-aware learners, and (b) to give students the tools to contribute to a multicultural, diverse society.
> —From the NAGC Pre-K–Grade 12 Gifted Programming Standard 3: Curriculum Planning and Instruction

The emergence and growth of gifted students' talents and interests are shaped by myriad factors and experiences. And, although the powerful influences on giftedness of family, culture, chance, and opportunity at times may lead teachers to wonder about the utility of their role in talent development, there is little doubt that gifted students' experiences in school can be an important force that shapes their journey into adulthood.

What then should teachers do to ensure that all students—in particular gifted students—encounter the meaningful challenges and opportunities needed to thrive in the classroom and beyond? They must choose carefully the knowledge and skills advanced learners will pursue in their classroom, using assessment data and professional judgment to weigh the options. The choices teachers make about content and curriculum are the cornerstone on which meaningful learning experiences are built, and with careful selection they enable teachers to close the distance between theory and practice. Moreover, these choices that teachers make about content, resources, and strategies ultimately determine the degree to which a student encounters knowledge, skills, and understandings, which are conceptually challenging, complex, and of an appropriate depth. Finally, whether at the elementary, middle, or high school level, decisions about content and curriculum must be focused on students and their needs so that gifts and talents can emerge and flourish.

The *Teaching for High Potential* articles selected for the Curriculum Content section provide research-based guidance from experts in the field of gifted education about how to make the most of the everyday choices that shape the learning opportunities offered in schools and classrooms. The articles have been organized into five categories, each representing key academic disciplines:

1. **Language arts**—These articles present a variety of strategies and resources for enticing advanced students to explore the rich complexities of language and literature. Recognizing the relationship between exposure to engaging texts and the identification and development of talent for both readers and writers (especially for students from traditionally underserved populations), these authors emphasize the importance of an intentional and robust language arts curriculum.

2. **Social studies and history**—The authors of these articles urge us to move beyond the simple recall of names, dates, and facts to tap into the true depth and complexity of the social sciences. Moreover, practical suggestions are provided that will enable teachers to challenge advanced students to interpret their world and draw meaningful connections that promote the skills and understandings needed to become informed global citizens prepared to act with compassion and conviction.

3. **Science**—Grounded in the Next Generation Science Standards (NGSS), these articles provide guidance about how to create opportunities for advanced students to explore the natural world in pursuit of authentic questions. In addition, the authors advise us to think broadly about the skills needed to excel in science (including creativity, communication, and collaboration), as well as the potential for innovative uses of technology in our explorations.

4. **Mathematics**—These authors remind us that mathematics classrooms should provide ample opportunities for students to actively engage in problem solving—preferably of the messy, real-world variety! They

also provide numerous useful strategies for helping gifted students persist and reflect as they work to develop new critical thinking skills and deeper mathematical understanding.

5. **Visual and performing arts**—These articles share insights about the universal appeal and applicability of art as process and product while also providing practical strategies for incorporating the arts into diverse classroom settings. In several cases, authors advocate for a multidisciplinary approach to designing learning experiences that inspire both creative and critical thinking.

Although the articles have been divided into five separate academic disciplines, this distinction is somewhat artificial. Rather than thinking of this information as being contained within separate "silos," notice the potential for interdisciplinary thinking and the ways in which the provided strategies and resources can be used to complement each other as well as the existing curriculum within an academic discipline.

As you read these articles selected from *Teaching for High Potential*, hold your students in mind and consider the following guiding questions and the choices you make about the content and curriculum your students will encounter:

▶ How might the content, resources, and strategies shared in this article connect to my current curriculum? In what ways might this information be used to extend or build upon my students' existing knowledge and skills?

▶ What evidence do I have to suggest that this learning experience would be appropriate for my students? What need would it fill for me and/or my students?

▶ Who in my classroom or school might be most excited to take on this challenge? What aspects of the author's recommendations for creating a learning experience would be most appealing to this individual or group? Why?

▶ What resources would I need to implement the author's recommendations? What concerns or pitfalls do I foresee with this implementation?

▶ With whom would I like to share this information?

Section I: Language Arts

Chapter 23

Readers for a Lifetime

by Susannah Richards

Reading is still a mystery to me. Although I understand the cognitive process of reading and know that it is an essential part of learning, there are many mysteries about "the formula" that makes one a reader. I have yet to determine why some people are born readers, some grow into readers, and others fight the invitation to read all of their lives. As a researcher, I am always interested in why people read. I watch and listen to readers and nonreaders everywhere, in my courses, at parties and events, and am regularly engaging with strangers on the NYC subway.

So, how do educators create an environment where students are more likely to be lifetime readers rather than only read because they are told to do so? We need to consider the conditions under which a talented reader (a student who reads at least 2 years above what you would expect for a child of that chronological age) would grow as a reader. Over the years, I have interviewed hundreds of kids and parents about the reading habits of children from ages 3–25. While not generalizable, my data does indicate a number of conditions that are likely to promote and sustain kids as readers for a lifetime.

Here is some advice to ignite, delight, and cultivate young readers.

Read Aloud

This includes reading to young children as well as reading to older children. Reading aloud promotes language development by increasing vocabulary, introducing different text structures, and developing comprehension. A person's listening vocabulary is greater than their reading vocabulary, so it is important to read books that are 2 years above what a child may be able to read independently. Audiobooks are another great option. A few recommendations for family read-alouds and/or audiobooks include:

- *The Crossover* by Kwame Alexander (middle grade)
- *The Mighty Miss Malone* by Christopher Paul Curtis (middle grade)
- *A Snicker of Magic* by Natalie Lloyd (middle grade)
- *We Were Liars* by E. Lockhart (young adult)
- *Greenglass House* by Kate Milford (middle grade)
- *Noggin* by John Corey Whaley (young adult)

Classroom Libraries

In order to read, kids need books. Ideally you want to have at least five books per child[4] available in your classroom.

- These books need to be at different reading levels. I suggest a range of 2 years below the grade level to 4 years above the grade level. Make sure to have audiobooks as well.
- The books should be varied in terms of genres (both fiction and nonfiction) and formats (picture books, graphic novels, etc.).

Let Students Read Anything

There is no formula for the "right books" that should be read. Magazines, newspapers, and comic books are some alternatives. A happy reader is better than a nonreader.

---

4   *Note.* For a dream library, the goal is 25 books per child or 625 books for a classroom of 25 students.

Don't Assume You Know Everything About the Reader

Behaviors and habits can differ greatly between home and school. When Elizabeth's teacher was reading *The BFG* as a read aloud in class, Elizabeth was reading it at home. She was hesitant, though, to share that information with her teacher, feeling that she would be given harder work. Get to know the readers you have in class. Just because a child has reached a certain reading level at school, this may not always indicate what he or she is capable of. Communication between home and school is important and should happen regularly. Reading assignments and projects can be used for all levels.

Avoid Telling a Child to Not Read Ahead

If children are reading, we want them to keep reading. If you are worried about a child "spoiling" the reading experience for other students, here are a few suggestions:

- ▶ Keep a pile of SPOILER ALERT cards that the child may write on to share his or her ideas without sharing them with the other members of the reading group.
- ▶ In your guidelines for literature discussions, discuss how some people may read faster, but, during a specific discussion, the students will focus only on what everyone has read.
- ▶ Work with the children to set their own timetables for reading a text and use phrases such as, "Before we discuss . . . you will have had to read at least to . . ."

Share Your Love of Books

Look at your classroom and celebrate reading with images of books, ideas from books, photos of readers (including your kids), and all things literary. For their spring break, my undergraduate elementary education certification students tweeted images of themselves reading, and they had a blast sharing images from here, there, and everywhere.

Chapter 24

Promoting Citizenship Development Through Biographies

by Mary E. Haas

Experts suggest various strategies to promote individual awareness of citizenship development, such as working with a guest mentor, shadowing role models, going to work with a parent, and becoming an intern. Other experts propose students learn by gathering and recording historical knowledge through interviews or working for political or social causes. Although these strategies may show limited success, more is needed. This article explores how using digital resources related to biographies can help teachers turn their classrooms into environments that value and promote democratic citizenship.

Traditionally, teachers of the gifted have approached social studies curriculum from a textbook-based approach. Textbooks generally teach about citizenship through sharing anecdotes about "outstanding citizens" whose leadership provided significant contributions to our nation. The NCSS curriculum standards (2010) shift the focus from reading social studies textbooks and answering questions about content to an applied focus on 21st-century skills, such as critical thinking and problem solving. An emphasis on critical thinking supports the building of citizenship skills as well as thinking skills. However, a psychosocial perspective, such as that advocated by Eric Erikson (1980), also must be emphasized if learners are going to be able to develop into participating citizens. Erikson's perspective focuses on the development of personal values and traits that people need to accept themselves and others. Developing this combination of skills calls for teachers to include a range of experiences and perspectives on life in social studies instruction—not just deeds that define a person as famous.

All effective teachers of the gifted want to create a classroom that encourages individual accomplishments, self-direction, and personal identity among their students; such a classroom setting is particularly important with the social studies curriculum, because social studies is the academic discipline that has the primary responsibility for examining and promoting citizenship. Using digital resources to teach social studies concepts provides students with a greater access to "model citizens" than traditional textbooks, offering opportunities to examine a larger number of careers and occupations gleaned from the biographies accessed.

The Non-Public Lives of Historical Figures

Let us now explore excerpts from the biographies of several historical figures and examine suggestions for helping gifted students develop into participatory citizens while expanding and supplementing their studies of these U.S. citizens' lives.

Collectors

Introducing consideration of personal use of time, such as collecting or practicing a hobby, into biographical studies raises new questions about historical figures and their times. Presidents Franklin D. Roosevelt and Theodore Roosevelt were known as collectors. The video, "The Stamp Collector in Chief" (http://www.smithsonianmag.com/videos/category/history/the-stamp-collector-in-chief), explains how stamp collecting played an important role in the life of FDR and programs he developed to answer challenges during his stressful political career. In systematically examining stamps, students do something that this busy and famous president did in order to understand the history, culture, and characteristics of places and nations. By observing the images on stamps, students encounter information clearly related to the NCSS Standards of People, Places, and Environments and Time, Continuity, and Change. Website resources at the Smithsonian Institution's National Postal Museum and the U.S. Postal Service provide information and projects for teaching about stamps.

Although stamps have a larger variety of designs, coins have a much longer history. Examining the changes in the appearances and production of both coins and stamps, the NCSS theme of Science, Technology, and Society can be analyzed and evaluated. Production, Distribution, and Consumption, another NCSS theme, is also related to the greater need for coins and money in meeting the needs of societies throughout the world.

In lessons related to collections and hobbies, students use skills associated with Dimension 3 (Evaluating Sources and Using Evidence) of the NCSS C3 Framework (2013) and arc of inquiry. Students identify and classify stamps and coins based on historical/cultural symbols, habitats, and natural landscapes of places, and products produced. In examining the production process of special coins and stamps, more questions associated with political decisions of whom and what to memorialize or honor are evaluated. Examining the right to request the issuing of new stamps and coins reveals changes in cultures and policies over time and among nations.

Naturalists

Theodore Roosevelt was noted as an energetic outdoorsman and environmentalist. Theodore began hunting and collecting animal species at the age of 9. Studying animals has changed greatly since the days when shooting and stuffing were the standard practices. As a youth, Theodore spent so much time collecting and preserving birds and animals that people complained that he smelled of the process. As president, Roosevelt signed the bill establishing the Smithsonian Natural History Museum. In 1909, after his presidency, he went on an expedition to Africa shooting and collecting animals. Even today the public can view and learn from his collection at the Natural History Museum in DC or online at http://naturalhistory.si.edu/onehundredyears/profiles/TR_profile.html.

Unlike Theodore Roosevelt, today's students have access to video presentations recorded by cameras with special lenses and protective devices to learn more about the lives and habits of species. In examining the changes technology has made in studying animals and their habitats, students gain new perspectives about the relationships between science, technology, and society, and perhaps a new understanding of the fascination people have with adventures and nature. As well as bringing enjoyment, the arts have a long history of recording and commenting on life. Nature films are a form of art, often using music when communicating the story. In learning to separate truth from creativity and imagination, the artist's perspective needs to be considered in interpreting data in social studies class and in life.

In today's digital world, it is very easy for students to become detached from the stimulating environment of the outdoors, replacing it with virtual environments. Simulated environments cannot replace the genuine questions, puzzles, and surprises that the real world offers to stimulate discovery, analysis, and sharing through cooperative efforts. Youthful outdoor interests prompt many individuals to study science. Famous scientists with youthful interests in the outdoors include Mae C. Jemison, Sally Ride, Ben Franklin, Marie Curie, Mary Leakey, E. O. Wilson, and Jane Goodall.

Painters, Inventors, and Other Hobbyists

From an early age, John James Audubon showed an interest in music, drawing, and nature. He turned his hobby into the pursuit of painting birds of North America. *The Birds of America* was Audubon's most famous book. His drawings portray birds dramatically and in life size. After 1838, Audubon turned to painting the wildlife of the American West. Copies of his books and paintings are still highly sought and reveal much about America's early West. Many of his paintings can be viewed at the website of the Audubon Society (http://web4. audubon.org/bird/BoA/BOA_index.html).

The concept of "invention" is much larger than electronic or mechanical devices. Inventions are well-represented in the traditional curriculum and the daily lives of today's youth. Most people do not know that the great inventor George Washington Carver's first interest was in art and that he continued to produce works of art throughout his long life. Carver developed ways to turn vegetation into paints and other usable products. Students might be interested to know that the dye in the crayons they use is attributed to the work of Carver.

Often careers in the arts do not lead to livable incomes and great fame. Skills in these fields often remain as hobbies, are combined with other more practical needs, or put away until retirement. Students might be interested to learn that painting as a hobby is associated with such recognizable names as Prince Charles of England, Winston Churchill, and Presidents Dwight Eisenhower and George W. Bush.

Teacher as Guide

Students usually enjoy learning about famous people, and reading biographies is integral to the school curriculum. With the increased call by the Common Core State Standards for reading nonfiction books, biographies are likely to receive an even greater use beginning in the elementary grades. Indeed, one might expect that some teachers could replace history textbooks with biographies. Trade books, including biographies, are by the nature of their narrative style and multiple illustrations better received than textbooks. However, simply handing a student a biography does not automatically encourage and motivate him or her to want to read or to learn beyond the gathering of isolated facts to gain meaningful learning. The reality for improved learning lies in promoting motivation and in-depth questioning; teachers need to play a major role in establishing these work habits in youth.

Linking a biography to student interests begins by presenting a carefully selected stimulus in the form of a statement, picture, or artifact that reveals the personal talents or interests of people. But it does not stop with that single act. Teachers must support the impact of the stimulus through two additional behaviors. First, asking questions designed to invite students into the lesson as questioners and encouraging students to look again until several possible answers have been suggested. Questions related to using stamps and coins as such a stimulus might include:

- Why might a person or place be selected to appear on coins or stamps?
- Who do you think helps to create a design for a coin or stamp?
- Sometimes people hold money up to a light and look carefully at it when money is returned to them in the store. Why do you think a person might do this?
- Why do you think there might be different rules or laws that regulate what is on the money or stamps in different countries?

Second, and of equal importance, is a teacher's skill in responding in ways that do not judge the correctness of individual responses. Developing this is a difficult skill for teachers who face time deadlines. Too much enthusiasm for one student's reply may cut short the potential for in-depth learning. "That could be," or "Does anyone have another idea?" are responses that encourage more questions.

At the beginning of a lesson students respond quickly and then begin to cast doubt on a reply. It is important for students to recognize their own need to rethink and evaluate answers without fear of failure or ridicule. Instead, they should view new uncertainties or questions as potential learning opportunities. Such a thinking skill needs practice throughout life, including while teaching. When necessary a teacher might help clarify the direction of students' thoughts with questions that prompt additional examination such as:

- ▸ What information do we need to determine if our ideas are accurate?
- ▸ Where can we find information to help us determine the accuracy of our ideas?
- ▸ What are other approaches we might use to find answers to our questions?

Constructing a Meaningful Lesson

The big questions and life lessons, unlike TV shows or isolated fact lessons, take longer than 20 to 45 minutes to master; only quiz shows reward the speed of recall. Meaningful learning also promotes and rewards learners with intrinsic satisfaction throughout life. In suggesting or providing opportunities for individual pursuits of interests and accomplishments within some lessons, teachers promote meaningful learning and feelings of accomplishment. Providing additional resources supports skills in research and the self-regulation of learning and time.

For students living in the 21st century, self-regulation of life and learning are objectives equal to, or perhaps more important than the standards and objectives listed in curriculum guides. The true art in teaching is improving the talents and interests of all students so they learn and grow academically and personally. This is a must for social studies teachers as citizenship belongs to all in a democracy. Citizens from a variety of backgrounds move forward together through respecting and employing their various talents and perspectives. Promoting civic ideals in lessons may begin with stating the objectives, but citizenship is greatly assisted by a classroom environment that encourages all students to address knowledge, skills, and interests in their classes, while at the same time respecting each other. When there is cooperation among teachers, administrators, and students, a school will successfully contribute to citizenship fit for democracy. Looking beyond the popular accomplishments of historical leaders is one way to begin.

References

Erikson, E. H. (1980). *Identity and the life cycle*. New York, NY: W. W. Norton.

National Council for the Social Studies. (2010). *National curriculum standards for social studies: A framework for teaching, learning, and assessment.* Washington, DC: Author.

National Council for the Social Studies. (2013). *College, career, and civic life (C3) framework for social studies state standards*. Silver Spring, MD: Author.

Chapter 25

Vocabulary Instruction in the Common Core State Standards Era

by Kimberley L. Chandler and Barbara Dullaghan

Students who are verbally gifted enjoy vocabulary instruction. Word play, vocabulary games, and learning Greek and Latin stems are all activities that can be engaging to even the youngest students. Beyond this, however, it is important to understand how crucial it is that vocabulary instruction is intentional and robust, especially for students from low socioeconomic (SES) backgrounds and/or who are learning English as a second language. It is estimated that first graders from low-SES settings come to school knowing about half as many words as more advantaged children (Beck, McKeown, & Kucan, 2008). In our efforts to spot and develop potential in underserved populations, it is crucial that we use deliberate strategies to promote vocabulary growth.

As school districts transition to using the Common Core State Standards (CCSS) as the basis for planning curriculum and instruction, it is incumbent on teachers to understand the importance of direct vocabulary instruction in social studies and science. The CCSS have a strong emphasis on informational text in the primary grades (K–3). Although vocabulary is explicitly listed only in the craft and structure strand, it is inherently part of the other reading and all writing strands as well.

Beck et al. (2008) provided a useful framework for vocabulary instruction that includes three tiers of words vital to comprehension and vocabulary development. The framework is based on research that indicates that while most vocabulary is learned indirectly, some must be taught directly (Partnership for Reading, 2002). The tiers, which are not hierarchical, are:

- **Tier 1:** Words commonly appear in spoken language and everyday speech. Because they are heard frequently in numerous contexts, Tier 1 words rarely require explicit instruction. Examples are kitchen, boy, sad, and run.
- **Tier 2:** Words are general academic words used across several content areas. Because of their lack of use in oral language, Tier 2 words present challenges to students who primarily meet them in print. Examples of Tier 2 words are evident, complex, determine, and validate. They often represent subtle or precise words to express ideas (saunter instead of walk).
- **Tier 3:** Words are not frequently used except in specific content areas or domains. Tier 3 words are central to building knowledge and conceptual understanding within the various academic domains. Science, legal, medical, and mathematics terms, such as octahedron and crustacean, are examples of these words.

According to Beck et al. (2008), teachers should concentrate on Tier 2 words because most students already know Tier 1 words; Tier 3 words should be taught at point of contact as they occur in reading. Because Tier 2 words appear often in student texts, these are the ones that are most important for vocabulary development. The concept of "robust" vocabulary instruction is focused on Tier 2 words. The key features of Tier 2 instruction and how those might be incorporated in a classroom for the highly able and "at-potential" (Coleman & Gallagher, 1995) students are:

- Introduction of a set of five to seven Tier 2 words each week with student-friendly definitions:
  - ▷ Explain the meaning of the word in everyday life.
  - ▷ Focus on the meaning used in the context being addressed.

- Daily analytic activities to engage students in using the word in a variety of formats and contexts:
  - ▷ Analyze the word structure (prefix-root-suffix).
  - ▷ Teach students Greek and Latin stems for understanding meaningful units of the word.

- End-of-week assessment:
  - ▷ Assess using a variety of methods, including word play.

TABLE 25.1

Tier 2 Word Chart

Word	Definition	Context	Prompt
Hypothesis	An educated guess about why something happens	The scientist made a *hypothesis* about why the storms were occurring.	What is your *hypothesis* about the reason for the change in temperature of our classroom?

- ▶ Maintenance activities:
  - ▷ Provide a context for the word and have students use it frequently.
  - ▷ Help the students find a prompt that will connect to a personal context for the word.

A chart such as Table 25.1 could be used to help students to record their Tier 2 words.

Although we agree with suggestions from the researchers that Tier 2 words are crucial to vocabulary development, we contend that for primary gifted learners, teachers should also introduce the Tier 3 words. We all know how these students love words such as Tyrannosaurus and polyhedron!

References

Beck, I. L., McKeown, M. G., & Kucan, L. (2008). *Creating robust vocabulary: Frequently asked questions and extended examples.* New York, NY: Guilford Press.

Coleman, M. R., & Gallagher, J. (1995). State identification policies: Gifted students from special populations. *Roeper Review, 17,* 268–275.

Partnership for Reading. (2002). *The Reading Leadership Academy guidebook: Presentations and resources about scientifically based reading research: Grades K–3.* Washington, DC: Author.

Chapter 26

Exploring Between the Pages

by Susannah Richards

Several years ago, *The New York Times* stirred up a lot of attention for picture books in the article, "Picture Books No Longer a Staple for Children" by Julie Bosman (http://www.nytimes.com/2010/10/08/us/08picture.html). The response was varied. It sparked a renewed discussion about the role of picture books in the development of a child. Picture books are an important part of childhood and have enormous potential to help young learners explore the world around them.

Recently, my attention has been captured by the wonderful mathematical and scientific stories that help to ignite my curiosity about mathematicians and scientists. For years, I have paid attention to the lists of great science books on the list of Outstanding Science Trade Books for K–12 published annually by the National Science Teachers Association (http://www.nsta.org/publications/ostb), but now I am also thinking about the books that may meet the criteria for the Bank Street College of Education Cook Prize (https://www.bankstreet.edu/center-childrens-literature/cook-prize), which honors the best science, technology, engineering, and math (STEM) picture book published for children aged 8 to 10.

In thinking about the picture books from the perspective of the Cook Prize, I am fixated on one of the 2014 winners—*The Boy Who Loved Math: The*

Improbable Life of Paul Erdös—as well as a few other picture books that have STEM potential. These picture books:

- ▶ extend mathematical and scientific thinking,
- ▶ jump-start an interest in math and science,
- ▶ stimulate curiosity by making the topic intriguing and accessible,
- ▶ enrich vocabulary by using the terminology of the discipline, and
- ▶ model that there are many different ways to share science.

The following books are examples of seemingly simple but delightfully complex picture books that deliver information and ignite curiosity. These books can jump-start a lesson, engage a child who already has an interest, and expose kids to new ideas. *The Boy Who Loved Math: The Improbable Life of Paul Erdös* by Deborah Heiligman is an exceptional informational book about one of the world's most beloved mathematicians. The book is a great read-aloud with quirky lines about Erdös's thinking (one time when a visitor told Paul when her birthday was and the time she was born, he quickly replied that she had lived for 1,009,152,358 seconds). The story is a textual and visual delight. The detailed text paired with LeUyen Pham's energetic illustrations really show a man, who, though a brilliant mathematician who wrote elegant proofs, only saw the world through mathematical eyes and needed help with daily mundane details like cooking, laundry, and paying bills.

Not all picture books provide as much information as *The Boy Who Loved Math*. In *Circle, Square, Moose*, the companion book to *Z is for Moose*, Kelly Bingham and Paul O. Zelinsky play with shapes even though Moose, once again, is determined to be the center of attention. Young children will appreciate the zany antics of Moose while exploring the characteristics of circles, triangles, rectangles, and other shapes. Even older children will appreciate the metafictional format that permits Moose to take over the story.

Math is not the only focus for today's sophisticated picture books. Science is also well-represented. Three current favorites for gifted kids are *Gravity* by Jason Chin, *Some Bugs* by Angela DiTerlizzi, illustrated by Brendan Wenzel, and *Tiny Creatures: The World of Microbes* by Nicola Davies, illustrated by Emily Sutton. For children who want to know what would happen without gravity, Chin weaves a visual story that explores the concept of gravity that serves as an introduction to the concept and/or a model for how students might demonstrate what they know about gravity. *Some Bugs* explores the world of bugs that may be closer than children think through the rhythmical text and exuberant illustrations. The quick-paced, short text will capture young readers before it has a chance to sting. DiTerlizzi sets the stage, using the familiar backyard territory to help young entomologists spy on the comings and goings of the insect world. Wenzel flies with it, capturing imaginations with images of not only bugs but also the other living creatures with which they share their world. The focus on the bugs in action "Stinging, biting, stinking, fighting, hopping, gliding, swimming, hiding, building, making, hunting, taking" supports the notion that bugs may be small, but are hugely fascinating.

Zoologist Nicola Davies knows how to communicate science by hooking the reader immediately in *Tiny Creatures: The World of Microbes*. She immediately gets down to the small details, giving readers the perspective on microbes. Did you know that there are as many as a billion microbes in a teaspoon of soil? She tells a story about tiniest microbes while sharing enormous amounts of information about them—where they live, what they eat and how they impact the world around us. Her tone is engaging, and the thoughtful visual illustrations set the stage for seeing microbes here, there, and everywhere.

With these great STEM titles, consider picture books as read-alouds or for literacy instruction as well as to supplement content area instruction. These are sure to ignite, delight, and cultivate the mathematician and scientist in many young learners.

Recommended Book List

Bingham, K. (2014). *Circle, square, moose*. New York, NY: HarperCollins.

Chin, J. (2014). *Gravity*. New York, NY: Roaring Brook Press.

Davies, N. (2014). *Tiny creatures: The world of microbes*. Somerville, MA: Candlewick.

DiTerlizzi, A. (2014). *Some bugs*. San Diego, CA: Beach Lane.

Heiligman, D. (2013). *The boy who loved math: The improbable life of Paul Erdös*. New York, NY: Roaring Brook Press.

Chapter 27

Differentiation in the English Literature Classroom Through Highly Moral Literature

by Scott J. Peters

The current state of education for many gifted and talented students involves many of them spending the school day in a standard general education classroom. In fact, it is not uncommon for the ability level in a typical classroom to range from conventional special education students upward through those in the gifted range. This situation has led to sometimes vague and nearly always clichéd practices of differentiation. Although ideal in nature, wide-ranging differentiation for the kinds of abilities mentioned above is often a daunting task. Teachers already have to remediate materials, which is difficult enough without having to accelerate and enrich them as well. In addition, some topics or materials are simply not well-suited to such differentiation and leave the teacher with little to work with and the student with even less to learn with. English literature curriculum for a given grade level serves as an excellent venue to differentiate activities for mainstreamed gifted students because it tends to be standardized within a state or district.

Issues Embedded in the Classics

In addition to the required grade-level classics, young adult (YA) novels have become a staple of the American English classroom. Such books cover student-friendly topics at an accessible level, albeit often at a level beneath that of a gifted student in the regular classroom. Instead of simply abandoning YA books and programs such as Accelerated Reader, teachers can employ specific selections dealing with highly moral topics, or direct gifted students toward addressing highly moral issues in their literature selections. The reason this can work so well is that young adult novels tend to address issues involving moral or ethical dilemmas such as a character doing what is right versus what is popular, choosing friends, death of a family member, racism, honesty, family relationships, law, religion, violence, and much more. Although these topics are popular because of the text-to-self connections they can create with all students, they can also serve as a means by which gifted students can investigate and question these issues beyond the scope of curriculum written for their age peers. For many schools, programs such as Accelerated Reader are required for all students regardless of ability level. This being the case, there are ways that educators can alter or add to such programs to make them beneficial to gifted and talented students.

These investigative methods can be applied to the "classic" or classroom canon novel as well. Books such as *Julius Caesar, Adventures of Huckleberry Finn, Catcher in the Rye, The Great Gatsby*, and *1984* present highly moral issues that are open game for gifted students, mainly because gifted students tend to be more emotionally sensitive, have a greater degree of empathy, a strong sense of justice, and greater interest in wide-ranging social issues (Davis & Rimm, 2004).

Updating Common Practice

In many cases, students are required to read a variety of the classics in order to pass a given grade. It must be noted that students must also read a book regardless of the match between interest, ability level, and level of emotional readiness. When a book is already chosen for the student, the teacher can direct the student's study toward higher order issues including those dealing with moral and ethical concerns. An example is warranted to better illustrate this concept of using highly moral literature with young adults.

Every year thousands of students read *To Kill a Mockingbird* and *Adventures of Huckleberry Finn* sometime between seventh and tenth grade. If *To Kill a Mockingbird* is an Accelerated Reader book, the student will need to remember key facts in order to pass a computerized test. These facts focus on basic comprehension without much attention to in-depth understanding or higher order thinking skills. Rather than simply leave gifted students at this basic level, teachers can engage them with additional activities.

Activities Related to Differentiation

Such activities can range from more in-depth questioning, allowing for extra credit or alternative assessment presentations on highly moral issues such as racism, to encouraging the student to take on an assignment of interest in place of a final unit paper. An example of such a differentiated activity could involve a gifted student being encouraged to develop a project connecting a young adult Accelerated Reader novel to a more classical one instead of writing a more traditional essay. Similarly, the student could be allowed to write a paper or create an alternative project such as a lesson on a more personalized or obscure interpretation of the book. In both of these instances, the student is allowed to choose the texts involved as well as the medium through which to demonstrate deeper understanding in addition to basic comprehension.

The point with these strategies is not simply to create more work, but to create more interesting and challenging work. Students can also expand on an area of interest while at the same time covering required topics or assignments. A student might address the moral issue of racism present in *To Kill a Mockingbird* by entering a writing competition in prose or poetry. Writing competitions are one medium that is starting to gain popularity as a means of motivating middle and high school students. Being able to see one's work in print is a powerful experience for any student.

Creating a cluster of more advanced students is also an option for the general education classroom. Students can discuss some of the larger issues in depth and engage in more in-depth exploration of a book beyond that of the general curriculum. Although some students might be reading *Bucking the Sarge*, a teacher might make a cluster of gifted students who can select a more advanced book such as *The Curious Incident of the Dog in the Night-Time*. This book has a number of topics for students to investigate as a group including things as close to some of them as education and honesty.

Huckleberry Finn is one of the most morally involved characters in all of world literature. This familiar 13-year-old boy deals with family struggles, honesty, right versus wrong, and issues of race. Today's students might not recognize the issues faced by Huckleberry as similar to their own. After such a classic novel is read, most students will be required to write an essay on some aspect of the book. Rather than dwelling on another person's literary interpretation of some aspect of the story, gifted students could be allowed to address the complexities of the human factor in a highly moral issue. For example, rather than being handed a teacher-made topic such as the Duke and the King as a metaphor for 19th-century carpetbaggers (a typical interpretation) to write about, gifted students can be encouraged to examine the relationship between Huck and his various forms of family. This can be developed into a critical analysis based on primary and secondary sources, or can be presented as a debate topic or other creative medium.

Differences in interpretations can in and of themselves serve as topics of interest in almost all novels and stories. The fact that books such as *Adventures of Huckleberry Finn* are controversial can serve as a topic for gifted student to investigate. Not only does such a topic allow for greater enrichment and depth in a topic, but some authors even advocate for moral and character education through such topics and activities (Bohlin, 2005; Lamme, Krogh, & Yachmetz, 1992; Mills, 1987, 1988). Although moral education is another issue altogether, being able to externalize some of these major issues for investigation can benefit the student long after the class is over. Small bits of encouragement and specialized direction on the part of the teacher can turn seemingly mundane and unenlightened activities into real learning for the gifted student in the regular classroom. Not only does such an idea allow for growth in a mainstreamed setting, but it also does so with minimal additional work on the part of the instructor.

One of the best places to start implementing differentiation strategies such as those proposed here is by always having alternate assessments available to interested students and by always allowing for students to incorporate their interests into as many assignments and activities as possible. This can start out as small as having students work in reading circles grouped by book of interest once every few weeks, or become as large as having students develop their own final assessment project including grading guidelines. Many highly moral topics are well-suited for such strategies because such topics are inherently applicable to many students' lives.

An option for allowing for student choice in assessment options could include a three-choice system. The first choice is the most standard for education and reaches out to those students who are good at research papers and for whom alternate assessment options would not be of much interest. This option works well for those students who are good at school. The second option involves nontraditional assessment such as a presentation, debate, or creative media to be used in place of a more traditional paper. In this case the instructor still lays out the guidelines, but the student comes up with exactly what type of project will be used to demonstrate comprehension and understanding. The third option is the most open and as such requires the most work from the student. However, this work is a tradeoff for almost complete student control. One veteran Golden Apple award-winning teacher termed this option Something More Important to You (SMITY). In this case, the student is allowed to propose nearly anything as a final assessment option. A formal proposal must be presented to the instructor that includes exactly what will be done and how the project is to be assessed. This final option is ideal for gifted students because it goes much more in depth into a topic than does writing a paper or presenting a PowerPoint. This kind of depth and focus is ideal for highly moral topics due to their depth and complexity.

Differentiation is a complex strategy with great potential to increase student learning. To keep from becoming overwhelmed by the idea of differentiating for 30 ability levels in every class, middle and high school teachers can begin by incorporating small strategies, such as those proposed by highly moral literature, into existing lessons and assignments. This strategy creates an additional level of depth to traditional lesson and assignments while also including opportunities for student choice and interest.

References

Bohlin, K. E. (2005). *Teaching character education through literature: Awakening the moral imagination in secondary classrooms*. New York, NY: Routledge.

Davis, G., & Rimm, S. (2004). *Education of the gifted and talented* (5th ed.) Boston, MA: Allyn & Bacon.

Lamme, L., Krogh, S., & Yachmetz, K. (1992). *Literature-based moral education: Children's books and activities for teaching values, responsibility, and good judgment in the elementary school*. Phoenix, AZ: Oryx Press.

Mills, R. K. (1987). Traditional morality, moral reasoning and moral education of adolescents. *Adolescence, 22,* 371–375.

Mills, R. K. (1988). Using Tom and Huck to develop moral reasoning in adolescents: A strategy for the classroom. *Adolescence, 23,* 325–329.

Chapter 28

Seney's Top 10

by Bob Seney

In 1985, I was working with a group of librarians who asked me, "What are your favorite young adult novels?" That question prompted me to create and to maintain a list that I now call my *Top 10 All-Time Favorite Reads* (see Table 28.1). When I was teaching a graduate level class, *Reading and the Gifted Adolescent*, the assignment that I gave myself was to review my list in terms of novels that I had read during the previous year. I still periodically review and share that list. The interesting thing is that there have been very few changes over the years. It may be because of the "pain" of removing a favorite to replace it with a new favorite. In the latest version of the list, Brian Selznick's *The Invention of Hugo Cabret* (2007, Scholastic Press), which waited in the wings for almost 2 years, took its place on my list. Now I am faced with another problem. Will another Brian Selznick graphic novel take its place?

Selznick has taken the picture book and the graphic novel to a whole new high and new place. Single handedly, he is redefining the genre of graphic novels with his use of text and illustration. This is most dramatically seen in his latest offering: *Wonderstruck: A Novel in Words and Pictures* (2011, Scholastic Press.) My first reaction was *Double Wow*! I am truly, well—wonderstruck!

Selznick tells the story of two characters, Ben and Rose, both who wish their lives were different. However, their stories are set apart both geograph-

TABLE 28.1

Top 10 List of All-Time Favorite Reads[1]

1. Caroline Cooney—*What Child Is This? A Christmas Story*
2. Robert Cormier—*Fade*
3. Lois Lowry—*Gathering Blue[2]*
4. Gary Paulsen—*Dogsong[3]*
5. Katherine Paterson—*Bridge to Terabithia*
6. Cynthia Rylant—*The Van Gogh Café*
7. Brian Selznick—*The Invention of Hugo Cabret[4]*
8. William Sleator—*Interstellar Pig*
9. Stephanie Tolan—*Welcome to the Ark*
10. Cynthia Voight—*A Solitary Blue*

1   This list was last reviewed on November 1, 2011.

2   Anne McCaffrey's *The Dolphins of Pern* was painfully removed in 2002 to make room for *Gathering Blue*. I love the whole Pern Series. Dropping *Dolphins* was the first change in several years. Adding *Cabret* was the first change since 2002. At this point there are more contenders.

3   At this point there are more contenders. I am considering removing Gary Paulsen's *Dogsong* and replacing it with John Flanagan's *Erak's Ransom*, Book 7 in *The Ranger's Apprentice* series (2007) to represent this whole wonderful series.

4   2010: I love the Redwall Abbey series, but I had to cut Brian Jacques's *Salamandastron* to make room for Selznick's *Cabret*. Most painful!

ically and in time. There is a 50-year difference in the time setting of the two stories. Ben's story is told in text, while Rose's story is told entirely through illustrations. The reader eventually discovers why Selznick has chosen to tell their stories in this way. The stories alternate with seemingly no connection until, as they say, "the plot thickens." The temptation is to tell too much, but part of the joy of this novel is the discovery and the problem solving required of the reader. Readers participate in the "writing" of this novel by the connections that they make.

The illustrations are as rich and as detailed as those found in *Cabret*, recently made into the movie, *Hugo*, which won several Oscars. Again, Selznick uses the media of pencil on watercolor paper, which helps create the almost dreamlike quality of the illustrations—matching and paralleling the almost dreamlike narrative. Again, he ties his stories, both narrative and illustrative, to interesting and perhaps compelling historical situations.

I am truly impressed with this novel. It makes me ache for a classroom of gifted middle or high school students with whom to investigate the treasures of this novel. I see so many possibilities: a study of literary style; studies prompted by the historical situations; the role of museums in our lives and histories; the role of art media in telling a story, etc., etc., etc.! If you have not experienced Brian Selznick, then I strongly encourage you to pick up *Wonderstruck*. I promise you, you will not be sorry.

Happy reading!

Section II: Mathematics

Chapter 29

Thinking Like a Mathematician

by Eric L. Mann

I suspect we have all done some variation of the water jug problem several times during our mathematical development. You know the problem. You have three unmarked jugs that hold various quantities of water and you need to accurately measure a different amount that can be obtained by some combination of the jugs you have. It is thought that Siméon Denis Poisson, a 19th-century mathematician, had his interest in mathematics sparked when he encountered the problem. "Two friends who have an eight-quart jug of water wish to share it evenly. They also have two empty jars, one holding five quarts, the other three. How can they each measure exactly 4 quarts of water?"

In 1942, Abraham Luchins created a series of water jug problems that he used in a problem-solving experiment. A subset of those problems was used by Derek Haylock (1985) with 250 11- and 12-year-old students. Before you read further, try to solve the problems in Table 29.1.

When solving problems we are often taught to look for patterns. In the problem above most people discover a solution that works for all six. However, while the solution pattern works it is not always the most efficient way to solve the problem. If you solve all six problems the same way (and odds are most of you did) take a moment to go back and see if there is a simpler way to solve any of the problems.

TABLE 29.1

Sample Problems

	Measure Out	Jug A holds	Jug B holds	Jug C holds	Your Solution
Ex	55 units	10 units	63 units	2 units	B − A + C
1	52 units	10 units	64 units	1 unit	
2	14 units	100 units	124 units	5 units	
3	3 units	10 units	17 units	2 units	
4	100 units	21 units	127 units	3 units	
5	20 units	23 units	49 units	3 units	
6	5 units	50 units	65 units	5 units	

What Luchins (1942) and Haylock (1985) found is that individuals tend to become mechanical in the way they approach a particular set of problems. This is known as the Einstellung effect, when a set successful procedure is applied consistently even when it is less efficient or inappropriate. In Haylock's study, 70% of the students used the same approach to solve all six problems, 11% discovered a simpler way to solve one of the problems, and 11% solved two of the problems using a more efficient approach (8% said the problems were too hard).

When I talk with teachers, I often hear stories about how students were taught a topic but later in the year seemed to have forgotten everything they were taught. Might this not be another version of the Einstellung effect? Many of the traditional approaches to teaching mathematics focus on one concept at a time and the practice problems are often a series of progressively more difficult problems employing the same solution strategy. We ask our students to learn an algorithm or master a procedure, give them practice problems, and then use similar problems to assess their skills. At some point students become mechanical in their approach. As a result, when they encounter a problem for which the procedure does not work they determine that the problems are too hard. Our students need opportunities to explore problems through a process of problem solving and not just by following a predetermined path. When we learn to write we are taught grammar and spelling and then are asked to apply what we learned in order to create a variety of products such as short stories, business letters, or sonnets. In teaching students to read, we ask them to look deeply into the choices the authors made to create the story they share with us. For math, students need the opportunity to move beyond the vocabulary, symbol usage, and computation to apply what they have learned in creative ways.

One way to involve your students in solving problems, not just finding answers, is to use problems that engage students in a search for meaningful solutions. The best problems are the ones that you create or tailor to meet the needs and interests of your students. Start by using some of the math competition texts. MATHCOUNTS publishes a yearly school handbook with great problems from which to choose. Each year there are a few Extended Activities that make great anchor activities or projects for your students. Samples are available on the MATHCOUNTS website at https://www.mathcounts.org/press-room. The time invested in providing your students with these types of opportunities will help them to develop metacognitive, computational, and procedural skills that mathematicians employ.

References

Haylock, D. W. (1985). Conflicts in the assessment and encouragement of mathematical creativity in schoolchildren. *International Journal of Mathematical Education in Science and Technology, 16,* 547–553.

Luchins, A. S. (1942). Mechanization in problem solving: The effect of *Einstellung. Psychological Monographs, 54*(6), i–95.

Chapter 30

Nurturing Mathematical Minds

Differentiation Strategies and Curriculum That Promote Growth

by Michelle Sands

Nora and Jack

Nora, a petite third grader, eagerly approached my desk during her recess break. "I want to learn long division. Will you show me?" After a few minutes of direct instruction using single-digit divisors, her eyes lit up and she skipped from the room. The following day Nora was at my door again. At home she had created a book of division problems for herself with double- and triple-digit divisors. "I made these for myself last night. Will you check them for me?" At her prompting, we met each day for a week and reviewed the latest additions to her self-made problem book.

Jack is a high-energy presence in his third-grade classroom. He continually looks for the humor in situations and is intensely curious. His number sense is strong, and he quickly calculates any math problem in his head. When number puzzles are presented that emit groans from classmates, Jack attacks the task with enthusiasm. Recently, during a class activity he began extending a number table that had been presented as an exercise. Jack grew excited as he identified the pattern and shouted, "The rule is number times 2 plus 2 always results in the answer!"

Characteristics of Gifted Math Students

Nora and Jack exhibit many of the learning behaviors that are characteristic of gifted math students. They learn information easily and discern patterns quickly. These students work efficiently and combine thought processes, often bypassing algorithms to solve multistep problems. Nora had internalized the patterns of necessary operations and extended this new information to division with double- and triple-digit divisors. Her passion, persistence, and aptitude were not unusual; she eagerly engages with all facets of mathematics in this way. Jack was able to describe the pattern presented in class and articulate it algebraically in a fraction of the time that it took other students to recognize even that there was a pattern. Mathematically gifted students are able to immediately extend new information to novel situations, and like Jack, are comfortable with abstract applications.

Bret

Bret is another gifted math student who differs from his classmates in unique ways. He recently grew excited as he collected and analyzed data during a probability lesson. Bret began recording the results from his experiment on small scraps of paper and as he arranged his data, a bell-shaped curve began to emerge. A neighboring student peeked over his shoulder and asked, "Why is it so high in the middle?" "Because that's the mean!" Bret declared enthusiastically. Bret had taken his data and connected it to the concept of the law of large numbers.

High-Achieving Students in the Era of Assessment

Every teacher is familiar with the struggle to provide an engaging and enriching environment that meets the needs of all students. The average classroom consists of children ranging from those with special academic needs to students who may be years ahead of their peers in specific content areas. The reality of these challenges can be daunting. According to a recent report, *High-Achieving Students in the Era of NCLB* (Loveless, Farkas, & Duffett, 2008), advanced students are not top priority in our classrooms.

In a national survey of teachers, the Fordham Institute found that 81% of teachers identified "academically struggling" students as those most likely to receive their one-on-one attention (Loveless et al., 2008, p. 12). High-achieving and gifted students are aware of these disparities. Nora, now a fifth grader, recently expressed her sensitivity to this: "I know the teacher can't spend a lot of time with me when I already know it."

At the same time, 86% of the teachers surveyed strongly believed that all children should receive an equal education regardless of academic ability (Loveless et al., 2008), including our highest achieving students. In the same report, Loveless examined achievement from 2000 to 2007 using National Assessment of Educational Progress (NAEP) data and found that while the lowest performing students made gains, the highest performing students had not made similar progress. The report credits teachers' attitudes toward equitable education as the reason for high-achieving students' performance remaining consistent rather than decreasing.

The reality, however, is that gifted learners are failing to make progress as teachers spend the majority of their time with students who are struggling academically. Teachers who are committed to equitable educational opportunities for all students find it challenging to meet the needs of all learners, particularly students like Nora, Jack, and Bret. Even in schools where support services for gifted students are in place, high-ability students spend the majority of their instructional day in heterogeneous classrooms (Reis & Westberg, 1994).

Curriculum Delivery

Gifted students have often already mastered the grade-level curriculum, or are capable of doing so at a much faster rate than their peers. They bring a unique set of learning behaviors to the classroom, requiring curriculum that provides advanced content and in-depth investigations enabling them to work beyond their current capabilities (VanTassel-Baska, 2003). Too often the grade-level curriculum is not challenging enough for students like Nora and Jack. Topics are revisited every year, investigated minimally, and contain repetition that other students may need to master rote skills.

This spiral approach to curriculum delivery is insufficient to address the accelerated pacing and depth of content necessary to stimulate the gifted math student. The repetition of topics rarely provides an application of concepts that provides new learning. As Nora demonstrated, after internalizing the processes of multiplication or division, it is not difficult for these students to transfer the mathematical concept to larger numbers or even decimals. Therefore, assigning more of the same work is not an appropriate way to address these students' needs. Tomlinson (2001) refers to this as a need for transformational experiences. When content comes easily to a student "they need information that shows them the intricacies about the idea. They need to stretch the idea and bend the idea and see how it interacts with other ideas to create a new thought" (Tomlinson, 2001, p. 46). As Bret demonstrated, gifted math students actively seek and intuitively make connections between content. Increasing depth and breadth of curriculum eliminates the frustration that occurs for students like Bret, who commented at the conclusion of their 2-week study of probability, "Just when we get to something interesting in math class it's time to move on to something else."

Curriculum Compacting

As Nora and Jack demonstrated, gifted math students learn material and transfer content at a faster rate than their peers. Like Bret, they need less repetition to master new skills, and intuitively know mathematical concepts prior to direct instruction. In order to "promote growth in learning, students must be working beyond their tested level of performance" (VanTassel-Baska, 2003, p. 20). In addressing differentiation for gifted math students, determining what they already know is a critical first step.

Curriculum compacting is an important strategy that allows teachers to assess student knowledge and skill development in particular content areas prior to instruction. Through pretesting, teachers can determine what material students have already mastered and therefore, can be eliminated. Such assessments, often found in textbooks and curriculum guides, can be brief and should include an application or extension of the mathematics to be taught. Open-ended assessments that require application of mathematical concepts rather than computational fluency provide insight into students' thinking and are effective in identifying students in need of acceleration. The integration of preassessment into the planning of mathematical units allows the teacher to identify and eliminate review of content skills that is unnecessary for gifted math students. This prescriptive approach allows for the substitution of curriculum that moves students toward greater complexity and challenge (VanTassel-Baska, 2003).

Flexible Grouping

Once levels of mastery have been determined, materials and activities can be provided that align to readiness levels. Flexible, within-class groupings based on preassessment allow teachers to address the appropriateness of content, process, and pacing for gifted students. In mathematics, research has shown that "within-class groupings of students in elementary classrooms results in higher achievement than whole-class instruction in heterogeneous classrooms" (Robinson, Shore, & Enersen, 2007, p. 124). Gentry and Owen (1999) found that differentiation strategies that address instructional groupings and content benefit all students in the regular classroom by creating small groups of students with similar educational needs. When students are grouped homogeneously based on skill level, in-depth investigation of content is possible. Students of similar achievement levels have the opportunity to grapple with challenging problems together (Sheffield, 1994). Ensuring that gifted students have opportunities to learn with and from intellectual peers reflects exemplary program design based on the National Association for Gifted Children Pre-K–Grade 12 Gifted Programming Standards (NAGC, 2010).

Emily

Emily is a talented student who benefited from this approach to differentiation. In the classroom Emily struggled with division and multiplication but was able to demonstrate advanced spatial skills in a preassessment for a geometry unit. Through curriculum compacting, Emily's math instruction was streamlined to provide time for an independent investigation. With the elimination of repetitive curriculum she was able to pursue three-dimensional geometry concepts not covered in the fourth-grade curriculum. Emily was able to use her strength area to investigate paper engineering and created a pop-up book using her new skills. This was accomplished through small mini-lessons twice a week and the opportunity to combine more divergent thinking skills during her geometry instruction.

Differentiated Curriculum Experiences

Once mastery has been determined through preassessment, and instruction has been individualized utilizing flexible grouping, differentiation of curriculum is necessary. Differentiation experiences for gifted math students should stress mathematical reasoning and the discovery of underlying principles within areas of study (Sheffield, 1994). Curriculum that moves students from concrete experiences to abstract applications, such as discovering and generalizing patterns, organizing data to reveal relationships, and articulating the formulas that describe them, requires higher levels of thinking skills and application of math skills (VanTassel-Baska, 2003). Bret's discovery of the law of large numbers could lead to more rigorous mathematical investigations of theoretical and experimental probability. The study of place value can focus on the analysis and creation of alternative number systems. The creation of number puzzles to determine the function that will establish any number in the sequence can replace rote practice of multiplication and division skills (Gavin, Chapin, Dailey, & Sheffield, 2006).

VanTassel-Baska (2003) stresses the importance of differentiation experiences for the gifted that utilize both creative and critical-thinking skills. Emily's pop-up book, creating original games, and designing a survey to collect and analyze class data are examples of these processes. The in-depth study of curriculum that occurs when pursuing these projects allows for the application of advanced concepts and creative, original responses. This open-ended approach to mathematics provides students with learning experiences that match their interest areas, readiness, and learning styles. Sheffield (1994) also recommends math competitions as a way of providing gifted math students with the content-based enrichment they require. She noted, "competitions offer students the opportunity to study math in greater depth, at a higher level, and with a broader curriculum than is offered in most school programs" (p. 23). Participation in programs such as Math Olympiad, Continental Math League, and the 24 Challenge provide opportunities where students are "challenged to use and explain logical, inductive, and deductive reasoning" (p. 23).

Putting It All Together

Appropriate learning situations for talented learners should include opportunities for them to learn at an appropriately challenging rate and pace, and encounter advanced content and learning challenges based on interests (Reis, 2008). Due to the unique learning behaviors of gifted math students, content should be accelerated when appropriate, pace of instruction should be expedited, and opportunities should be provided to allow for creative applications of open-ended tasks.

Pretesting, curriculum compacting, and flexible grouping provide differentiation opportunities for gifted math students by determining what skills are developed, developing, or undeveloped (Driscoll, 2005). Once teachers identify specific gaps regarding knowledge and skills, instructional decisions can be made in order to create more time for alternative curriculum.

Within these flexible opportunities young mathematicians have the opportunity to apply critical and creative-thinking skills that move students toward abstract applications of content. When Bret's math curriculum was compacted to allow for the exploration of probability in greater depth he was able to explore new topics. As he discovered the connection between probability and the law of greater numbers he exclaimed, "I love learning new things. It makes my brain hurt." These transformational experiences provide challenging learning experiences for all children, including our gifted math students.

References

Driscoll, M. P. (2005). *Psychology of learning for instruction* (3rd ed.). Boston, MA: Allyn & Bacon.

Gavin, K. M., Chapin, S. H., Dailey, J., & Sheffield, L. J., (2006). *Project M3: Mentoring mathematical minds*. Dubuque, IA: Kendall Hunt.

Gentry, M. L., & Owen, S. V. (1999). An investigation of the effects of total school flexible cluster grouping on identification, achievement, and classroom practices. *Gifted Child Quarterly, 43,* 224–243.

Loveless, T., Farkas, S., & Duffett, A. (2008). *High-achieving students in the era of NCLB.* Washington, DC: Thomas B. Fordham Institute.

National Association for Gifted Children. (2010). *NACG Pre-K–Grade 12 Gifted Programming Standards: A blueprint for quality gifted education programs.* Washington, DC: Author.

Reis, S. M. (2008, December). What parents need to know: Current research about gifted and talented students. *Parenting for High Potential,* 19–22.

Reis, S. M., & Westberg, K. L. (1994). The impact of staff development on teachers' ability to modify curriculum for gifted and talented students. *Gifted Child Quarterly, 38,* 125–135.

Robinson, A., Shore, B. M., & Enersen, D. L. (2007). *Best practices in gifted education: An evidence-based guide.* Waco, TX: Prufrock Press.

Sheffield, L. J. (1994). *The development of gifted and talented mathematics students and the National Council of Teachers of Mathematics Standards* (Report No. RBDM9404). Storrs, CT: National Research Center on the Gifted and Talented, University of Connecticut.

Tomlinson, C. A. (2001). *How to differentiate instruction in mixed-ability classrooms.* Alexandria, VA: ASCD.

VanTassel-Baska, J. (2003, September). Differentiated curriculum experiences for the gifted and talented: A parent's guide to best practice in school and at home. *Parenting for High Potential*, 18–21.

Chapter 31

How to Lie With Statistics

by Eric L. Mann

The title for this column is borrowed from Darrell Huff's 1954 book, *How to Lie With Statistics*. The book was revisited in a 2005 issue of *Statistical Science* and acknowledged as "the most widely read statistics book in the history of the world" (Steele, 2005, p. 205). Although laced with humor and written in a casual style, the text also contains substantial intellectual content. A quick Internet search for the text listed it as required reading on recent courses such as Quantitate Reasoning 32 at Harvard University and Statistics 21 at the University of California. The first illustration in the book is a cartoon of two men talking and the dialogue reads, "Don't be a novelist, be a statistician. Much more scope for the imagination." Listening to my graduate students talk about their struggles with statistics classes I suspect more than a few view the subject as an imaginative creation designed to challenge their intellect. In our sister publication, *Gifted Child Quarterly*, the authors take great care to present their data accurately and to support their findings and recommendations with sound statistical reasoning. Most K–12 students probably do not encounter such in-depth statistical analysis in their readings but they still need the skills to understand the data they encounter.

The American Statistical Association's (AMSTAT) *Guidelines for Assessment and Instruction in Statistics Education* (GAISE) Report seeks statistical literacy for all (Franklin, et al., 2007). Although you may not know (or remember from your stats classes) all of the different statistical terms and tests you read about in research journals, our world is such that we consistently encounter data as part of an effort to influence the choices we make.

In their 2004 book, *Math Through the Ages*, Bertlinghoff and Gouvêa describe probability and statistics as two sides of the same coin. Probability seeks to understand characteristics of an unknown sample of a known collection (What is the chance of . . . ?), while statistics seeks to extend our understanding of an unknown population from data collected from a small sample. Unfortunately the distinctions between the two sides of the coin are often blurred.

Statistics and probability first appear in the Common Core State Standards for Mathematics in the middle school curriculum and include the following topics and skills:

Grade 6
> ▸ Develop understanding of statistical variability.
> ▸ Summarize and describe distributions.

Grade 7
> ▸ Use random sampling to draw inferences about a population.
> ▸ Draw informal comparative inferences about two populations.
> ▸ Investigate chance processes and develop, use, and evaluate probability models.

Grade 8
> ▸ Investigate patterns of association in bivariate data.

High School Statistics and Probability
> ▸ Interpreting categorical and quantitative data.
> ▸ Making inferences and justifying conclusions.
> ▸ Conditional probability and the rules of probability.
> ▸ Using probability to make decisions.

Waiting until middle school to introduce the statistical tools and concepts children need to make sound decisions does a disservice to all and denies our gifted students the opportunity to engage in critical thinking and seek answers to their research questions. AMSTAT offers additional resources for K–12 classroom teachers. Information on their programs is summarized in a

PDF flyer at http://www.amstat.org/ASA/Education/K-12-Educators.aspx#classroom?hkey=09d2addb-f9d1-42a8-bb71-3f395265b531.

As a discipline, statistics is young. Bertlinghoff and Gouvêa's (2004) chapter on the history of statistics (pp. 215–222) begins with an English shopkeeper's work in 1662 and the new field of "Political Arithmetic." Others who shared an interest in developing an understanding of the "mathematics of uncertainty" include Halley, Bernoulli, Fisher, Galton, Gauss, Laplace, Legendre, Pearson, Quetele, and Tukey, among many others. Fisher's 1925 book, *Statistical Methods for Research Workers*, served as guide for many generations. Fisher writes about a summer tea party in Cambridge, England, and a woman who tells the guests she could detect a difference between a cup of tea that had milk added after the tea was poured and one in which milk was added to the cup first. Dismissed by most in attendance, Fisher designed an experiment to test her statement. It is a great conversation or lesson starter for your students, and for you! For more on the growth of statistics as a discipline see *The Lady Tasting Tea: How Statistics Revolutionized Science in the Twentieth Century* by David Salsburg.

References

Bertlinghoff, W. P., & Gouvêa, F. Q. (2004). *Math through the ages: A gentle history for teachers and others*. Washington, DC: Mathematical Association of America.

Franklin, C., Kader, G., Mewborn, D., Moreno, J., Peck, R., Perry, M., & Schaeffer, R. (2007). *Guidelines for assessment and instruction in statistics education (GAISE) report: A pre-K–12 curriculum framework*. Alexandria, VA: American Statistical Association.

Huff, D. (1993). *How to lie with statistics*. New York, NY: Norton. (Original work published 1954)

Salsburg, D. (2002). *The lady tasting tea: How statistics revolutionized science in the twentieth century*. New York, NY: Holt Paperback.

Steele, J. M. (2005). Special section: How to lie with statistics turns fifty. *Statistical Science, 20,* 205–209.

Chapter 32

Mathematics Olympiads for Elementary Students

Nurturing Young Talent

by Keri M. Guilbault

The National Association for Gifted Children (1994) stated in its position statement on differentiation that providing challenging coursework means ensuring opportunities for advanced classes beginning as early as the elementary years. Currently, most gifted children spend the majority of their time in regular classrooms without access to challenging coursework or teachers knowledgeable about the special learning needs of our most highly able learners.

A Personal Connection

As a gifted education specialist in an elementary school, I noticed that this lack of appropriate opportunity for advanced classes and challenging coursework was particularly evident in mathematics. Mathematically gifted fourth-grade students reported that they were spending much of their time memorizing multiplication facts in the regular mathematics classroom. Preassessments and above-level testing showed that many of these gifted students were ready for prealgebra.

After meeting with the intermediate grade-level teachers, I realized that even those educators who had a good grasp of differentiation were unable to effectively plan challenging experiences due to the wide range of ability levels in their heterogeneously grouped mathematics classes. Several teachers indicated that they realized they had a handful of "really bright students" who already knew most of the lessons, but were not sure what to do for them; others were not confident that they could juggle multiple lessons at a time.

In addition to providing planning assistance and support for in-class differentiation and coteaching during the mathematics block, I wanted to ensure that we were challenging our mathematically gifted learners by providing opportunities for both acceleration and enrichment. To that end, 28 mathematically gifted learners were identified and selected for participation in a weekly Mathematics Olympiads program.

The Program

Mathematics Olympiads for Elementary and Secondary Students (MOEMS) is an international program in which students explore a topic or strategy in depth and utilize creative problem-solving strategies. Over the course of an academic year, students participate in five contests that include non-routine problems. After meeting with the administrative leadership team, we decided that this program was aligned with our state standards for mathematics, the Common Core State Standards, a county STEM initiative, and the NAGC Pre-K–Grade 12 Gifted Programming Standards (2010).

Intervention

Participants

Twenty-eight talented mathematics students in grades 4 and 5 were selected for participation in the school's Mathematics Olympiads club. Students were selected using the following criteria: (a) scoring at the *above proficiency* level on the most recent state mathematics assessment, (b) performing in the top 10% on *Scholastic Math Inventory* when compared to grade-level peers, (c) teacher recommendations, (d) quantitative scores at or above the 90th percentile on the *Otis-Lennon School Ability Test*, and (e) top 10% on the end-of-year grade-level mathematics benchmark assessment. Due to a limit on the number of students who may compete on a school team, the pool of candidates identified based on the above criteria was then ranked. The top 16 fifth graders and the top 12 fourth graders were selected. Efforts were made to select a diverse team representative of the school demographics as well as an even number of male and female students. Letters were sent home to the students' parents explaining the program and requesting their permission for their child's participation. All parents allowed their child to participate in the program.

Implementation

The gifted education specialist met with selected students on Fridays during their regular mathematics flextime for up to 60 minutes per week for 5 months. During flextime, classroom teachers provide hands-on learning stations for students to practice different math skills taught during that week. This is one form of differentiation that is worked into the schedule on a regular basis.

During the Mathematics Olympiads meetings, students worked in pairs and in small groups to solve challenging mathematics problems similar to ones they would be presented with during competition. Strategies were taught to help students think creatively about problem solving. Students took turns explaining their strategies to the class and evaluated their efficiency for problem solving. Class meetings were also utilized in an effort to motivate students, encourage risk-taking, and help them set personal goals for success. Students tracked and graphed data from each contest and analyzed school contest statistics, comparing their achievement to the national data provided to all participants after each contest.

The gifted education specialist also utilized several different forms of technology to enhance student learning and to communicate with parents. One tool was a personal learning system called Edmodo (https://www.edmodo.com). The Edmodo site allowed each student to download PowerPoint presentations with class notes and explanations of homework assignments, as well as visit math websites for practice, respond to brain teasers and math enrichment problems, and view links to Khan Academy math tutorial videos (https://www.khanacademy.org). Animoto (https://animoto.com) was also used to create video slideshows set to music to inspire students and to lower the affective filter prior to contests. Prezi, a popular presentation editor, and PowerPoint presentations were used during each class meeting to demonstrate sample problems using highly visual images.

Because the Mathematics Olympiads program was used as a form of enrichment for highly able math students and did not count toward their report card grade, the gifted education specialist opted to issue weekly homework consisting of five practice problems and awarded extra credit in the form of a points system for the teams. Students who attempted the homework were given credit toward a team "math game day," and select problems were reviewed in class with students taking the lead to explain their work and their thinking to teammates. Parent involvement was encouraged through the teacher's school website, by utilizing Edmodo, and by providing answers and explanation sheets with homework so parents could help their children review and check work. Mathematics enrichment websites and community events were also shared.

Students were encouraged throughout the program to celebrate each other's success and to work as a team. Each week, the gifted education specialist recognized one female and one male student with a certificate for displaying a positive attitude, effort and perseverance, achievement, and/or leadership. Students were recognized for showing growth in their learning as measured by contest scores and active participation in class. High scorers also received recognition after each contest. Praising effort and encouraging collaboration and unique approaches to problem solving during practice sessions fostered a safe environment for risk-taking as well as positive behavior and attitudes.

Survey of Attitudes

An anonymous midpoint survey was administered to all MOEMS participants to assess student attitudes toward math and their self-perception as math students. The survey consisted of 20 items that were intended to measure (a) student self-perception of mathematics ability, (b) student attitude and motivation in mathematics, and (c) student feelings about their current mathematics instruction in the general classroom and Mathematics Olympiads club. The survey was adapted from existing valid and reliable questionnaires of elementary student attitudes toward mathematics. The questionnaire was administered in a group setting, and students were informed that their responses were anonymous so that they would answer as honestly as possible.

Questions on the student survey included negative value statements (i.e., "Mathematics is dull and boring") as well as positive value statements ("I am happier in a math class than in any other class") in order to differentiate student attitudes. Basic statistical analysis available in the Microsoft Office Excel program was conducted on the summary results.

Student Self-Perception of Mathematics Ability

Results from the questionnaire showed that the Mathematics Olympiads intervention had a positive impact on student confidence in their math ability. Eighty-six percent of students ($n = 24$) indicated that they "strongly agree" to the statement, "Since I started Math Olympiads, my confidence in my math ability has grown"; the balance of the students indicated that they "agree" with this statement. Fifty-four percent of students ($n = 15$) reported that they "strongly agreed" they were among the top math students in their general education class, and 46% of students ($n = 13$) indicated that they "agreed" with the statement. Informal conversations and anecdotal data suggested that just being selected for participation in Mathematics Olympiads boosted student self-esteem.

Student Attitude and Motivation

Students were asked whether or not they enjoyed using the Edmodo learning system at home to extend their math practice. A four-point Likert scale was used ranging from 1 = "strongly disagree" to 4 = "strongly agree." This item was used to evaluate the technology resource and to assess student motivation. If students were invested in the contests and wanted to practice to improve their scores, they might utilize Edmodo. The average rating for this item was a 3.04 on the 4-point scale, indicating, "agree." A frequency analysis, however, showed that five students out of the 28 did not enjoy Edmodo (4%, $n = 1$ "strongly disagree" and 15%, $n = 4$ "disagree"). It is not clear why those students did not like to use Edmodo or if they did not have access to computers at home. Eighty-two percent of students ($n = 23$) did report enjoying using Edmodo at home. This form of technology has many possibilities and should be considered in the future as an additional, optional resource.

Student Feelings About
Their Math Classes

One of the items tapped students' perceptions about the rigor of their general education mathematics class, specifically stating "I feel challenged in my regular math class at school." Results from this item indicated that 68% ($n = 19$) of the advanced math students strongly disagreed with the statement, while another 21% ($n = 6$) reported they disagreed with the statement.

At this elementary school, students are not grouped by ability for mathematics instruction as they are for language arts. There is also no formal cluster grouping of gifted and talented learners in mathematics class. This may contribute to an increased challenge for the classroom teacher who must work with up to eight or more grade levels of ability in the heterogeneously grouped classroom. Informal conversation with teachers indicated that they were feeling some stress and lack of ability to adequately meet the needs of the highest achievers in math when they had such extreme differences in ability in the classroom, particularly the teachers who had students with IEPs in the classroom.

Conclusion

Participation in advanced mathematics courses is frequently reported by policymakers and education researchers as one of the keys to success for individual students and for the continued competitiveness of our nation (Loveless, 2008; National Mathematics Advisory Panel, 2008; Saul, Assouline, & Sheffield, 2010). In order to ensure our most able math students reach their potential, interventions that include opportunities for enrichment and acceleration are required.

Differentiation for mathematically gifted learners should consist of purposeful, deliberate, planned experiences that extend the core curriculum (Saul et al., 2010). A blend of enrichment and acceleration in mathematics that provides increasingly rigorous curricular experiences, peer collaboration, abstraction, and complexity can contribute to student growth.

Overall, the Mathematics Olympiads program was able to meet some of the advanced learning needs of this group of talented students. One additional benefit was the time with intellectual peers who shared a common interest. An additional action research project will be conducted to investigate the effects of the

Mathematics Olympiads on student achievement, as well as the transfer of skills and motivation to the regular classroom. The questions to be asked include: Are Mathematics Olympiads participants participating more frequently in the regular math class? Are their grades and math benchmark test scores improving? Will their state standardized math assessment scores show gains? These are all questions that should and will be investigated.

References

Loveless, T. (2008). *The misplaced math student: Lost in eighth-grade algebra.* Washington, DC: Brookings Institute.

National Association for Gifted Children. (1994). *Differentiation of curriculum and instruction* [Position statement]. Washington, DC: Author.

National Association for Gifted Children. (2010). *NAGC Pre-K–Grade 12 Gifted Programming Standards: A blueprint for quality gifted education programs.* Washington, DC: Author.

National Mathematics Advisory Panel. (2008). *Foundations for success: The final report of the National Mathematics Advisory Panel.* Washington, DC: U.S. Department of Education.

Saul, M., Assouline, S., & Sheffield, L. J., (2010). *The peak in the middle: Developing mathematically gifted students in the middle grades.* Reston, VA: National Council of Teachers of Mathematics.

Section III: Visual/ Performing Arts

Chapter 33

Teaching Visual Art History and Appreciation to Young Children

by Gail N. Herman

"Who's coming to visit us today?" asked one kindergarten student as he eagerly bounded into Joan Boor's art room and pointed to the little yellow house on the wall.

I met artist Joan Boor at the Synergy Arts Conference in Hagerstown, MD. Boor is an example of the first requirement of a gifted and talented program. She provides a basic program that motivates all her students to do their creative best, 500 students in kindergarten through grade 2. When I discovered how creative she and her students were, I invited her to be interviewed for this column.

Boor was motivated to build a puppet theater in her art room because of mandated requirements to teach her students art from a historical perspective. Knowing these young students are strong proponents of creative play, she wanted to meet them on their terms, rather than on those of older elementary students. So, to teach in a creative, playful, and interesting way, Joan began using and making puppets. She soon discovered that this way of teaching art appreciation and history was a big hit.

During her preparations, she remembered the book *The Yellow House*, the story about how van Gogh invited his artist friends to come and stay with him in his little yellow house. Because she often uses the classroom wall as a "stage" for teaching, she thought, "I can make a little yellow house on the wall where artists come to visit my students and me." So that's exactly what she did. Many of the artist puppets "live" in little boxes around the edge of the bulletin board; reproductions of their work are glued to the covers of their boxes, although some of the puppets are too large to fit, so Boor bought a hanging shoe holder to store them in. The shoe holder resembled an apartment building so she transformed it into one: "I was struggling with a way to teach the concept of time to kindergarteners, so the 'apartment' became the 'Timeline Apartment'" where the ascending levels of boxes represented time periods.

Here's an example of how this works. When Boor teaches a unit to second graders about Roy Lichtenstein, she introduces him by going over to the Timeline Apartment and knocking at his door. Then she takes the Lichtenstein puppet, and a discussion of the time period in which he lived follows. Boor made the puppet to look like a very simple cartoon character complete with Ben-Day dots. Ben-Day dots involve a printing process used in comics that combines two or more different small, colored dots to create a third. It is this method that Lichtenstein used to create his style.

Then, Boor tells her class a story about how Roy Lichtenstein's sons gave him motivation to try a different style of painting, using Ben-Day dots on a large scale.

At this point, a PowerPoint of Lichtenstein's work is shown and accompanied by instruction about some basic drawing techniques related to the medium. Boor believes the drawings the students created after the training were true to form because of the added appreciation for the artist's life and times.

Currently, Boor has puppets for Romare Bearden, Mary Cassatt, Alexander Calder, Joyce Scott, Vincent van Gogh, Hokusai, Piet Mondrian, Rembrandt, and Andy Warhol. In addition to her little yellow house and apartment building, Boor has also made a lighthouse, which she plans to use to teach the students about the "Masters of Light." This is still a work in progress.

Boor would remind teachers that many young children are natural storytellers and like to repeat the stories about artists. Therefore, she also provides lessons for her kindergarten students to make puppets and toys. They especially like to make things they can play and interact with.

She says, "I believe teaching is a creative, associational process. [Teachers] need to listen to the children as they talk and work and to respect their love for imagination, fantasy, creativity, and playfulness."

What an exciting and unique opportunity Boor has created for her students. Perhaps you could incorporate some of her ideas into your classroom today. Hopefully some of your students will soon be asking, "Who's coming to visit?"

Chapter 34

Infusing Thinking Skills Into Visual Arts Instruction

by Juliana Tay

Art instruction and education has been generally considered an activity-based subject that caters to those who are talented and passionate in the area. It is also viewed as being focused on art production skills and techniques. However, there is more to the art classroom than creating visual artworks. A study by Sabol (2006) examined the differences among the criteria used by art teachers, art students, and artists to assess and evaluate works of art. Both students and teachers listed skills-focused criteria such as Elements of Art, Principles of Design, and Technical Skills, the usual curricular plan, for evaluating artworks. The artists, however, were more concerned about the conceptual and cognitive aspects of art such as the originality of their works, demonstration of their development and growth, overall creativity, and how the finished work reflected the original idea. The results present a clear case for why familiar curricular instruction, infused with creative thinking skills development, should be the route taken by educators if they are to ensure lasting knowledge that carries over into other fields. Art educators, or those that use art instruction in their classes, must seek ways to adapt curriculum to include key thinking skills. One possible approach is to draw both teachers' and students' attention to the cognitive activities (thinking, questioning, etc.) that are taking place within the art classroom. For this, I looked to the Talents Unlimited Model, which presents classroom-based practices that mirror the artistic creative processes, and a differentiation strategy known as tiered assignments (see Figure 34.1).

Thinking Skills: The Talents Unlimited Model

The Talents Unlimited Model (TU) by Carol Schlichter (1986), based on the work of Calvin W. Taylor, was designed to engage students in thinking and questioning during their learning process to generate new knowledge. Schlichter listed five components of TU, which can serve as the foundation for thinking during art instruction: productive thinking, decision making, planning, forecasting, and communication (see Table 34.1).

My experience during my training as an art teacher was focused on the different types of craft for art production, art history, and art critique. This focus was similar to that of the teachers in the Sabol study (2006). Thinking skills were implied throughout the modules, but they were not taught explicitly, nor did the lecturers make any direct connections between thinking skills and the art activities. Although I felt that I was challenging my students and found success in my lesson plans, which included suggested conceptual reflection and a push for originality, it was not until I was introduced to TU that I began to see the similarities between the theory's framework and the artistic processes in which my students were engaged as they created. I was now able to use and apply various forms of higher order thinking skills intended for this purpose.

Differentiating Within the Model: Using Tiered Instruction

Tiered instruction, or the process by which teachers accommodate the learning differences of the students by assessing their ability and crafting assignments with ascending levels of demand, fits quite well with the TU model. In my case, tiered assignments provided students with the appropriate challenge for the task, while TU was able to provide the structure required by the students to help them develop their thinking skills. The concepts of TU, coupled with differentiation strategies, such as tiered assignments, can be used in the art class-

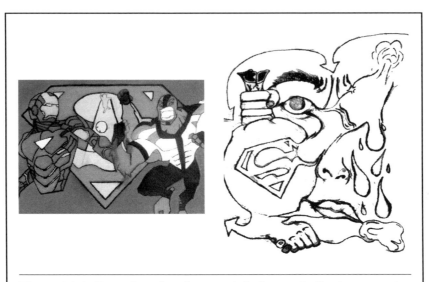

Figure 34.1. Examples of student work before and after incorporating Talents Unlimited Model.

TABLE 34.1

Components of the Talents Unlimited Model

Talent Areas	Definition
Productive Thinking	generate varied and unusual ideas or solutions and to add interesting and value-added details
Decision Making	outline, weigh, make final judgments; defend a decision on the many alternatives to a problem
Planning	design a means for implementing an idea by describing what needs to be done, identifying the resources needed, outlining a sequence of steps to take, and pinpointing possible problems in the plan
Forecasting	make a variety of predictions about possible causes and/or effects of various phenomena
Communication	use and interpret both verbal and nonverbal forms of communication to express ideas, feelings, and needs to others

Note. Adapted from Schlichter (1986), p. 120.

room to teach students a set of skills that allow them to take control of the art making process, regardless of the level of mastery with which they begin. Let's look at a classroom example.

A Printmaking Class

In a printmaking class, my eighth-grade students were to create self-portraits, and the activity began with a short presentation on the visual arts task and included some examples of self-portraits in various media created by different artists. Schlichter (1986) referred to productive thinking as a way "to generate many, varied and unusual ideas" (p. 120), which is an important step at the beginning of most creative assignments, so I began with idea generation. The students then began by brainstorming the concept of self-portraits: what the words meant to them and what forms a portrait can take. By engaging in this type of productive thinking, the students generated ideas as a class, questioning and challenging the notion of self-portraits. Students having more experience with or exposure to the medium linked the idea of the portrait to the concept of self-identity and began questioning the various ways self-portraits were approached by the masters. Students less familiar with the medium benefited from the discussions as they listened, sought clarification, and questioned the various ideas generated through the interactions. By allowing the class to work together in the beginning, the students were able to reflect and build upon each other's artistic insights and to question and interpret the theme to the best of their abilities.

Once the students were satisfied with the range of ideas generated, they moved on to the decision-making, planning, and forecasting phases of TU. This involved considering the different options available for materials, space, and design, deciding upon the focus and theme they would take, planning out the work ahead of them while considering possible issues or problems, and seeking to understand how their work might be critiqued to include originality and creativity. The students had to ensure that the designs for their self-portraits communicated their individual ideas and intentions. It is important to note that the TU model does not present a linear process, as students often move between phases, reflecting and revising their ideas, and thinking about what they wanted their works to communicate.

Table 34.2 illustrates the difference between the characteristics of students and the activities they took part in and were evaluated on. Students who needed the most help were given more direct questions to encourage them to think about themselves and their preferences. Those who needed less direct instruction were tasked to think about their roles in society and relate them to their sense of identity.

TABLE 34.2

*Characteristics of Students and Activities Used
in Printmaking Tier Assignment*

Tier	Talent Areas	Definition
1	Below average success or students lacking drive and focus in their work	▶ Focus on one printmaking technique— lino-printing ▶ Given a variety of symbols and icons as examples, which they will be able to choose and modify to suit their creative expressions (a starting point in order not to overwhelm them with a blank slate)
2	Average students who have shown some mastery of printmaking techniques and understanding of self	▶ Choice of which printmaking technique they want to employ ▶ Given a set of questions to guide them in their thinking and development of work
3	Advanced students who have shown mastery of most printmaking techniques and self-awareness	▶ Must make use of more than one printmaking technique to create their work ▶ Independent research on the ideas that they want to express for their self-portrait

For example, students in Tier 1, those who lacked drive and focus or had below-average success, were given examples of icons and motifs to start them thinking on what the patterns could symbolize, while students in Tier 3, those who had shown strong mastery of printmaking techniques and good sense of self-awareness, were given only the theme to work with; they also received the additional challenge of incorporating more than one printmaking technique in their final product. In this manner, the students were engaged in the processes of decision making, planning, and forecasting at a level appropriate for their ability.

Figures 34.1 and 34.2 illustrate examples of student work and how they differed after the TU model was introduced. Although art is subjective in nature, and the examples are fine pieces, it is clear that after the introduction of TU, there was increased depth, intricacy, and originality exhibited in the product.

Combining tiered instruction with TU allows the teaching of various thinking skills to be directed at the appropriate level for each group of students. This combination, TU with a differentiation strategy, can be useful in helping both teachers and students to change their perceptions of what art is within the classroom and make the thinking processes more explicit. Once your students are familiar with the processes such as productive thinking, decision making, and planning, they will be more likely to use them during their art making pro-

Figure 34.2. Examples of student work before and after incorporating Talents Unlimited Model.

cess. This will help the students gain a stronger sense of self-autonomy and the ability to take charge in their creative works.

Encouraged by the components of TU to think about and question their work, students will be able to explore a larger context of this field of study and carry the lessons learned to others that they may be exposed to. Educators can assist in laying the foundation for the importance of thinking and questioning during any learning process. It will set students on a path to discover how they will approach other learning experiences, and possibly to a greater perspective of themselves as learners.

References

Sabol, F. R. (2006). Identifying exemplary criteria to evaluate studio products in art education. *Art Education, 59*(6), 6–11.

Schlichter, C. L. (1986). Talents Unlimited: An inservice education model for teaching thinking skills. *Gifted Child Quarterly, 30,* 119–123.

Chapter 35

Opening A Digital Art Gallery

by Kevin D. Besnoy

This edition explores the hybridization of artistic abilities and digital technology. In order to prepare artistically gifted students for postsecondary settings, teachers must create a robust digital ecosystem that weaves together digital technologies, art, and career readiness. Even though many artistically gifted students might not pursue a career in a technology-specific field, a majority of jobs in contemporary and future economies seek employees capable of using digital technologies for creative-productive purposes. The ideas suggested here are written for the visual arts. In future columns, I will describe ways to create a robust digital ecosystem for other mediums.

In the field of visual arts, teaching artistically gifted students to sell their art online is a process-oriented approach that requires students to think about how they can leverage digital media to share their artistic expression. A great start for these learners is to create a digital art gallery that allows them to promote and sell their creations. There are many online sites available for budding artists. One of my favorites is ArtPal (https://www.artpal.com).

ArtPal

ArtPal is a user-friendly site that allows members to create a personalized digital gallery. ArtPal enables artists to show and sell their art across the globe, thus creating a truly authentic audience. Learning how to successfully take artistic works to market is a valuable skill.

Step 1: Read Advice Articles and Peruse Existing Digital Galleries

One helpful feature with ArtPal is the advice articles about how to successfully create a personalized digital art gallery. Topics of these articles range from "Getting Started with ArtPal" and "How to Make Your Art Stand Out Online" to "Improving Your Online Portfolio" and "The Power of Persistence." I suggest that students read a few articles and view existing digital galleries. By doing this first, your students will begin to brainstorm ideas about the look of their own digital gallery.

Step 2: Create an ArtPal Free Gallery

Creating a personal digital gallery can be accomplished by clicking on the "Sell Art" tab. After registering for a free account, students will be taken on a tour of their personal digital gallery where they can personalize the look, name, and items they wish to sell. This is the point where students begin to upload digital images of their work. They will also want to set up specific functions of their gallery.

Step 3: Identifying an Audience

Finding an audience to whom students can promote and sell their work is an essential element to creating a successful personal digital gallery. Of course, students will want to share their galleries with their peers, but their peers likely will not be purchasers of their works of art. As such, students will want to expand out of their comfort area and find ways to connect with other artists and galleries that showcase and sell similar works of art.

Step 4: Promote Your Personal Gallery

In previous columns, I have described how to create videos to promote a Public Service Announcement or a crowdfunding campaign. This is another opportunity for students to create short videos promoting their digital galleries. At the same time, students will want to use other social media outlets to generate excitement. For example, students can create a series of short videos of themselves creating their art and post them on YouTube. Another idea would be to use the built-in Facebook feature that automatically posts status updates to a Facebook page.

There are several other digital art galleries that can be found through an Internet search. One popular e-marketplace example is Etsy (https://www.etsy.com), where artists can sell crafts, clothing, art, or photography. Another example is ArtFire (https://www.artfire.com), which serves as an e-marketplace for those interested in selling their works of art. Each of these sites charges a fee for posting items and collects a percentage at the point of sale. For detailed information about associated fees, please see each site's Frequently Asked Questions page.

Conclusion

Regardless of the site used, Internet safety precautions must always be considered. Whether selling personal art, posting, or blogging about the visual arts, keeping students engaged in activities that hybridize technology and art for creative-productive purposes will provide skills for today and transferable skills needed to have a successful model of career readiness.

Chapter 36

Building Class Kindness and Concern Through Chant and Storytelling

by Gail N. Herman

Supporting text on the NAGC website (2008) regarding the NAGC Socio-Emotional Guidance and Counseling Standards states that

> Gifted learners who are comfortable with their abilities are more likely to use their talents in positive ways. High-ability students need specific curriculum that addresses their socio-emotional needs and enhances development of the whole child, rather than just focusing on cognitive development.

As a teacher of primary gifted children and as a regular classroom teacher, there were weeks during the start of school when I ran out of time trying to solve all of the social problems that cropped up. Students were often preoccupied with hurt, anger, and worry about not being liked.

The grumps spread like weeds among flowers until not a flower or a smiling child was left. Insults had a withering effect on any budding talent. But, luckily, my young students learned to support one another. They found it rewarding to end the cycle of insults and effect changes in people's negative behavior.

How did this happen? A little story and some information about behavior helped.

The transformation happened after I used my monkey puppet to create Sylvester the grumpy monkey and a story called, *Sylvester and the Grumps* (Herman, 2008). The story uses a "wrap-around" story structure in which the monkey begins a cycle of put-downs: Monkey wakes up with the grumps and insults Turtle, who becomes grumpy and then insults Parrot, who becomes grumpy and then insults Alligator. But a little mouse puppet decides to reverse the cycle of put-downs by changing them to put-ups. The vicious cycle is reversed by Mouse. But what about tomorrow morning? Mouse decides that to avoid the grumps from starting the next morning, she will teach them a Put-Up Chant to "dump the grumps." As soon as they wake up she chants:

I've got a put-up inside of me
And it goes like this.

The Mouse gives one puppet a put-up and then returns to the chant, after which she gives another puppet a put-up. This technique creates a musical form called a rondo: A . . . B . . . A . . . C . . . A . . . D . . . until all of the puppets receive a put up. The A is the chant that all of the students learn to say. The letters B, C, D, stand for the individual contributions of put-ups that the Mouse (individual children) gives to the puppets. Later we gave put-ups to each other.

I saw the change in my second-grade gifted students when I first started using this story. The "I'm better than you" statements (put-downs) slowly changed to "I like the way you do that" statements (put-ups) as children gained an awareness of each other's talents, feelings, and growing potential.

I noticed that my primary grade students were able to take more creative chances, perhaps because of a gradual lessening of fear and peer criticism. They learned to receive and give affirmations as well as protect their classmates on the playground from barbed put-downs.

Several other books are helpful in creating positive climates for creative work. One that I use with elementary students is called *Simon's Hook* (Burnett, 2000). The author helps students see how to avoid "biting the hook" when put-downs are thrown out. Burnett offers practical strategies to deflect barbs without returning the put-down, and so continuing the cycle.

Another book that hits home with many children is *Don't Laugh at Me* (Seskin & Shamblin, 2002). A portion of the proceeds of this book goes to an organization to rid bullying through malicious laughter.

Because the effectiveness of a group depends in part on the feelings members possess about themselves and their place in the group, I want the students to recognize each other's potential for improvement, accomplishment, and kindness. I want the students to develop a classroom atmosphere where each receives recognition and encouragement from others.

Meanspiritedness is often learned from TV or peers. It is not the destiny of classrooms. When teachers consciously develop strategies for demonstrating other ways of behaving, the cycle of put-downs can be reversed and we can make classrooms accepting of all students' demonstrated strengths as well as their approximations toward excellence. High-ability students will thank us.

Resources

Burnett, K. G. (2000). *Simon's hook: A story about teases and put-downs.* Felton, CA: GR Publishing.

Herman, G. N. (2008). *Sylvester and the grumps: How to dump the grumps.* Available from the author at 166 Lodge Circle, Swanton, MD 21561.

National Association for Gifted Children. (2008). *Pre-K to Grade 12 gifted program standards.* Retrieved from http://www.nagc.org/resources-publications/resources/national-standards-gifted-and-talented-education/pre-k-grade-12

Seskin, S., & Shamblin, A. (2002). *Don't laugh at me.* Berkeley, CA: Tricycle Press.

Chapter 37

Moving Beyond Traditional Investigations and Role-Playing

by Sara Newell

New and emerging technologies have changed the way educators think about instruction and classroom activity. The old-fashioned methods of student research, collaboration, participation, and delivery of work have been replaced by digital tablets, cloud computing, and near-instantaneous access to resources and materials. Just as the typewriter gave high-ability writers a venue for exciting change and speed at which to create, the digital tablet has done the same for the gifted historical researcher and role-player. Speed, interactive interface, a variety of formats, and relevant (dare I say "entertaining") applications are all a part of the tablet user experience. As all of these techno-tools become available, my challenge as a classroom teacher in a center for highly gifted students is to ensure that I maintain strict standards for rigorous instruction and depth of knowledge while keeping my students' attention. My fifth graders are accustomed to having the latest technological devices at home and expect a similar level of engagement at school. My role is to merge the universal appeal of new devices with the high level of instructional quality that gifted students need and deserve. I found a way to get the best of both by using digital tablets to reenact the dramatic trial of Sacco and Vanzetti. It is a lesson I had done for years as a debate, but is now transformed into a challenging 21st-century simulation.

From Traditional Approach
to Something New

The infamous trial of Italian immigrants Nicola Sacco and Bartolomeo Vanzetti was one of the key events of the 1920s and is an important part of our fifth-grade social studies curriculum. The questionable conviction and execution of the men is symbolic of the issues of class struggle, the Red Scare, ethnic tensions, and social injustice that society faced in both the U.S. and abroad. For years, I led students through investigations of the key players and debates over the guilt or innocence of the men charged with robbery and murder. Students enjoyed the debates, but I always felt that the standard curricular materials and writing prompts, along with a limited number of print-based materials and access to resources, left my gifted students wanting more depth and understanding. It is as if they were missing the evidence and detail needed to truly evaluate the fairness of what occurred in that Massachusetts courtroom. Their high levels of questioning and involvement demanded more than an oversimplified debate about the issues.

This year, the availability of new tablets for instructional use completely changed how I approach this unit. We now use the tablets and Moodle (an online, secure course management system) to analyze primary sources such as complete court transcripts and documents to reenact portions of the trial in detail. The students are able to get out of their seats and "become" the key players in the case—experiencing the true complexity of the contradicting testimony, sympathetic characters, red herrings, and outside influences affecting the controversial conviction. Where before they had written or typed transcripts, pieced together in a notebook or simple word processing program, they now have online collaboration tools to complete the effort and handheld access to the script. Work with the tablets also allowed for a discussion of online etiquette and behavior.

The Sacco and Vanzetti Lesson

Students begin by reading a one-page summary of the case and ask to be part of either the prosecution or defense team. They then locate the actual transcript from the trial (available on several sites online) and cut each person's section down to a maximum of two pages in length. The entire trial could be acted out, but our allotted time limited the reenactment to two class periods. Next, the "attorneys" organize a forum thread on Moodle for each argument, prepare the text for rehearsal of testimony with witnesses, and, of course, prepare for the closing statements. The end result of this "copy and paste" is a complete, student-edited transcript that will be analyzed, rehearsed, and performed.

Once the script is created, students begin a series of tasks related to analysis and evaluation. This demands the type of higher order thinking skills and lines of questioning expected from gifted students. Initially, students must analyze key questions such as: *Why is the lawyer asking this question? Why is "my" character answering this way? What are the motives at play here?* Then they evaluate: *Is this crucial evidence in the case? Is this an example of bias on the part of the attorney or witness?* The in-depth discussions the students have while working through this process are extremely valuable to their understanding of the motivation of each of the main players, providing them with a real-world application of critical thinking skills. Additionally, the reading and cutting of the transcripts requires students to evaluate text for a number of criteria: bias, purpose, motive, and connection to the "plot" or sequence of events. As students continue to read through the transcripts, it is fascinating to witness the results of their evaluation of the court documents and the detail to which they "become" their character. I have observed students explain to their attorney how the prosecutor bullied them or how they were attacked on the street and dragged to the police station to be interrogated. They quickly switch from saying, "my character" to "I." It is a transformative process, made even more real as they now have digital access to enough detail to make emotional connections to the case.

As students complete their transcripts, they utilize the tablets to edit and post their pieces on the forum thread on Moodle in the order in which the original witnesses testified. This means that the whole thread will represent the edited script of the entire trial, which usually takes two, one-hour class periods to act out. At this point in the project, we take time to discuss online etiquette. The positive and polite manner in which students conduct themselves with others is just as important in a virtual environment as it is when speaking face to face. In addition, students need to understand that there are deadlines to meet and if not, others' work, which is dependent on their own, may suffer. Next, an entire class is dedicated to rehearsal, allowing the students to get into character, using what they learned about each person involved in the trial. (And yes, costumes are allowed and encouraged— Sacco's cap is a must-have piece of evidence.) Presiding as Judge Thayer, the teacher can help with organizing, troubleshooting, and occasionally directing. Then, it is time for the trial.

This is when the simplicity and size of the tablets really make a difference. Although the research and preparation could have been done on laptops or desktop computers, use of the tablets streamlines the reenactment. They also add a bit of technological excitement that helps motivate the students. The judge, the defense team, the prosecution, and the witness on the stand all used the tablets, following along using the same "live" script in the Moodle forum thread. Attorneys "object" and the judge "rules" using the exact words from the actual trial without anyone having to memorize pages of testimony. The students were even quick to hand off the tablets when a new witness took the stand. The process is virtually seamless and the dramatic quality created by students able to "live" their research as historical figures are brought to life as the trial moves along.

Upon the conclusion of the trial, students were asked to reflect and write about the verdict—*Was it fair? Was the defendants' immigrant status an issue? What about his or her political views and activities?* Rather than generalizations and unfounded opinions, the gifted students cited evidence and supported their responses by pointing out actual events and quoting specific characters, participating in the type of high-level discussions one comes to expect when working with this population. Even though I have had similar student experiences with the previous method of presenting this lesson, the addition of the tablets has incorporated a new, often crucial technological aspect into the mix.

Extending the Idea

This process can be easily applied to reenacting other trials, both historical and literary. Thurgood Marshall's victory in *Brown v. Board of Education* would make a dramatic impact presented using this method. Gifted middle or high school students could write and perform a trial of Boo Radley for the murder of Bob Ewell as an extension of their study of *To Kill a Mockingbird*. I plan to apply tablet-facilitated analysis of primary source documents in additional units. For instance, utilizing the DrawCast app (http://drawcast.com) provides the perfect method for creating blackout poetry (http://newspaper-blackout.com) with original newspaper articles found on the National Archives website (https://www.archives.gov). There are myriad possibilities; however, I am careful to remember that rigorous, meaningful content and a clear, relevant purpose must always provide the foundation for gifted classroom instruction, no matter the technology available. Incorporating the latest digital technology into well-written and implemented curriculum is essential if we are to instill 21st-century skills in our students. The use of digital tablets provides just one of many possibilities.

For a classroom example of the trial, please visit http://prezi.com/5jhlsryphzdr/using-ipads-to-reenact-the-sacco-and-vanzetti-trial/?auth_key=23d6faa09d14ebfd4943b974f9330191fe7653bf .

Resources

D'Attilio, R. (2007). *Sacco-Vanzetti case*. Retrieved from http://www.writing.upenn.edu/~afilreis/88/sacvan.html

Linder, D. (2000). *The trial of Sacco and Vanzetti*. Retrieved from http://law2.umkc.edu/faculty/projects/ftrials/SaccoV/SaccoV.htm

Chapter 38

The Silent "A"

*Why Art Has Always Been
Part of STEM Expertise*

by Kenneth J. Smith

> If I had an hour to solve a problem I'd spend 55 minutes thinking about the problem and 5 minutes thinking about solutions.
>
> —Einstein

The acronym STEM (science, technology, engineering, math) is in vogue as an educational buzzword. Nevertheless, the idea of adding an A for art, changing STEM to STEAM, has been picking up a lot of, well, steam. The reasons for this addition seem twofold: First, art adds to the scientist's toolbox as a different way of perceiving concepts, and second, it complements the creative components of STEM. I contend that art has always been an integral part of STEM, and therefore there is no need to consider adding it as a component. In this context, art presents the opportunity to think visually and spatially. In projects it is expressed through activities by manipulating two- and three-dimensional objects, converting data into charts, sketching, and designing blueprints.

A da Vinci or an Einstein?

The definition of STEM seems to be in flux. For me, the definition is operational: Teachers who develop STEM curriculum should understand the behaviors of gifted and expert adults in the relevant content areas and then develop curriculum that fosters this kind of thinking (Smith, 2014). Therefore, to understand how STEM experts think, I looked at two of the field's luminaries, da Vinci and Einstein. Da Vinci was the consummate polymath, his giftedness manifesting itself in numerous disciplines. Einstein, in contrast, was a more specialized genius, focusing his efforts on physics and music. Both, however, saw art as integral to their thinking. Da Vinci advised us to "[s]tudy the science of art and the art of science."

Da Vinci analyzed human movement and then systematically applied his understanding of anatomy to the design of machines, often going though many iterations of the same design (Baeck, 2008). The mathematical notations in his drawings illustrate the integration of STEM and art that permeated his work. Da Vinci often used his anatomical and mechanical drawings to define his procedural knowledge.

Einstein's cognitive processing paralleled da Vinci's in that both manipulated mental images when reasoning how the physical world operated. When Einstein was asked to describe his thinking during the inventive process, he often commented that images were much stronger than written language.

It is likely that there was more to Einstein's and da Vinci's thinking than manipulating images and translating these into words near the conclusion of the problem. It does seem that being able to visualize possible solutions and to mentally manipulate images are essential to success in STEM fields. The longitudinal findings of Project TALENT (e.g., Coxon, 2012; Lubinski, 2010) support the essential role spatial thinking plays in developing expertise in STEM careers. In 1960, Flanagan gathered data from 100,000 high school students and followed their academic and career choices into the 1970s (Flanagan, Shaycroft, Richards, & Claudy, 1970). Students who demonstrated the strongest spatial and math skills in high school were significantly more likely to be drawn to STEM fields while their counterparts with lower scores in these areas tended to be drawn to such fields as education, arts, and social sciences. Moreover, even though evidence suggested that these spatial and visual skills can be taught, instruction focused on creative and spatial ability development is uncommon (Coxon, 2012; Mann, 2006). Thus, by examining the skills and strategies in which Einstein and da Vinci engaged, we learn how spatial manipulation, visual arts, and creativity can be woven into STEM instruction and have a positive impact on our students.

Ill-Constructed Problems: da Vinci and Einstein in our Classrooms

There are specific skills and content that students need to master to solve STEM challenges, yet classroom projects, as in the lab or the field, often need to be ill-structured rather than well-structured. In well-structured problems, regardless of their complexity, X includes all information needed to find a singular best answer. Ill-structured problems, in contrast, have open constraints (or options) in one, two, or all three aspects of the problem. The more open constraints, the more complexity the solver must handle. For example, Reitman's (1965) seminal analysis of a composer creating a fugue showed that the abstraction of any problem can be expressed as X $\rightarrow$ Y in which X represents the problem statement, Y represents the acceptable solution(s), and $\rightarrow$ represents all of the available paths to get from X to Y.

Einstein said that solving a problem was easy; defining it was hard. More recently, Davidson and Sternberg (2003) wrote that ill-structured problem solving is an essential educational goal. Strangely, even though the kinds of problems most frequently encountered in STEM professions are ill-structured, the ones most frequently encountered in school are well-structured ones (Daniels, Carbone, Hauer, & Moore, 2007).

Providing our students with Einstein and da Vinci-like strategies adds to their toolbox for solving ill-structured problems and leads to expertise. The following two classroom examples, third graders designing a fort for the founders of Jamestown and middle schoolers designing and constructing a miniature golf course, are used as examples to illustrate a suggested series of guidelines (all containing a visual or spatial component) intended for use with high-ability students in the regular classroom.

1. Spend time planning or defining the problem. Einstein alluded to the essence of expertise in STEM fields. When faced with an ill-structured problem, invest cognitive effort in defining and then redefining the problem statement. Novel solutions are the result of bringing structure and detail to the problem statement, breaking it down into smaller, interrelated problems; deciding what to include and what is extraneous; and tentatively providing the specifics that close open parameters.

STEM classrooms should mirror STEM careers. Therefore, initial information given to students should be minimal, with a combination of open-ended and some specified parameters. Asked to design a fort for the Jamestown settlement, students were told that they could only use materials and machinery available to the settlers. In building the miniature golf course, students were told that it must be possible to achieve a hole in one, yet there must be an obstacle that prevents a straight tee-to-cup shot.

Students generated lists of questions they needed answered before they could draw an initial blueprint of their solution. Regardless of the project, students' initial questions fall into three categories: materials, details, and use. Students who ask questions about the use of the project have a higher level of understanding about what drives the decision process. Sample questions asked by students in past include:

Jamestown Fort
- ▶ How tall will it be?
- ▶ How long will it take to build?
- ▶ Does it have a chimney?
- ▶ Do we need to cut down stuff?
- ▶ How big will it be?
- ▶ Who will live in it?
- ▶ What would be inside?
- ▶ What is the skill level and specialty of those involved in construction?

Miniature Golf Course
- ▶ How much can we spend?
- ▶ How much space do we have?
- ▶ Where do we put the course?
- ▶ What materials can we use?
- ▶ How hard will it be to find plastic golf clubs for safety?
- ▶ What is the skill level of the people who will use it?
- ▶ What will be the circumference of the holes?

A discussion about the relationships among the questions follows and helps students realize that solutions to different problems impact each other. For example, when planning the golf course, students discuss the relationships among materials, geometry of the hole, obstacles, and trajectory of the hole-in-one. The shape of the hole foundation and the determined path create angles that limit the placement of obstacles.

2. Make several attempts. Persevere. You aren't wrong until you give up. Systematic perseverance is a hallmark of STEM, and da Vinci personified this. He was a pioneer in the field that has come to be known as anthropometry (Baeck, 2008): the measuring of the human body, both in static position and during movement. One of da Vinci's well-documented projects in this area was the building of digging machines for the Arno River diversion. Da Vinci studied many men before concluding that in one hour, a good worker could move 500 shovels of soil a distance of six arms. He then used his findings to develop many iterations of digging machines, several of which were failures. But failure is a misnomer as each ineffective iteration led to a better version, moving him closer to his goal. Rather than allow students to give up after one try, stress that this is a part of the discovery process. Perseverance is related to problem definition because each attempt allows one to restructure variables and redefine an aspect of the problem. As teachers, it is often difficult not to give students the correct answer to their questions. Students building the golf course had to build a catapult to see how levers worked and often asked how they should construct it. Isolating variables through trials is an integral part of the STEM creative processes; therefore, respond with "Try it and find out."

3. Focus on cause and effect. Einstein developed his Theory of Relativity by interpreting how a body appeared to slow down as it entered the frame of reference of an observer. Da Vinci's drawings for his inventions are replete with his empirically discovered reasons to refine cause-and-effect sequences. Their expertise came as a result of procedural knowledge, where a specific sequence combined with trial and error lead to new understandings.

Although students need years to develop expertise, teachers can guide them to practice thinking like experts. This means providing questions and activities that require them to focus on cause and effect and if/then situations intended to move them toward solutions. As with many aspects of STEM problem solving, art provides a useful tool for developing this focus.

Specifically, visual representations and experimental trials can help advance student understanding of procedural knowledge in the following ways:
- turning two-dimensional into three-dimensional shapes;
- breaking objects into component shapes and manipulating them into new forms;
- predicting paths of objects placed into motion; and
- changing variables in a scientific experiment.

In the fort project, several lessons are dedicated to turning two-dimensional shapes into three-dimensional ones. In one lesson, students draw a 4 x 4 inch square centered on a sheet of construction paper and then add five more squares with the same dimension to create a cube. Students are told that each of the squares had to share at least one edge with another square. Feedback given after unsuccessful attempts should focus on "Why do you think it didn't work?" "How can you solve that problem?" "Why do you think that will solve the problem?" and "I don't know; try it."

This leads to the second spatial thinking exercise: breaking objects into component parts. In the fort activity, students break down the original Jamestown Fort into component basic shapes: How many squares, cubes and rectangles (e.g., walls, gates, buildings)? How many cylinders (e.g., bulwarks, wells, cannons)? Students then calculate and estimate to determine the area of the original fort. Students work in groups to use their three-dimensional shapes to create a facsimile of the original fort. Next they rearrange components to illustrate their hypothesized improvements to the original triangular fort.

In the golf course project, students place a large sheet of paper against a wall. Using a yardstick and pencil they draw predicted paths a golf ball will follow when hit from point A on the paper off the wall toward point B on the paper. Students then roll a golf ball in tempera paint and hit the ball off the wall. They can compare the path left by the ball with their predicted path and discover the actual path is always an isosceles triangle. This is essential to designing their hole and the discovery of the pattern is part of visualizing procedural knowledge.

4. Be innovative. Although there are aspects of STEM fields that have a single correct answer (e.g., math facts), the same can be said about art class (e.g., two complementary colors make gray). All STEM projects should be creative; if they aren't, they aren't STEM. This is because there should not be one single correct answer to be "discovered," rather, an innovative solution should be one of the defining measure of success. If, for example, students were simply creating a scale model of the original Jamestown fort, it would not be considered a valid STEM assignment. Solving an ill-structured problem should require creative thought. Visual-spatial skills are tools for the engineer just as they are for the sculptor. I recently asked a group of eighth graders to name a creative profession. Their first responses were not surprising: fashion designer, musician, playwright. No one mentioned scientist (unless you count app designer) or mathematician. Part of our challenge as teachers is to get STEM professions added to this list. As DeHaan states, "Creativity is the creation of an idea or object that is both novel and useful." Yes, this could be a painting or a play, but it could also be a prosthetic limb that allows one to climb mountains or a new way of defining the relationship between energy and mass.

Conclusion

The case is sometimes made that STEM lacks a visual or creative component that can be supplied by integrating aspects of art into instruction. There is some validity to this claim as descriptions of STEM programs can fail to reference innovation or visual-spatial skills. Still, by studying the work of da Vinci and Einstein, we see that these skills can be essential to accomplishments in STEM professions and the development of expertise. These two members of STEM royalty, though as unique from each other as the times in which they lived, have commonalities. They both began with ill-structured problems that required systematic experimentation to define and focus on cause and effect. Both men were innovators and used visual and spatial thinking to consider aspects of and solutions to problems. Our role as educators demands that we help students discover how art can enhance each phase of the STEM experience—as it has for generations.

References

Baeck, A. (2008). *How Leonardo da Vinci invented (and can reinvent) our design process*. Retrieved from http://www.chi2008.org

Coxon, S. V. (2012) Innovative allies: Spatial and creative abilities. *Gifted Child Today, 35,* 277–283.

Daniels, M., Carbone, A., Hauer, A., & Moore, D. (2007). *Ill-structured problem solving in engineering education*. Paper presented at the 37th ASEE/IEEE Frontiers in Education Conference, Milwaukee, WI.

Davidson, J. E., & Sternberg, R. J. (Eds.). (2003). *The psychology of problem solving*. Cambridge, England: Cambridge University Press.

Flanagan, J. C., Shaycroft, M. F., Richards, J. M., Jr., & Claudy, J. G. (1971). *Five years after high school*. Palo Alto, CA: American Institutes for Research.

Lubinski, D. (2010). Spatial ability and STEM: A sleeping giant for talent identification and development. *Personality and Individual Differences, 49,* 344–351.

Mann, R. L. (2006). Effective teaching strategies for gifted/learning disabled students with spatial strengths. *Journal of Secondary Gifted Education, 17,* 112–121.

Reitman, W. R. (1965). Cognition and thought: An information processing approach. New York, NY: Wiley.

Smith, K. J. (2014). From pop-up books to Shakespeare: Writing as problem solving across the grade levels. *Gifted Child Today, 37,* 222–234.

Section IV: History/ Social Studies

Chapter 39

Uncovering History in the Elementary Grades

by Suzanna E. Henshon

How do you make teaching history fun? Is there a way to make the subject exciting and three-dimensional within your classroom? Where do you start?

Ask people what they think of history and most will tell you that it is just dates and factual information. In truth, history is far more interesting than names, dates, and famous events. When you bring history to life in a three-dimensional way, your students will see history everywhere they look. Studying Ancient Egypt presents the opportunity to not only study, but also to bring this field into your classroom through a plethora of resources. Through exploration you can help your students develop critical thinking and research skills, engage them in methodological tasks, and incorporate writing skills.

How do you begin a study of Ancient Egypt? In order to be effective, you can introduce your class to the fields of archaeology, Egyptology, and historical research. In order to fully understand this historical era, students must engage in a multidisciplinary study.

"Smart Cookies" by Bess Wilson

Engaging Your Students as Archaeologists

Archaeology presents a way to study the past through artifacts and architectural remains. During the past 100 years, archaeology has transitioned from a treasure-seeking field to a field in which researchers seek information that will lead to a better understanding of the past.

Students are naturally fascinated by the field of archaeology. You can turn your classroom into a mini-Indiana Jones adventure with a little imagination and planning. One kit that I recommend is *Lift the Lid on Mummies: Unravel the Mysteries of Egyptian Tombs and Make Your Own Mummy!* (Running Press). Using the knowledge they have uncovered about Ancient Egypt, students can discover a mummy and its artifacts. What could be more exciting than uncovering the treasures of a mummy and learning about its life?

Introduce Egyptology

Egyptology is the study of Ancient Egyptian artifacts including mummies, pyramids, and decorative objects. Since researchers began deciphering hieroglyphic writings in 1823, Egyptology has evolved from a souvenir-collecting enterprise to a dynamic academic subject.

There are myriad ways to bring Egyptology into your class in a three-dimensional setting. You can build the pyramids with sugar cubes, or you can develop theories about how the pyramids were constructed. You can also lead your class to the discovery of King Tutankhamen's tomb by reading about Howard Carter's discovery. Just flipping through a book about King Tutankhamen will give your students a better understanding of the burial practices and art of Ancient Egypt, for images relating to this subject are usually rich in visuals. One of the best ways to introduce your students to this field is to show them hieroglyphics. Until 1823, researchers couldn't read and interpret hieroglyphics. But today your students can read and write their own hieroglyphics, developing a better understanding of the language and culture of Ancient Egypt. One kit that I recommend is the Metropolitan Museum of Art's *Fun With Hieroglyphics* (Simon & Schuster). What could be more fun than writing a message with hieroglyphics?

Working With Historical Research

Historical research is the study of the past through written records and documents. Your students can decipher primary documents and add to their understanding of the region.

Historians read primary documents and make interpretations about the past. Your students can engage in this process by reading books like *Egyptology* (Candlewick Press), a fun adventure in which a young woman heads to Egypt in the early 1920s in search of a tomb. Your students can read along with this adventure and make their own interpretations.

Encouraging Your Students as Writers

How can you incorporate creative-writing skills while studying history? While Ancient Egypt is a great entry point to the worlds of Archaeology, Egyptology, and historical research, you can also teach your students writing skills. Kay Winters's *Voices of Ancient Egypt* (National Geographic Society) is a dynamic volume of poetry, a collection of voices from the past that might serve as a good model for your students, who might enjoy writing in the voice of King Tutankhamen, a pyramid architect, or Queen Nefertiti. You can use Winters's book as a launching point to a discussion about history and how it encompasses many voices, while focusing on the art of writing.

Supporting Student Exploration

As a teacher, you can support numerous fields of study in your classroom. To fully engage students in these fields, you need to take a risk as an educator; you need to allow your students to create knowledge and to draw their own conclusions about the past. Make the past come alive for your students. As their teacher, you have the opportunity to guide and support every experience in dynamic and exciting ways.

Resources

Dineen, J. (1998). *Lift the lid on mummies: Unravel the mysteries of Egypt tombs and make your own mummy!* Philadelphia, PA: Running Press.

Hart, G. (2008). *Ancient Egypt (DK Eyewitness Books)*. New York, NY: Dorling Kindersley.

Putnam, J. (2009). *Mummy (DK Eyewitness Books)*. New York, NY: Dorling Kindersley.

Sands, E. (2005). *The Egyptology handbook: A course in the wonders of Egypt*. Cambridge, MA: Candlewick.

Steer, D. (2004). *Egyptology*. Cambridge, MA: Candlewick.

Winters, K. (2003). *Voices of ancient Egypt*. Washington, DC: National Geographic Society.

Chapter 40

Inquiry-Based Learning for Gifted Students in the Social Studies Classroom

by Timothy Lintner and Arlene Puryear

Today's public schools are as diverse as ever. Students enter the classroom with a broad and complex range of skills and struggles, diligence, and distractions. Into this rich and challenging mix stands the teacher who is charged with creating relevant and engaging learning opportunities for all students.

Although creating such opportunities is important, it may be doubly so for students who are gifted. Curious by nature, students who are gifted often seek to scratch below the proverbial surface to unearth new insights and understandings of the content at hand. In this article, we illustrate how social studies classrooms premised on inquiry and creativity can support and enhance the inquisitive nature of students who are gifted.

Defining Students Who Are Gifted

The National Association for Gifted Children (2010) estimates that up to 10% of K–12 students are academically gifted. Although there is no universal exemplar of students who are gifted, such students differ in cognitive and language abilities; interests; learning preferences; motivation; personality; and general behavior. Given the unique learning interests and abilities, how can these characteristics be both evidenced and utilized in an exemplary social studies classroom?

The Inquiry-Based Social Studies Classroom

The National Council for the Social Studies (NCSS, 2010) states that, "The aim of social studies is the promotion of civic competence—the knowledge, intellectual processes, and democratic dispositions required of students to be active and engaged participants in public life" (p. 9). To become civically competent, students must possess a foundational knowledge of one's community, nation, and world. Students must be curious and inquiring. They must be able to gather and evaluate sources, collaborate, make sound evidence-based decisions, and employ problem-solving strategies to grapple with the complexities inherent in social studies.

In 2013, NCSS published the *College, Career, and Civic Life (C3) Framework for Social Studies State Standards*. The purpose of the C3 Framework is to provide cognitive and application-based suggestions as to how students should learn, represent, and apply social studies content. The C3 Framework is rooted in four dimensions of informed inquiry: developing questions and planned inquiry, applying disciplinary concepts and tools, evaluating sources and using evidence, and communicating conclusions and taking action.

Developing questions and planned inquiry. A cornerstone of exemplary social studies instruction is developing (and asking) thoughtful and probing questions that further inquiry. Questions can be compelling ("Why was the Suffragist Movement so important?") or supporting ("Who were the leading supporters of the Suffragist Movement?"). Regardless of scope, questions foster curiosity and critique and lead to more substantive understandings of the social studies content.

Applying disciplinary concepts and tools. Social studies consists of four core content areas: history, geography, economics, and political science/civics. Students can analyze selected historical writings and measure their influence upon future events or actions. When studying geography, students can interpret and/or create maps. To understand consumer preferences, students can create and then "pitch" a product or service they designed; the civics classroom is the perfect place to simulate a mock trial.

Evaluating sources and using evidence. Exemplary social studies classrooms ask students to both use and evaluate multiple source types (e.g., print, visual, auditory, tactile) when analyzing information and forming resultant conclusions. Such claims must be evidence-based and naturally lead to further inquiry.

Communicating conclusions and taking action. At its core, social studies is both active and collaborative. Students need multiple opportunities to demonstrate their newfound understandings.

The vast majority of social studies classrooms provide few opportunities for students to create and ask deep, probing questions (Chapin, 2013). Nor do they foster sustained analysis, evaluation, curiosity, or collaboration. For the most part, students in K–12 social studies classrooms are not being intellectually or creatively engaged (Gibson, 2012). So how can social studies teachers create purposeful, applicable, and challenging learning opportunities for all students, including students who are gifted? One way is through inquiry-based learning.

Inquiry-Based Learning in the Social Studies Classroom

Inquiry-based learning is a teaching method in which students work to develop deep and layered understandings of complex questions, problems, or ideas. This method of instruction hits home for many gifted students and is in line with the advanced level of thinking so often sought out. Students investigate, explore, and interpret interrelated themes and concepts parsing out both commonalities and differences. Inquiry-based learning creates classrooms that are alive with curiosity and creativity and rooted in authentic application.

Though specific to project-based learning, Larmer and Mergendoller (2010) provide seven essential components that serve as theoretical and pedagogical pillars in an inquiry-based classroom. An overview of each component is provided along with an example of how teachers can use each component to create engaging and challenging inquiry-based learning opportunities in exemplary social studies classrooms.

1. **The need to know:** How do we initially engage or "hook" our students? Although many gifted students are naturally curious and, thus, naturally engaged, it is still important to light the proverbial fire of interest. Using the American Civil War as our fictitious unit of study,

have students read the Gettysburg Address or excerpts from Frederick Douglass or Mary Chesnut. Students can analyze and evaluate battlefield maps or contextualize and interpret battlefield photographs. With appropriate permission, show scenes from *Gettysburg* or Ken Burns's documentary *The Civil War*. The key is to provide students with a sweeping yet admittedly cursory "overview" of the Civil War in an effort to pique initial interest.

2. **The driving question:** A driving question serves as the conceptual foundation in the inquiry-based classroom. It provides students a sense of purpose and an intellectual and creative challenge. The question should be compelling, open-ended, complex, and linked to the objective of the unit of study. Questions can be abstract ("Can the Civil War be justified?"), concrete ("Was Lincoln *really* the Great Emancipator?"), or focused on solving a problem ("How could religious institutions have done more to end slavery?").

3. **Student voice and choice:** Once student interest is generated by the driving question, allow students options in both how to explore and present their newfound understandings. Students can access text and/or digital-based sources, the Internet, oral histories, or artifacts. They can write papers, create posters or digital media, write brochures, or film a short video. Ideally, students will decide what resources they will use and how they will use these resources to gain a better understanding of the Civil War.

4. **21st-century skills:** An inquiry-based classroom allows students to collaborate, think critically, communicate, and use technology, all emphasized in the NCSS C3 Framework. Working in pairs or in small groups, students can role-play the arduous life of a slave. They can analyze a military recruitment flyer and discuss its role in fostering wartime propaganda. Lincoln's suspension of habeas corpus can be debated. Fostering such skills serves the gifted student well in the social studies classroom, and also develops skills all students need to be successful outside of the classroom.

5. **Inquiry and innovation:** Questions invariably lead to more questions. In the inquiry-based classroom, the Driving Question often spurs other avenues of inquiry. New questions are generated and alternate and provocative conclusions reached. Inquiry into the Civil War may lead students to consider previous or contemporary acts of forced servitude. Students may explore the moral implications of slavery. The role of leaders and leadership in times of crises may be examined and

addressed. The role media played—and continues to play—in shaping public sentiment can be debated.

6. **Feedback and revision:** The inquiry-based social studies classroom should naturally challenge student-held perceptions ("All Southerners supported slavery"). By presenting students with multiple interpretations and manifestations of a topic, students come to question both the origin and the validity of what they may have once held as dogma. Arguably, nothing is quite as rewarding as a student who challenges, questions, evaluates, and reevaluates his or her "position."

7. **Presentation:** How can students present their understandings of the Civil War? For classroom presentations, students can argue a position, role-play, create a skit or media display, draw, paint, or rap. Allow students flexibility in how they display their understandings. Outside of the classroom, students can advocate for equality, assume leadership roles, or petition for the end of global violence. Sound social studies pedagogy encourages students to become concerned, participatory global citizens. Such participation may simply begin with a scratch of the head, a pique in interest, and a desire to explore the seminal questions.

Conclusion

Although social studies is often presented as a series of disconnected faces and places, a more dynamic and engaging way to intellectually invigorate all students is by rooting instruction in inquiry-based learning. Knowing particularly that students who are gifted possess an innate desire to both excel and explore, inquiry-based learning fosters creativity of expression and representation and pushes students toward a deeper, more complex understanding of the social studies content. It is in such an exemplary classroom that all students, not just students who are gifted, can imagine and explore all of the possibilities that social studies has to offer.

References

Chapin, J. R. (2013). *Elementary social studies: A practical guide* (8th ed.). Boston, MA: Pearson.

Gibson, S. (2012). "Why do we learn this stuff"? Students' views on the purpose of social studies. *Canadian Social Studies, 45,* 43–58.

Larmer, J., & Mergendoller, J. R. (2010). Seven essentials for project-based learning. *Educational Leadership, 68,* 34–37.

National Association for Gifted Children. (2010). *Redefining giftedness for a new century: Shifting the paradigm* [Position statement]. Retrieved from https://www.nagc.org/sites/default/files/Position%20Statement/Redefining%20Giftedness%20for%20a%20New%20Century.pdf

National Council for the Social Studies. (2010). *National curriculum standards for social studies: A framework for teaching, learning, and assessment.* Washington, DC: Author.

National Council for the Social Studies. (2013). *College, career, and civic life (C3) framework for social studies state standards.* Silver Spring, MD: Author.

Chapter 41

Deliberations

Giving Voice to High-Ability
Social Studies Students

by Ed Robson

When you think of a high-ability social studies student what comes to mind? Someone who can see connections and patterns between facts? Someone who has a passion for history? Someone who can tell you more about an historical topic than you ever cared to know? These students can present unique challenges in the classroom. They can become easily bored as they finish assignments well ahead of everyone else. They can be argumentative and overly confident that their opinion is the truth. They may not value the ideas of classmates and their instructors. How can we address the needs of these students in social studies?

What Is Social Studies?

Bolinger and Warren (2007) concluded that "the modern goal of social studies is to develop citizenry and productivity" (p. 71), and discussed how successful people must have interpersonal skills, allowing them to make decisions and solve problems. Clearly, these skills reach far beyond the stereotypical memorization of names, dates, and facts that so often characterizes social studies classrooms. If the goal of social studies is to develop these skills, then students must have opportunities to practice and refine them.

Best teaching practices from Interstate New Teachers Assessment and Support Consortium (INTASC), the National Council for the Social Studies (NCSS), as well as the Indiana Professional Standards Board (IPSB), and the NAGC Gifted Programming Standards include involving students in considering multiple perspectives, critically analyzing appropriate source material, constructing new knowledge, and making sound interpretations. Bolinger and Warren (2007) suggest that debate, Socratic seminars, and individual research can be used as strategies to encourage the development of values and multiple perspectives. Through my involvement in the Integrating International and Civic Education (IICE) project (2007) I have learned how the process of deliberation can be incorporated into the classroom to meet the needs of the high-ability students in my social studies classes, for it targets the core purpose of social studies courses.

6 Steps in the Deliberation Process

1.   Identify a topic of interest.
2.   Define the possible options and their effects.
3.   Investigate the background information.
4.   Deliberate the options.
5.   Reflect on the best option.
6.   Make a civic outcome based on the reflection.

According to the IICE group (2007), deliberation involves: considering the merits of different alternatives, weighing the tradeoffs of each alternative with the use of research, collaborating in ways to involve multiple perspectives, sharing perspectives, and making the best possible choice. The process of deliberation helps high-ability students heighten their critical thinking skills, see the importance of considering multiple perspectives, and develop research skills so that these learners become civically involved in order to create positive changes. The teacher's role in deliberation is to generate student interest in a topic, guide students in the research of the topic, and create a safe atmosphere in which to deliberate.

The following example from my own teaching illustrates how to incorporate deliberation into the social studies classroom.

Identify a Topic of Interest

Per Indiana state standards, my seventh graders were to learn about the Eastern Hemisphere. To teach about East Africa, I decided to use an article from *National Geographic* magazine on zoonotic diseases (Quammen, 2007), pathogens that can jump from animal species to humans. The key question for our class was, "What should the United States do to stop the spread of zoonotic diseases?" We also created the following prompts from opposite viewpoints to help frame the various options for the United States:

1. The United States should not spend time and resources on combating the spread of zoonotic diseases from other countries to the United States.
2. The United States must be vigilant in stopping the spread of zoonotic diseases.

Define the Possible Options and Their Effects

After reading the article, students brainstormed and listed various options that fell between the above prompts. Some of the options included spending more money on research, increasing security on the borders, and raising money to help fight the spread of zoonotic diseases in other parts of the world. Others suggested doing nothing about the movement of people and goods coming into the U.S. After listing the options, students chose the option they wanted to research and present to the rest of the class. They formed groups based on their selections and decided appropriate questions to study to gain an understanding of their option.

Investigate the Background Information

The students then researched the issues surrounding their option. For example, a number of groups wanted to research the trade connections between the countries in the article and the United States. I also asked the students to research basic statistics related to their topic (e.g., per capita Gross Domestic Product, percent of urban population) because the state standards require that students compare various statistics from countries in the Eastern Hemisphere. The English teacher on our academic team used words from the article as part of her spelling and vocabulary tests. Future interdisciplinary approaches could include asking the health or science teacher to share more information on zoonotic diseases, such as Ebola or Hendra. Math teachers could have students create graphs using the statistics they researched about the countries being studied.

Deliberate

Each group then presented its option and research to the rest of the class. Presenters began with their option, told what was positive about the option, explained evidence that supported their findings, gave possible consequences for doing the option, and gave a possible course of action for the class if they supported the option. Students took notes during the presentations and afterward engaged in a "fishbowl activity," an organized, student-run discussion designed to allow students to ask probing and/or clarifying questions of one another in small groups.

To begin a fishbowl, organize students into groups and have a member of each group sit in an inner circle of chairs. Members of the inner circle have 5 to 8 minutes to ask probing and/or clarifying questions of one another. The teacher monitors key comments while students on the "outside" take notes about what is said. Students utilize these notes when it becomes their turn in the inner circle. Guidelines for the fishbowl activity can be found in Figure 41.1.

Reflect

After the fishbowl, each student, based on his or her own unique perspective and deliberation, reached a position concerning what option he or she

---

Conducting a Fishbowl Activity

1. **Reference all research that is shared.**
   ▸ Emphasizes the importance of keeping the discussion focused on fact rather than opinion.

2. **Listen to hear and not to respond.**
   ▸ Allows students the opportunity to develop interpersonal skills.

3. **Ask questions to probe and clarify.**
   ▸ Develops higher-order thinking skills.

4. **Recognize the importance of silence.**
   ▸ Encourages students to reflect on what is being discussed instead of just reacting.

5. **Refrain from interrupting.**
   ▸ This is tough for many adolescents to do.

6. **Avoid labeling the viewpoints of others.**
   ▸ Develops interpersonal skills.

7. **Keep an international perspective.**
   ▸ As our world becomes more interdependent, it is crucial that students develop a broader outlook.

Figure 41.1. Guidelines for the fishbowl activity.

---

believed was best. Students then wrote a summary of what option they thought was best and gave their rationale for their judgment. In addition, I also required them to include evidence from the deliberation in their rationale. For example, one student felt strongly about the option she chose due to the fact that she knows of a family who travels to Africa as missionaries, and her research made her realize the danger visitors to other parts of the world can face.

Civic Outcome

Finally, students participated in a civic response. The goal of this step is to actively involve the students in an issue. The three methods of civic engagement include educating others, affecting policy, and taking action. For the topic of zoonotic diseases, some of the students wrote a letter to our local congressman asking that more research dollars be allocated toward finding a cure for Ebola and West Nile. Some students created posters to educate others on ways to prevent the spread of zoonotic diseases. Additional opportunities to get involved include: following local, state, and national current events; writing letters to the editor; voting in local, state, and national elections; attending school board meetings; or promoting community awareness of social needs and issues.

Assessment

Although not part of the deliberation process, assessment is a necessary component to any form of learning. I assess student participation in the deliberation stage through participation in the fishbowl and the quality of students' civic response. Their deliberation scores become part of a unit grade that includes tests and reading assignments, as well as other unit activities.

Get Started With Deliberations

Deliberation is a way to invigorate high-ability students in social studies. The students enjoy the opportunity to discuss "real" issues and have their perspectives valued. I enjoy seeing the interactions among my students and between the students and myself, and also seeing the acquisition and application of the interpersonal skills students need to become successful in the fishbowl, and in life.

If you want to start using deliberations in your classroom and need more guidance, the Choices Program at Brown University has units designed for use in social studies classes. They offer workshops on the topic and can be contacted via http://www.choices.edu.

References

Bolinger, K., & Warren, W. J. (2007). Methods practiced in social studies instruction: A review of public school teachers' strategies. *International Journal of Social Education, 22,* 68–84.

Center for the Study of Global Change. (2007). *Integrating international and civic education: An invitation to deliberate.* Retrieved from http://www.indiana.edu/~global/iice

Quammen, D. (2007). Deadly contact. *National Geographic, 212,* 78–105.

Chapter 42

Dramatic Social Studies Monologues That Stir the Gifted Soul

by Thomas N. Turner

Many gifted students want to be superstars. They love to perform, share their work, and be praised for their creative efforts. Monologues, whether delivering famous historic or theatric speeches or specially written orations for dramatic purposes, allow and encourage this kind of outlet. They give vent to anger, angst, frustration, hilarity, exuberance, and hubris.

Monologues are dramatic speeches designed so that the actor addresses him- or herself directly to the audience. They can take several forms. Most types of monologues are standalone "bits" for which little specific context is needed. However, there are heavily contextualized monologues that depend on situation. Setting up opportunities where students can deliver and develop monologues is one effective way of igniting the potential and involvement of gifted learners (Willis, 2006, 2010). Gifted students may find drama exciting because it presents a source of story sequence as well as characterization. In addition, it requires students to become involved in an active away, engaging them in thinking about language in abstract ways.

Communication, as a skill, is present in Dimension 4 of the C3 Framework as a means of expression after inquiry. Dramatic monologues also can provide an exciting way for students in social studies classrooms to exhibit their knowledge of history and historical figures.

Connecting Dramatic Social Studies Monologues to the Gifted Curriculum

Dramatic monologues allow students to utilize their skills and interests in ways that encourage active participation and engagement in the social studies curriculum (VanTassel-Baska, 2013). This assessment enriches the standard social studies curriculum as students explore topics and individuals in more depth. Students are also integrating different facets of learning as they research, write, and perform their monologues. Dramatic monologues utilize an interdisciplinary approach to learning, which is critical for all students, especially gifted learners (VanTassel-Baska, 2014).

Dramatic monologues challenge gifted students. The different components involved in these activities embody the best intentions of the NAGC Pre-K–Grade 12 Gifted Programming Standards (2010). For example, dramatic monologues are fitted to the qualities described in student outcomes 3.4 and 4.5 in that they develop students' literacy skills through research and writing. Many of the other standards are met as well. In the next sections, we will look at four dramatic social studies monologue activities: *Historic Infomercials*, *Anachronistic Phone Calls*, *Brags*, and *Whines*.

Infomercialing Like Paul Harvey and Billy Mann

By age 10, most Americans know about infomercials and the glib, convincing product "pitches." Infomercials have identifiable elements that make them effective models for monologues. These elements include:

- ▶ Introduction of a product claimed to be both unique and different.
- ▶ A "hard sell" to convince the viewers that the product will make their lives easier and better. Claims are exaggerated but not to the point of absurdity.
- ▶ An attempt to seduce the audience into an immediate purchase by showing them that they need the product right away, they cannot get it anywhere else, and that they are getting a terrific deal.

Historic infomercials are easy for teachers and gifted students to construct and fun to deliver as dramatic monologues. They encourage humor and research. Students become involved in working with primary documents and develop both literacy skills and knowledge of history and biography.

To help students write their own infomercials, include criteria relating to length, inclusion of facts, and structure with the assignment. Table 42.1 shows products for which infomercials may be developed, each relating to a different period of history.

The following is a model of a monologue infomercial selling the crossbow.

The Everyman Crossbow

Have you practiced and practiced until your arms and shoulders ache with pain trying to master the long bow? You pull and you strain, shooting at the butts for hours every week, yet you don't get any better. Those short bows may be easier, but you can't hit anything with them. You're never going to win the prince's archery contest, no matter how hard you try. Well, say good-bye to the aches and pains, the wide misses, and the feeling that you always fail. You won't hunt without game again when you buy the new and improved Everyman Crossbow.

Bullseye! You'll score a perfect shot with the Everyman Crossbow. At 30 yards, 50 yards—just point and shoot. The bolt will fly true—we guarantee it. You don't have to be Robin Hood or the King's Archer to use this sweet weapon.

There is no better time to try the Everyman Crossbow. And this amazing weapon is not five, not four, not even three pence—for just two silver pennies you can buy your own handcrafted Everyman Crossbow if you contact us at Castle Arms 1066. We'll send it next fortnight delivery to your hut or hovel.

But Prithee, wait—if you order today, we'll add two bones of Saint Sebastian and one of the arrows that killed him.

Act right now and for the first 300 customers we'll also include three turtledoves with feathers perfect for fletching absolutely free.

But don't wait—order now! This Everyman Crossbow is not available in shops or local armories!

TABLE 42.1

Examples of Infomercials

Period	Product
Ancient Roman Times	The Aqueduct
The Middle Ages	The Crossbow
Colonial America	The Franklin Stove or the Lightning Rod
The Age of Invention and the Gilded Age	The Electric Light Bulb and the Telephone

Waking the Dead With a Phone Call

The telephone has been around just more than 100 years. However, just imagine what it would have been like if phones *had* existed through history. Anachronistic phone calls are a teaching device that accomplishes just that illusion. They imagine a conversation between a historic figure and someone else, either a real or fictitious person. Of course, you can only hear one side of the phone call, but the other side can be imagined. Constructing anachronistic phone calls includes a few facts and a little humor to create an attention-catching dramatic device to teach history. Gifted students can both deliver these conversations as dramatic monologues as well as creating their own. Teachers can scaffold the construction of these one-sided dramatic conversations. Here is an example of an anachronistic phone call between William Shakespeare and his "agent."

Anachronistic Phone Call With William Shakespeare

B-R-R-R-ing: "Will, baby. Wally Iago here. How 'ya doing, baby?"

Pause . . . "Wally Iago, your agent, don'tcha know."

Pause . . . "Yeah, old 15% Iago, - big joke. Ha, Ha! How's "Venus and Adonis" doing?"

Pause . . . "Oh, I got the commission check. Small bones. What can I say? It's about a bunch of Greek gods and the pretty boy prefers hunting to kissing. Londoners want action and suspense. And the love part is just cheesy."

Pause . . . "Yeah! Yeah! Yeah! I know it's a great play, and you're better than Marlow and Johnson rolled together. But Willie, this stuff just isn't drawin' the pit crowd, and you, if anybody, ought to know you've got to play to the pit, the yard, the cheap seats, capisce? The hoot and holler gang, the roaring boys."

Pause . . . "Never mind—I'm here for you. I've got a play request, almost a commission you might say."

Pause . . . "Who from? You're not going to believe this. You personally have got a request from Good Queen Bess herself—on the Q-T of course."

Pause . . . "What's the catch? Oh, nothing much, our beloved queen wants you to write a play about—wait for it—King Richard the Third."

Pause . . . "Here's how we pitch it. You make Richard a real bad guy, mean and ugly, grasping and greedy. You make him a murderer—then Grampa—Henry VII, I mean, is the good guy, the hero who saves England."

Pause . . . "Do I think it will work? Will, if this isn't pure gold, I'll refuse my commission. We are going to cash in on this, my man. The names Wally Iago and William Shakespeare will go down in history."

Bragging Like Hulk Hogan and Whining like C-3PO

Once in a while, everybody wants to blow his or her own horn, to crow, to brag. At other times, we feel like moaning, crying, and whining. Brags and whines are monologues constructed to vent such feelings. Because brags and whines are written in the voices of historical and fictional characters, students can let out the emotions without guilt. Such monologues encourage student creativity (Russell, Waters, & Turner, 2014). Monologists can assume the role of any character, whether it is people, events, places, or things. Below is an example of a Madison Square Garden Brag and an Andrew Jackson Whine.

Madison Square Garden Brag

Madison Square Garden here. I don't like to brag, but I am the "Sports Mecca of the World." All of the major sporting events happen inside me in the heart of New York City. I host the Knicks for all of their home games. The first WrestleMania that saw the epic team of Hulk Hogan and Mr. T clash with Roddy Piper and Mr. Wonderful was held inside me. Do not think that I lack musical taste. Elvis and Led Zeppelin were invited to perform at my place multiple times. Unfortunately, there have been bad musicians, if I can call them that, which I will never host again. Yes, Justin Bieber, I am talking about you. I also have acting chops as I appeared in *Godzilla*. Not bad for a place only 46 years old?

Andrew Jackson Whine

Those no-count scoundrels cost me the election in 1824. It just ain't right. I was gonna be the president of these here United States, but I was robbed by Henry Clay and John Quincy Adams. Their corrupt bargain is a dark cloud over these United States. I was supported by more folks so I should be President. However, those dishonorable double-dealers made a horse swap that gave Adams the support he needed in the House to become President. Those low-down varmints are corrupting the ideas of Washington, Jefferson, and all those other folks. But I will be back. You just wait until the next election. I will whip Adams and all of his cronies.

Conclusion

Historically-based dramatic monologues fit the needs and passions of many gifted students. The four types of monologues represented here bring history alive as gifted students use their imaginations to recreate events. Such monologues make both creative writing and dramatic reading doubly valuable in the classroom. Reading fluency and comprehension are developed by multiple read-alouds. Writing dramatic monologues involves gifted students in research by extending their knowledge, and it also challenges them to explore their creativity, even cleverness. Such monologues encourage humor and the application of writing skills in an enjoyable way. All four of these dramatic activities relate to life experiences and engage gifted students to observe life around them more closely. Dramatic historical monologues are lively performance activities that create an exciting classroom environment for gifted students in the social studies by sparking their imaginations.

References

National Association for Gifted Children. (2010). *NAGC Pre-K–Grade 12 Gifted Programming Standards: A blueprint for quality gifted education programs.* Washington, DC: Author

Russell, W., Waters, S., & Turner, T. (2014). *Essentials of middle and secondary social studies.* New York, NY: Routledge.

VanTassel-Baska, J. (2013). A commitment to excellence. *Gifted Child Today, 36,* 213–214.

VanTassel-Baska, J. (2014). Back to the future: Differentiated curriculum in the rearview mirror. *Gifted Child Today, 37,* 200–201.

Willis, J. (2006). *Research-based strategies to ignite student learning: Insights from a neurologist and classroom teacher.* Alexandria, VA: ASCD.

Willis, J. (2010). *Inspiring middle school minds: Gifted, creative and challenging.* Tucson, AZ: Great Potential Press.

Chapter 43

Applying Differentiation Strategies to AP Psychology Curriculum

by Rebecca N. Landis

Educators of the gifted are continually seeking new and effective ways to engage and challenge their gifted learners. As students progress through school and into adolescence, this ambition becomes more difficult because their interests begin to extend beyond school. At the secondary level, students crave increasing independence and face distracters, with the educator's role in the students' lives becoming further removed, making it particularly challenging to provide enticing and effective services.

At the elementary school level, gifted programming is flexible, and can take many different forms. Pull-out programs are the most common service delivery model (Davis & Rimm, 2004; Duke Gifted Letter, 2004) allowing educators of the gifted a good deal of license. Thus, at this level, the programming setup is conducive to integrating appropriate strategies for gifted students. However, at the high school level, gifted programming often takes the form of acceleration and honors and Advanced Placement (AP) courses (Gallagher, 2001). Although these courses typically include more advanced curriculum, this level of service does not necessarily accommodate the many possible learning characteristics of gifted students, such as emotional intensity, creative thought, and independence (Davis & Rimm, 2004; Frasier et al., 1995; Piechowski, 2006; Silverman, 1993). That is, the advanced content of this type of course work is not necessarily sufficient. Strategies for adapting the curriculum are still needed to effectively serve gifted secondary students and promote their continued achievement and growth.

VanTassel-Baska (2001) points out that AP curriculum has several advantages for gifted students, including opportunities for using higher order thinking skills and learning domain-relevant skills, among others. One AP course that may be particularly attractive to gifted students is AP Psychology. The field of psychology is concerned with studying and understanding human behavior; thus its content may be very compatible with the inherent nature of many gifted students. For example, characteristics acknowledged as distinctive in some gifted students include self-reflection, empathy, and intense curiosity (Davis & Rimm, 2004; Piechowski, 2006; Silverman, 1993), which may be stimulated through the study of psychology. AP Psychology also allows students to earn college credit, which may be enticing for ambitious gifted students. Finally, psychology is a field with great capacity for rigorous and extended academic study.

In light of the connection between psychology content and the characteristics and needs of gifted students, it can be useful to apply teaching strategies to AP curriculum that have been recommended for gifted students. For example, problem-based learning (PBL) is one specific strategy that has been suggested for engaging and educating gifted learners (Gallagher, 2005). PBL is an approach that requires students to independently solve problems without concrete answers by taking on the role of an expert or stakeholder in the problem. Given certain similar traits and abilities of both gifted students and field experts, the skills used in PBL activities can be very appealing to gifted students (Gallagher, 2005).

The lesson provided in Table 43.1 is an activity that uses PBL principles, and can be used in the weeks leading up to or following the AP Psychology exam. Completing this activity near the end of the semester will be necessary due to the amount of prior reading and learning that students will need. There are several potential benefits: First, because many of the students will be entering college in the near future, this activity may guide them in career searching. Additionally, the use of PBL principles allows them to integrate fields of psychology into other relevant fields. Finally, this approach requires self-directed learning (Gallagher, 2005), which will be vital to students in future endeavors.

The scenarios included (see Table 43.1) are simply models and may be modified for your classroom needs. They were devised with consideration of the topics covered on the AP Psychology exam, touching on the topics of developmental, abnormal, and social psychology (College Board, 2006). If you choose

TABLE 43.1

Exploring Psychology in Careers

Estimated time needed: Five 50-minute class periods

Objectives
▶ Students will demonstrate an understanding of the psychological area assigned.
▶ Students will demonstrate an understanding of how psychology plays into everyday professions and situations.
▶ Students will solve problems through self-directed learning.

Procedures
Before lesson:
▶ Contact local private attorneys, second-grade teachers, and human resources specialists and explain your lesson to them, as well as what you would like them to do. Later, after the students have completed their projects, send them to the corresponding professionals along with instructions for feedback.

During lesson:
▶ Tell students: *Psychology is more than what you learn for the AP exam or what is in your textbook. Psychology plays into a number of professions, aside from those of the psychiatrist and the psychologist. This week we'll explore some of those professions.*
▶ Divide students into three groups.
▶ Pass out note cards with individual scenarios to groups. Tell students they will be using their psychology knowledge to develop plans to solve the problem given to their group.
▶ After students have read the scenarios, tell them they are welcome to use any resources they would like. Also tell them you will be contacting various professionals to give them feedback on their proposed plans and strategies.
▶ Be available to provide guidance.
▶ Monitor participation and progress.

Materials
▶ Note cards with individual scenarios on them
▶ Psychology textbook
▶ Library and Internet access for students
▶ Phone numbers and e-mail addresses for relevant professionals

Evaluation
Students will receive feedback from professionals who actually work in the roles they are assuming. You should ask the professional to comment on how realistic their product is. You should also read students' plans to ensure that they did the work, but formally grading the assignment is not necessary.

TABLE 43.1, *Continued.*

Three Potential Scenarios

Jim Chambers is a second-grade elementary school teacher who is trying to create both challenging curriculum and appropriate disciplinary boundaries for a particular student, Jenna. Jenna has been acting out in class and not finishing her homework. Jim does not currently have penalties in place for late or unfinished homework. Jenna's test scores indicate that her academic potential is much higher than her current performance. Using what you have learned about developmental psychology create a plan for Jim to help Jenna and other students who might be having similar problems.

    Cheryl Newman is a prominent private attorney who deals with clients who plead "not guilty by reason of insanity." One of her current clients is on trial for assaulting a store clerk. The client claims that the store clerk has been plotting to kill her for months. Cheryl believes her client may have a psychological disorder. Using what you have learned about psychological disorders and the "not guilty by reason of insanity" plea, help Cheryl develop a plan to defend her client.

    Jaime Young is a Human Resources Specialist for the state of Georgia, working on issues related to fair treatment in the workplace. Jaime has received several complaints of an employee who is rumored to have made several gender-insensitive remarks around the office. Jaime wants to offer remediation and education for the employee in order to create an environment in which everyone is comfortable. Use what you learned in our unit on attitudes to help Jaime develop a plan for working with this employee and creating a comfortable work environment.

---

to modify these scenarios, you should examine the College Board guidelines to ensure that your topics are relevant.

The pursuit of appropriate education for gifted students must continue to be an objective for dedicated teachers of the gifted. Applying certain strategies to enhance existing curriculum is an excellent way to provide challenge and stimulation. With continued perseverance, educators can help gifted students in every class to reach their potential.

References

College Board. (2006). *Course details.* Retrieved from http://www.collegeboard.com/student/testing/ap/psych/topics.html?phych

Davis, G. A., & Rimm, S. B. (2004). *Education of the gifted and talented* (5th ed.). Boston, MA: Pearson.

Frasier, M. M., Hunsaker, S. L., Lee, J., Mitchell, S., Cramond, B., Krisel, S., . . . Finley, V. S. (1995). *Core attributes of giftedness: A foundation for recognizing the gifted potential of minority and economically disadvantaged students* (RM95210). Storrs, CT: National Research Center on the Gifted and Talented, University of Connecticut.

Gallagher, J. J. (2001). Personnel preparation and secondary education programs for gifted students. *Journal of Secondary Gifted Education, 12,* 133–138.

Gallagher, S. A. (2005). Adapting problem-based learning for gifted students. In F. A. Karnes & S. M. Bean (Eds.), *Methods and materials for teaching the gifted* (2nd ed., pp. 285–311). Waco, TX: Prufrock Press.

Piechowski, M. M. (2006). *"Mellow out," they say. If I only could: Intensities and sensitivities of the young and bright.* Madison, WI: Yunasa.

Program delivery models for the gifted. (2004). *Duke Gifted Letter, 5*(1). Retrieved from https://blogs.tip.duke.edu/giftedtoday/2006/08/27/program-delivery-models-for-the-gifted

Silverman, L. K. (1993). The gifted individual. In L. K. Silverman (Ed.), *Counseling the gifted and talented.* Denver: Love.

VanTassel-Baska, J. (2001). The role of advanced placement in talent development. *Journal of Secondary Gifted Education, 12,* 126–132.

Section V: Science

Chapter 44

The Next Generation Science Standards and High-Ability Learners

by Alicia Cotabish, Debbie Dailey, Rachelle Miller, Steve V. Coxon, and Cheryll M. Adams

New science standards for K–12 classrooms were developed through a collaborative, 2-year, state-led process managed by Achieve, Inc. The Next Generation Science Standards (NGSS) are rich in content and practice, and are arranged in a coherent manner across disciplines and grades to provide all students an internationally benchmarked science education. Similar to the Common Core State Standards in mathematics and English language arts, the adoption of the NGSS is cause for gifted education as a field to reflect on its role in supporting gifted and high-potential learners appropriately in the content areas. The field of gifted education has not always differentiated systematically in the core domains of learning, but rather has focused on interdisciplinary concepts, higher level skills, and problem solving, typically across domains. With the new NGSS and its national focus, it becomes critical to address how teachers can meet the needs of gifted science students. Integrating the Arts through a STEAM (science, technology, engineering, arts, and mathematics) instructional approach, securing administrative support and resources, and engaging in professional development that will best support the implementation of the NGSS are equally important considerations. Furthermore, it is imperative to have a roadmap for meaningful national, state, and local educational reform, elevating learning in science to higher levels of passion, proficiency, and creativity for all learners. We address several key questions below.

How Is Giftedness Addressed in the NGSS?

The NGSS for grades K–5 address specific grade-level expectations. Unless teachers are already well-versed in how to differentiate curriculum for gifted learners, the grades K–5 science standards may limit opportunities for those students who have mastered the grade-level content. However, there are two formats in which to access the standards, by topic or by Disciplinary Core Idea (DCI). Along with the science and engineering practices and the crosscutting concepts, these formats allow teachers to differentiate for gifted learners by following the progression of standards for a particular concept.

To assist teachers with making decisions about how to use the NGSS with diverse learners, Appendix D of the NGSS (http://www.nextgenscience.org/appendix-d-case-studies) provides seven case studies describing how effective instruction using the standards might look in today's classrooms. Each case study focuses on a different type of learner for whom instructional modifications may be necessary, one being gifted learners. Although it is commendable to provide this information, Appendix D, unfortunately, is the only place in the standards document that specifically addresses the needs of diverse learners, including gifted students. The authors of the NGSS (NGSS Lead States, 2013) indicate that although the standards

> provide academic rigor for all students, teachers can employ strategies to ensure that gifted and talented students receive instruction that meets their unique needs as science learners. Effective strategies include (1) fast pacing, (2) different levels of challenge (including differentiation of content), (3) opportunities for self-direction, and (4) strategic grouping. (Appendix D, p. 1)

A number of evidence-based practices, essential for working with gifted learners, are mentioned throughout the vignette in Appendix D such as preassessment, compacting, independent study, flexible grouping, advanced ideas, teacher as facilitator, faster pace, and challenging content. Some limitations still exist. For example, if the reader does not know what curriculum compacting is, he or she might not understand what the teacher in the vignette is accomplishing. There are also some inaccuracies such as the misidentification of a practice as an "anchor activity." The strength of the vignette, however, is that it clearly demonstrates how the DCI, performance expectations, crosscutting concepts, and science and engineering practices are used together to provide lessons that allow advanced learners to show mastery and move beyond the grade-level standards.

How Can Teachers Meet the Needs of Gifted Science Students?

Although the NGSS are a step forward in meeting the needs of the gifted in science education, they are not a roadmap for addressing specific needs of talented learners. The authors of the standards acknowledge that pathways must be created for students with special learning needs. To that end, little can be accomplished to meet the needs of the gifted without excellent teachers using gifted education pedagogy grounded in research-based models and methods. Several well-established models and methods lend themselves to quality teaching utilizing the NGSS, including higher order questioning, scientific habits of mind, and project- and problem-based learning. In combination, existing models, methods, and differentiation can provide a pathway for teachers to implement the NGSS with gifted science students.

Higher Order Questioning

The phrase "higher order questioning" is usually referenced to indicate the upper four levels of Bloom's Cognitive Taxonomy (Anderson et al., 2000): Application, Analysis, Synthesis, and Evaluation. Although most teachers are familiar with Bloom's taxonomy, few utilize it in practice. The NGSS appropriately move beyond lower level practices; yet, too few curriculum units of study integrate higher order questioning techniques. Therefore, teachers must be able to create or revise existing curricula. This can be accomplished by creating higher order questions in advance of implementing a lesson, unit, or book. Using a chart of question stems at each level of classification will ensure a variety of student responses. Several examples of question stems are available online,

including at http://www.bloomstaxonomy.org/Blooms%20Taxonomy%20
questions.pdf. With effort, higher order questions and corresponding higher
order thinking can become habits that are part of the regular classroom routine,
similar to scientific habits of mind.

Scientific Habits of Mind

Paul and Elder (2008) describe scientific habits of mind as cognitive skills,
affective skills, and attitudes that help lead the learners toward scientific thinking. These habits include curiosity, creativity, objectivity, and openness to new
ideas, skepticism, and tolerance for ambiguity. Teachers can help model habits
of mind by including inquiry-questioning techniques when sharing their thinking with students via think-alouds (e.g., I wonder . . .). Other habits of mind,
including tolerance for ambiguity, have been suppressed under No Child Left
Behind and the accompanying state standards. These standards and the corresponding, single-answer, multiple-choice test formats suggest that science is a
quantifiable known (certain) body of facts. In reality, science is often composed
of explorations and investigations of theories. The former is often modeled in
science classrooms where only well-trodden experiments are conducted with
known answers (Kim & Coxon, 2016). To facilitate exploration and scientific investigations, problem-based learning (PBL) and project-based learning
(PrBL) can be employed to develop students' scientific habits of mind.

Problem-Based and Project-Based Learning

Problem-based learning (PBL) is an instructional method in which students are given a real-world, ill-structured problem statement. Students generally work in teams and must determine what they know, what they need to
know, and how they plan to find out using resources such as experts and processes such as scientific investigation, critical thinking, and research. The application of these processes is generally not only hands-on, but minds-on. That is,
students are often conducting experiments of their own design in PBL. This
is a shift from other hands-on experiments in which students blindly follow
teacher-provided steps, acting as technicians, not scientists. When they simply follow steps correctly, they arrive at a known answer. Intervention studies involving PBL units in K–12 schools have demonstrated gains in student
learning. For example, VanTassel-Baska, Bass, Ries, Poland, and Avery (1998)
and VanTassel-Baska, Avery, Hughes, and Little (2000) examined science units

utilizing PBL. Both found significant gains in student learning, particularly of the scientific process. Many science units can be reorganized as PBL tasks by creating a problem-statement, providing students with some background knowledge, and providing ample time for students to conduct research, especially scientific experimentation. Ultimately, it is ideal if students create an end product to share what they learned.

A similar concept, project-based learning (PrBL), is an instructional strategy in which students work cooperatively over time to create a product, presentation, or performance. The fundamental difference between PBL and PrBL lies in the application. The two essential components of PrBL are an engaging and motivating question and a product that meaningfully addresses that question. PrBL can be very engaging for students, especially when an audience is involved for the product presentation. An example would be to have students present their PrBL end products in a scientific-conference setting (e.g., papers or posters are presented to a group). To increase motivation, students should be presented a variety of choices or formats for presenting their products.

Through PBL and PrBL teachers can engage students with the NGSS in meaningful ways that may improve motivation and standardized test scores, as well as scientific habits of mind and higher order thinking. For these methods and models to be well understood and utilized by teachers in the classroom, significant professional development should be undertaken.

Integrating the Arts Into STEM Curricula

Integrating the arts can enhance academic achievement and increase the participation of students in the STEM disciplines. Rinne, Gregory, Yarmolinskaya, and Hardiman (2011) suggest that art integration can improve students' long-term memory when educators incorporate activities that encourage students to (1) rehearse information and skills, (2) elaborate content through the use of artistic activities, (3) generate information instead of receiving it in written or oral form, (4) physically act out material, (5) produce information orally, (6) provide effort in order to create meaning, (7) express emotional responses to content, and (8) present information in the form of pictures.

Resources such as *From STEM to STEAM: Using Brain-Compatible Strategies to Integrate the Arts* (Sousa & Pilecki, 2013) and *STEAM Point: A Guide to Integrating Science, Technology, Engineering, the Arts, and Mathematics Through the Common Core* (Riley, 2012) offer planning tips and sample lesson plans for primary and secondary teachers who are interested in creating a STEAM curriculum.

What Professional Development and Administrative Support Will Be Needed?

For teachers and schools to effectively implement the NGSS, both district and building administrators need to provide administrative support through encouragement, resources, scheduling, and professional development. In *A Framework for K–12 Science Education: Practices, Crosscutting Concepts, and Core Ideas*, the National Research Council (NRC, 2012) declared "The school leaders' expectations, priorities, and decisions establish a climate that encourages or discourages particular pedagogical approaches, collegial interactions or in-service programs" (p. 243). In other words, the school administrators set the stage for how well a program will be adopted and the NGSS is more likely to become a part of the overall school climate if the administration deems it a priority.

Teachers will be expected to establish an investigative classroom where students engage in scientific and engineering practices spanning the disciplinary core ideas of physical science, life science, earth and space science, and engineering, technology, and applications of science (NRC, 2012). When implementing a new program or innovation, teachers need quality professional development that involves extended contact time, follow-up support, explicit instructions on teaching practices and the classroom-based curriculum, and active participation in learning. Extended contact is often necessary to promote real change in a classroom. The Council of Chief State School Officers (Blank, de las Alas, & Smith, 2007) found the most effective professional development programs provided 45+ contact hours with teachers.

Stakeholders, including state officials, school district administrators, and teachers, should examine quality professional development programs to support teachers in gaining the needed knowledge and skills to successfully implement the new science standards. If teachers are not provided with necessary support, the NGSS will follow the path of other science initiatives and gather dust on classroom shelves.

Time and scheduling is another major obstacle in conducting investigative science. This is especially true in elementary classrooms where the focus is on literature and mathematics. It takes much longer to lead students through inquiry and investigation than to read a story and do a worksheet covering knowledge-based facts. Time and scheduling is also a concern for upper-level grades where teachers often worry they will not cover all required content if they devote time to investigations. For example, teachers are expected to cover an enormous amount of content when preparing students for an Advanced Placement exam. A recent intervention study conducted by Dailey (2013) demonstrated that when teachers were provided with support in implementing a new program, their concerns shifted from logistic matters (e.g., time, resources) to more student-focused matters (impact of the program on students).

Conclusion

The adoption of the NGSS provides an opportunity for gifted education as a field to consider how it can support gifted and high-potential learners appropriately in the content areas. There are a number of strategies that teachers can use to implement and support the new standards for advanced learners at all stages of development in K–12 schools.

Educators need to provide the appropriate level of rigor and relevance within the new standards as they translate them into experiences for gifted learners. Educators also need to create innovative opportunities to nurture the thinking, reasoning, problem solving, passion, and inventiveness of our best students in this subject area; however, successful implementation of the NGSS cannot occur effectively without the support of both district and building administrators. Providing teachers with encouragement, resources, time-in-the-day, and professional development opportunities will permit teacher concerns to be focused on student needs rather than logistic needs. Finally, it is imperative to elevate learning in science to higher levels of passion, proficiency, and creativity for ALL learners. Through talent development efforts focused on developing motivation and readiness to learn within the domain of science and deliberate efforts to increase rigor for talented science-prone students, teachers can cultivate the next generation of scientists.

To learn more about these strategies in action visit Edutopia's Project-Based Learning videos at https://itunes.apple.com/us/itunes-u/project-based-learning/id395540445.

References

Anderson, L. W., Krathwohl, D. R., Airasian, P. W., Cruikshank, K. A., Pintrich, P. R., Raths, J. . . . Wittrock, M. C. (2000). *A taxonomy for learning, teaching, and assessing: A revision of Bloom's taxonomy of educational objectives.* Boston, MA: Allyn & Bacon.

Blank, R. K., de las Alas, N., & Smith, C. (2007). *Analysis of the quality of professional development programs for mathematics and science teachers: Findings from a cross-state study.* Washington, DC: Council of Chief State School Officers. Retrieved from http://programs.ccsso.org/content/pdfs/Year_2_IMPDE_Fall_06_Rpt_with_errata-041708.pdf

Dailey, D. (2013). *The effects of a STEM professional development intervention on elementary teachers* (Unpublished doctoral dissertation). University of Arkansas at Little Rock, Little Rock, AR.

Kim, K. H., & Coxon, S. V. (2016). Fostering creativity using robotics among students in STEM fields to reverse the creativity crisis. In M. K. Demetrikopoulos & J. L. Pecore (Eds.), *Interplay of creativity and giftedness in science.* Rotterdam, The Netherlands: Sense.

National Research Council. (2012). *A framework for K–12 science education: Practices, crosscutting concepts, and core ideas.* Washington, DC: The National Academies Press.

NGSS Lead States. (2013). *Next generation science standards: For states, by states.* Washington, DC: The National Academies Press.

Paul, R., & Elder, L. (2008). *Scientific thinking (for students and faculty).* Tomales, CA: Foundation for Critical Thinking.

Riley, S. M. (2012). *STEAM point: A guide to integrating science, technology, engineering, the arts, and mathematics through the Common Core.* Westminster, MD: Education Closet.

Rinne, L., Gregory, E., Yarmolinskaya, J., & Hardiman, M. (2011). Why arts integration improves long-term retention of content. *Mind, Brain, and Education, 5,* 89–96.

Sousa, D. A., & Pilecki, T. (2013). *From STEM to STEAM: Using brain-compatible strategies to integrate the arts.* Thousand Oaks, CA: Corwin Press.

VanTassel-Baska, J., Avery, L. D., Hughes, C. E., & Little, C. A. (2000). An evaluation of the implementation of curriculum innovation: The impact of William and Mary units on schools. *Journal for the Education of the Gifted, 23,* 244–272.

VanTassel-Baska, J., Bass, G., Ries, R., Poland, D., & Avery, L. D. (1998). A national study of science curriculum effectiveness with high ability learners. *Gifted Child Quarterly, 42,* 200–211.

Chapter 45

Curiosity for All

by Steve V. Coxon

Curiosity is a *curious* subject. It's often mentioned as a trait common to scientists, for scientists certainly need it. And, although curiosity is considered fundamental to creativity and innovation, the term rarely appears as a focus in education, and is often lost as individuals age. Science is a natural stimulant for curiosity and science class is the perfect place to foster it.

Picture a room full of kindergarteners studying live, wriggling worms, bubbling over with curiosity, and peppering their teacher with questions and stories of their own experiences with worms. Now picture those same kids as middle schoolers. Although we shouldn't expect them to act like 5-year-olds, our hope should be that their curiosity has matured as their education progresses and has not disappeared. They now may be curious about what factors led worms to evolve five hearts or hypothesize about what would happen if all worms disappeared from Earth. Unfortunately, I don't often find this to be the case. Too many older students are disinterested in science. I've come to think that the way we teach may have a lot to do with it.

In the traditional science classroom, curiosity is not fostered. Students are generally led through the curriculum with great breadth, but little depth and little chance to pursue what they are particularly curious about. Professional scientists, on the other hand, often spend their lives researching a topic of interest in great depth. If students are fortunate enough to be in a setting where their teachers are both willing to lead them in experiments and have the budget for needed supplies, they will follow step-by-step instructions that, when completed, produce a result long known to their teacher and to science. Professional scientists, on the other hand, develop novel experiments to help answer yet-unanswered questions. To foster curiosity, the science classroom should be preparing curious students in a manner more attuned to the work of practicing scientists. There are many ways this can be accomplished. Two of my favorites are through questioning and field experiences.

Questioning

Teachers asking higher order questions in class is important, but it is when the students ask those kinds of questions—and try to answer them—that the stated goal can be reached, and curiosity deepened. Some answers may come from the library or Internet, although others may be the subjects of student-designed experiments, such as those used in problem-based learning or pondered in a Makerspace. When students are able to focus their curiosity on an area of interest, they begin to think and work like scientists.

Field Experiences

In this period of hyperfocus on minimum competency testing, field trips and other experiences outside of the regular classroom setting often have been removed from the science curriculum. Not only is this a shame from a curiosity standpoint, but it also affects student scores on those very tests. When aligned with the curriculum, field experiences have a greater impact on student learning than any other science teaching method (Schroeder, Scott, Tolson, Huang, & Lee, 2007). And they are likely to invoke curiosity.

I organized many trips with my fourth- and fifth-grade scientists to a nearby national park, aligning our study of animal adaptations and food webs to the national standards. Half of the group begins with a volunteer forester, touring around a large pond with plenty of opportunities to get their hands in the water, observe wildlife, and see the natural world in action—more memorable than any worksheet. The other half is taken on a hike along a stream to a point of significant beaver activity. Students have the opportunity to touch (and trip over) gnawed-down tree trunks and to observe beaver dams, the results of both behavioral and structural adaptations. After a few hours, the groups switch. This experience is revisited during different seasons, presenting students with additional learning opportunities and inquisitive questions. Such trips also could be coupled with stream monitoring, surveying of macroinvertebrates, and plant studies scaled for any age group. In addition, the trip was nearly free, amounting to less than $3 per child for the bus. If you don't have a national forest nearby, use whatever outdoor resources are available in your area. Monitoring of an urban stream or observing insects on an empty lot can be just as stimulating for student curiosity.

Curiosity isn't just a thing for young children. It is, and may be, the most important trait for success in the sciences and of science talent development. As such, it shouldn't be left to chance, but fostered and nurtured in the curriculum throughout a child's education. I'm curious to see what happens when more science teachers take on that challenge.

Reference

Schroeder, C. M., Scott, T. P., Tolson, H., Huang, T.-Y., & Lee, Y.-H. (2007). A meta-analysis of national research: Effects of teaching strategies on student achievement in science in the United States. *Journal of Research in Science Teaching, 44,* 1436–1460.

Chapter 46

Using the Digital Ecosystem to Improve Nature's Ecosystem

by Kevin D. Besnoy

Sound environmental education pedagogical strategies stress the authentic use of critical thinking skills to engage in the scientific process of testing hypotheses and disseminating findings. In order for gifted children to learn about climate change's impact on their environment, they need to experience nature firsthand, documenting the changes taking place in their local environment, and engaging in global discussions. Climate change is a major topic that could be tailored into curricula that address local issues.

Louv (2005) commented that many of today's youth suffer from "nature-deficit disorder," which negatively influences their understanding of nature and is an obstacle to them solving the environmental problems plaguing our world today. The etiology of "nature-deficit disorder" is brought on in part because young people spend too much time immersed in digital technology. However, digital technology tools can be used to document climate change, identify solutions, and disseminate findings. A robust digital ecosystem combines content-specific pedagogy strategies with purposeful technology applications and involves students in meaningful instruction (Zambo, 2009). There are several ways to embed digital technology tools into environmental education pedagogy.

Step 1: Find a Global Community Project

A global community project leverages hands-on projects and social media to connect classrooms across the globe. There are several projects where students can use their talents to test novel hypotheses and report innovative findings. One aspect to consider when evaluating a prospective project is the ability to easily connect with others who are investigating the same questions.

One community site that focuses on climate change is the Women's Earth & Climate Action Network, International (WECAN; http://wecaninternational.org). WECAN strives to halt the acceleration of climate change by empowering women to research and apply sustainable solutions that promote proenvironmental actions. This organization offers sustainable solutions while accelerating the implementation of sustainability solutions through women's empowerment, partnerships, hands-on trainings, advocacy campaigns, and political, economic, social, and environmental action. The Solutions Forum on the website is a place where teachers and students can join one of eight working groups, engage in discussions, and research tangible solutions to many climate change topics.

Step 2: Evaluate the Project's Technology Requirements

Using digital technology tools to investigate the impact of climate change on the environment is a critical element of this process. Each global project will have different technology requirements, many of which are available in most classrooms. Many projects require access to Twitter or Facebook, although others require the use of vlogs (blogs where postings are in a video form). There are some that also require participants to post pictures of their local environment. It is essential that you make sure your class has the proper resources before beginning.

Project Noah (http://www.projectnoah.org) is a global online community designed to allow people to investigate and document natural organisms. The Missions section offers numerous investigations that span the life sciences spectrum. Although information can be shared through the website, a mobile app allows classrooms to participate in citizen-science research projects.

Step 3: Registration and Participation

Registering your classroom to participate in the global online science project connects your students with others who are investigating similar environmental issues. For example, mushrooms are guardians for local ecosystems because they break down animal material and assist with plant growth. Documenting and sharing the types of mushrooms growing in their local environment, students can compare the health of their local ecosystem to others around the globe.

The Great Nature Project (https://www.nationalgeographic.org/projects/great-nature-project) is one global online community that leverages smartphone and tablet apps (download for free to Android and Apple devices). Through this project, students learn how to record and disseminate environmental observations in a scientifically sound way that permits the global community to help identify local ecosystem characteristics. As a result, students learn about biodiversity and develop a greater understanding of the impact of climate change.

Step 4: Creating Missions

Robust Digital Ecosystems ultimately yield gifted students capable of creative-productivity. Once students have mastered the basic precepts of scientifically sound environmental investigations, they need to design and lead their own projects to share with the global community.

One site where students can create and engage global citizens in environmentally based missions is iNaturalist.org (http://www.inaturalist.org). iNaturalist.org is a crowdsourcing website where users record their environmental observations and share ideas for making a stronger, healthier natural environment. Under the project's page, students utilize their creative-productive skills to design their own citizen-science project.

Technology-rich, digital ecosystems can prepare gifted students to be leaders in reversing the impact of climate change. Whether they are recording evidence of climate change taking place in their local ecosystems or designing projects for others to join, today's students can utilize digital technology tools and reverse the effects of "nature-deficit disorder." Hopefully in the process, today's gifted students will be leaders in the crusade to protect the environment.

References

Louv, R. (2005). *Last child in the woods: Saving our children from nature-deficit disorder.* Chapel Hill, NC: Algonquin.

Zambo, D. (2009). Gifted students in the 21st century: Using Vygotsky's theory to meet their literacy and content area needs. *Gifted Education International, 25,* 270–280.

Chapter 47

Rocks Rock!

Teaching Geology to Elementary School Students

by Suzanna E. Henshon and Alyssa Del Campo

How do you get students interested in science? How do you engage students in a subject you might not feel comfortable teaching? Many elementary school teachers end up teaching multiple subjects outside their comfort zone. It is challenging to bring science to your students, and geology is a wonderful subject to bring into your classroom.

What Is Geology?

Geology is the study of the earth and earth processes that includes a wide range of fields including biology, astronomy, and physics. Geology encompasses other academic fields such as mathematics, language arts, and a variety of the natural sciences. The study of geology lends itself to many interdisciplinary subjects, and as a result, you can bring geology into your classroom in myriad ways.

Where Do You Live?

Is your school located near an ocean shore, a pond, park, or woods? When bringing science into your classroom, think about the natural resources that are available in your unique geographic setting. Begin by utilizing places that your students are most familiar with and sights that they visit every day. Should you be fortunate enough to take a field trip, you can venture out, taking students on a tour of new and exciting places. You can also visit natural places on your own, collecting rocks for use in your classroom.

Bring Where You Live
Into the Classroom

Before studying geology with your students, you may want to have a general discussion about geology. Amassing a wealth of print and online materials in preparation is a great idea. You can then begin by reading a book about rocks and minerals. Check out some field guides from the library specific to rocks and minerals and have the students identify the rocks you collected. They can then start to make inferences about the geologic history of your location. Reading up on the geographic and geologic setting where your school is located is also a good idea. Each state has a state geologist and office of geology. You could invite him or her to your class or find a university professor or member of a local science-based organization or company to share his or her expertise.

A Lesson Plan Idea

Here is a quick sample plan for a geology lesson that you can use with your students. First, the students travel to a beach, collect sediments, take them back to class and view the different grains under a microscope. In this way the students will learn about how sediment is formed by weathering and erosion. Next, the class will look at sedimentary rock from one area and see how sediment over time turns into rock and shows geological history. Lastly, the class will be exposed to a fossil reef and make observations about how the setting has changed.

In *Enriching the Young Naturalist: The Nature of a Science Classroom* (Prufrock Press, 2009), Jeff Danielian recommends allowing students time to explore their interest base within natural settings. Many students have a first encounter with geology through their interest in dinosaurs; this can be a natural launching pad for an introduction to geology. Many students are also fascinated by volcanoes, which are easy to discuss and recreate in the classroom. Depending upon what your students are most interested in, you might end up studying the history of Pompeii while creating your own volcano or end up "discovering" dinosaur bones in class while later visiting a nearby science museum. As you plan a mini-curriculum for your students, keep in mind that ordinary geologic processes can be just as interesting as big events.

Let's Go

Exploring geology through a variety of lenses is exciting for both the student and the educator. So, get out there, collect some samples, acquire some materials, and begin your expedition into all that earth science has to offer.

Chapter / 48

Global Climate Change

Motivated High School
Students Gain Their Voice

by Paul Bierman, Peter Gould, Jasmine Lamb, Christine Massey, Simon Norton, Jean Olson, Luke Reusser, and John Ungerleider

With the snow-less winter of 2007, 3 years after Hurricane Katrina, and now coming to the end of a winter with brutally cold weather in the Midwest and record snow in the Northeast, human-induced climate change is on everyone's mind. Release of the authoritative United Nations-sponsored Intergovernmental Panel on Climate Change report in February 2007 confirmed for policymakers what most scientists have known for years: Humans are changing the world's climate by running the biggest uncontrolled global experiment in history. Burning fossil fuels and slashing tropical forests, we have increased atmospheric levels of CO_2 by more than 30% since the dawn of the industrial revolution and unless something changes quickly, CO_2 levels will have doubled or tripled by century's end. Climate models suggest the world will by then be 2 to 10°F warmer on average, permanent sea ice will have vanished, and the great ice sheets of Greenland and Antarctica may be in irreversible decline.

How does an exceptional young person deal with such a dire forecast without losing hope, and how does he or she avoid becoming mired in a cycle of inaction and helplessness? To address these issues, faculty of the Governor's Institutes of Vermont, a seven-program group of summer residential institutes tailored to high-potential learners, developed a weekend climate change program. The program brought together 70 of Vermont's most motivated high school students, nearly a dozen staff, and 18 visiting specialists for a winter weekend of learning and action. The overarching theme of the weekend was to understand global climate change from a variety of perspectives while also getting a sense of the science as well as the politics involved. After learning the basics, the students worked with faculty and outside specialists to learn about solutions—personal, local, and global. Throughout the weekend, we stressed the importance of not giving up hope, of taking action, and of finding one's own voice to speak about this compelling issue.

Our Approach

We explicitly designed the Focus on Global Climate Change Weekend to crossdisciplinary boundaries and to build on previous programmatic knowledge. We had seven objectives for the weekend:

- ▸ increase student awareness of human-induced climate change;
- ▸ increase student knowledge about the science underlying changes in climate, catalyze student reflection on new information and ideas to which they are exposed;
- ▸ provide skills, knowledge, and support to allow students to make changes in their lives and their families' lives that minimize human impact on climate;
- ▸ catalyze action by students to provide positive societal change;
- ▸ model ways of learning outside the classroom setting; and
- ▸ support students as they accept and acknowledge the problems posed by human-induced climate change.

Over the past decade, the Governor's Institutes of Vermont residential winter weekends have always had students and faculty working in separate, topically focused groups. The integrated approach we took this year was the result of both faculty and student interest in approaching the pressing problem of climate change through an interdisciplinary lens. Crossing disciplines allowed us to attract a variety of students and appeal to a variety of learning styles. Recruiting was done on a first-come/first-served basis through high school guidance counselors. The demand for the program greatly outstripped the number of available spots with registration closing weeks ahead and numerous students and teachers turned away.

The planning process for staff required several group meetings and conference calls to create cohesion among the faculty, discuss curricular goals, create a working schedule, and discuss reading materials for the students. We created a preweekend packet of activities for all students and staff to complete before arriving that included: (1) a short reading packet with science, newspaper, and popular book excerpts; (2) a graphic "footprint" collage of household energy use on 11x17 paper; and (3) a calculation of household carbon emissions. Staff also created a carpool list for students and visiting speakers to encourage the reduction of carbon emissions. All of these materials are available at the Winter Weekend website (http://www.uvm.edu/~givsat/givwinter2007/index.html). The overall structure of the weekend moved students intellectually from learning facts toward reflection and then taking action. Students arrived on Friday afternoon and were immediately immersed in the issues and the science. We opened the weekend with a local champion of climate change action, the President Pro Tempore of the Vermont State Senate. The senator was followed by a local expert, a geologist who studies regional climate change and climate history. We used the carbon footprinting exercise as an icebreaker for the students and closed the evening with *Too Hot Not to Handle*, a movie that moved beyond statistics to action and solutions. By the end of the first evening the problem was clear, the importance of taking action had been well articulated, and the students were starting down the pathway from learning facts to taking the steps necessary to make change.

The footprinting exercise provided information we used immediately. For example, from the footprints, we calculated the number of lights contained in all of the student and faculty homes (see Figure 48.1). Of the nearly 3,000 installed bulbs, more than two thirds were still incandescent. A simple calculation showed the students that just by swapping out these incandescent bulbs and replacing them with energy-efficient compact fluorescents, we could save approximately 40,000 kilowatt hours of electricity each year, equal to the average annual electrical use of six Vermont households. If we use the estimate that 2 pounds of CO_2 are released per kilowatt hour of electricity used, then changing these 2,000 light bulbs could reduce our collective emissions by 80,000 pounds per year. That's the equivalent of between one and two households' average yearly carbon emissions—a big change, simply done.

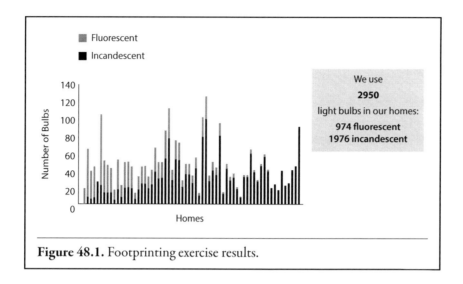

Figure 48.1. Footprinting exercise results.

Exposure to Multiple Perspectives

A very important aspect of the interdisciplinary winter weekend, not only pedagogically, but in terms of empowering students to respond to critical global issues in their own lives, was providing them with intensive exposure to different perspectives that would allow them inroads for learning about the reality of global climate change and finding ways to appropriately take action in their own lives and communities. On Saturday morning, students worked closely with faculty in disciplinary groups considering the Science of Climate Change, gaining a voice in Performing Arts, understanding themselves in the ecopsychology of the Body-Earth relationship, and learning about policies in Current Issues and Youth Activism. These four strands provided students with the scientific foundation to understand potential policy advocacy and social action responses at a political level. The strands also allowed them to explore the reactions and emotions that can create denial or paralysis in the face of an overwhelming environmental threat. Students experimented with artistic expression as a holistic and inspiring medium for raising consciousness and mobilizing local action to this global threat. During the afternoon, the students rotated between disciplines so they all met and worked with faculty having different expertise.

In Performing Arts, theatre skills helped young people confront this daunting problem by helping them acquire a clear, persuasive voice and project a positive, open attitude even to the last row of the audience. Students learned specific techniques to access our own emotional experiences, as a way to identify and work with feelings that a global problem of such immensity brings up in us. They tapped into energy that will help them be leaders in the coming social changes that global warming requires.

In the Science of Climate Change, students investigated the global carbon cycle, current and future fuels (their characteristics and carbon intensity), and the greenhouse effect. They worked in small groups and created large posters in order to do peer teaching. A subgroup of students used portable wattmeters to measure the electrical power use of common household and campus appliances—assuming the persona of guerrilla energy efficiency experts as they monitored soda dispensers and microwaves. These meters allowed a graphic demonstration of the efficiency of compact fluorescent lighting.

Through the strand Body-Earth, students connected climate change to their own lives, to who they are, and to how they interact and experience the environment around them. Through engaging all of their senses, the students experienced the reality that we are living organisms in relationship to and part of the planet, that reducing our carbon footprint is not an action to fix some big problem beyond us, but to address our own health and well-being and the health and well-being of everything we hold dear. Activities included movement, discussion, and quiet reflection, being in the woods, and possibly the silliest and most fun activity, eating cake to connect and appreciate how our bodies rely continuously on what the Earth provides. This strand helped bring balance and integration to the students by providing them a place to express and experience their feelings amidst a packed schedule of electives and presentations on global climate change.

In Current Issues and Youth Activism, students assessed how they could take effective political and social action locally to respond to this global threat. They practiced being able to speak knowledgeably and convincingly about the scientific evidence to skeptics or to the uninformed, and role-played strong verbal arguments for policy changes. In Socratic discussion, they explored the disconnect between the overwhelming scientific evidence for global warming and the apparent inaction, denial, and/or paralysis of politicians who are not addressing the threat. They deepened this understanding by analyzing the perspectives, interests, and motivations of various stakeholders in the debate by role-playing. In small groups, they researched the efforts of those who have been taking political action. Students made recommendations for action at the national and state policy level and by designing peer education programs.

Outside specialists were an important part of the curriculum and brought new and different ideas to the Institute. We recruited local specialists who could speak with the students in small groups regarding "solutions" to the problem of climate change. Students were able to choose and spend 35 minutes each in six of the 22 workshop offerings. These workshops touched on diverse aspects of politics, policy, science, conflict resolution, communications, outreach, media, alternative energy, conservation, transportation, sustainability, local farming, and the arts (http://uvm.edu/giv/givwinter2007 has a complete list of speakers and their topics). The goal of these rotations was to expose students to a wide range of ideas and people while showing that many people were already taking meaningful actions to address climate change.

We ended the activities with Five Steps Forward, an exercise where the students developed personal action plans detailing what positive steps they would take personally and in their communities to effect change. We closed the weekend with a ceremony and celebration where students presented to their peers using a variety of means including puppetry, murals, and performance. The ceremony concluded with the students and faculty standing up to declare their commitments for change followed by a graduation where each student received their diploma, an energy-efficient compact fluorescent light. Students left with the feeling that they were on their way to developing enough self-confidence to be effective public speakers for this issue about which they feel so passionate.

Outcomes

The outcomes were overwhelmingly positive and can be evaluated two ways. We did formal assessment that blended knowledge and attitude surveys administered before and after the weekend. Students were asked to self-assess their knowledge and attitudes on a 1–5 scale that ranged from "I don't have a clue" to "I know exactly" (see Figure 48.2). From these surveys, we learned that the weekend cohort was already motivated and knowledgeable. Their biggest gain (1.5 pts.) was in their knowledge of evidence for climate change in New England, the topic of our keynote speaker. Students came into the weekend very willing to take action (4.6 pts.) and made least gains there (0.1 pts.). They made large gains in their understanding of how humans change climate (the science strand), how climate change could affect Vermont (the keynote speaker), how to take action (all strands and workshops), and how to reduce emissions (specialist workshops).

Anecdotal written student responses tell the story and repeatedly mention the amount they learned, how the winter weekend changed them personally, and how it primed them for action.

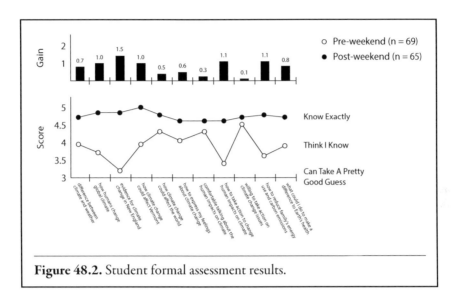

Figure 48.2. Student formal assessment results.

This weekend was the most motivating, inspiring, incredible weekend of my life. With the information I gathered, I will be prepared to create positive change. I feel enlightened.

This weekend gave me more faith in my generation. It was nice to be with people who are all working for the common good.

It was depressing and encouraging, liberating and frustrating, hard and fun.

That the adults had so much confidence that we could change the world. Enjoyed learning the ways I could help personally.

I met incredible, passionate students and collaborated with them to make change. Incorporating art and science was important. It's great to see it addressed with different subjects.

Issues for the students and some faculty included a change in approach from previous winter weekends as well as information overload, lack of sleep, a need for more hands-on activities, and requests for more time to openly discuss issues with their peers.

The broader community responded well to our program. The President of the Vermont Senate asked to speak to the program's young adults, taking time out of his very busy schedule to open the Winter Weekend. Our recruiting efforts for outside specialists generated much interest. The adults who presented workshops felt it was an important goal for them to reach a young, motivated audience. We provided a small honorarium and invited the specialists to meals, but the fact that most took time on a weekend to be with the students, speaks volumes. The media also responded to press releases, with at least one onsite newspaper reporter and one local television crew appearing over the weekend. We encourage anyone interested in running a similar program to examine the Winter Weekend website at http://uvm.edu/giv/givwinter2007 and to contact the article authors. Putting this all together took many people, many months but the results were worth it. We are catalyzing change and empowering students to make change. Here's how one student summed up the weekend.

> [The] weekend was excellent and changed my life . . . I'm inspired; I want to make people listen to me and listen to global warming. Before I came here I didn't know a lot about global warming. We hadn't spent a lot of time talking about it in school and I wasn't very concerned. I want to walk out of here and start to make a difference, and I want to get started NOW.

Important Links

The Governor's Institutes of Vermont (http://giv.org), a member of the National Conference of Governor's Schools (http://ncogs.org), has served more than 7,000 highly motivated students from virtually every high school in the state since the Institutes were established in 1982. Many gained the confidence and encouragement to be the first in their families to go on to college. All came away knowing themselves better, more clearly defining their capabilities and goals, and seeing the world in a new and brighter light. The Institutes open the world to talented Vermont students.

Chapter 49

From Consumer to Producer

DIY and the Maker Movement

by Brian C. Housand

One might argue that the field of gifted education has been built firmly upon the foundation of constructivism. The ideas of Dewey, Vygotsky, and Bruner seem to be alive and well in gifted education in the form of hands-on, project-based, and problem-based learning. I think few would argue that learning by doing is not a noble goal for most gifted learners. However, learning by doing is not in and of itself the means to an end. If we look at this through the lens of Renzulli's Enrichment Triad Model, what we desire is for students to move toward self-selected independent or small-group investigations of real-world problems. This idea is echoed in Betts's Autonomous Learner Model and many other models of gifted education. Yet, there is another idea building on the principles of CONSTRUCT-IVISM and gifted pedagogy that I would like to bring to your attention: CONSTRUCTION-ISM.

Instead of having students learn by doing, constructionism focuses on learning by *making*. Constructionism is an idea inspired by constructivism and is typically attributed to Seymour Papert who also happens to be one of the creators of Logo, a computer programming language for kids designed in the 1960s that utilized a "turtle" to create line graphics. Constructionism posits that learning can happen most effectively when students are involved in the process of constructing tangible objects in the real world. The principles of constructionism have been actualized in what is commonly referred to as the "Maker Movement," a subculture of individuals fueled by imagination and innovation that typically involves new and unique applications of existing or new technologies. Many associate the Maker Movement with the origination of *MAKE* magazine, which was first published in 2005, and the blog Boing Boing (http://boingboing.net). Not content to construct for the sake of constructing, "makers" seem to be in constant search of audiences with which to share their creations. In 2006, this need gave rise to Maker Faires, which have become regular events held around the world. The 2012 Maker Faire in San Mateo, CA, was visited by more 120,000 people interested in learning firsthand more about robots, 3-D printing, and other do-it-yourself creations.

As I look at the Maker Movement, I see a subculture of innovative grown-up gifted kids continuing to explore their creative sides. I imagine that as you think about the gifted students with whom you currently work that there are several who immediately come to mind and fit the profile of a maker.

One of the most fascinating web resources that I have encountered is DIY (https://diy.org) because it embraces the Maker Movement and provides a venue for kids to explore a variety of interests and develop talents in a wide range of areas. According to the website, "DIY is a place for kids to share what they do, meet others who love the same skills, and be awesome." DIY is a community of creators designed for kids to develop skills through completing a series of challenges. Skills range from animator to zoologist in more than 100 different areas. Each skill area is made up of a series of challenges. For example, geologist has 11 challenges and includes activities, such as making a seismometer, conducting a soil test, and making a glacial simulation. Interestingly, specific instructions are not provided as to how to complete the challenges. Instead, each individual is left to decide how to complete the challenge. Proof of completion is documented through photos and videos that are uploaded either online or with the free app for iOS devices (https://itunes.apple.com/us/app/diy.org/id519308960). Once three projects are completed in a skill area, a patch is earned and is displayed on the user's profile page. If six activities are completed, then the user is considered to have mastered the skill. Although the patches exist online, DIY has begun selling actual patches for $5 each. As of now, this is the only cost that is associated with this online community.

Although DIY began as an online community, the site has begun promoting the idea of groups coming together to form DIY Clubs in your neighborhood or sharing skills in your classroom (https://diy.org/guides). This seems like a perfect way to construct a series of enrichment clusters or even an after-school club focusing on individual interests. As the founders of DIY state on the About Us page, "The big idea is that anyone can become anything just by trying—we all learn by doing." By developing skills and interests of their own choosing, gifted kids can work to construct their own world.

PART / III

Meeting Student Needs

by Thomas P. Hébert

My career as an educator began in a high school social science classroom. Years later I transitioned to facilitating K–12 programs for gifted students. I was blessed with opportunities to teach a variety of student populations. The more I worked with highly able students, the more I was drawn to understanding the social and emotional components of their giftedness. I went from being passionate about U.S. History to being passionate about developing my students' talents and supporting their psychosocial development. My work in gifted education classrooms helped to prepare me for my career as a university researcher interested in examining the affective development of highly able students.

I have been pleased to join other scholars in my field who conduct research in this area. Together we have reached an understanding of the social and emotional characteristics and traits evidenced in gifted students. We understand that intelligent young people maintain high expectations of self and others in their lives. They may also be perfectionistic. We know that they can be emotionally sensitive, empathic, and intense in dealing with others. They are capable of reaching advanced levels of moral maturity and may insist that people behave according to their values. Within this population of young people, the process of identity formation may be complex and there is a strong need for self-actualization. Moreover, we understand that resilience is often an evident trait in gifted children.

Understanding these characteristics and how they intersect with giftedness can be helpful for educators. Such knowledge helps teachers in designing curriculum in which academic and affective skills are interwoven. Awareness of these characteristics also enables them to design classroom environments that encourage motivation and self-efficacy in young people. These classrooms also support the emotional well-being of students, nurture their identity formation, provide them space for positive social interaction and offer opportunities to develop cultural understanding.

To assist teachers with this challenge, the editors of *Teaching for High Potential* have brought together authors who share their thoughtful perspectives and offer approaches from their classroom practice that permit them to address the academic and affective needs of their students. This rich collection of contributions includes articles that explain how teachers have woven academic and affective skills in their curricula, supported students in their efforts to engage in social action projects, guided young people in managing stress and perfectionism and helped students maintain healthy motivation. This collection also includes contributions to assist teachers in their collaborative work with school counselors and parents.

As you examine these contributions, you will appreciate that the authors honestly describe their experiences and reveal their frustrations and successes. As you delve into these articles, you will naturally identify with their challenges and benefit from the compelling stories of the young people featured. You will develop a better understanding of the social and emotional components of giftedness, as well as acquire an appreciation for how it influences the school experiences of students. You will gain new insights in guiding young people with their identity development. Moreover, you will be challenged and inspired to design supportive classroom environments for gifted students and become proactive in your efforts to work with counselors and parents. I am envious! As a novice teacher, I would have benefitted from this significant anthology. I encourage you to enjoy it and support you in your work with gifted students.

Section I: Supporting Social-Emotional Development

Chapter 50

When Bright Kids Become Disillusioned

by James T. Webb

> It's very hard to keep your spirits up. You've got to keep selling yourself a bill of goods, and some people are better at lying to themselves than others. If you face reality too much, it kills you.
>
> —Woody Allen

Bright children are often intense, sensitive, idealistic, and concerned with fairness, and they are quick to see inconsistencies and absurdities in the classroom, in their families, and in the world. They are able to see issues on a universal scale, along with the complexities and implications of those issues. Children with high expectations and idealism are often disappointed, and disillusionment seems to occur mainly among the most idealistic children. They may become disillusioned only in some areas, or they may become completely disenchanted with life, which often leads to feelings of loneliness, unhappiness, anxiety, and even depression.

During childhood, the world seems simple, straightforward, and uncomplicated. The expectations and rules of daily life within the family are clear, and their awareness of the world is generally limited to their immediate family. Unless they live in a chaotic, confusing, abusive family, life for most young children is generally consistent, predictable, and emotionally comfortable. They trust that they are safe.

When children enter school, they are exposed to differing expectations and rules from their teachers, and as they see how other children, parents, and teachers behave, they begin to question the previously steadfast illusions. They discover that they are not the main focus, as they are at home; they are expected to fit in with other children and act like them. They learn, too, that other families live their lives according to different rules. Although, for instance, their parents insist that the children obey them unquestioningly, other families may let their children talk back to adults and question and challenge them. Perhaps a child's family is concerned with helping others, supporting charities, and preserving the environment, but other families focus on conspicuous consumption and attaining wealth, power, and prestige. A child in a family that is critical and judgmental of others' shortcomings may discover that other families are more accepting. Children begin to realize that families and teachers vary in their views of the world and of how one should live one's life. The simple innocence of childhood becomes perplexingly complex, and, in adolescence, even more so. These bright youngsters wonder which way is the "correct" way of living and often worry about what they will want to do with their lives. As they grow gradually into young adulthood, they question which values and behaviors they will live by as an adult. Will they follow a teacher's guidelines, their family's example, or will they cast off some of those behaviors and take up new ones?

Their brightness, sensitivity, and idealism make them likely to ask themselves difficult questions about the nature and purpose of their lives and the lives of others. Even very young gifted children may ask questions like "Why do people hate and kill others because they look or act different?" or "Why did my friend, who was a good person, die when he was only 7 years old?" Teachers and parents find these questions to be challenging and uncomfortable.

These are not idle questions; these children focus on issues of fairness, wonder how they should live their lives, and want to know the rules of life and of the universe. "Who am I, and where do I belong?" are questions they may ask themselves repeatedly because the answers devised in childhood and adolescence were inaccurate or incomplete. Quite early in life, bright children develop the capacity for metacognition—thinking about their thinking—often even before they develop the emotional and experiential tools to deal with it successfully.

As bright children hear the evening news, they see that the idealistic world does not exist. Instead, there are stories of intolerance, assault, robbery, and murder. It is not uncommon to hear reports of people hurting or taking advantage of others. People in positions of trust, such as politicians, clergy, scoutmasters, teachers, and even parents, engage in dishonesty, neglect, or abuse. We live in a world where many people do not take responsibilities seriously and where there seems to be little concern with quality. Poverty abounds, and the environment is ravaged daily. So few people seem to care. It is not the idealistic world we try to present to our children. And bright children often find that their age peers and even many adults do not share their concerns.

Teachers and parents may try to reassure these children by saying something like "You can make a difference in the world when you grow up." But such statements are seldom comforting because these bright minds are keenly aware of so many issues and needs around them, and they feel helpless to fix the many troubling problems they see. As a result, they can become disillusioned and depressed even at a young age.

How frequent and how strong are these feelings? A teacher friend described what she observed in her second-grade gifted cluster classroom:

> I had three students initiate conversations with me about wanting to die. Two of these conversations were ignited by a particular situation occurring in the child's life connected with death and dying. The third seemed to be connected to ongoing issues in the child's life concerning his self-image and place within the family. Some teachers may have been horrified by such disclosures, but I felt more empathy than horror. As a teacher I felt helpless as to how I could help these children cope with their feelings, since I felt the same way as they did. What is the essential piece of life (relationships, family structures, personality characteristics, future life situations) that can help them cope with these existential thoughts and steer them toward mental health as opposed to a life filled with depressive thoughts and possible suicide? There are little children sitting nicely in their desks and at the dinner table who are thinking of killing themselves. They may let these feelings show, or they may keep them hidden. They may tell someone, or they may not. These feelings can be devastating to a child so young, as she feels there is something wrong with her. She may feel as if her existence is more of a burden on her family than it is a pleasure to experience life.

Among bright and caring children, disillusionment is not rare, and it can lead to feelings of despair and aloneness. As these individuals examine themselves and their place in the world, they can see how things might be and should be. They start out believing that others share their idealistic concerns, but they end up feeling like Don Quixote, tilting at windmills. Sometimes they are fortunate enough to find a few other idealists, but all too often they feel alone in their struggles. Many find themselves accused of being too much of something—that is, their friends, families, and even teachers repeatedly say to them: "You are too serious," "You think too much!" "You are too sensitive," "too idealistic," "too impatient with others," "expect too much of the world," "focus too much on what is wrong in life." Disillusioned idealists battle with feelings of loneliness, sadness, emptiness, self-doubt, and, often, an intense search for meaning.

The Loneliness of Being Disillusioned and Different

A 6-year-old who frets about war or helping the homeless or victims of natural disasters, or a 12-year-old concerned with her life purpose rather than with the latest fashion or rock star is likely to find herself being one of the "cafeteria fringe" who is unwelcome at any lunch table, or she may be bullied or teased and called "loser" on a daily basis because of her serious interests. In the classroom, the student with unusual ideas or demanding questions may well find himself sitting by the wall, outside of the teacher's line of vision to reduce his participation in the class. I knew of a kindergarten teacher who invited a behavior modification team into the classroom to help with a boy who was proud when he had learned to ask just one question every hour.

Any person who is in a minority group is particularly likely to feel outside of the mainstream and, as a result, is apt to struggle with issues of feeling different, left out, or ostracized—all of which can result in disillusionment. Any member of a minority, whether based on race, ethnicity, sexual orientation, gender identity, looking different, or being idealistically concerned with life-purpose issues, is at risk for a minority experience. Being different can lead to feelings of disappointment and a lack of connectedness with others; in other words, being thoughtfully gifted can be a very lonely experience.

Many people, whether young or old, with such weighty personal concerns are hesitant to share them, fearing that others will see them as bad-mannered or that they will not be understood. And that may, in fact, be the case. Friends and family may try to reason them out of such thinking, making comments like "You have friends. You are doing well in school (or at work). You should just enjoy your life right now," or "Of course you are doing important things to help the world; you have a good job and a good family." In my experience, most people are reluctant to talk with others about their existential concerns of disillusionment because they doubt that other people will care enough to listen and because of their own discomfort. They are not yet ready to experience the angst that can arise if they begin thinking carefully about their lives.

What Can Teachers Do?

Teachers face a dilemma. On the one hand, they are supposed to educate the whole child and to help each child find his or her place in the world. On the other hand, teachers are limited in what they can do and say. They are customarily prohibited from discussing values in the classroom, except for seemingly universal ones, and they are evaluated for students' accomplishment and content mastery of basic minimal standards. Despite attempts at differentiation, so much of the curriculum in age-grouped classrooms is lock-step and focused on basic minimal levels—something that quickly raises issues of fairness for gifted students. Treating everyone the same is not fair; just because one child in a classroom needs braces, will we put braces on the teeth of all of the children? Disillusionment with the educational experience typically results. So what can you do as a teacher? Here are a few ideas.

- ▶ **Recognize the process of disillusionment.** If you understand, you will be able to think of ways to be helpful both in and outside of the classroom.
- ▶ **Don't try to argue a child out of his disillusionment.** It won't work, and you run the risk of losing the most important thing you have with the child—your relationship.
- ▶ **Listen and understand the child's concerns about unfairness and aloneness.** Intense, sensitive, disillusioned idealists usually feel very alone, and one teacher, parent, or other caring adult can be a lifeline.
- ▶ **Use developmental bibliotherapy and cinematherapy.** As alternative reading, suggest books where the characters are bright youngsters dealing with disillusionment, or movies featuring a gifted child with such concerns. Then you can use those individuals as the basis for further discussion and relationship-building.
- ▶ **Help these youngsters find other idealists.** Feeling alone, disillusioned, and powerless can be truly miserable. When these children are with other idealists, they feel less alone and more empowered, perhaps able to find new ways of viewing the world.

- ► **Remember that a gifted child's age peers are not necessarily her intellectual or idealistic peers.** If allowed, these children often gravitate toward older playmates and adults in their search for friends.
- ► **Bridge the gap between home and school.** Parents of gifted children typically welcome contact with a caring teacher, and teachers can suggest books, websites, and other resources where parents can better understand the concerns of their children and foster their relationships.
- ► **If a child seems severely disillusioned, alone, and depressed, do not hesitate to bring the matter to the attention of the school guidance counselor, psychologist, or someone else in a helping position so that a suicide assessment can be made.** Ideally, you accompany the student; if the student refuses that offer, you make the report regardless. Of course, teachers do not want to obligate a school financially by suggesting specific diagnoses or treatment. However, they can note what they have observed and encourage the parents to explore appropriate websites or books.
- ► **Take care of yourself.** Teachers who advocate for gifted children often find themselves being in a minority, becoming disillusioned, and being at risk for burnout. Often this is referred to as "compassion fatigue." When your battery has run down, you have nothing left to give.

Disillusionment implies dissatisfaction with the status quo. As such, it can be an opportunity to gain wisdom and a positive life lesson that can lead to personal growth and sometimes a newfound feeling of belonging and purpose.

Suggested Readings

Galbraith, J. (2009). *The gifted kids' survival guide: For ages 10 and under.* Minneapolis, MN: Free Spirit.

Galbraith, J., & Delisle, J. (2011). *The gifted teen survival guide: Smart, sharp, and ready for (almost) anything.* Minneapolis, MN: Free Spirit.

Halsted, J. W. (2009). *Some of my best friends are books: Guiding gifted readers from preschool through high school* (3rd ed.). Scottsdale, AZ: Great Potential Press.

Webb, J. T. (2014). *Searching for meaning: Idealism, bright minds, disillusionment, and hope.* Tucson, AZ: Great Potential Press.

Webb, J. T., Gore, J. L., Amend, E. A., & DeVries, A. R. (2007). *A parent's guide to gifted children.* Scottsdale, AZ: Great Potential Press.

Chapter 51

Resilience and Gifted Children

by Barbara A. Kerr

Until just a decade ago, most psychologists thought resilience—that is, "bouncing back" to normal after trauma or other negative events—was rare. They assumed that most children exposed to frightening events were traumatized and needed psychotherapy, because those were the children they saw in their offices. Similarly, those of us who provide psychotherapy to gifted children are also likely to get a warped view of the gifted child when all we see are those most in need of our services. The popularization of the idea that gifted students are highly sensitive and intense has also led to misperceptions that they are more vulnerable to trauma than are other students. The research says otherwise. George Bonanno (2004) began to conduct large-scale studies of people who had experienced traumatic events and loss, and found, surprisingly, that the majority of people are fairly resilient. Bonanno and his colleagues found that humans across cultures have remarkable abilities to bounce back after adversity. In addition, they found that high intelligence contributed to greater resilience, an important finding for those who serve gifted and talented students.

Since then, psychologists have studied resilience in children, adolescents, and adults across a wide variety of situations ranging from bullying to natural disasters, with similar findings. We have, however, learned that resilience is a complex phenomenon; it's not just a character trait, or a situational element, or a result of parenting. Resilience is an interaction of all of these.

Resilience Is Common Among Gifted Children

Because gifted children are so often characterized as "highly sensitive" or "intense," teachers may mistakenly believe that gifted students are less resilient than other students, but the opposite is true. In fact, as psychologist Maureen Neihart (2002) notes, many of the characteristics of resilient people have been found to be similar to those of gifted people—that is, intelligent, adaptable, good problem solvers, and able to take a larger perspective on current problems. It is important, therefore, to assume that your gifted student is resilient until there are clear signs that he or she is not returning to normal after crises or losses, even when others similarly affected have moved on. One sign that a gifted child is not resilient is being chronically frightened, anxious, angry or sad long after relatively common crises or losses—for example, a 10-year-old still sad and resentful several weeks after losing a school music competition or a 6-year-old crying about leaving home for kindergarten each morning of the first semester. These situations usually indicate that the child has a temperament different from other children, such as being more introverted or more anxious. A particular crisis or loss may also be too extreme for that child's developmental level. Most gifted children actually adjust rather quickly to developmental challenges—sleeping alone; going to preschool and kindergarten; losing a pet; having a peer say something mean; getting a lower-than-expected grade; or moving to a new neighborhood or school. Teachers who use careful strategies for building resilience can often help even anxious or traumatized children to heal and thrive.

Positive Emotions Are a Strong Protective Factor

A clear finding from positive psychology research is the importance of positive emotions as a protective factor during and after a crisis or loss. Barbara

Fredrickson, one of the best-known researchers on positive emotions, and her colleagues have shown that emotions such as gratitude, hope, love, and humor are powerful forces for building resilience (Fredrickson, Tugade, Waugh, & Larkin, 2003). Families where expressions of positive emotions are much more frequent than negative emotions tend to have more resilient children. Families that encourage children to feel and express gratitude for good things in their life are also likely to build resilient children. During stressful periods, parents can read and tell stories that are happy, go to funny movies, and express warmth and affection frequently. Studies of divorce and resilience show that it is not the divorce, but the negative emotions and conflict that precede it that increase the risk for poor adjustment. Parents who model humor in the face of difficulties—finding small, funny things even in the middle of frightening events like a severe storm—also build resilience. I remember that as my family sat in a dark basement during the most devastating tornado to hit my city, my mother and father made a picnic on the floor and let the dog, birds, and even fish in their bowl join us for dinner.

As part of a longitudinal study of resilience, Lucy Bowes (2010) and her colleagues at Magdalene College in the U.K. studied the characteristics of children who were resilient to bullying between ages 8 and 10. She found that a mother's warmth, a sibling's warmth, and a positive family atmosphere were the crucial variables in determining whether children were resilient after experiencing bullying. This study may have special meaning for gifted children who are bullied because of their higher achievement, unusual interests, or advanced vocabulary.

Planning and Problem Solving Build Resilience

Gifted children, by virtue of their intelligence, can be excellent problem solvers, but sometimes we neglect to show them how social and personal events need as much planning and creativity as schoolwork. Making friends, dealing with mean kids, and creating a good relationship with a teacher are all tasks that require planning. When Jean Peterson interviewed bullied gifted children, she learned that some applied self-calming learned in karate, gave a recording of bullying to the principal, devised clever comebacks, moved to a different social group, or offered responses in class less often. Adults who help bright children develop strategies for protection and coping and praise them for good interpersonal planning help build resilience. For example, if a gifted girl worries that her teacher doesn't like her, a parent can talk with her about the "psychology of liking"—that is, we like people who we think are similar to us, who express positive emotions both nonverbally and verbally, and who seem to like us. Parent and child can develop a plan together for changing the teacher's attitudes—perhaps smiling and looking at the teacher when she speaks, and offering help when the teacher asks for volunteers. Of course, one can't plan for natural disasters or accidents, but parents can talk about how they have a plan for keeping the family as safe as possible from scary events.

Helping Gifted Children Live With Ambiguity and Unpredictability

Children vary in their ability to tolerate ambiguous, unpredictable situations; some children seem to need to know all of the details of a coming event, and some are happy to simply jump in. Parents of children with a cautious temperament (sometimes called "inhibited personality") are familiar with their constant questions: "Who will be there?" "What if I have to go to the bathroom?" "How long is it?" "What will we eat?" Gifted children, because of their ability to read advanced material, may extend their fears about unpredictability to societal and world events. The gifted child who reads about war may ask, "Will there be a war here?" "If we were refugees, where would we go?" Resilient gifted children are likely satisfied with simple, straightforward answers, but those with a cautious temperament may find ever more reasons to be fearful.

Although building the characteristic of openness to experience, a protective factor, may be difficult, it is worth trying gradual exposure to unpredictable experiences that are likely to turn out well. Sometimes this means insisting on a new experience and praising the child for success in trying something new. For the gifted child who is overwhelmed with existential uncertainty, the solution may not be simple or rapid. Because it is often avid reading or attention to news online that leads to worry and fear, teachers can turn to appropriate literature to help the gifted child see how wise people throughout time have approached suffering, loss, and death.

Inoculation With Small Amounts
of Stress Builds Resilience

Even for children whose temperaments are open to new experiences, a challenge like summer camp or moving to a new school brings mixed emotions of fear and anticipation. Children who have had gradual, small experiences of separation from parents or being with a new group of children tend to be resilient during longer separations and permanent moves. This "stress inoculation," first discovered in primates, was then confirmed in children: short separations inoculated babies against experiencing trauma during a longer separation. Sir Michael Rutter (2006), of Kings College, London, reviewed evidence for what he called the "dynamic" nature of resilience and showed how children grow resilience when parents reward children for coping with difficulties, and children develop ability to face crises on their own—that is, through challenge and support. Resilient children tend to come from families that allow them to take risks and to sometimes fail—all within the context of loving support. In a study I led, on the characteristics of happy families (Kerr, & Chopp, 1999), we found that the families allowed children to take risks that were unusual for their age. For example, a 10-year-old was allowed to pass out blankets to homeless people. Because gifted children are advanced intellectually, they are often excited about opportunities to learn that take them away from home, require learning a new language, or require physical and emotional daring. Happy families provided both "prospect"—challenging their child to learn about what lies beyond their home and community—and "refuge"— the promise that if the child fails or is overwhelmed, home and family will be there for them. Teachers can also make their classroom a place of prospect and refuge.

Teaching Agency

Another strong finding about resilience is a sense of agency—control over many aspects of life. How is agency acquired? A teenager once told me, "My parents always told me I was the author of my own story." The comment is interesting, given the frequency, in the study of happy families, of children keeping journals and telling stories around the dinner table. Most gifted children are eager writers, and keeping a journal not only enhances their writing skills, but also teaches them how to author their own stories. Gifted children need to take control of the narrative of their lives, and learning the art of story can help them do that.

Agency is also built through solving problems independently. Much has been made in the media about helicopter parents who insist on solving their children's problems, even in college. Too often parents of gifted kids are stereotyped in this way when they advocate for an appropriately challenging education for their children. It is possible, however, to take too much control. Parents should consider whether the child might solve a problem at school by discussing and brainstorming solutions, rehearsing new behaviors, and then evaluating how the new strategies worked and improving them. Even in cases where the child is bored and wanting more learning opportunities, it is possible to use these steps to inform the teacher of the problem in a positive way; ask for reasonable changes; and give feedback. In this way, the parents are resources, not the ultimate problem-solvers.

"Knifing Off" Some Traumatic Experiences

In a world where wars, refugee crises, domestic and public violence, and natural disasters are increasing, it is likely that many of us will teach or parent a child who has experienced severe trauma. Although gifted children on average are resilient because of their greater capacity for problem solving, reflection, and openness to experience, some experiences are too difficult for even the most resilient child to overcome quickly. In both Rutter's and Bowes's studies of refugee children and children who have been adopted after experiencing abuse and neglect, one common factor seemed to indicate successful healing. The "knifing off" effect refers to a clear cutoff between the old life, in which the traumatic incident took place, and the new, safe life. Adopted children who are moved away from families where they suffered extreme abuse heal more quickly and demonstrate greater resilience than those who have continuing contact or reminders of the negative events. Refugee children taken into safe homes in completely new environments fare better than those who return to the site of their losses. Parents and teachers of gifted children who have experienced trauma should try to remove whatever cues remain of the old losses and terrors.

Can a Gifted Child Be *Too* Resilient?

In my three Smart Girls books, each covering a decade of research between 1985 and 2014, is an underlying theme: that gifted girls may be too well-adjusted for their own good. I learned that gifted girls' emotional intelligence, cognitive abilities, and feminine socialization often led them to compromise their own dreams and goals in order to "fit in" and to give precedence to others' needs—from childhood through womanhood. Gifted young women who are constantly adjusting to sex-role expectations that they be pretty, popular, and giving as well as smart may find themselves giving up learning and career opportunities. In reviewing the lives of today's eminent women for *Smart Girls in the 21st Century*, Robyn McKay and I learned that these women often were *not* accommodating, emotionally sensitive, and compromising. Instead, their life's passion, rather than their adaptability, was the source of their resilience. When gifted girls fall in love with an idea, they seem to grow the "thorns" of sharp humor, verbal self-defense, and refusal to adapt to inequity or injustice.

Interestingly, Sandy Cohn and I, in our research on eminent men for *Smart Boys: Talent, Manhood, and the Search for Meaning*, found that gay, bisexual, and transsexual men, as well as men who chose nontraditional careers in fine and performing arts, writing, and care work, often had to use the same defenses as gifted girls and women do.

Although most gifted children are resilient, parents and teachers can build resilience in anxious and traumatized children by attending carefully to what the research teaches us about resilience. Sometimes strategies are intuitive—like creating a warm and positive classroom. Some are counterintuitive, requiring that we allow children to take risks that we are uncomfortable with. Whether it is insisting on the summer camp when a child wants to back out at the last minute, or letting a child play outside after dark, teaching for resilience can sometimes be more daunting for the teacher or parent than the child. It may be counterintuitive for teachers to encourage our girls and nontraditional boys to disagree with peers, to challenge authority, and to refuse to compromise their dreams and goals. Sometimes the key to resilience is *not* to adapt, adjust, and give in to others' expectations. Sara Ellis, who wrote the first parenting book for mothers in the 19th century, said that the best preparation for the adversities of adulthood is a happy childhood. We need to modify that just a bit: The best preparation for the adversities of adulthood is a happy *and* daring childhood.

References

Bonanno, G. A. (2004). Loss, trauma, and human resilience: Have we underestimated the human capacity to thrive after extremely aversive events? *American Psychologist, 59,* 20–28.

Bowes, L., Maughan, B., Caspi, A., Moffitt, T. E., & Arseneault, L. (2010). Families promote emotional and behavioural resilience to bullying: Evidence of an environmental effect. *Journal of Child Psychology and Psychiatry, 51,* 809–817.

Fredrickson, B. L., Tugade, M. M., Waugh, C. E., & Larkin, G. R. (2003). What good are positive emotions in crisis? A prospective study of resilience and emotions following the terrorist attacks on the United States on September 11th, 2001. *Journal of Personality and Social Psychology, 84,* 365.

Kerr, B., & Chopp, C. (1999). Families and creativity. *Encyclopedia of Creativity, 1,* 709–715.

Kerr, B. A., & Cohn, S. J. (2001). *Smart boys: Talent, manhood, and the search for meaning.* Tucson, AZ: Great Potential Press.

Kerr, B. A., & McKay, R. (2014). *Smart girls in the 21st century: Understanding talented girls and women.* Tucson, AZ: Great Potential Press.

Neihart, M. (2002). Risk and resilience in gifted children: A conceptual framework. In M. Neihart, S. M. Reis, N. M. Robinson, & S. M. Moon (Eds.), *The social and emotional development of gifted children: What do we know?* (pp. 113–122.) Waco, TX: Prufrock Press.

Rutter, M. (2006). Implications of resilience concepts for scientific understanding. *Annals of the New York Academy of Sciences, 1094,* 1–12.

Chapter 52

Helping Gifted Students Move Beyond Perfectionism

by Thomas S. Greenspon

We seem to be living in a winner-take-all, second-place-is-for-losers culture. Learning from mistakes and doing a worthy, effortful, ethical job take a backseat to the goal of being Number 1. Intense competition for the best grades and for entry into the best schools and careers has made anxiety common—possibly most pointedly among gifted students. Fear of failure is rampant. In this atmosphere, although some students take mistakes or failures in stride and learn from them, others are devastated by them, becoming full of worry and self-reproach. What insights into this problem might allow you as a teacher to help such students?

What we're talking about here is perfectionism—a simultaneous intense desire for perfection and intense fear of imperfection. We see it in many "flavors": the overworked, overcommitted, straight-A, award-winning high achiever who is always ahead of schedule and always volunteering for more work; the quiet, hesitant student who doesn't try new things for fear of getting them wrong or looking foolish; the procrastinator, who we discover puts off doing assignments because of fears that something won't be done perfectly. Our impulse is to say, "Don't worry so much! The effort is what's important. Everyone makes mistakes. Who says you have to be perfect?" We're appalled when such reasonable suggestions have so little effect. Why is this?

In my decades-long practice of psychotherapy with individuals, couples, and families—the majority of whom are in the gifted community—I've learned that perfectionism is more than just what we can observe of a person's behavior or thoughts. To understand perfectionism, and therefore to be more able to help, we need to understand its psychology. That is, we need to understand a perfectionistic person's emotional or affective world. If we continue to analyze from outside of an individual's perspective, we are prone to misconstrue the perfectionism in highly successful perfectionistic people as "healthy" or "adaptive," and we are likely to confuse the many positive personality characteristics of perfectionistic people, such as conscientiousness, persistence, and dedication, with some kind of positive perfectionism. Perfectionistic people, though, do not see their chronic, pervasive anxiety about mistakes as positive or healthy. Instead, their experience is like what the author Anna Quindlen once referred to as a "backpack full of bricks."

To understand perfectionism, let's consider three basic elements of human psychology.

1. Human beings are meaning-makers. Although it isn't with conscious effort, keeping our everyday world consistently organized and meaningful allows us to go about our business in a coherent way so that we can accomplish what we set out to do. The particular way we organize and make sense of our experience is profoundly shaped by our interactions with others, particularly with those to whom we most closely and consistently relate. These consistent relationship patterns point us toward a set of emotional convictions about who we are and how we fit in during our developmental years. As we grow, these patterns become firmly established as our sense of reality. If we feel liked and understood, we see ourselves as healthy and competent, with many reasons to feel hopeful about life. If we feel judged or disliked—or if people around us seem happiest only when we succeed at something—we tend to see ourselves as only conditionally acceptable. Then we believe we have to be highly successful to be most accepted. Perfectionistic people have particular emotional convictions about mistakes. Making a mistake means being inherently defective and therefore personally unacceptable. That's their sense of reality.

2. Affects, or feelings, are the essential motivators of human behavior— not internal drives or developmental potentials. In the simplest terms, we act to obtain comfort, safety, connection, affirmation, and pleasure, for example. We also act to avoid feelings such as pain, sadness, disgust, fear, and loneliness. This behavior is called affect regulation, and we do it both on our own and with the help of others. The chronic struggle for perfection is a means of regulating the fear of making a mistake, for mistakes imply defectiveness and rejection. It is also a way to manage—or to avoid—the feelings of shame that this sense of defectiveness and difference reflects.

3. Connection to others is vital to emotional and even physical well-being throughout life. Our ability to experience mutual bonds, based on our capacity for empathic attunement to the experience of others, is what allowed us to survive as a comparatively small, slow, weak species. Connection is what has allowed us to build societies and cultures. Threats to our sense of connection and acceptability to others have powerful effects on our self-esteem and sense of self. Because of intellectual differences from others, and all that implies, gifted kids can be quite vulnerable to threats of disconnection and being treated as an "other." For perfectionistic people, an emotional conviction that making mistakes threatens acceptability and connection to others powerfully motivates the struggle to be perfect.

In summary, perfectionism is, emotionally, a self-esteem issue, with a sense of shame at its roots. Perfectionistic people understand mistakes to mean that something is wrong with them, and that they are therefore less acceptable to others. The resulting anxiety about failure is what motivates them to push, relentlessly, for perfection. It is this anxiety that sharply differentiates a person who strives for excellence from one who is perfectionistic. Perfectionism is like an airplane wing with leading and trailing edges. The leading edge is conscientious effort, commitment to doing something well, and growing as a result. The trailing edge, without which there is no wing, is the intense anxiety about what it means to be less than perfect or to fail. It is this pervasive anxiety that makes rational suggestions to change their thinking so difficult for perfectionistic people to hear. Such suggestions are usually experienced as one more expectation, or judgment, and one more reminder that they aren't good enough.

There is no evidence that gifted individuals are more perfectionistic as a group than others, and there is certainly no evidence that perfectionism is an essential part of giftedness itself. That said, many gifted students come from families that have high expectations for achievement. The message they hear, or sense, is, "You're very smart, so there must be something wrong with you if you aren't doing exceptionally well." Societal expectations of gifted people frequently echo these messages. In addition, emotional threats perceived by the gifted kids who are highly sensitive can motivate perfectionistic strivings as a way to contain anxieties. These perceived threats can range from parental displeasure, to feelings of differentness from others, to feelings of powerlessness, and to loss of personal agency regarding life at school or in the world at large. Although perfectionism is pervasive in most perfectionistic people's lives, some gifted students may seem perfectionistic only in school because that's where they have the best chance for perfection.

How to Help: Antidotes to Perfectionism

With this understanding of the psychological origins of perfectionism, what can you as a teacher do to help? It is certainly reasonable to explain to students that you are not expecting perfection, and that putting forth effort, grappling with problems, and learning from mistakes is actually the royal road to growth and competence. Beyond this message, however, you can more directly address the self-esteem issues and the anxieties perfectionistic students are likely to have. What follows is not a list of discrete interventions, but rather the elements I consider necessary for creating an environment of acceptance. These elements can help you develop a sensibility about the problem of perfectionism in the classroom. The idea is that if students can feel a sense of acceptance and connection, they will feel more comfortable with the risk-taking involved in learning and growing.

Empathy. Although perfectionism looks irrational and self-defeating to an outside observer, helping perfectionistic children needs to begin with an exploration of how they experience their world—what it means to them to fall short of perfection. A famous post-Freudian psychoanalyst called this kind of empathic exploration "vicarious introspection." If private conversation is possible, ask a perfectionistic student questions like these: "What makes being perfect seem so important?" "How does it feel to make a mistake?" "What would others (parents, teachers, friends) think if you made a mistake?" Ask about feelings that you might observe: "You seem nervous when you're answering a question. Is that how you're feeling?" "Can you say what it is that you're afraid of?" You can ask with an attitude of curiosity rather than judgment. The fears and shame felt by perfectionistic people may be based on perceptions that can be challenged, but they are also very real. Recognizing and accepting these feelings is an important step toward having a student feel more understood, personally accepted, and capable of change.

Self-reflection. Gifted high schoolers who are straight-A students sometimes make this kind of complaint: "If I make a B on a test, I'll come into class and the teacher will say, 'What happened to you?!' like I've suddenly become incompetent!" It's important to encourage kids to achieve their potential; however, it's also important to avoid implying that something is broken if mistakes are made. It helps when teachers can summon the courage to self-reflect about whether they might be contributing to a child's perfectionism. It's not a blame game; many things contribute to a child's character and personality. However, as a teacher you can attempt to figure out how the situation for a perfectionistic student developed. Then you might be able to figure out how to help them move in a different direction. You can ask yourself, "Am I frequently judgmental? Do I focus more on what can be done better than on what has been done well?" Your self-awareness may help you help a student move past perfectionism. If you aren't sure, you can ask yourself, "Do I seem to be saying that if a student makes a mistake, it's not OK?" If that is true, an apology to the perfectionistic student is a strong message that mistakes are simply mistakes, and that we can pay attention to them, learn from them, be OK with each other, and work together to move on.

Encouragement. Feeling liked and accepted forms a secure emotional base for trying new things and risking failure. Creating this sense of security can be as simple as remembering to tell students often what you like and appreciate about them. Give them sincere and genuine feedback. Focus on who they are rather than what they do. It's fine to celebrate accomplishments. However, noticing and affirming a student's conscientiousness, persistence, taking things seriously, thoughtfulness, and real effort—all qualities present in the leading edge of perfectionism—goes a long way toward building the secure base from which the student can risk doing something new. Affirmation also makes it easier for a student to hear critical comments as something directed at their work, rather than at their person. This shift in perspective may be a major step toward dealing with mistakes without shame and toward healing an existing sense of shame.

Dialogue. Healing takes place in the presence of dialogue. Conversations conducted on an ongoing basis can consist simply of brief check-ins about feelings, expectations, and concerns. These conversations can help students feel heard, understood, accepted, and affirmed. In that safe environment, you can suggest that they relax a bit and begin to learn from inevitable mistakes. If your time and the student's attitude make conversation possible, remember to check in again as time goes on. You can ask if the checking in feels intrusive; your continuing interest will probably feel supportive instead. Teachers have a steep climb in their efforts to help perfectionistic students. The origins of perfectionism are outside of the classroom, and the roots are deep. It is helpful to involve parents in the ongoing dialogue. They may or may not be willing to help. Remember that they may have their own perfectionistic burdens, and hearing that their child is having a problem may be difficult for them. Often, though, parents are already aware of the issue and welcome a joint effort to work on it.

You might tell them that you have noticed that their child has some anxiety about tests, or assignments, or class participation, and that you're wondering if they observe these behaviors at home. You might also suggest some reading. Ideally, they will note and talk about helpful suggestions with each other and with their child. Such conversations can be a good way to acquaint them with resources and also a good way to form empathic bonds and a joint sense of purpose and to set the stage for growth.

You can find more information about perfectionism and these suggestions in the books listed below. It takes courage to initiate the conversations described here. Because immediate results are unusual, you may have to struggle with your own perfectionistic tendencies while you wait for change. However, you may have launched a process that will ultimately allow students to begin to think differently about themselves. This result will be well worth your efforts.

Suggested Readings

Greenspon, T. S. (2007). *What to do when "good enough" isn't good enough: The real deal on perfectionism*. Minneapolis, MN: Free Spirit Publishing. For middle schoolers and their families.

Greenspon, T. S. (2012). *Moving past perfect: How perfectionism may be holding back your kids (and you!) and what you can do about it*. Minneapolis, MN: Free Spirit Publishing. For parents, teachers, and families.

Chapter 53

The Buddy Bench

*Supporting the Emotional
Well-Being of Others*

by Thomas P. Hébert

Welcome to "Heart to Heart," a column that will explore the social and emotional development of gifted and talented young people. Here, we look at sensitivity, which is often present in this population. I would like to introduce you to a second grader named Christian Buck.

Christian and his family were planning an international move. When he and his father went online and explored possibilities for international schools he might attend while living in Germany, he came upon a school playground with a designated bench for friendship. Christian's family ended up not moving; however, he was inspired to make a change in his school. He approached Matthew Miller, the principal of his elementary school in York, PA, with his idea for a "buddy bench."

Christian recognized that some children at Roundtown Elementary felt lonely during recess and had difficulty finding friends. He explained to Mr. Miller that his buddy bench would be established as a designated seating area where kids who were lonely or upset could seek companionship. He pointed out that, for some children, recess could be intimidating. He thought having a buddy bench where kids could go if they did not get picked for games or did not have anyone to play with would be a big help. Christian thought the bench would encourage other children to include them in a game, teach them to play, and become friends.

Christian suggested painting an outdoor playground bench in bright, inviting colors with cheerful lettering to designate this special seating area. Mr. Miller was delighted with the idea and together they began to shop for suitable benches. Following their work in designing the bench, the principal requested that Christian share his idea with all students at Roundtown Elementary. With his prepared speech and digital presentation he stood before the entire school community at a special assembly and unveiled the plan for the buddy bench. Christian explained the objectives of the bench and proposed a plan for how it would be implemented. He explained to his peers how the bench would support the school's mission of being a place of "caring, sharing, and respect." Christian specified three different ways the bench might work for kids. It would become a place where children might invite others to play. It could also serve as a place where children could meet and offer to "talk and walk" together on the playground. The bench could also serve as a place where children might sit and meet someone new to the school.

When Christian was finished responding to questions from the audience, students and teachers applauded and cheered. Soon after, the new buddy bench was installed.

An Idea Spreads

When *The York Daily Record* reported the news of the buddy bench and the *Huffington Post* picked up the story, Christian's family and friends were delighted when the *Today* show called with news that Christian and his buddy bench would be featured in a segment on the morning news program. When it aired, Matt Lauer called Christian his "new favorite kid." News of the second grader's idea went viral and elementary schools in more than 30 states have followed his example and established designated spaces for fostering friendship. For more details, visit http://buddybench.org.

Christian's story reminds educators to become aware of characteristics that are often evident in the social and emotional development of gifted children. Sensitivity is a depth of feeling that enables children to identify with others. Such sensitivity influences their daily experiences. Children like Christian cannot stand to see others suffering and are highly aware of the needs and emotions of others. Empathy as a characteristic often accompanies sensitivity. It is understood as an other-oriented emotional response that brings about the need to improve another human being's welfare. If a young person is thought to be in need, an empathic child responds emotionally and experiences an altruistic motivation to help that person. Such qualities in gifted students need to be supported.

Christian Buck was fortunate in having a school principal who listened closely to what he had to offer and supported him in following through on his buddy bench idea. Mr. Miller's response validated Christian's emotional well-being and his view of self. He was teaching Christian that it's a good thing to be a second-grade boy who sees that others may be lonely and in need of friends and that he could make a difference in their lives.

Christian's story reminds educators of the value of classroom projects involving reaching out to others in need. As teachers and counselors working with gifted students observe characteristics such as sensitivity and empathy, a rather natural approach to supporting these qualities is to implement social action projects or campaigns in the classroom. With a generation of young people strongly influenced by the media, students are very aware of serious societal issues and want to address the pain and suffering of others. With the support of dedicated educators, children like Christian Buck can become effective voices for change. An online blog response to Christian's story says it best:

> How many playgrounds are there in this country? How many kids feel alone on those playgrounds? How many parents worry about their kids being one of those lonely kids on the playground? This little dude came up with a solution. And we think it's rather brilliant. The beauty of this story is it's simple. Way to go Christian! We'll be your buddy any day of the week. (Food Bank of the Rockies, 2013)

Reference

Food Bank of the Rockies. (2013). *Buddy bench*. Retrieved from http://www.foodbankrockies.org/kung-food-fighters-kids-club/buddy-bench

Chapter 54

Helping Gifted Students Discover Daily Pockets of Joy

by Thomas P. Hébert

Melissa Howard ended her day of classes at Carver High School with her Advanced Placement American Literature students. As her students were engaged in reading, she enjoyed a few quiet moments from the back of her classroom and reflected on the gifted teenagers in her class. She smiled to herself for she was proud of what they had accomplished in just a few months. She was impressed with their dedication to their work and how they managed to negotiate demanding schedules. At times she worried that they were overscheduled. A dedicated teacher, Melissa enjoyed working with some of the brightest students at Carver; however, she did not have a real understanding of the complexity of the adolescent lives of her students.

That afternoon Sean was concerned about the trigonometry exam he had not been prepared for earlier in the day and worried how the results may affect his overall course grade. He thought back to his father's questions about his GPA last night at dinner and shuddered silently. Bethany had managed to find a few minutes of conversation with her guidance counselor about her scholarship applications and was embarrassed when Mrs. Jordan raised her brow when she noticed a recent selfie of her and her boyfriend on her cell phone. Determined to make the varsity squad this year, Nolan ran extra laps in morning gym class to make certain that Coach Ryan noticed his workout. Haley was dreading soccer practice after school because she knew that she would have to deal with more drama when her best friends confronted each other over hurtful comments in their Instagram postings.

Educators like Melissa Howard must understand that adolescence is a complex stage of life that involves many stressors. In our high-tech frenzied way of life, young people experience increased levels of stress in their academic, athletic, social, and emotional lives. Gifted young people characteristically known for their intensity may experience stress differently from typical adolescents. Because of this they need to be made aware of how stress is influencing their lives and learn effective coping strategies.

Amanda Enayati, an expert in the field of stress management indicates that not all stress is harmful. She differentiates toxic stress from tolerable stress and good stress. She explains that good stress is the lifesaving energy that enables one to jump out of the way of a speeding car. It enables one to ace a test, deliver a great speech, or lean into the excitement of a first kiss! Toxic stress is harmful over time in that it is unrelieved stress that is not accompanied by any buffers. Tolerable stress is healthier than toxic in that it involves breaks and alternates between high and low periods during the course of a day. Enayati maintains that we need to create buffers or "protective factors" that enable us to cope with the alternating waves of daily stressors. She encourages us to "discover daily pockets of joy." Taking time out to do something pleasurable in the course of a hectic day—an instant mini-vacation—enables us to better manage the tolerable stress in our lives (Enayati, 2015).

With just a bit of planning, educators can facilitate class discussions about how stress impacts daily living and guide students in generating a rich collection of ways they can discover daily pockets of joy. Some enjoyable possibilities for teenagers include:

- ▸ Listen to relaxing music.
- ▸ Read a good book; read a funny book.
- ▸ Take a walk in the woods, along the beach, in the city park, or on local nature trails.
- ▸ Watch a favorite television show.
- ▸ Spend time talking or playing a board game with a good friend.
- ▸ "Dump daily stressors" by writing about them in a journal.
- ▸ Go to a special quiet place to think alone.
- ▸ Find a quiet place to draw or enjoy a coloring book.
- ▸ Spend daily time with a pet.
- ▸ Find enjoyable physical activities and build them into a daily routine.
- ▸ Burn off excess energy by dancing to fast, upbeat music.

- ▸ Learn relaxation exercises such as abdominal breathing and muscle relaxation techniques.
- ▸ Meditation.
- ▸ Blow bubbles or dandelion fuzz and watch them float away.
- ▸ Soak in a hot tub or a relaxing bubble bath.
- ▸ Write poetry.
- ▸ Play a musical instrument or enjoy another hobby.

Dedicated educators such as Melissa Howard may serve their gifted students well by providing them intellectually challenging curriculum; however, they may need our help in calling attention to just how complex and stressful the adolescent experience may be. They may need to consider looking beyond the required curriculum and incorporating classroom guidance activities on topics such as coping with stress. Gifted education specialists may want to offer professional development sessions with middle and high school teachers and guide them in helping their students discover daily pockets of joy.

Reference

Enayati, A. (2015). *Seeking serenity: The 10 new rules for health and happiness in the age of anxiety*. New York, NY: Random House.

Chapter 55

Motivating Adolescent Gifted Learners

by Richard M. Cash

Adolescent gifted learners are some of the most complex students a teacher will encounter in his or her career. Not only are they experiencing adolescent development, which has its own issues, but they are gifted on top of it. Trying to keep adolescent gifted learners motivated, engaged, and productive is a never-ending battle. This article shares some of the reasons adolescent gifted learners underachieve, as well as practical ideas teachers can employ to keep their students on track.

Why Do Adolescents Underachieve?

Successful students have learned to adapt to the educational setting through the many challenges they encounter. Gifted students often don't encounter sufficient academic challenges for them to build the skills they need to adapt to a rigorous setting. This lack of challenge can be a reason they have too little or too much of what is required to thrive in school. Additionally, there are many reasons students can run into the "can'ts." (See Table 55.1.)

TABLE 55.1

Reasons for Underachievement

Reasons for Underachievement		
Too Little	**Too Much/Many**	**Cant's**
▶ Motivation ▶ Challenge ▶ Interest ▶ Self-efficacy ▶ Impulse control ▶ Perseverance ▶ Ability to control perseveration ▶ Balance in life ▶ Product orientation	▶ Self-confidence ▶ Other activities ▶ Procrastination ▶ Self-pity ▶ Dependency on others ▶ Distractions ▶ Ideas	▶ Can't determine the individual tasks from the greater project ▶ Can't put thought into action ▶ Can't follow through ▶ Can't fail ▶ Can't get organized

Note. Adapted from Sternberg & Grigorenko, 2000.

Unlocking Underachievement

This article focuses on the one challenge most prominent in the battle of underachievement: motivation. Overwhelmingly, the underachieving adolescent gifted learners I've worked with tell me they don't feel the need to achieve. They don't find the work valuable or interesting. To help teachers develop students' intrinsic drive to learn, I propose five principles of curriculum and instruction.

Principle 1: Make It Relevant

Adolescence is a time for personal growth and development. During the middle school and early high school years, youth are struggling to develop a sense of identity, are growing into their bodies, and are working out mood and emotional reactions. The adolescent brain is also undergoing enormous amounts of change through circuit refinement, pruning, and connection-making. These cognitive changes signal a shift in how adolescent youth approach learning. The connections made during the teen years will most likely hard-wire the brain for the future. For instance, youth exposed to theater, dance, music, and the arts during adolescence will stay attuned to them in later years. Conversely, students who are disengaged academically, socially, or physically during the adolescent years most likely will stay this way for years to come.

It is essential that middle school and high school teachers help students find themselves in the curriculum. For instance, in social studies students can identify a social issue that is important to them. With assistance, they can map out ways they can impact the situation either directly or indirectly. Another way to help students connect with the curriculum is through interest-based surveys or discussions. This will help you as the teacher focus your topic discussions or project work toward what interests students. Suggestions for making curriculum and instruction relevant:

▸ Allow students to share themselves or their passions with the class.
▸ Provide time in your day for students to meet in interest-based small groups to find commonalities and develop bonds.
▸ Have students start thinking about career pathways—built on their personal interests—then contact experts in those fields and bring them into the classroom to share their schooling careers.

Principle 2: Make It Meaningful

When students find curriculum and instruction meaningful and relevant they are more likely to engage in the learning. Meaningfulness in curriculum occurs when learners are able to see themselves in the learning or find the information they are learning immediately useful. Lessons that incorporate personal experiences, authentic productions, and self-reflection can bring the curriculum alive for the adolescent gifted learner. For instance, a child may connect with a situation experienced by a character in a novel, or feel open to express his or her feelings during a role-playing activity.

Suggestions for making curriculum and instruction meaningful:

▸ Use metaphors, similes, and analogies to make unfamiliar topics familiar.
▸ Use mnemonic devices, acronyms, or acrostics to help learners with lists and orders of items so that they can map or visualize the decision-making process.
▸ Use mind maps to connect seemingly unconnected topics.
▸ Use elaborative rehearsals such as mock trials, role-playing, and simulations.
▸ Integrate personal stories (both the students' and yours) into the content.
▸ Connect the content to what is current (use the media and/or Internet).

Principle 3: Make It Rigorous

Rigor involves the advancement of intellectual engagement that requires learners to stretch beyond their comfort zone to reach what Vygotsky termed their "zone of proximal development." A student's zone of proximal development is defined as the difference between what a child can do with help and what he or she can do without help (Morris, n.d.). Rigor also involves the use of complex thinking, which is the cognitive process that requires sophisticated forms of and interactions between creative thinking, critical reasoning, and advanced levels of inquiry, problem-solving strategies, and metacognition skills. Bloom's taxonomy provides an excellent scaffold for building a framework of increasing rigor. Curriculum that is created for gifted learners must extend to the higher levels of Bloom's taxonomy (analysis, synthesis, and evaluation).

Suggestions for making curriculum and instruction rigorous:

- ▸ Teach critical, creative, and effective thinking strategies throughout your content areas—and encourage students to use them. (See Edward de Bono's CoRT Thinking Program: http://www.edwdebono.com.)
- ▸ Teach the metacognitive skills of self-reflection, summarization, and effective memorization strategies (see mnemonic devices, acronyms, or acrostics).
- ▸ Use brainstorming and SCAMPER techniques to help students create new and original products.
- ▸ Help students apply content knowledge to applications across disciplines using authentic products.
- ▸ Use more complex/abstract concept development to encourage deeper investigation and understanding. Example: For the concept of "cycles," students can examine the simple/concrete examples of water, air, and the seasons in order to examine what characteristics define the concept. Following this would be a discussion of the complex/abstract examples of the concept found in politics, economics, and philosophy (see Table 55.2).

Principle 4: Make It Safe for Intellectual Risk-Taking

Many gifted adolescent learners were not exposed to learning experiences that required sustained intellectual effort during their elementary years. The lack of true challenge early did not provide them the opportunity to learn how to struggle, make mistakes or persevere at tasks that require complex thinking. Teachers working with adolescent gifted learners must create safe and support-

TABLE 55.2

Concept Development: Cycles

Concept Development: Cycles	
Simple/Concrete	**Complex/Abstract**
Water	Political
Air	Economic
Seasons	Philosophical

ive learning environments that allow learners to take intellectual risks. Students should be exposed to strategies and techniques for dealing with failure, keeping organized, and maintaining persistence.

Suggestions for making curriculum and instruction safe for intellectual risk-taking:

▶ Show learners how making mistakes leads to incredible inventions (share the book *Mistakes That Worked* by Charlotte Foltz Jones and John O'Brien).

▶ Play up problem-solving techniques—give them many types and help them identify when to use them.

▶ Encourage students to work outside of their preferred learning style.

▶ Offer learners appropriate strategies for dealing with stress: meditation, exercises, the arts, taking deep breaths, or listening to soothing music.

By offering instances of "failure" and allowing for the reworking of solutions through positive criticism, the teacher can strengthen the overall comfort ability of being incorrect.

Principle 5: Make Choices

Students are motivated to learn when meaningful choices are offered. Student ownership and responsibility for the learning increases, and creative production is strengthened. Choices can be accomplished in a variety of ways:

▶ Allow for students to choose different ways to demonstrate what they know.

▶ Allow students to develop and investigate topics of interest.

▶ Allow students to use a variety of materials and resources to complete projects and assignments.

▶ Provide for various seating arrangements or grouping arrangements in the classroom. Allow students to create their own evaluation rubrics and types of assessments.

Choice Menus

An excellent way for teachers to provide for choices in the classroom is to create choice menus, which are a formatting strategy for differentiating curriculum and instruction. Choice menus should allow students to:

▶ use their preferred learning style,
▶ incorporate their personal interests into their learning, and/or
▶ study a topic in depth.

The first step in constructing choice menus is to decide what the "essential learning" is in the unit or project students are to complete. Essential learnings are the big ideas, concepts, themes, or generalizations that make the topic/unit of study important to future learning. Second, decide how the menu will be arranged. Teachers can arrange the menu so that it focuses on learning profiles/styles, interests, or students' need to go into greater depth. Choice menus for gifted students can be created to either replace or supplement the regular curriculum. Remember that choice menus are not intended to be *more* work, but to be more engaging work.

Third, build your choice menu by integrating Bloom's taxonomy and Gardner's multiple intelligence theory (or other learning styles you prefer). Ensure the learning experiences scaffold to higher, more complex activities that move to authenticity. For an excellent template for constructing choice menus, see the Matrix Plan or Integration Matrix in Diane Heacox's book *Differentiating Instruction in the Regular Classroom* (2002, pp. 80–83).

Finally, keeping gifted students motivated to learn can be accomplished through engaging, interesting and rigorous challenges.

Key to getting and keeping gifted adolescent students motivated is by building the drive to achieve from extrinsic to intrinsic. Teachers can begin with external rewards (such as prizes, passes, and so forth), but they must move toward developing the learner's internal drive to succeed. As Sternberg and Grigorenko state in *Teaching for Successful Intelligence* (2000), "Internally motivated individuals are able to maintain their motivation over the rising and falling of external rewards" (p. 85). Developing internal forces comes from the learner's passions and engagement with content. Hooking the gifted adolescent through their interests will build the skills necessary to do well in future challenging courses.

Resources

Erwin, J. C. (2004). *The classroom of choice: Giving students what they need and getting what you want.* Alexandria, VA: Association for Supervision and Curriculum Development.

Feinstein, S. (2004). *Secrets of the teenage brain: Research-based strategies for reaching and teaching today's adolescents.* San Diego, CA: The Brain Store.

Jensen, E. (2005). *Teaching with the brain in mind* (2nd ed.). Alexandria, VA: Association for Supervision and Curriculum Development.

Reis, S. M., Burns, D. E., & Renzulli, J. S. (1992). *Curriculum compacting: The complete guide to modifying the regular curriculum for high-ability students.* Mansfield, CT: Creative Learning Press.

Tomlinson, C. A. (2001). *How to differentiate instruction in mixed-ability classrooms* (2nd ed.). Alexandria, VA: Association for Supervision and Curriculum Development.

VanTassel-Baska, J., & Little, C. A. (Eds.). (2003). *Content-based curriculum for high-ability learners* (2nd ed.). Waco, TX: Prufrock Press.

Wolfe, P. (2001). *Brain matters: Translating research into classroom practice.* Alexandria, VA: Association for Supervision and Curriculum Development.

References

Heacox, D. (2002). *Differentiating instruction in the regular classroom: How to reach and teach learners, grades 3–12.* Minneapolis, MN: Free Spirit.

Morris, C. (n.d.). *Lev Semyonovich Vygotsky's Zone of Proximal Development.* Retrieved from http://www.uf.bg.ac.rs/wp-content/uploads/2015/10/Master5.2015.pdf

Sternberg, R. J., & Grigorenko, E. L. (2000). *Teaching for successful intelligence: To increase student learning and achievement.* Arlington Heights, IL: SkyLight Professional Development.

Chapter 56

Critical Intelligence

Teaching Social and Emotional Awareness

by Bronwyn MacFarlane

When students arrive at the schoolhouse door, they bring with them their bags full of books, spirals, and pencils along with their collective experiences. The social-emotional development of students has been an area overlooked as classroom time has centered on instructional content and test preparation. However, social-emotional development is a critical area impacting overall growth as children strive toward their own potential. Educators working with students must be knowledgeable not only in subject content and effective instructional methods, but also in the affective domain. Educators must provide affective services at each developmental stage by assessing where and how the curriculum can be adapted to enhance student affective awareness.

Cultivating Critical Social-Emotional Development

Gifted students have unique combinations of characteristics and differentiated curriculum can help develop their critical understandings about specific affective areas, such as feelings of being different, high expectations of self and

others, sensitivity, developing relationships, handling criticism, academic planning, career planning, perfectionism and fear of failure, and introspection and
introversion (VanTassel-Baska, 2008).

But affective curriculum should be more than just fragmented collections
of affective activities. To empower talented students to reach new goals, integrating social and emotional education within the academic learning experience
is essential. Growth opportunities for gifted students to develop self-awareness
and talent development plans for a fulfilling future can be incorporated through
a variety of curriculum units of study across the disciplines. Furthermore, curriculum writers may consider collaborative learning experiences to promote social
awareness, such as with the use of group discussions and activities, connecting
content curricula with the humanities, providing a specific focus on listening for
content and reading situations with a variety of people, reflective interpersonal
debriefings, and collaborative social activities.

Curriculum units can integrate social and emotional activities while connecting with the holistic learning goals of the unit. For example, in a curriculum
unit about the *Titanic*, the overarching concept could be Systems and within the
set of Essential Understandings, there could be Essential Questions relevant to
social-emotional learning goals, such as (1) how did egotism impact the Titanic
disaster, (2) how did the ship construction decisions and ship operations fail the
passengers and the crew, and (3) how did the tragedy of the sinking influence
classism in Western culture? The use of a tic-tac-toe choice board could provide
a learning activity about the social and emotional perspectives of the Titanic's
passengers and owners.

Psychosocial Development in Relation to Gifted Education

Erik Erikson's Theory of Psychosocial Development outlined eight stages
of development in which a crisis must be solved at each stage without carrying
forward issues tied to the previous crisis. Erikson's theory provided a framework to understand the typical psychosocial developmental patterns of people
across the lifespan, and he postulated that conflict may arise from a person's
interaction with his or her environment. The eight stages occurring at specific
age frames include: (1) trust versus mistrust (occurs during year one); (2) autonomy versus shame and doubt (occurs during the second year); (3) initiative ver-

sus guilt (occurs during years 3–5); (4) competence versus inferiority (occurs during elementary school years); (5) identity versus role confusion (occurs during adolescence); (6) intimacy versus isolation (occurs during young adulthood); (7) generativity versus despair (occurs during middle adulthood); (8) integrity versus despair (occurs during late adulthood).

Cross (2005) noted the significance of Erikson's theory of psychosocial development in relation to the development of gifted children and recommended parents, teachers, and counselors pay great attention to the conflicts Erikson described as occurring during the first 18 years of life. These same adults should also be aware that while the same developmental stages occur in all children, they often occur at a younger age in gifted children (Webb & Kleine, 1993), and furthermore that gifted children could be affected by a psychosocial conflict at an earlier age than Erikson proposed (Cross, 2005). Some needs and problems, however, may appear more often as characteristics among gifted children, such as uneven development, difficult peer relations, excessive self-criticism, perfectionism, avoidance of risk-taking, and frantic multipotentiality.

There are a variety of curriculum strategies for promoting affective development that may be used to integrate Erikson's theory into the curriculum. The following strategies fit well with Erikson's stages and include the use of moral and ethical dilemmas, modeling, role-play and simulation, targeted readings and discussion (e.g., bibliotherapy), sanctions and rewards, use of the arts (different media and partner dance), and counseling.

Schoolwide Approach

In addition to integrating social-emotional learning goals into academic curriculum units in each classroom, a schoolwide approach should be articulated. Schools can assist with social-emotional development with a comprehensive curriculum implemented across grade levels to meet the affective needs of gifted students. Schools also need a fully functioning counseling team trained in the characteristics and issues of gifted children. Peer counseling groups are positive ways for like-minded students to discuss interests, problems, and other issues that arise. Supplemental services for underachieving gifted students should be readily available with corresponding training for teachers in meeting social-developmental needs.

All of these curricular recommendations can increase students' knowledge of social-emotional issues. Educators can proactively serve all children and gifted children by increasing their understanding and awareness of the unique social-emotional development of gifted children, purposefully planning curricular approaches intended to help students learn about positive decision making for a lifetime.

References

Cross, T. L. (2005). *The social and emotional lives of gifted kids: Understanding and guiding their development.* Waco, TX: Prufrock Press.

VanTassel-Baska, J. (2008). *Social-emotional curriculum with gifted and talented students.* Waco, TX: Prufrock Press.

Webb, J. T., and Kleine, P. A. (1993). Assessing gifted and talented children. In J. Culbertson & D. Willis (Eds.), *Testing young children* (pp. 383–407). Austin, TX: Pro-Ed.

Section II:
Meeting Students'
Academic Needs

Chapter 57

Ungifting the Gifted Underachiever

by Jennifer Ritchotte

Much to her parents' delight, Rebecca was identified as gifted in reading and math at the end of second grade. Throughout elementary school, she made excellent grades and never had an issue keeping up with her schoolwork; she was the "typical" gifted student, not only meeting, but also exceeding her teachers' expectations. Yet, in sixth grade her parents noticed a change. Rebecca began earning C's in Language Arts, her favorite class. When they asked Rebecca to explain her below-average grades, she just shrugged her shoulders and muttered inaudibly under her breath. Frustrated, but still hopeful, Rebecca's parents met with her language arts teacher and were told it was probably just "a phase." The next year, however, the pattern continued and extended into other classes. Rebecca's parents scheduled a meeting with all of her teachers. This time they were told they should consider exiting their daughter from the gifted program. The gifted label was no longer appropriate for Rebecca.

This scenario begs the consideration of an important question: Should only academic "achievers" be considered gifted? Passow (1981) posed this question as he pondered the nature of giftedness and talent. And although the answer to this question should not be followed by a simple "yes," many educators, especially those without gifted and talented training, would not hesitate to answer this way. If asked, their explanation might have something to do with how their

The Original Gifted Underachiever

"Smart Cookies" by Bess Wilson

school district defines giftedness, perhaps a focus on achievement and performance. Or, their explanation might concern the needs of other students. For example, if Rebecca were not going to take advantage of gifted programming, a high-achieving student without the gifted label would benefit from taking her place. Another plausible explanation might concern how educators perceive the "typical" gifted student who may be viewed as highly motivated to do well in school. Although, on the surface, these appear to be valid explanations for why only "achievers" should be considered gifted, they each are flawed in some way.

Giftedness = Academic Achievement

There is no fixed definition of giftedness; it is continuously evolving. Although Terman (1925) most famously defined giftedness as the top 1% of general intelligence (*g*) measured by an IQ test, in more recent decades, researchers have proposed broader definitions. These definitions recognize other attributes in addition to intellectual ability. For example, Passow, Goldberg, Tannenbaum, and French (1955) defined giftedness as the *potential* for superior achievement in any area of study that is valuable to society. The federal definition (No Child Left Behind Act, 2001) also includes students with *potential* to perform at high levels of accomplishment. Renzulli (1978) contended that gifted students are *capable* of developing such traits as task commitment, above-average ability, and creativity. Further, Sternberg (1999) posited that "successful intelligence" means "the ability to balance the needs to adapt to, shape and select environments in order to attain success" (p. 438). Educators can *nurture* a student's successful intelligence by capitalizing on the student's strengths and finding ways to compensate for his or her weaknesses (Sternberg, Torff, & Grigorenko, 1998). Gifted underachievers most likely have the potential for superior achievement, but that is not where the story ends. They may require extra help from teachers to develop other aspects of giftedness like task commitment and the components of successful intelligence.

Making Room for "High Achievers"

If Rebecca were not going to take advantage of gifted programming, a high-achieving student without the gifted label would benefit from taking her place. The issue with this statement has to do with the gifted label itself. Once a student is labeled "gifted," can or should that label ever be taken away? If the answer is "yes," what are we saying about giftedness? Is giftedness episodic, meaning you may be gifted now, but no longer gifted at a different stage of your life? It should be noted that many prominent researchers have argued that gifted programming options should be made available to high-achieving students and students who demonstrate potential for high achievement (e.g., Callahan, 1982; Peters, McBee, Matthews, & McCoach, 2014; Renzulli, 1978). Can high achievers receive gifted programming options without displacing gifted students who need extra help achieving at a level commensurate with their ability? The answer is "yes." There do not need to be winners and losers in gifted education. Rather, the focus of gifted education should be on whether or not children's needs are being met by the general curriculum, and ensuring that enrichment and special programming are available to those who need them. If students are underachieving due to boredom, lack of appropriate challenge or interest—only a few of the factors that may contribute to a gifted student's underachievement—these factors might be mitigated through modifying special programming to make it more engaging and challenging.

The "Typical" Gifted Student

The "typical" gifted student does not exist. Although useful lists of the traits and characteristics of gifted students have been compiled, educators should not believe that an individual student should embody all or even the majority of these traits and characteristics. Gifted students are unique. For example, they may or may not be motivated to achieve in school, or their imagination and creativity may not be highly original. They may have heightened sensitivity, or their reaction to emotional stimuli may not be very strong. The characteristics of a gifted child depend on the gifted child. Davis, Rimm, and Siegle (2011) cautioned that not all gifted students display the same characteristics, and stated that "sometimes teachers make the mistake of assuming that gifted children who are not self-directed, persevering, and motivated should not be considered gifted" (p. 43). A byproduct of this mindset is that "underachieving or troublesome gifted students are too easily eliminated from gifted programming" (p. 43). Instead of eliminating gifted students who underachieve from gifted programming, efforts should be made to target the source(s) of the students' underachievement and develop individualized interventions based on this information (Rubenstein, Siegle, Reis, McCoach, & Burton, 2012).

Thoughts From Gifted Students

Before educators make the recommendation that an underachieving student should be removed from gifted programming, they should read what gifted students themselves have to say concerning this topic. The following comments were compiled from gifted students who will graduate from high school this year.

> If gifted students are not achieving to [their] potential, be encouraging. Do not disown them and say, "If at first you don't succeed, give up." To take away the gifted label is to teach that giving up is acceptable.
>
> —Katie

> Natural aptitude or appreciation is not something that can be given or taken away. Why then, can a gifted label be slapped on a student like a sticker and just as easily ripped off?
>
> —Gracie

> By taking away students' gifted label, you are not helping them reach their true potential, you are hindering their growth.
>
> —Andrew

> I was removed from the gifted math program in eighth grade because my end of the year exam score did not meet a certain cut-off point. That year I was forced to take prealgebra, which was essentially the same class I had taken in seventh grade. Taking away my gifted label only delayed my progress in math and made me feel frustrated.
>
> —Alayna

It takes a great deal of effort to achieve in a gifted environment, and even a student who may not be achieving will be forced to work harder and, due to the nature of the class, be encouraged by his peers. When the gifted label is removed, this is lost.

—Bryan

Removing a student with gifted potential from the gifted programming on the grounds that he [or] she is not achieving would imply that his or her success in the program is impossible.

—Elizabeth

Strategies for Combatting Underachievement

Underachievement is a complex phenomenon. One factor or a combination of factors may contribute to a student's underachievement in school. For example, poor self-efficacy (i.e., belief in one's ability), negative environmental perceptions, low task meaningfulness (i.e., not finding value in the task at hand), and poor self-regulation (e.g., thinking about thinking, planning, studying, evaluating one's progress) are just a few of the factors that may cause academic underachievement (Siegle & McCoach, 2005). Because there are many reasons a student may underachieve, there is no single cure for reversing underachievement (Reis & McCoach, 2000). Educators working with students exhibiting one or more factors contributing to their individual underachievement might find success with them by utilizing some of the strategies listed below.

For Students Struggling With Poor Self-Efficacy

▸ Emphasize a growth mindset over a fixed mindset (learning over performance).
▸ Provide feedback specific to effort as opposed to just the finished product.
▸ Embed small projects/assignments into larger projects/assignments so students have the opportunity to experience success.

For Students With Negative Environmental Perceptions

- If appropriate, modify curricula, the classroom environment, and increase teacher feedback.
- Encourage students to take ownership of the choices they make.
- Be consistent with advice and feedback.
- Stress the importance of effort over a final grade.
- Provide time for self-reflection.

For Students With a Lack of Motivation

- Assign projects that address real-world problems or have a real-world application.
- Provide an authentic audience for student presentations.
- Explore connections to other content areas.
- Preassess and compact the curriculum when appropriate.
- Connect class content to individual interest and goal setting.

For Students With Poor Self-Regulation

- Introduce different study methods to determine what works (e.g., flashcards, peer tutoring, participating in study groups).
- Schedule one-on-one conferences to discuss organization.
- Guide the writing of long- and short-term goals.
- Create a system for monitoring the progress of goals.

Helping Rebecca and Those Like Her

Remember Rebecca? Rebecca should not be "ungifted" because she does not fit the mold of the "typical" gifted achiever. Like any child struggling with underachievement, she needs teachers who will help her to develop her gifts and compensate for her areas of weakness and believe in her potential. She also needs teachers who take the time to understand the reason(s) behind her under-achieving behaviors and who are willing to put forth the effort to help her attain success in school.

A single teacher can make all the difference in the life of a student like Rebecca. Instead of "ungifting" the underachiever, educators should work to identify the root cause(s) of a student's underachievement and select appropriate interventions for them.

Resources

Siegle, D. (2012). *The underachieving gifted child: Recognizing, understanding, and reversing underachievement.* Waco, TX: Prufrock Press.

Supplee, P. L. (1990). *Reaching the gifted underachiever: Program strategy and design.* New York, NY: Teachers College Press.

References

Callahan, C. M. (1982). Myth: There must be "winners" and "losers" in identification and programming! *Gifted Child Quarterly, 26,* 17–19.

Davis, G. A., Rimm, S. B., & Siegle, D. (2011). *Education of the gifted and talented* (6th ed.). Boston, MA: Pearson.

No Child Left Behind Act, 20 U.S.C. §6301 (2001).

Passow, A. H. (1981). The nature of giftedness and talent. *Gifted Child Quarterly, 25,* 5–10.

Passow, A. H., Goldberg, M. L., Tannenbaum, A. J., & French, W. (1955). *Planning for talented youth: Considerations for public schools.* New York, NY: Teachers College Press.

Peters, S., McBee, M., Matthews, M., & McCoach, D. B. (2014). *Beyond gifted education: Designing and implementing advanced academic programs.* Waco, TX: Prufrock Press.

Reis, S. M., & McCoach, D. B. (2000). The underachievement of gifted students: What do we know and where do we go? *Gifted Child Quarterly, 44,* 152–170.

Renzulli, J. S. (1978). What makes giftedness? Reexamining a definition. *Phi Delta Kappan, 60,* 180–184, 261.

Rubenstein, L. D., Siegle, D., Reis, S. M., McCoach, D. B., & Burton, M. G. (2012). A complex quest: The development and research of underachievement interventions for gifted students. *Psychology in the Schools, 49,* 678–694.

Siegle, D., & McCoach, D. B. (2005). *Motivating gifted students*. Waco, TX: Prufrock Press.

Sternberg, R. J. (1999). Successful intelligence: Finding a balance. *Trends in Cognitive Sciences, 3,* 436–442.

Sternberg, R. J., Torff, B, & Grigorenko, E. L. (1998). Teaching triarchically improves school achievement. *Journal of Educational Psychology, 90,* 1–11.

Terman, L. M. (1925). *Genetic studies of genius: Mental and physical traits of a thousand gifted children* (Vol. 1). Stanford, CA: Stanford University Press.

Chapter 58

We Teach Great Minds

by Felicia A. Dixon

> Great minds discuss ideas; average minds discuss events; small minds discuss people.
>
> —Eleanor Roosevelt

Recently I was part of a group of volunteers that was invited to tour a new health care facility for low-income citizens in the city where I live. I was very impressed with the artwork on the walls of this facility, and in addition to wonderful paintings, the designer used quotations from famous people. One of these quotations was the Eleanor Roosevelt quotation included here. I found myself borrowing a piece of paper so that I could copy some of the quotations to use later—and this is the later!

It occurred to me that we teach students who are capable of all three types of discussions that Eleanor Roosevelt includes in her quotation. The power of a strong classroom for gifted students is certainly one that focuses on ideas. We are reminded of the importance of ideas in the work of many of the great scholars in our field. Feldhusen, Kaplan, VanTassel-Baska, Renzulli, and Gallagher all speak of the power of great ideas as organizers of lessons appropriate for gifted students. My own work has focused on how secondary gifted students need to work with ideas, debating the issues surrounding them, and synthesizing the thoughts that they suggest into new guiding principles. Indeed, part of the unique experience of working with great minds is that they are capable of creating new understandings.

We may not be aware of how important discussions are for these great minds, but our students can tell us of their importance, and they can remember the exact situation that prompted them in class—or out of class in those impromptu discussions that characterize our work with them. A "remembrance of times past" (to cite Proust) happened for me this past month. I attended a reception for a former student who has written the screenplay for a film, which has been doing well at regional and national film festivals. She reminded me that I had advocated for her in her quest to take a senior English class instead of the required freshman one and that it had worked very well for her. But it was not really her comments about my class or the residential school, but rather the interactions she described with her fellow classmates out of class that especially snagged my attention. She described several life changes she made as a result of the deep discussions she had with her classmates. Further, she retained these friendships, and their encouragement and critical help convinced her to move her novel to a screenplay. She described the 27 drafts it took to complete the task and the invaluable help from a classmate who currently works with independent films in Los Angeles. Their friendship was formed in the discussions they shared over issues, and the ideas derived from these interactions were instrumental in forming the great minds they have today.

This student and her classmates did not center their discussions on events or on people. What characterized their friendships were the ideas that frequently came from meaningful time spent together and their ability to be creative. The second quotation that I copied from the walls on that tour focused on creativity and read as follows:

> Creativity is just connecting things. When you ask creative people how they did something, they feel a little guilty because they didn't really do it, they just saw something. It seemed obvious to them after a while. That's because they were able to connect experiences they've had and synthesize new things. —Steve Jobs

Reading his thoughts reminds us of Jobs's great mind. They also remind us that forging connections is relatively easy and "normal" for creative people. Additionally, it reminds us that occurrences in class in which students are asked to "connect experiences" are worthwhile in many ways. They allow the chance to synthesize information and experiences, providing the elements that lead to their creation of "new" ideas. It seems to me that these are productive expenditures of class time.

Indeed, as Jobs reminds us, gifted and talented students "connect things" because they see things differently from the norm and are able to synthesize these new perceptions with their existing experiences. I agree with both Eleanor Roosevelt and Steve Jobs. If teaching centers on events and people, it sells students short with average to small possibilities to use their knowledge. It is through the sharing of individual ideas through discussion that new ideas emerge from these great minds.

Chapter 59

Mindsets Over Subject Matter

How Our Beliefs About Intelligence Impact STEM Talent Development

by Lori Andersen

As a nation, we do not nurture enough scientists and engineers to fill the needs of high-tech industries, a situation that has become critical. Much of America's science, technology, engineering, and mathematics (STEM) workforce is foreign-born (Adams & Pendlebury, 2010) and educated at U.S. institutions of higher education. Greater numbers of our youth must be guided toward STEM careers. However, the severe underrepresentation of females and minorities in STEM fields mandates that we go further than merely increasing numbers; we must systematically identify and develop interest and ability in the STEM content areas. In recent years, there have been numerous calls for national attention to STEM education in the United States and for methods to resolve these problems. The identification and development of STEM ability in American children is an urgent need, essential to nurture the future innovators that will resolve critical global issues and the technicians that will maintain all of the gadgetry used in our high-technology world. An important part of solving this problem is taking explicit action to change students' beliefs about the nature of math/science ability, including the relationship between ability, effort, and performance. The National Association for Gifted Children (NAGC) Pre-K–Grade 12 Gifted Programming Standards (2010) emphasize the importance of teachers assisting high-ability students in developing "identities supportive of achievement" (p. 8). Beliefs about ability and effort affect student decisions to exert effort and to pursue challenging coursework. Effects of student beliefs can also be insidious, causing inaccurate results on standardized assessments by compounding the effect of stereotype threat (Good, Aronson, & Inzlicht, 2003). The long-term impact of these student beliefs contributes to the persistence of wide achievement gaps and underrepresentation of females and minorities in gifted education and STEM programs.

Math/Science Intelligence Mindsets

Potential STEM talent within many American students remains unidentified and undeveloped because possession of a fixed-ability science/math intelligence mindset dissuades students from pursuing challenging STEM courses. What are mindsets? Mindsets are attitudes and beliefs about the connection between personal intelligence and related success. There are two basic mindsets: fixed and growth. The fixed mindset is based on a belief that intelligence is an in-born quality that you have or do not have and which inhibits motivation and learning, especially for female and minority students The growth mindset is based on a belief that intelligence can be developed through hard work and effort. Children's mindsets are influenced by parent and teacher mindsets. Approximately 40% of students have a fixed mindset, another 40% have a growth mindset (Dweck, 2008). How can the growth mindset be cultivated in students? One way is to utilize praise messages through feedback and evaluation.

Praise Messages and Mindsets

Ability Praise

The feedback that children receive from parents and teachers is important to the development of their mindset. Statements used for student praise foster either a growth or a fixed mindset. For example, if a child is praised for ability, the child tends to associate success with a fixed intelligence. This type of praise has negative effects because failures are often attributed to a lack of ability, which can lead to avoidance of challenge. If intelligence is a part of the child's identity, the child does not want to fail at a task because it endangers that identity. Gifted students may be prone to adopt the fixed-ability mindset because they have been praised for years about their outstanding abilities. For a child who has yet to be identified as gifted, a fixed mindset engenders a fear of failure that could possibly discourage the pursuit of challenging areas of interest. For the child who is already identified as gifted, an aversion to challenge indicative of the fixed-ability mindset might be reflected in students that drop out of gifted programs. Thus, although 80% of parents think that it is important to praise a child's ability (Dweck, 2006), ability praise is counterproductive and should be avoided. Ability praise promotes the fixed mindset, prevents children from seeking challenge, and may restrict the potentially gifted from even attempting to stretch their cognitive boundaries.

Process Praise

How should we praise children? The growth mindset can be fostered through process praise. If a child is praised for the process of effort and hard work, the child develops a growth mindset (Dweck, 2006). The child learns that intelligence can be developed through hard work and that effort is valued. Failures are attributed to lack of effort; increased effort is identified as a viable path to success. This growth mindset fosters persistence and resilience. Failure is accepted as part of learning, and when failure occurs it is not attributed to a lack of intelligence, but rather that more effort is required to be successful (Dweck, 2006). Potentially gifted students with a growth mindset thrive on challenge, which permits educators to identify that potential by observing the child working through challenge. Students with a growth mindset are not afraid of failure and are more willing to exert effort in challenging domains such as STEM. Therefore, nurturing a growth mindset in children is important for developing high achievement in all domains and for reaching our nation's goal of increasing the numbers of students who train for STEM careers.

Growth Mindset and Talent Development

The hallmark of the growth mindset is the capacity to respond to failure in a positive way, by interpreting negative feedback as information to use for improvement rather than as an evaluation of intelligence. The growth mindset fosters persistence and resilience, qualities needed for individuals to progress from novice to expert within a talent domain (Subotnik & Rickoff, 2010). In other words, differences in individual achievement within a talent domain depend more on psychosocial factors than ability. According to Subotnik, talent development techniques that build the tacit knowledge necessary for success in performance domains, such as music, should be formally included in STEM talent development programs. Elements of tacit knowledge include how to recover from failure, which is related to the growth mindset. Subotnik's conclusions are based on studies of college-aged students in STEM and music programs; however, the importance of the growth mindset extends to much younger children. I contend that a child's fixed mindset may prevent the development of maximum potential because the avoidance of challenge leaves observers little evidence of the child's cognitive ability during the identification of giftedness. Therefore, before this student can be identified as gifted and long before talent development can begin, a student must possess a growth mindset and be willing to engage with challenge. Thus, strategic measures must be taken by schools to identify and reshape fixed mindsets.

Growth Mindset Negates the Effects of Stereotype Threat

One of the more insidious effects of the fixed-ability mindset is seen in the susceptibility of females and minority students to stereotype threat. Stereotype threat (ST) is a phenomenon where individuals perform poorly because of the discomfort they feel when there is a perceived belief that members of their subgroup do not have the ability to do well within a domain (Mangels, Good, Whiteman, Maniscalco, & Dweck, 2011). The effect of ST can yield testing results that consistently underestimate the abilities of female and minority students (Carr & Steele, 2009). Individuals with the fixed mindset are highly susceptible to the effects of ST, although research has shown the growth mindset is a protective factor (Good et al., 2003). Stereotype threat creates an environment where students are anxious about how their performance will compare to an expectation based on race or gender. For example, a female student in an advanced mathematics class can experience ST if she perceives a belief that women are not as able as men in mathematics. On a test, she worries that she will not do as well as the men and she thinks about how to prevent others from seeing her anxiety. It is thought that the processes individuals use to cope with ST use some working memory capacity, thereby reducing the cognitive capacity that remains to work on the test. This effect is exacerbated by seemingly innocuous details such as having to indicate her gender on the test or the attribution of ability differences to genetic factors. The effect is alleviated when the test-taker has the growth mindset (Good et al., 2003) or when ability differences are attributed to experiential factors (Dar-Nimrod & Heine, 2006). Thus, instilling a growth mindset in students can protect them against ST and may help increase identification of potential talent in underrepresented groups.

Instilling a STEM Growth Mindset

Individuals who pursue STEM careers must be able to respond positively to challenges, failures, and setbacks that are inherent in many research-based professions. The proclivities to take on challenge and recover after setbacks are associated with the growth mindset, making it important to cultivate this mindset in all our children, beginning at an early age so to start them on a lifetime journey of intellectual growth.

Because mindsets are flexible, teachers and families can help young people develop positive, successful mindsets and ultimately, increase achievement. The models adults provide through their own response to challenge can affect a child's position on the mindset spectrum and in turn student outcomes.

Educators and parents need to take action to prevent challenge avoidance in children by personally holding the growth mindset and instilling it in students. For teachers, presentation styles and student feedback should be crafted in a way to provide environmental support for a growth mindset. Therefore, I propose teachers should (1) learn about their individual mindset and the mindsets of their students; (2) increase their awareness of the effects of praise on children and develop appropriate process praise techniques; and (3) increase their awareness of methods to change student mindsets and the potential impacts of mindset development.

Incorporating social-psychological interventions to encourage and develop the growth mindset (Dweck, 2006) in late elementary school and early middle school could help create a new generation of students motivated to learn and stimulated by challenge. However, one intervention will not be sufficient to sustain these new growth mindsets. American culture is filled with fixed mindset messages such as "work smarter, not harder." Therefore, it is imperative to change our cultural mantra. It is important, not only for our students, but also for our future, that Americans believe—and act accordingly—that intelligence can be developed, that failures are caused by a lack of effort, and that people with high ability still need to work hard to develop expertise.

References

Adams, J., & Pendlebury, D. (2010). *Global research report: United States* (pp. 1–12). Leeds, England. Retrieved from http://researchanalytics. thomsonreuters.com/m/pdfs/globalresearchreport-usa.pdf

Carr, P. B., & Steele, C. M. (2009). Stereotype threat and inflexible perseverance in problem solving. *Journal of Experimental Social Psychology, 45,* 853–859.

Dar-Nimrod, I., & Heine, S. J. (2006). Exposure to scientific theories affects women's math performance. *Science, 314,* 435.

Dweck, C. S. (2006). *Mindset: The new psychology of success.* New York, NY: Ballantine Books.

Dweck, C. S. (2008). *Mindsets and math/science achievement.* New York, NY: Carnegie Corporation of New York.

Dweck, C. S. (2010). Mind-Sets and equitable education. *Principal Leadership, 10,* 26–29.

Good, C., Aronson, J., & Inzlicht, M. (2003). Improving adolescents' standardized test performance: An intervention to reduce the effects of stereotype threat. *Journal of Applied Developmental Psychology, 24,* 645–662.

Mangels, J. A., Good, C., Whiteman, R. C., Maniscalco, B., & Dweck, C. S. (2011). Emotion blocks the path to learning under stereotype threat. *Social Cognitive and Affective Neuroscience, 7,* 230–241.

National Association for Gifted Children. (2010). *NAGC Pre-K–Grade 12 Gifted Programming Standards: A blueprint for quality gifted education programs.* Washington, DC: Author.

Subotnik, R. F., & Rickoff, R. (2010). Should eminence based on outstanding innovation be the goal of gifted education and talent development? Implications for policy and research. *Learning and Individual Differences, 20,* 358–364.

Chapter 60

The Social and Emotional Benefits of Nature

by Steve V. Coxon

As a child growing up in East Tennessee, it was a joy to have woods in my backyard and streams nearby. Science was everywhere. My sister and I learned about praying mantises, frogs, and turtles—often bringing snakes in to show off to our parents. My friends and I learned about the power of water while attempting—and failing—to stop the flow of water in the creek in our yard during heavy rains. We learned about physics while sledding in the winter, spraying the bottoms of our plastic sleds with cooking oil (and occasionally running into trees or the rocky, dry creek bed). We learned about poison ivy, ticks, and mosquitoes. We benefited from minimal adult interference. And although we didn't think about it at the time, we also experienced tremendous social and emotional benefits.

Working and playing outside is joyful, engaging, and exciting for children. The social and emotional benefits of being in the natural world have been well-documented for children through observation and empirical research (Thompson & Thompson, 2007). These benefits include sociability, teamwork, responsibility, empathy, and self-control as well as self-defined play, increased creativity and curiosity, and self-awareness and self-esteem. Massive, longitudinal research also clearly indicates that these so-called soft skills offer tremendous future benefits in quantifiable ways, including increased educational attainment and future earnings (Chetty et al., 2011).

Not every child has the benefit of growing up near a forest, but learning in nature can occur in any region, and nature can be brought inside, too. Science and gifted teachers can lead the way in providing these experiences.

School Gardens

Although I have seen very impressive—and expensive—school gardens, it doesn't take a fortune to create something wonderful. A sunny location and access to water is all that is needed. Raised beds are an easy way to avoid digging. Untreated cedar fencing boards are inexpensive and work well and can be stacked to create a deep raised bed on asphalt in even the most overpaved urban schoolyard (though ideally, your raised beds are planted on the ground). In my own school garden, we utilize quick growing vegetables that can be harvested before the end of the school year.

School gardens can also focus on local, native plants, many of which can be grown from seed. Such gardens can also focus on attracting butterflies, bees, and other important pollinators. I encourage any teacher in the monarch migration path, which covers most of the country, to plant milkweed—the only plant monarch caterpillars can eat.

Students should have as much say in the garden location, design, and plantings as possible. And they should do as much of the work as possible, getting their hands dirty, finding worms and insects, and working together to accomplish tasks like weeding, watering, and harvesting. Gardens can be tied in with deep observation, art projects, and problem-based learning, including student-designed experiments, and can tie into the standards relating to ecology, botany, pollinators, life cycles, along with weather and math.

Your students will not only learn the content better than in-class activities alone, but they'll also likely be better off socially and emotionally as well as developing responsibility and empathy in caring for the plants, self-esteem in seeing the benefits of their hard work, and deepening their curiosity.

Soda Bottle Terrariums

One of my gifted program teachers taught me how to make terrariums in soda bottles, and I've been making them ever since. You only need a clear soda bottle with the label removed, potting soil, and small seedlings or seeds (see Figure 60.1).

Students can learn many of the same things with a terrarium as with a garden, and they are ideal for learning about the water cycle as a closed system. As they each create their own terrarium, they will likely experience pride in their accomplishment and sustained interest in following the progress of their plants.

The natural world is such an exciting place. Bringing your students to nature or bringing nature to your students can lead not only to great academics, but to positive social and emotional development as well.

Resources

"Build Raised Beds from Cedar Fencing": http://preparednessmama.com/build-raised-garden-bed

"Designing a School Garden": http://www.kidsgardening.org/designing-a-school-garden

"Growing Milkweeds": http://www.monarchwatch.org/milkweed/prop.htm

"How to Build a Pop Bottle Terrarium": https://www.youtube.com/watch?v=69hYV9ti_R8

Louv, R. (2008). *Last child in the woods: Saving our children from nature-deficit disorder*. Chapel Hill, NC: Algonquin.

Skenazy, L. (2010). *Free-range kids: How to raise safe, self-reliant children (without going nuts with worry)*. San Francisco, CA: Jossey-Bass.

References

Chetty, R., Friedman, J. N., Hilger, N., Saez., E., Schanzenbach, D. W., & Yagan, D. (2011). How does your kindergarten classroom affect your earnings? Evidence from Project Star. *The Quarterly Journal of Economics, 126*, 1593–1660.

Directions for Making Soda Bottle Terrariums

1. Start by piercing a hole in which to insert your scissors and then cut the bottom of the soda bottle off about a third of the way up the bottle. To the bottom, you may choose to add an optional inch of aquarium gravel and/or a single layer of activated carbon (sold at aquarium stores).
2. Fill the rest of the bottom with potting soil.
3. Add 1–3 very small plants or a few seeds. Anything that likes a moist, humid environment will do. I've even used avocado pits. Dandelions, grass, clover, and other lawn plants all work well.
4. Water the plants moderately; don't create soupy soil.
5. Gently work the top portion of the bottle into the bottom. Cutting some small slits may help.
6. Terrariums can be placed in a shaded area or a sunny window, but should not be outside in full sun on a warm day as they may get too hot.

Figure 60.1. Soda bottle terrariums.

Thompson, J. E., & Thompson, R. A. (2007, November/December). Natural connections: Children, nature, and social-emotional development. *Exchange*, 46–49.

Chapter 61

The Case for Affect in Mathematics

by Scott A. Chamberlin

What many people refer to as the social and emotional needs in the world of gifted education is referred to as affect in the larger world of educational psychology. In fact, experts in the field of mathematics education have often been noted as conducting pioneering research that formalized the construct of affect. In mathematics education, the term *affect* is often considered globally to be comprised of feelings, emotions, and dispositions (McLeod, 1994; McLeod & Adams, 1989). Although not all education decision makers are aware of its prominence and importance, affect, whether good or bad, exists in literally every learning situation. That is because as students engage in learning scenarios, they have emotions about the situation.

The failed approach thus far to improving mathematical performance is often more of the same, with increased emphasis on standardized tests. This approach has resulted in the equivalence of talking louder and slower to English language learners in hopes that they will understand. Most likely, one of the keys to facilitating deep conceptual understanding of mathematics, something espoused in the Common Core State Standards, is the consideration and attention to student affect in mathematics.

Policymakers often will not address affect in school mathematics for several reasons. First, standardized instruments are not readily available to assess affect.

Second, affect is a "fuzzy construct," implying the notion that emotion is difficult to quantify. Third, given the rather nebulous nature of affect, policymakers are not entirely sure what it is and how to deal with it. Lastly, affect is something with which they may not be familiar, and it is easier to continue to neglect it altogether, rather than embrace it to facilitate legitimate learning.

An example of using affective data to guide teaching and learning decisions may be as simple as asking students if they enjoyed an activity. If the activity is one that is embraced by students, they may like doing similar ones in the future, and students in future years may enjoy the activity. If they did not enjoy an activity, then it may be worthy of eliminating, given the positive byproducts that often accompany positive affect. Certainly, teachers are the ones that make decisions in their classroom, but using actual data to make curricular decisions is a solid educational tactic.

One may wonder about the potential outcome if affect is assessed and subsequent changes are made to the learning environment through curricular and instructional approaches. The outcome may be quite evident. For example, the country of Singapore, often held up as the gold standard in mathematics, is one in which 20% of the emphasis in mathematics is student affect (Young, Yee, Kaur, Yee, & Fong, 2009). Clearly, policymakers in Singapore realize that students' feelings, emotions, and dispositions are important in the learning equation. *Singapore Math* (http://www.singaporemath.com) is an actual curriculum adopted by various school districts throughout the world, and may provide some guidance for those seeking to emphasize affect in the curriculum. Investing resources and attention to student emotions in mathematics and problem solving scenarios has not occurred on a large scale in the United States yet.

Finally, if educators do not consider affect in the learning equation, we may expect two results. Educational results, determined by standardized assessments, will likely stagnate, and a high percentage of the most promising pupils, may risk academic peril due to disengagement (Chamberlin, 2002). When learners are perpetually force-fed a diet of disengaging learning scenarios, the likelihood for boredom may increase, and with it a host of outcomes, notably underachievement.

References

Chamberlin, S. A. (2002). Analysis of interest during and after model-eliciting activities: A comparison of gifted and general population students

(Doctoral dissertation, Purdue University, 2002). *Dissertation Abstracts International, 64,* 2379. Retrieved from http://docs.lib.purdue.edu/dissertations/AAI3099758

McLeod, D. B. (1994). Research on affect and mathematics learning in the JRME: 1970 to the present. *Journal for Research in Mathematics Education, 25,* 637–647.

McLeod, D. B., & Adams, V. A. (1989). *Affect and mathematical problem solving: A new perspective.* New York, NY: Springer-Verlag.

Young, W. K., Yee, L. P., Kaur, B., Yee, F. P., & Fong, N. S. (2009). *Mathematics education: The Singapore journey.* Toh Tuck Lik, Singapore: World Scientific.

Section III: Support for Educators

Chapter 62

Professional School Counselors and Gifted Educators

Working Towards Solutions

by Susannah M. Wood

Samantha is a gifted eighth grader who is highly driven in her academic and extracurricular pursuits. She carries a full honors load including French, advanced language arts, math and history. Samantha is an active participant in debate and speech clubs and is a competitive cello player. Samantha has been described as having perfectionist tendencies, a label that triggered even higher levels of studying and performance in Samantha. Recently, however, Samantha's honors English/Integrated Language Arts (ILA) teacher has noticed a decline in Samantha's participation in class, a reduction in the quality of submitted assignments, and a general sense of confusion and fatigue.

Educating a gifted student of any age can be exciting and rewarding for gifted educators. Gifted educators may find themselves wearing multiple hats and occupying multiple roles as they strive to provide the best academic environment in which gifted students can receive a rigorous education, while also working to meet the social, emotional, and career needs these students have throughout their school-age years. Identifying, programming, teaching, and working with gifted students can also be challenging and stressful, requiring great amounts of time, energy, commitment, and motivation. Over time, feelings of lack of support, time for planning and effective teaching, and multiple student issues can begin to accumulate in a stressful and problematic nature for gifted educators (Pelsma, Richard, Harrington, & Burry, 1989). Gifted educators have a useful ally in the professional school counselor who can help with student concerns, act as a support, and can find resources that alleviate stress and enhance teaching. Through their roles as counselors, consultants, collectors of information, coordinators of services, and collaborators in multiple partnerships, professional school counselors play a vital part in the talent development of their gifted students and in the support of their gifted educators. Together, gifted educators and school counselors can provide the necessary supports and structures needed for the whole gifted child to learn and thrive in the classroom.

School Counseling and Gifted Education

Although the National Association for Gifted Children is the primary professional organization with which gifted educators affiliate, the American School Counselor Association (ASCA) is the parent organization for professional school counselors. Gifted educators may be more familiar with the traditional three "C's" of the school counselor's role: counseling, consulting, and coordinating. However, ASCA's new National Model has strengthened and expanded the school counselor's role with the equitable promotion of achievement and access to education for all students as a central focus (ASCA, 2003; Stone & Dahir, 2006). Professional school counselors are leaders, advocates, and specialists in delivering comprehensive developmental guidance and counseling curricula that provide an array of services and collaborative partnerships and whose effectiveness and impact on both student achievement and school culture can be measured (ASCA, 2013). The professional school counselor is also a key person in the advocacy of special populations in schools and an integral part in the talent development of gifted students (ASCA, 2003).

Originally developed in 1988 and subsequently revised, the ASCA position statement (2013) on the school counselor's involvement with gifted students asserts that, in general, the professional school counselor assists in "providing technical assistance and an organized support system within the developmental comprehensive school counseling program for gifted and talented students to meet their extensive and diverse needs as well as the needs of all students."

Specifically, the position statement articulates the roles and responsibilities school counselors can assume when serving gifted students, including identification of gifted students, advocacy for counseling activities that address the academic, career, and personal/social needs of the gifted through individual and group guidance, provision of resources and materials, raising awareness of gifted issues, and engaging in professional development activities in order to facilitate the continuing education of the psychology and development of gifted students (ASCA, 2013).

School counselors who utilize the model to shape their identity and roles, can also refer to the socio-emotional guidance and counseling standards in NAGC's (2010) Pre-K–Grade 12 Gifted Program Standards for the development of services for gifted students. The program guidelines, which outline standards for services, interventions, scope and sequence, and provisions for at-risk and underachievement in gifted youth, work in tandem with the ASCA model, which stresses equity and access of educational provisions for all children, advocacy for students without voice, partnerships and collaboration with multiple stakeholders to support services, as well as the demonstration of effectiveness in services and interventions rendered.

The three "C's" have not left the professional school counselor's repertoire; they have been reenvisioned in a more comprehensive manner, including other "C's that gifted educators can call upon when working with their gifted students. These roles include, but are not limited to, the following:

▶ counseling,
▶ consultation,
▶ collecting information,
▶ coordinating services and resources,
▶ collaboration and partnerships, and
▶ 'countability.

School counselors actively occupy each of these roles in order to provide the necessary services to meet gifted students' academic, career, and personal/social needs. Gifted students can present a wide array of gifts, talents, and challenges. Concerns that gifted educators often have on behalf of their students are typically related to the challenges tied to the traditional developmental milestones, as well as challenges resulting from the students' asynchronous development, their ability to regulate their emotional and psychological responses based on typical characteristics, and/or as a result of belonging to a special population (Robinson, 2002). A few common concerns include multipotentiality, perfectionism, heightened intensity and sensitivity, and existential depression. By assisting in one or many of the roles described above, the school counselor may be able to help alleviate the stress gifted educators experience when working to meet the needs of the whole gifted child. These roles are described more thoroughly through the case of Samantha given below.

Counseling

Probably the most recognizable role for professional school counselors is that of counseling. Counseling in schools can be done in different venues including individual sessions, small-group counseling, and classroom guidance activities. Every professional school counselor is trained in student development, child and adolescent-specific issues, critical cases, and multicultural competency. In addition, each counselor brings a unique perspective on student needs, development, and counseling theories and techniques. Counseling sessions in any venue are typically a result of a student self-referral, a parental referral, or a referral by an educator. In this case, Samantha's father has contacted Ms. Richardson, the eighth-grade counselor, to discuss his concerns about his daughter's recent behavior. He describes Sam as a "fun loving" young woman who is conscientious about her work. However, in the past week, Samantha burst into tears while practicing both her speech for her team and again while practicing her cello. When her father voiced his concern, he was greeted by an outburst of "I just don't know, okay?!" which he described as uncharacteristic of his daughter. It is probable that when Samantha meets with Ms. Richardson, she will already know that she has been referred. Teenagers can be challenging clients and resist counseling for many reasons including their perception that their counselor cannot "relate," coming to counseling under duress, resentment of "interfering" parents or teachers, and the desire to cope with their own problems individually or with peer help as a signifier of the normal developmental desire for autonomy. However, with an explication of what counseling is and that Samantha can choose or not choose to participate, and with time, patience, and humor, Ms. Richardson can develop a rapport with Samantha and a solid, working alliance that can facilitate positive changes. A solution focused counseling session in which Sam will be "blamed" for her past success in ILA, and asked to "scale" her problem in ILA, might include the following scene:

Ms. Richardson: So, Sam, you've told me that in general, you typically turn in all your assignments on time, and that you're generally proud of them. I'm really impressed by your dedication to your homework and classes!

Sam: Thanks, I guess I never thought of it like that. It wasn't until recently that they got a lot harder.

Ms. Richardson: You're saying that the problems in English are recent? Can you tell me more?

Sam: Yeah. I feel bad for disappointing Mrs. Bonney for not turning in good stuff the past few weeks. But the assignments are harder than she knows. Especially right now.

Ms. Richardson: Sam, if I were going to follow you around with a video camera and I could see what you do when you get ready to do an assignment for Mrs. Bonney, and then actually doing the assignment, what would I see?

Sam: Hum . . . well, getting started is pretty easy. I usually do work in the library or at home. I look at the assignment, and I start, using the writing mode. I get through the first paragraph or so and then I just . . . I just get confused.

Ms. Richardson: So about halfway through the assignment you get stuck.

Sam: Yeah. I mean, I know what I have to do. I just look at the main paragraph and elaborate. But it just seems like I could go any different direction. Like right now we're reading and talking about heroes and heroines and all of these people who . . . did something significant. And in speech we're talking about role models and how they can influence our thinking. So when Mrs. Bonney asked us to write about the heroes, I thought about Yo-Yo Ma and the speech I wrote about him. I thought maybe he could be my hero. And I got halfway through the assignment last week, but then I got to thinking . . . I don't know if I want to do cello for the rest of my life. I don't even know what I want to do. Jonathan's writing on Nelson Mandela, and Traci on Mother Teresa, and I got to thinking, these are really great people who made a difference and I haven't done anything! I'm not even sure if Yo-Yo Ma is my role model, you know? I think my heroes are more fantastical, but they do more than play the cello. They make a difference.

Ms. Richardson: So, when you're writing these assignments, you're thinking about some really tough topics, some really important ideas and questions about who you are.

Sam: Exactly. And then I just lose track of what I've written. I could write about anything, but when I try to, nothing makes a lot of sense.

Ms. Richardson: Sam, can you tell me, with your English assignments, on a scale of one to 10, one being not a big problem, to 10 being a very, very big problem, where are you?

Sam: Oh . . . oh, maybe a seven? It's not all bad. It'd be better if my cello tutor would stop pressuring me to study more and to do all of these competitions this year. . . .

Ms. Richardson: Okay, a seven, so it's a pretty big problem. And your cello tutor is stressing you out. So, let's talk about where you would like to be on that scale. . . .

Ms. Richardson has discovered several things. Samantha is generally a hard worker, for which she was positively "blamed," but the assignments concerning heroes and role models have created frustration and anxiety. Using videotalk, Ms. Richardson began to understand that Sam's struggle to create a coherent paper about her role model was due in part to confusion of who she wanted to be, what she could do with her talent, and the overwhelming need to have to choose "the" career path. This, coupled with her cello tutor's urging Samantha to increase practice and make decisions about future competition, has exacerbated Samantha's existential crisis. By nature of her giftedness, Samantha is wrestling with questions of "Who am I?" and "What do I do with my life?" at an earlier age and can conceptualize and "see" various paths and pursuits that look equally valid and attractive. At this point, Ms. Richardson can inquire if Samantha feels comfortable sharing some of these concerns with Mrs. Bonney, her ILA teacher, which will alleviate anxiety and frustration concerning Samantha's work.

Consultation

When working with a fellow educator on behalf of a student, most likely the professional school counselor will be acting as a consultant. School counselors who employ the solution-focused method of consultation will underscore the fact that when working with teachers, administrators, or other personnel, the nature of the consultation relationship is one of equals. A primary characteristic of this model is the collaborative nature of the consultation relationship—Mrs. Bonney, Samantha's ILA/English teacher, and Ms. Richardson form a strong working alliance on behalf of Samantha (Kahn, 2000). Solution-focused consultation, an application of brief, solution-focused counseling (de Shazer, 1985; Murphy, 1997), orients consultation in term of solutions, future instead of past, inherent strengths and past successes, and emphasizes the fact that language plays an important role in the construction of meaning and reality. In addition, a solution-focused orientation empowers the gifted educator as an agent of change by collaboratively identifying strengths, reframing problems, brainstorming solutions, and evaluating changes made. In a solution-focused consultation framework, Mrs. Bonney is the expert on her classroom and her students, while the school counselor acts as the facilitator of the consultation process.

The stages of consultation are fluid; however, they generally progress through presession and initial structuring, establishing consultation goals, examining attempted solutions and exceptions, deciding on a solution, enacting the solution, evaluation, summarization, and complimenting. In essence, Ms. Richardson will first discuss the nature of consultation with Mrs. Bonney. Then, together they will explore the strengths and resources each brings to the process of consultation. They will then identify goals, and examine attempted solutions and exceptions to the "problem." Next they will decide on a solution or course of change, and, over time, evaluate the progress of that solution. Finally they will summarize their journey together and any needed plans to continue the changes made:

Ms. Richardson: So it sounds like this is really new behavior for Samantha. Can you tell me a little more about how and when this change occurred?

Mrs. Bonney: I wouldn't say it was overnight, but I'd say it's been downhill for about 2 weeks now. Samantha was always punctual about finishing her assignments, and even if she didn't like them she always completed them well, and followed the instructions. Recently, they lack focus if they're turned in at all, and Samantha seems . . . confused. I'm concerned.

Ms. Richardson: You care very much about Samantha, and your concern says a great deal about how you work with your students. If a miracle happened overnight and tomorrow Samantha was doing everything she needed to do in your class to make her successful, what would she be doing?

Mrs. Bonney: She would at least turn the assignments in, just to get the credit. That would be a great place to start. We can always work on the content later.

Ms. Richardson: Okay, so Samantha would at least turn in the assignments. How do we start working toward that goal?

Collecting Information

Several options present themselves to Ms. Richardson as the result of talking to Mrs. Bonney. One option is to meet with Samantha's teachers individually to gain a better understanding of Samantha's progress in her other classes. This information will help Mrs. Bonney determine whether or not the sudden decline in Samantha's work is unique to her class or is occurring elsewhere. A second option, should Mrs. Bonney decide that a "two heads are better than one" approach is warranted, is that Ms. Richardson can also be called upon to coordinate a group meeting with Samantha's teachers.

The counseling sessions with Sam have also given Ms. Richardson food for thought about other aspects of Samantha's concerns. With Samantha's permission and beginning with Mrs. Bonney, Ms. Richardson can pursue a few different options to gather information. First, is Sam the only one evidencing these identity and career concerns via their assignments in Mrs. Bonney's class? Second, are there other members of the speech team that also are struggling with theses issues? Mrs. Bonney and Mr. Banks reported that no, they had not seen any evidence of career or identity concerns with their other students. However, Mr. Banks also told Ms. Richardson that there were some very bright students in the speech class that were agonizing over their writing and seemed to be struggling with finding the "right" words. Samantha had not, up until recently, demonstrated that concern; however, she was very exacting and could be highly critical of herself if her speeches did not come out quite the way she wanted. Could Ms. Richardson consider working with students whose perfectionism was beginning to interfere with positive performance? Third, Mr. Williams, the high school gifted education coordinator, had recommendations of other gifted students who were underachieving or who were embarking on the college and career decision-making journey and having a difficult time.

Coordinating Services and Resources

The information Ms. Richardson has gathered has caused her to consider how she would meet several different types of needs that the gifted students in her building are experiencing. Ms. Richardson's planning and programming for these students are limited only by her imagination. However, they will require the help and creativity of multiple stakeholders. Her first decision is to coordinate a series of small groups for gifted students focusing on healthy and unhealthy perfectionism, interests, values, and the decision-making process for the future. To do this she will have to elicit the volunteer participation from the students themselves, the willingness of the teachers to allow them out of class if an afterschool group cannot be arranged, parent permission, and the career and values inventories suggested by Mr. Williams that meet the cognitive needs of these students. Her second decision is to hold parent meetings to help parents communicate with their gifted students, assist gifted students in understanding the struggles they may face with competing expectations about the use of their talents, and aid teachers in interpreting inventories and assessments that can be used to provide differentiated instruction for these students. Third, Ms. Richardson thinks that all students would benefit from classroom guidance topics including stress reduction.

Collaboration and Partnerships

To help run the groups, Ms. Richardson has enlisted the help of school counseling interns from a nearby university. She will train them on the use and interpretation of career and values inventories, and in return they will help students process the results and talk about their thoughts and feelings pertaining to career choices. The same university hosts a center for gifted education. Ms. Richardson has investigated possibilities with Mr. Williams, the gifted education coordinator of her building, and Dr. Phillips, the director of guidance, regarding workshops and in-service possibilities concerning social and emotional needs of gifted students. Ms. Richardson's colleagues, fellow counselors and assistant specialists in the building, have also suggested the use of online software that can compare colleges for their career and college fair at the end of the school year. Last, Ms. Richardson has decided to utilize the power of the hero and heroine as explored by the English and ILA instructors in eighth grade. Part of being a hero is the ability to cope with struggle positively, and the teachers have promised to brainstorm possible activities, modeling, and writing assignments as extensions of their curriculum with this idea in mind.

'Countability

The time, energy, and programming that Ms. Richardson has been putting into helping the gifted students in her building is admirable. However, it will mean little without documentation of effect. Accountability is an integral part of the school counselor's profession. The effects of interventions, counseling, partnerships, and consultation can be demonstrated through a variety of measures. The use of pre- and postassessments of student learning and progress in counseling groups and monitoring grade point averages and attendance are all viable ways of measuring effectiveness. In the case of Samantha, Mrs. Bonney will be evaluating Sam's progress on assignments, and her fellow group members will report on what they have learned, what was helpful and what was not. Mrs. Bonney can also provide her unique assessments and report on changes made as a result of consultation. Classrooms in which Ms. Richardson conducted classroom guidance sessions on stress reduction and/or in which positive methods for coping with struggle and internal conflict were modeled and discussed will be given postassessments to determine if positive change has occurred since the administration of the preassessment. Ms. Richardson has given thought to piloting a schoolwide assessment of gifted needs at the end of the year, and interviewing her teachers, other school counselors, and the district coordinator in order to plan for the next year.

As seen in the example of Samantha, professional school counselors can play several vital roles in the talent development of their students. Through counseling, consultation, collecting information, coordinating services, and establishing collaborative partnerships, school counselors can aid gifted educators in their remarkable teaching and service to their gifted students so that they do not suffer from unnecessary stress. Demonstrating accountability through evaluations and assessments provides both gifted educators and school counselors with proof of positive change and the information needed to move forward with additional programming and services. Working together to find solutions, gifted educators and school counselors can make the difference to gifted students.

References

American School Counselor Association. (2003). *The ASCA National Model: A framework for school counseling programs.* Fairfax, VA: Author.

American School Counselor Association. (2013). *The school counselor and gifted and talented student programs.* Retrieved from https://www.schoolcounselor.org/asca/media/asca/PositionStatements/PS_Gifted.pdf

de Shazer, S. (1985). *Keys to solutions in brief therapy.* New York, NY: Norton.

Kahn, B. B. (2000). A model of solution-focused consultation for school counselors. *Professional School Counseling, 3,* 248–255.

Murphy, J. J. (1997). *Solution-focused counseling in middle and high schools.* Alexandria, VA: American Counseling Association.

National Association for Gifted Children. (2010). *NAGC Pre-K–Grade 12 Gifted Programming Standards: A blueprint for quality gifted education programs.* Washington, DC: Author.

Pelsma, D. M., Richard, G. V., Harrington, R. G., & Burry, J. M. (1989). The quality of life survey: A measure of teacher stress and job satisfaction. *Measurement and Evaluation in Counseling and Development, 21,* 165–176.

Robinson, N. M. (2002). Introduction. In M. Neihart, S. Reis, N. Robinson, & S. Moon (Eds.), *The social and emotional development of gifted children: What do we know?* (pp. xi–xxiv). Waco, Texas: Prufrock Press.

Stone, C. B., & Dahir, C. A. (2006). *The transformed school counselor.* New York, NY: Lahaska Press.

Chapter 63

Social and Emotional Needs

Is There a Curriculum Connection?

by Jennifer Beasley

Recently I met with colleagues to discuss integrating strategies and techniques that address both our students' social and emotional and their academic needs. Story after story shared in our small group revealed that whether we planned for it or not, our students had a need to discuss issues and concerns in our classrooms. Through our discussions, we began to talk about where this would fit into our perfectly planned lessons and activities. Was there a curriculum connection?

In a recent article in *The New York Times*, high school students discussed the pressure they feel over grades and competition for college admissions and testing, leading some to abuse prescription stimulants in order to give them focus during tests and study sessions (Schwarz, 2012). This stress and pressure is not isolated. Students in our classrooms today are under stress from testing, parents, their peers, and themselves. Jean Peterson (2009) noted that although research does not establish that gifted individuals are more or less likely to have mental health concerns, there is quite a bit of evidence to suggest that those "gifts" can impact students in both positive and negative ways. How then, do we help our students with pressures and stress while at the same time attending to curricular standards in the classroom?

Creating a Space for Learning

A great place to start is by creating a classroom community in which students feel welcome and ready to learn. In order for students to feel like they can share their worries and struggles in the classroom, a teacher must create that environment for learning. Teachers can do this by giving students an opportunity to have a voice in the classroom, by giving students choice in assignments as well as opportunities for feedback throughout the assignment. In classrooms where students feel like they have to know the answers to look good in the eyes of their peers, some students may not feel comfortable raising their hands or telling you how they feel. Placing a "Question Box" in a discreet area of the classroom allows students to pose questions anonymously or in private and get their questions and concerns addressed. For more information on learning environments, please access Standard 4 of the NAGC Pre-K–Grade 12 Gifted Programming Standards (http://nagc.org/resources-publications/resources/national-standards-gifted-and-talented-education).

Using Your Resources

Teachers often feel that when they are presented with an issue in the classroom, it is their job to conquer it alone, but this need not be the case. When faced with students experiencing stress in testing situations as well as in peer groups, I reached out to my school counselor. I was fortunate to have a school counselor who could point me to some great resources as well as teach with me as we addressed stress management. One book that was incredibly helpful was *Fighting Invisible Tigers* by Earl Hipp, which helped me weave strategies for dealing with stress into my classroom. One great strategy that I use in my own life is "Front Burner, Back Burner." I gave students paper that looked like the top of a four-burner stove. We talked about how there are some things that are "front burner issues" and others that don't demand our immediate attention that we can leave for the "back burner." Students wrote their issues on their burners and we discussed issues that we really don't have any control over, which we can take off the stove completely. As students faced stresses throughout the year, I knew they continued to use this strategy because I often heard them say, "I don't think this is a front burner issue!"

Whether teachers have access to a school counselor, fellow teacher, an article or book, or even a Pinterest page (yes, there are pages devoted to social and emotional needs! See: http://pinterest.com/kimberlielewis/aig), there are resources out there that can help us integrate affective education into the classroom.

Making the Connection

Teachers are not counselors, but they do have a responsibility to get to know their students. Not only does this make sense for meeting academic needs, but affective needs as well. Until a child feels that the classroom is a safe environment in which to explore new concepts and new ideas, real learning cannot take place. When it comes to addressing the social and emotional needs of learners, there truly is a curriculum connection.

References

Hipp, E. (2008). *Fighting invisible tigers: Stress management for teens* (3rd ed.). Minneapolis, MN: Free Spirit.

National Association for Gifted Children. (2010). *NAGC Pre-K–Grade 12 Gifted Programming Standards: A blueprint for quality gifted education programs*. Washington, DC: Author.

Peterson, J. S. (2009). Myth 17: Gifted and talented individuals do not have unique social and emotional needs. *Gifted Child Quarterly, 53,* 280–282.

Schwarz, A. (2012). Risky rise of the good-grade pill. *The New York Times*. Retrieved from http://www.nytimes.com/2012/06/10/education/seeking-academic-edge-teenagers-abuse-stimulants.html

Chapter 64

The Role of Teachers When Gifted Students Experience Negative Life Events

by Jean S. Peterson

Life happens. When negative life events happen in the lives of gifted students, inner turmoil is likely. However, in the study of life events presented in the *Gifted Child Quarterly* article, school-related challenges were retrospectively the most unsettling for graduates, not deaths, illnesses, accidents, or family upheaval. But that finding should not suggest that teachers be unconcerned about students experiencing negative events. Characteristics associated with giftedness may exacerbate distress: sensitivity, excitabilities, intensity, and perfectionism, for example. Suddenly being unable to control situations by applying intellectual nimbleness, feeling pressure to problem solve, being reluctant to ask for help, and not feeling permission to express negative emotions may also contribute.

I offer some thoughts about the role of teachers when in contact with high-stress students, as well as some perspectives about assumptions, resilience, and loss. Teachers, activity directors, and coaches may actually spend more time with students than parents do, sometimes with sustained contact for several years. Those relationships give teachers opportunities to be supportive.

Common Assumptions

I once made a videotape of a panel of gifted underachievers, which I use when training school counselors. These adolescents did not fit common stereotypes of either gifted kids or underachievers. Each time I watch the tape, I am reminded how idiosyncratic underachievers are. I also hear, once again, one sensitive girl's story about how a teacher humiliated her in fifth grade about her unorganized desk and changed her attitude toward school "forever." One severe underachiever tells about fourth grade, when his teacher "thought I should have more friends." He said his teachers' perception that he was a "loner" with depression, and the uncomfortable "fuss" that followed, contributed to his negative attitude. His comment was that "everyone is different in what they need in friends."

It is unwise to assume that gifted students have fewer problems than other students or that high ability means being able to make sense of interpersonal and emotional complexities. Change and loss occur for everyone. It is important to remember that school transitions, family relocation, parental unemployment, family reconfigurations, tension at home, or having a sibling leave for college may be particularly stressful for sensitive, intense gifted students. Those life events may not seem "traumatic," but such situations may feel disorienting and represent significant loss. Yet gifted students may project a positive image by hiding uncertainties and emotions. In spite of smiles and success, some may be quietly experiencing post-traumatic stress disorder (PTSD).

Trauma is not limited to war or abuse. Trauma might be related to an acrimonious parental divorce, chronic bullying, witnessing violence, a horrific accident or fire, or the death of a classmate, for example. Symptoms of PTSD are pervasive fears and feelings of powerlessness, anger, humiliation, intrusion, emotional confusion, and lack of trust. PTSD, regardless of age, may be reflected in a frantic need for control, possibly manifested in disordered eating, self-medication with illegal substances, self-mutilation, a violent temper, or dominating social behaviors. It can also mean isolation, depression, physical complaints, an impaired sense of self, and interpersonal difficulties. However, none of these might be obvious to a parent or educator.

Teachers may assume that smiling, pleasant, handsome, organized, high-performing students are comfortable with themselves and others and are happy and satisfied. Teachers may therefore miss opportunities to validate gifted students' complexity, distress, and worth. During the years I facilitated over a thousand small-group discussions with gifted students about nonacademic concerns, I learned that few felt confident in all contexts. Many felt inferior to peers. They had no problem naming situations where they felt inept. Many believed that adults and peers did not understand that they were more than just performers or nonperformers.

High achievement may actually be the one controllable component in a life that otherwise feels chaotic and uncontrollable. Furthermore, academic achievers may not feel satisfaction in their work. Academic *under*achievers may be happy and satisfied, although my own research has found that underachievement can also reflect distractions, negative life events, difficult family situations, or a learning disability—and a consequent inability to concentrate in school. Underachievement may also reflect "developmental stuckness" related to incorporating giftedness into their identity, finding direction, developing a mature relationship, incrementally increasing autonomy, and coming to grips with sexuality and even sexual orientation. High achievers may also struggle with any or all of these areas, of course.

Change and Loss for Gifted Students

Change is constant. Nothing, bad or good, stays the same. That idea may offer hope when despair feels permanent. However, in the midst of life-altering events, change can be frightening. Change means loss. Something is left behind. There may be grief for "the way it used to be."

Gifted youth may have losses that others do not, and they may experience these losses differently from other similarly aged peers. For example, being able to consider many options for university, major course of study, and career may be stressful, especially when any choice means the loss of all other options. Relationships might be lost when a gifted adolescent pursues interests in extracurricular activities and finds new friends. Embracing giftedness may mean losing a mainstream identity. Perhaps more than others, they may grieve the loss of childhood, of familiar roles as siblings arrive or families blend, of no longer having "one main teacher." For a target of bullying, a sense of safety may be lost. Awareness of peers' extreme circumstances may mark a loss of innocence. When parents are preoccupied, children miss nurturing. If a parent is deployed overseas or becomes unemployed, changes at home may be huge. When natural disasters "take everything," the sense of loss may prevail. If there is a break-in or vandalism, a sense of privacy and security may be lost. With asynchronous development, young gifted children may struggle with existential questions when "events" happen, without the wisdom of age and experience to put them into perspective.

Teachers also may consider losses related to achievement. Achievers may "lose" fun, time, play, friends, and opportunities to differentiate themselves from family. Underachievers may lose the approval of parents, scholarships, teacher support, opportunities to validate ability, and academic skills normally honed through challenge. When parents abdicate responsibility and a gifted child moves into a parental role, there may be no real childhood. When children's lives are overstructured by protective parents, again there might be a loss of childhood play, in addition to little chance to learn how to cope with boredom and choice.

Teachers Responding

It is important not to assume that grief resulting from change and loss has a beginning and an end, and that there is an "appropriate amount of time" for grieving, after which someone should simply be "over it." Even if children and adolescents do not seem to *stay* in grief, it may be intense, long-lasting, and even hidden. However, "rescuing" children from grief is not the answer. Validating their feelings with statements is important ("This is a very sad time." "I know you're missing Grandma." "It's OK to cry. People cry when they're sad."). When students are given permission to freely express sad feelings, the ability to cope increases, even as situations bring up feelings of loss. "It's OK to feel" is an appropriate statement of support. It might be appropriate to ask, if there is evidence of severe distress, "Should I worry about you?" A referral to a school counselor is appropriate if the answer is yes.

Teachers can help children to cope and develop resilience, but what they say to distressed students needs to be credible. A few years ago, my college roommate, a long-time therapist, remarked that shallow cheerleading ("feel-good talk") by teachers and parents generates "a phony sense of pride and strength"—something she associated with difficult, young adult clients. She said they speak of being proud of themselves, but may be unable to connect with other people who value this trait. She said, "Life is hard. When kids grow up with a sense of entitlement because they do not receive credible, accurate, observant feedback, they are at a disadvantage when hurt. They are vulnerable when experiencing loss." A sense of confidence is best when it is well-founded and has humility.

However, she emphasized that teachers and other significant adults should not hesitate to compliment children and adolescents who have exceptional ability. The life events article attests to the reality that gifted youth may have self-doubt. They need compliments—from people whose opinion matters. When criticized by hard-edged, perfectionistic parents or teachers, they may accept the criticism too harshly and/or accept it as fact. In hearing only criticism, they miss crucial feedback, affecting their sense of self. Their own self-talk may be unrelentingly negative. They need to hear about their desirable qualities, including non-performance-related strengths. They need compliments about their smile, kindness, insights, sensitivity, ability to prioritize, thoughtful comments, sense of style, ability to express feelings, ability to take feedback (e.g., in a talent area), perseverance and steadiness, or creativity. Ultimately, confidence and humility can coexist. My friend summarized an ideal outlook: "This is what I am and can do, but I know I'm not the most important person in the universe. I need to be respectful of others. We all have something to contribute."

Informed teachers and school counselors can help students make sense of feelings and behaviors by providing psychoeducational information about social and emotional aspects of giftedness, "normal" responses to change, and resilience. Information about nonacademic aspects of giftedness can also counter arrogance and entitlement. Teachers and school counselors can advocate for adding books related to giftedness to the school library—for their own and students' use.

It is a rare gift when teachers can meet gifted kids, nonjudgmentally, where they *are*. An effective teacher posture when working with gifted students, including during times of high stress, is one that remains open to their humanness. They are developing, feeling, dealing with complex situations, wondering about the future, and perhaps having self-doubt. When teachers are comfortable with giftedness, they can interact with gifted students without positive (being "in awe") or negative ("needing to put them in their place") biases interfering.

Teachers can build relationships—with good boundaries, without needing the gifted child or teen to fill a need, and without so much personal investment that objectivity is lost. Teachers can avoid pouncing on mistakes or weaknesses. They can keep the focus on the child, not talking about themselves. They can resist impulses to "fix" the student. They can beware of controlling the conversation, instead being open to what the student has to say.

Being alert to changes in demeanor, attitude, or behavior may provide an opportunity to ask, "You seem kind of quiet lately. How is your life going?" or "You don't seem to have your usual energy. Is anything getting in the way?" or "You seem to be working hard at getting our attention lately. What's going on?" or "School is pretty stressful, these days, huh." Teachers who stay open to complexity can affirm that a gifted child is "interesting and complex." Even if only for 30 seconds between classes, listening carefully and validating feelings ("It sounds frustrating" or "I can see that you're angry") may be a much larger contribution to well-being than is apparent at the time.

Positive Events

The *GCQ* life events article did not discuss the experience of *positive* events, which the study also explored. In short, academic challenges, highly invested teachers with good humor and effective teaching approaches, academic awards, and college acceptances validated students' efforts and strengths. For many, extracurricular activities provided social contacts (e.g., "a family of friends," a "place to belong"), skills, and a sense of accomplishment. Service locally or far away sparked career interests and introduced them to other cultures. Some students mentioned that spiritual growth had led to purpose, peace, and direction. The students who completed the study all mentioned positive experiences, which likely helped to balance the negatives so many had experienced during the school years. In order to achieve a healthy balance in the classroom, teachers, in supporting students during difficult times, should seek to provide positive experiences as well.

Chapter 65

The Evolving Benefits of Teacher Collaboration

by Meg Strnat and Robin Young

Picture this. You're the only gifted/talented teacher at your grade level in the building. You have occasional meetings with all of the gifted/talented teachers in the district, but the focus of meetings is mainly to discuss testing and scheduling. You are left to develop most of your teaching materials on your own. Worst of all, you are overwhelmed and isolated.

You know that collaboration is the ticket to solve your problems. Richard DuFour and Robert Eaker (1998) note that collaborative structures promote opportunities for peer evaluation of teaching practice and use of educational strategies, nurture stronger decision making through increased support, and encourage risk-taking. Lawrence and Pauline Leonard (2003) stress, "Prevailing thought suggests that improved student performance may be fully realized only when teachers routinely function as teams and abandon their traditional norms of isolationism and individualism" (p. 1).

Our Situation

We are two fourth-grade gifted/talented teachers in two separate schools in the same district who decided that isolation wasn't working. Collaboration was the answer. Our intent was simple: Share materials and ideas. This required each of us to ask a couple of questions of ourselves including, "What is not working?" and "How can I be more effective?" which naturally led to sharing our successes and failures. Early benefits were limited to the simple sharing of resources and materials. However, we quickly realized that these minimal "sharing" times did not adequately meet our needs. We decided to work together to design common units and activities. Despite scheduling and time constraints, the higher level of collaboration produced exponential results.

Begin with a common vision or goal. Finding a common vision usually requires teachers to share what they are already doing in their classrooms. We met once a week before school to share ideas and materials we were using for current units because we followed the same curriculum map. We quickly found that both of us were strong believers in inquiry-based learning across the curriculum, which allowed our gifted/talented students to reach their potential in an engaging environment.

Pinpoint areas of weakness. Until 4 years ago, our district provided a pull-out gifted program. Now every elementary school in the district has a third- and fourth-grade, self-contained gifted classroom. As a result, curriculum guidelines are just that—guiding principles providing extensive latitude for individual teachers to develop programs. Although this freedom is a plus for the creative teacher, it also forces each teacher to develop a large number of study units. It can be an overwhelming and isolating process because even though we teach in K–4 schools, our gifted and talented curriculum is above grade level in the areas of language arts and math. Our intermediate schools use curriculum geared specifically to grade level, and so collaboration is not a possibility there. The natural solution is to collaborate with each other across our two schools, creating joint units.

Each year we noticed that the students in both of our gifted classes seemed most engaged when they were given opportunities for lots of movement, creativity, and choice. Thus, our joint units needed to include options for many open-ended, hands-on activities. We also observed that many of our students needed more social encounters outside of the classroom with gifted students like themselves.

Develop solutions. The solution seemed apparent to both of us when we saw what was missing in our classrooms. We needed some sort of social apparatus that brought both of our classes together doing similar study units, so we created a quasi-club for the students to share, experience, and broaden learning on a joint study unit. It would involve an electric circuitry contest, a joint field trip to a museum in a nearby city, and a "Meeting of Minds" show (Allen, 1989) where students discuss social studies topics in the role of a famous scientist, mathematician, author, poet, or artist. Grant monies provided primary references, kits from Jackdaws, which include primary source photographs, reference guides, and lesson materials, and science biographies, K'NEX building materials, which allow for three-dimensional construction projects, and a variety of other hands-on materials to engage, solidify, and broaden learning.

Our first meeting was a family night, which allowed students to showcase their knowledge and understanding of electricity through original Snap Circuit brand projects. Before the first meeting, students participated in an electricity unit developed by both teachers. The real fun and deeper investigation began when small groups of students in each class explored Snap Circuits Electronic kits, and used Sidney Parnes's Creative Problem Solving Model (Duling, 1984) to determine the best approach to invent a new use for Snap Circuits. They created PowerPoint presentations and display booths to market the circuit inventions, which were presented at this family night. A local engineering expert judged the competition.

Preparation for the second meeting required little effort. We arranged for a joint field trip to a science and engineering museum. The trip greatly enhanced and enriched the curriculum. Students were able to experience, firsthand, applications of the materials they had been discussing and using during class. It was clear through observation that the students enjoyed this venture outside the walls of the school environment.

Assessing Student Learning

For the third meeting with our students, we developed planning materials that were used in both classrooms, but settled on different culminating projects to meet the different needs in our classrooms. At one school, student projects were presented by individual students to other classes and parents during the school day. At the other school, students performed skits written by their groups. The skits were videotaped and then shared with the other teacher's class. We shared student responses to the video to improve the project for the following year. Through this process we found that reflection is considerably easier when students and teachers can view the work of others in a nonthreatening atmosphere. Imagine our students' reactions to learning beyond their own classroom walls. They worked harder knowing that the results of their learning were shared, and they questioned from a different perspective than just within their own classroom. Videotaping is also an easy alternative for collaborating teachers separated by large distances, and with the advent of new media technology, videoconferencing alternatives are endless.

Synergized Collaboration

▶ **Establish a common vision.** Vision might include finding your common teaching style or teaching philosophies.

▶ **Pinpoint areas needing improvement.** Curriculum development is a common starting point, but student needs (particularly in a gifted/talented classroom) and social considerations are also relevant.

▶ **Select and develop a way to implement improvement.** Often, teachers select a joint study unit. Other possibilities include facilitating joint speakers, field trips, grants, or synthesizing understanding of a new teaching approach. Many teachers might be inclined to divide the work in order to shorten both the project and its evaluation, but the true benefit of collaboration occurs only when the strengths of each teacher are integrated, with both partners putting forth 100% effort.

▶ **Create assessment tools.** Pre- and postassessments are critical tools that not only allow teachers to evaluate the success of their joint curricular units, but also help document and report on the success of student learning.

▶ **Reflection.** This important step allows for necessary adjustments during and after completion of the course of instruction. Student and parent feedback through observation and surveys is a vital component of this step.

Reflection: What's in Store Next Year?

Next year we anticipate our collaboration will continue to evolve. Several teachers have heard about our efforts, seen the results, and wish to join the team. Two of the new members teach in regular education classrooms. The collaboration will now encompass three schools within the district. It will be interesting to see how the larger number of collaborating teachers affects our focus, closeness, and effectiveness. An immediate benefit will be the perspectives gained from returning students. Students will now represent multiple grade levels and they will receive a continuum of services throughout the time spent at our school.

Collaboration is a learning process that has led to exponential growth in benefits, both to us and our students. Next year's collaboration may look different, but we anticipate that it will involve the same positive results for everyone involved. New teachers wishing to join the collaboration team are aware that everyone is expected to bring new perspectives to the meetings, where everyone learns from each other.

References

Allen, S. (1989.) *Meeting of minds: The complete scripts, with illustrations, of the amazingly successful PBS-TV series, first series*. Buffalo, NY: Prometheus Books.

DuFour, R., & Eaker, R. (1998.) *Professional learning communities at work: Best practices for enhancing student achievement*. Bloomington, IN: Solution Tree Press.

Duling, G. A. (1984.) *Creative problem-solving for the fourth little pig*. Buffalo, NY: DOK Publishers.

Leonard, L., & Leonard, P. (2003). The continuing trouble with collaboration: Teachers talk. *Current Issues in Education, 6*(15). Retrieved from https://cie.asu.edu/ojs/index.php/cieatasu/article/view/1615

Chapter 66

Helping Your Students Take the Challenge

by Meg Strnat

Nothing's better than a wish that comes true, right? I recently won a grant that paid the publishing costs for a book of my train poems. When the moment arrived when I had to push the "submit" button for 175 copies of the book, self-doubt consumed me. Questions began to flow. Who am I to judge the quality of my poems? What if curators of the local museum I promised copies of the book to said they weren't interested in displaying the books now? I even committed to sharing this book in a presentation to all of the teachers of the gifted in my district and at a statewide conference. What was I thinking? This book that I looked forward to writing suddenly had the potential to undermine my reputation with fellow teachers. The fun ends when one is on the defensive. Well, maybe not.

One of my favorite children's books comes to mind: *A Bird About to Sing* by Laura Nyman Montenegro (Houghton Mifflin, 2003). The main character is a little girl, Natalie, who revels in her poetry. Natalie's poetry teacher invites Natalie to read one of her poems at a local poetry reading. The little girl freezes when it's her turn to read saying, "I feel like a bird who's lost its voice, and like a bird I wish to fly far, far away. . . ." Haven't we all been there? The real pleasure came when Natalie truly challenged herself and succeeded in an area in which she might fail.

Teachers of the Gifted:
The World's True Superheroes

It's a bird...
It's a plane...
It's THE GIFTED TEACHER!

"Smart Cookies" by Bess Wilson

The fear I felt when I realized I might fail helped me recognize that I subject my gifted students to possible failure on a daily basis. I push my students to do their best with realistic goals. But does the fact that I view the goals as realistic provide reassurance to my students?

Tips to Foster Confident Students

I have found many ways to foster confidence in the students seated before me. I have found that when I provide the appropriate goal-setting techniques, praise of work, scaffolding, and positive and constructive feedback on a regular basis, each student becomes more self-confident.

1. **Goals must be realistic.** Setting realistic goals can pose a challenge. Keep in mind that goals need to be modified for each student as skill and concept mastery will vary. I use S.M.A.R.T. goals (http://www. topachievement.com/smart.html) that are specific, measureable, attainable, realistic, and timely. When working on goal setting with a group of students, the dynamics of the cohort can become a concern, as a mixture of learning styles and personalities are presented. Lessons found in the text *Comprehension and Collaboration: Inquiry Circles in Action* (Heinemann, 2009) can be helpful when working with more than one student.

2. **Students must believe that the goals are realistic.** Messages to the students must be clear. Stating, "I wouldn't ask you to do this if I didn't think you could do it" is a great place to start. Sharing the theme of the value of taking risks can be accomplished through reading aloud the texts *A Bird About to Sing* and *Love That Dog* by Sharon Creech (Scholastic, 2001).

3. **Personalized praise is vital for student success.** Students may have tested into a self-contained class for the gifted, but that does not mean they are gifted or confident in every way. When meeting with students individually or in small groups, the first focus should be on what each student does well. General praise should be replaced with positive

comments about specific attempts to use and master new skills and concepts. Praise is important even if a child fails in the attempt of a new skill, or misuses the skill. Celebrate the use of new skills and recognize that misuse, and at times overuse, is part of the learning process. Keep track of student progress in reaction to positive praise. Recall that mastery of the skill is the goal.

4. **Scaffolding needs to be quick and specific.** Conferencing with students should typically last no more than 5 minutes. At the end of each conference, students should know what the skill is and how to employ and practice it. The goal is to model through demonstration or provide an example for them to reflect on. Scheduling a time to meet again during an upcoming class is necessary to verify success with the skill. If mastery has occurred, try to introduce a new skill.

5. **Know the limits of feedback.** Criticism and comments made about skill development and work can make or break a student's growth. It is up to the educator to gauge the student's current level and projected level of mastery. Feedback should always be constructive so that an individual student sees a level of success each time he or she attempts a task.

An Example: One Student's Story

One year a student transferred into my class at the midpoint. The rest of the students were wrapping up a short-story project, so I asked the student to free write as an informal assessment. He watched as the other students hung their stories on the bulletin board, and I could tell he was envious. I asked if he wanted to expand one of his entries into a short story, and he was delighted. We set a series of small realistic goals and worked toward mastering the skills that my other students had developed over the school year, which he missed out on. During short meeting times and the submission of writing samples, the student and I identified several easy ways to improve his writing skills in a dramatic way. In only one week he was comfortable with many of the techniques.

I could see the student's pleasure with the published version of his story from a smile that reached his eyes. I asked him if he wanted to staple it on the bulletin board, and suddenly he was squirming. I recalled now just how he was feeling, that reluctance to expose himself to criticism from peers. I told him that it would be a shame if others didn't see his story, but that it was up to him. He hesitated. Then he picked up the stapler and took the risk.

In this student's experience, the child took a risk not only then, but every time he met during a conference and when attempting to implement new skills. Educators are helpful in providing direction, but ultimately the student needs to make all decisions. In creating a classroom that fosters goal setting, praise of work, scaffolding, and positive and constructive feedback, students learn to value their success, as in the end, it is their work. Help them take the challenge!

Chapter 67

Getting Excited About Learning

Promoting Passion Among Gifted Youth

by Jennifer A. Fredricks, Kate E. Flanagan, and Corinne J. Alfeld

In our article "Developing and Fostering Passion in Academic and Nonacademic Domains" (Fredricks, Alfeld, & Eccles, 2009), we describe findings from interviews we conducted with gifted and talented adolescents. These students were part of a larger study of adolescent development and were selected because they were in a gifted program or because they were highly involved and successful in a nonacademic domain, such as sports or the arts. We interviewed 25 youth who were in gifted programs when they were in elementary school about their experiences growing up gifted. We also interviewed 41 high school youth who had demonstrated high ability and involvement in athletics or the arts during elementary school. We examined these interviews for evidence of passion, or a qualitative difference in the way the youth talked about their involvement in school or in their talent domain. Youth whom we rated as passionate talked about wanting to participate in the activity all of the time, getting completely wrapped up in the activity, persevering in the face of challenge, experiencing positive emotions such as excitement and joy, and defining themselves in terms of their involvement in that activity.

We had expected to find evidence of passion in both groups of participants. However, there was little evidence of passion among the gifted youth. This finding was both unexpected and troubling, especially because these youth were highly able and demonstrated high achievement (defined as a grade point average over 3.7). Although we were able to rate 13 out of 41 of the youth in sports and arts as passionate, we could not identify any gifted youth who talked with the same level of passion about their schoolwork. Instead, many of the gifted students had difficulty identifying aspects of school that interested or excited them. Here we share what some of these gifted youth said about their school experiences, why we think they exhibited so little passion, and some suggestions for ways that teachers and schools can foster excitement and passion among gifted youth.

Lack of Challenge in the Classroom

We found little evidence of positive affect toward school among the gifted youth. Instead, many of the students talked about feeling bored and unchallenged in school. We saw evidence of this boredom and frustration stemming from the structure of the classrooms and curriculum. Many of the gifted students felt that what they were learning in school had little relevance to the real world or their lives. A female taking a year off of college describes the problems with schools:

> There are so many things school can do to help kids think that learning was fun. I think kids are naturally inclined to want to learn, but it kind of gets killed off slowly, through school. If they could just have teachers who wanted to be there . . . and more dedicated stuff for each kid . . . and see what each person is interested in . . . they don't treat you like a real person.

Some of the gifted participants did talk more positively about interests outside of school such as writing poetry, learning history, or making films. For example, a male in college talked about his outside interests:

> I watch the history channel constantly. I'm a history junkie . . . I'll go run out and get an encyclopedia and just soak it all up and I'll read so much.

However, in these cases there appeared to be little attempt by either the teachers or students to connect these interests to the school curriculum.

Maintaining the "Smart" Image

One thing that did appear to motivate these youth was getting good grades and keeping up the image as the "smart" kid. However, they seemed more concerned about looking smart then about learning or mastering new skills. Prior research suggests this emphasis on performance is not the most optimal or adaptive form of motivation. The following quotes from two gifted students in our study illustrate this point.

> I don't think I was always that interested (in school), but I think I still did my schoolwork because I was the kind of person that had, like I had to get it done, and then I had to do it well. (Female taking a year off of college)

> I've always had good grades . . . I know looking at my grades doesn't tell very much about me or how I am as a person or a student . . . but I know that a lot of time that is what people think because that's all they have to go on . . . so you may as well make that look good. (Female in college)

Many of the youth talked about the stress of living up to expectations imposed by both themselves and others. Maintaining the image of the smart kid appeared to have a particularly negative impact on the emotional and academic adjustment of some of the female youth. In fact, four females in our sample had decided to take time off from college as they questioned their identity and experienced disillusionment with their educational experience.

Although many participants felt pressure to maintain an image as smart, others talked about how their academic interests were not supported by their typical peers and that it was not cool to be perceived as gifted or passionate about learning. For example, a female in college described her peers:

> Everyone had their cliques set and then I was this new, little dorky kid, and I was made fun of the first day of school for reading on my own. . . . They totally made fun of me, and so I never brought a book to school again until like senior year.

The gifted students talked most negatively about their regular classrooms, where they felt that the teachers had to water down the curriculum and cater instruction to typical students. A common frustration expressed was that some of the teachers and other students in their classes lacked enthusiasm and did not care about learning. Two students even talked about being able to sleep through these classes and still be successful. The following quotes express the feelings held by many of the gifted youth about their regular classrooms.

> I felt like I was 20 times smarter than everyone! You can always tell when you're in an easier class . . . a required class. (Female starting college)

> And those (required) classes were all insufferable, they were just horrible. We spent one day learning about the industrial revolution by coloring in little squares on pieces of paper and passing it to the left so that we could understand what it was like to work on assembly line. (Male in college)

GT Classes: A Safe Haven

In contrast to the regular classroom setting, the youth talked more positively about their gifted programs and advanced classes. In these classes, they felt they had more opportunities to work on challenging and varied tasks and had greater opportunities to make choices about what to work on. Prior research referenced in the *Gifted Child Quarterly* article suggests that challenge, variety, and autonomy are related to increased motivation.

Another reason these youth had more positive affect in these classes is that they were around other students of similar ability who cared about learning. A female taking a year off of college talked about the more positive social environment in gifted programs.

> I felt, more like I belonged when I was in (gifted programs) during school because you didn't have to feel like you were showing off or anything like that. You didn't have to feel limited there. It's like you're real smart but the other kids are real smart too, so you felt like you were more on level with them.

Many of the youth also talked about finding a more positive social environment in college than they had experienced in high school. They felt it was easier in college to meet intellectually engaged peers and find a group where their academic interests were both supported and encouraged. Creating a positive social environment for gifted students is critical for many reasons, especially for the development of passion. If being smart or showing excitement about learning draws negative reactions from peers, passion will likely be hidden and may ultimately disappear.

In contrast to the negative portrayal of school from the gifted students, many of the youth we interviewed in sports and the arts talked with excitement about their activity, how they wanted to do it all of the time, and how important it was to their identity. They talked about being supported and encouraged by teachers and peers, having opportunities to make choices, and receiving public recognition for their ability and accomplishments. In contrast, gifted youth did not often feel supported by teachers and peers. They also were given fewer choices and less frequent and positive recognition for their academic talents. This raises an important point about what we can learn from these contexts that can be realistically applied to the school setting.

Classroom Strategies That Foster Passion

Teachers play an important role in identifying students who appear bored or off task. Gifted students in particular, especially in classes with unchallenging curricula, are often at risk for becoming distant or mislabeled. Not only does this intellectual disengagement impede the development of passion, but it can also lead to poor grades and underachievement in which a student's actual level of performance is far below his or her potential.

To protect against boredom, teachers should ask themselves if there are times during the day when these students are more excited and engaged and what is it about that context that is changing their affect and level of involvement. Teachers can also try to discover students' individual interests, and ask their students questions about their hobbies and extracurricular activities. As we discovered in the interviews, some of the gifted students showed areas of high interest outside of school. By asking about these interests, teachers can use this information to help create real-world connections to academic materials. In addition, teachers can incorporate open-ended activities that allow youth to explore their interests through the curriculum.

For example, a female taking a year off from college suggested:

> There should be more emphasis on real life experience. Like you could have an apprenticeship with people, I mean something more interesting than just the same classes for 180 days.

Whenever feasible, it is important to give gifted students real opportunities to make choices about what they work on and how they complete tasks. For example, instead of assigning a final paper, teachers could offer students alternative choices such as writing and performing a brief play, developing a children's book, offering a multimedia presentation, or designing a "free choice" idea in which students work with the teacher to find a unique way to show that they have mastered the material. Although choice is helpful for all students, gifted students may particularly benefit from the opportunity to use creativity in demonstrating mastery of the curriculum. Prior research suggests that gifted youth prefer more unstructured and flexible assignments, as opposed to activities selected by the teacher, and this may be one way to foster passion in the classroom.

Project-based learning is one instructional strategy that combines these suggestions and may be particularly beneficial for gifted youth. This instructional approach is learner centered, less structured and more flexible, and encourages autonomous thinking. In these instructional environments, students either work individually or in teams over a period of time on a cognitively complex and real-world problem. They choose a driving question to investigate, which culminates in a personally meaningful and authentic product, presentation, or performance.

The social environment plays an important role in the development of passion in the classroom. Excitement for learning is contagious. Teachers can model passion by demonstrating their enthusiasm for learning and sharing examples of their own passions with their students, which may reduce the stigma associated with being smart or passionate. Teachers should also encourage students to take intellectual risks in the classroom by emphasizing individual learning and improvement over performance whenever possible. It is important to provide students with frequent, preferably immediate feedback on their growth and improvement. For example, several assessments over the course of a semester or unit will help students track their own progress.

Our findings also underscore the significant benefits of separate and differentiated instruction by ability. Gifted students describe more positive experiences in their advanced classes and gifted programs where they felt they were more likely to be supported by peers of similar ability and interest, where they felt adequately challenged, and where there were opportunities to work on varied and more cognitively complex tasks. Although there is some concern that separate instruction is not egalitarian, the results of our interviews demonstrate the negative consequences of neglecting both the academic and social needs of gifted youth. All students deserve to be challenged at school, and it appears that gifted programs are more likely to be structured in a way to challenge these students and support the development of passion. Furthermore, such programs appeared to largely protect against the negative labeling and peer reactions associated with being gifted or passionate at school.

In summary, the gifted youth in our sample have high ability and began school with high interest and excitement for learning. Unfortunately, this passion for learning appears to have been undermined by their overall school experiences. Instead, these youth seem to be motivated primarily by appearing smart and demonstrating their ability relative to their classmates, and some seem to have lost motivation entirely. It is unfortunate that so many of our young people, especially those with high potential, end up disillusioned with school and are put at risk for underachievement. Findings from our study suggest that the school context may play a large part in undeveloped passion among gifted youth. Educators need to pay more attention to the specific academic needs of gifted students and provide educational environments in which they can thrive intellectually and pursue their interests passionately.

Reference

Fredricks, J. A., Alfeld, C., & Eccles, J. (2009). Developing and fostering passion in academic and nonacademic domains. *Gifted Child Quarterly, 54,* 18–30.

Section IV: Support for Parents

Chapter 68

Note to Teachers

A Few Pointers for Parents

by Bob Schultz

As the school year winds back up again, I thought it would be thought provoking to provide teachers (and parents) with some input from GT kids about giftedness. The points that follow come from teens and are based on responses to questionnaires and personal interviews.

Q: What advice would you give to parents of a student who has just been identified as gifted/talented?

A: "Nothing changes. Your child hasn't mysteriously turned into some whiz kid overnight. They will still want to play the same way, do the same activities, and are going to be as goofy as regular. Enjoy them for who they are." (Cherie, 13 years old)

"Start to get information. Most people get identified, but don't know that this means the emotional side of life is just as important as the academic side. It's time to take action to know more . . . a whole lot more." (James, 14 years old)

"Start asking questions. Is there a special program or class? Who is in charge of it? Is there a parent group for GT families? Do GT kids and their families get together and do things?" (Sandy, 13 years old)

Q: What do you think is the most important thing that parents do not know about being a gifted kid?

A: "There is a lot of pressure on kids who are GT. They are expected to know everything by everyone at school. Most GT kids put a lot of pressure on themselves since they really don't know what being GT is really all about." (Brenda, 14 years old)

"Stress. Most GT kids are expected to do more. This includes more work in regular classes, depth in answers, and helping other kids who don't understand by tutoring. This stress is really painful." (Abigail, 14 years old)

Q: What do you wish parents would say to GT kids?

A: "I love you for who you are, not what other people expect you to do and be." (Tawnie, 14 years old)

"Go ahead, make mistakes. Fall down, trip up. Make a mess. Wallow around and see what happens. Life is supposed to be explored and lived based on your terms. Try something new and see what happens. Don't always try to do your best—sometimes good enough is good enough!" (Dale, 14 years old)

"It's just a label. This doesn't make you better than other people. It shows you are different and that you need different things to be happy and content." (Debbie, 13 years old)

Q: What do you wish parents would do with their GT kids?

A: "Try new things and grow together in adventures. Read with me and share the story. Help me try to overcome my fears, and maybe yours too." (Val, 13 years old)

"Teach me how to get other people to take me seriously. I'm tired of being the cute little kid with the big ideas. I want to turn some of these ideas into reality and I need your help to do it." (Elizabeth, 12 years old)

"Help your GT kid feel like a regular human being. Trying to be best or perfect only paralyzes us and we stop taking chances out of fear." (Francis, 14 years old)

Much of my life's work has been focused on learning about giftedness from the perspective of children and teens bearing the label. They have not often had their voices heard over the "noise" of the experts and adults around them.

Take the time to listen to your students and your children. They hold the key to understanding the social and emotional side of giftedness that guides the growth and development that is key to becoming a responsible and responsive adult.

In these troubled times of program cutting and accountability, gifted and talented students are our only chance of overcoming the burden of our myopic society, for they tend to see more broadly and deeply into issues that plague our society. As Alysha (13) shared, "If we [GT kids] are the future, how come everyone seems to tell us what to do, but no one ever seems to listen?" Let's start by listening!

Chapter 69

We're Going Where?

Providing Rich Learning Experiences
Through Family Enrichment Activities

by Katherine B. Brown and Diane J. Bresson

It is a cool, clear February evening. Johan, a fourth grader, reads through his library book about Saturn for the eighth time as he and his mother ride the bus through town. They reach the college campus, and the bus stops near the Physics and Astronomy Building. Johan's teacher has told their class that there are a number of telescopes on the roof of this building through which they will have the chance to see the wonders of space close-up. Johan jumps out of the bus, barely able to control his excitement. With his eyes fixed on the sky, Johan wonders what he will see tonight. Will he be able to see his favorite planet? What would the moon look like? Could he see other galaxies?

He arrives at the observatory just in time to be greeted by his teacher and a number of other classmates and their families. Throughout the evening, Johan and the other families from his class soak up the information from the astronomer. Some of the information they had already heard from their teacher in class, but somehow it takes on new meaning under the star-filled sky. The highlight of Johan's night is when he gets a turn to gaze through the enormous 24" telescope, keying in on Saturn. When Johan gets back to school, he is more passionate than ever about the wonders of space.

An Underserved Student

Johan, a minority student of low socioeconomic background, displays many characteristics traditionally related to giftedness such as being highly inquisitive, having a fluent vocabulary, and possessing the ability to catch on to new topics very quickly. Johan's mother sees how smart he is and desires to expose her son to more experiences outside of the classroom. However, she does not know where she can take him for rich experiences on a very limited budget.

Although Johan displays gifted characteristics, he has not been identified based on the traditional measures of intelligence and achievement used in a majority of schools/school systems. His teacher attempts to differentiate for Johan within the classroom, but feels that he would benefit greatly from additional services. She fears that underachievement may be in Johan's future if he is not exposed to a challenging and engaging curriculum, but wonders how much more she can help Johan in the regular education classroom.

Many teachers have students like Johan in their classroom. These high-ability students from culturally diverse populations or of low socioeconomic status demonstrate giftedness, but are unable to receive gifted services due to their inability to succeed on standardized or normed tests, or by a general lack of access to gifted and talented services. In many cases, these students are lacking the experiences or background knowledge necessary to achieve on traditional measures. Rather than the typical "drill and kill" strategy, which has been found ineffective in engaging students from low socioeconomic backgrounds, teachers must find ways to provide enriched learning experiences that will lead to increased achievement (Hébert, 2002).

Unfortunately, many schools no longer organize field trips due to tough economic times (Polochanin, 2008). However, family enrichment activities allow for teachers to plan hands-on learning for their students within the community without having to ask the school system or families for money.

Importance of Parent Involvement

Although many factors influence student achievement, parental involvement plays an important role in providing students with experiences that will enhance their learning potential (Ford & Harris, 1999). Children whose families are involved in their learning tend to achieve higher grades and scores on standardized tests, take more academically rigorous courses, have better attendance, earn more credits, enroll in postsecondary programs after successfully graduating from high school, and avoid harmful activities such as alcohol use and violence (Mapp, 2004).

Family enrichment activities are an innovative way to involve families in the school environment and to expose them to rich learning experiences in the community. These activities are voluntary excursions that teachers can offer to families outside of school in order to enhance the learning that is happening within the classroom. In a nutshell, teachers invite students and their parents to meet them at special locations within the local community, including nature centers, art museums, symphonies, or as in Johan's case, an observatory. These enrichment activities seek to provide families with a connection to the child's education and enrich his or her learning through community resources during time away from the classroom.

Planning Family Enrichment Activities, AKA "Field Trips for Families"

Teachers can offer family enrichment activities at a variety of intervals. Some teachers offer them as frequently as every month, while others offer opportunities just twice a year. When planning, it is important to keep several things in mind about the activities.

1. Fees. Admission should either be free or available at minimal cost to ensure the highest participation.

A quick online search or a phone call to the local Chamber of Commerce can help develop a list of free community resources. Teachers can also delve into travel books written about their city, call their local parks and recreation departments, or contact the community convention and visitor's bureau for ideas.

2. Location in close proximity to the school is crucial. Some families will have difficulty traveling long distances, assuming they can travel at all. In order to make these trips accessible to all families, activities should be located no farther than 30 minutes away and, if possible, located on a public transit route. Easy-to-read directions should be given to all. Teachers could also encourage families to carpool.

3. Student interest should direct activities. Providing families with community resources from various disciplines not only increases student knowledge about numerous topics, but also gives students a sampling of interest in areas they may not previously have been aware of. Many of the activities will be preplanned by teachers at the beginning of the school year; however, the teacher may choose to leave a few activities open for experiences based solely on student interest.

4. Survey your population. An appreciation for cultural awareness can only lead to an accepting classroom environment. Allow students to take pride in their culture and develop a positive mindset that can continue throughout the school year.

5. Take note of state and national standards whenever possible. Enrichment activities can promote meaningful learning experiences when related to the curriculum, thereby deepening their knowledge of and interest in a content area.

The Impact

On a sunny morning, Johan, his friend, Ana, and their parents are carpooling to a farm located about 15 minutes away from their school. The farm contains a plantation home, a graveyard with tombstones dating back to the early nineteenth century, and a cotton gin. The kids have been studying the life of Americans in the 1800s and chat in the backseat in anticipation of what they will experience today. In the front seat, the parents discuss the amazing places they have visited lately, which they never realized existed.

Like many of his classmates, Johan's interests have grown, his love of learning has been ignited, and his experiences have been deepened, all because of a teacher who showed her students the possibilities for learning right in their own backyard. Family enrichment activities provide students with rich learning experiences, and help to promote a classroom of acceptance and learning. Parents and their children are able to spend time together in a positive atmosphere outside of the traditional classroom. Most importantly, relationships are strengthened on all levels: between parents and children, teachers and parents, teachers and students, and students and their peers.

Getting Started: 20 Ideas for Family Enrichment Activities

The local newspaper is a great place to start in finding the resources below.

▸   Appreciate diversity by visiting a culture fair.

- ▸ Visit an art museum or gallery.
- ▸ Experience a different era by visiting a historical home.
- ▸ Honor great Americans through historic sites and statues.
- ▸ Have a reading day in a local park.
- ▸ Discover the past with a visit to a historic cemetery.
- ▸ Listen to beautiful music at a community symphony.
- ▸ Delight in the drama of a play or puppet show.
- ▸ Learn about plants at a state or local botanical garden.
- ▸ Explore the wilderness at a state or national park.
- ▸ Dive under the sea at a local aquarium or aquatic center.
- ▸ Become stargazers at an observatory.
- ▸ Find out where food comes from by visiting a farm or an orchard.
- ▸ Learn about local or state government with a tour of government buildings.
- ▸ Help others by volunteering as a class to work at a food bank or soup kitchen.
- ▸ Encourage lifelong learning with a trip to a library.
- ▸ Learn about conservation through a class stream cleanup.
- ▸ Create a scavenger hunt throughout your town to showcase some student hotspots.
- ▸ Attend a lecture at a local university or community event.

References

Ford, D. Y., & Harris III, J. J. (1999). *Multicultural gifted education*. New York, NY: Teacher's College Press.

Hébert, T. P. (2002). Educating gifted children from low socioeconomic backgrounds: Creating visions of a hopeful future. *Exceptionality, 10,* 127–138.

Mapp, K. L. (2004). Family engagement. In J. Smink & F. P. Schargel (Eds.), *Helping students graduate: A strategic approach to dropout prevention.* Larchmont, NY: Eye on Education.

Polochanin, D. (2008, March 25). The disappearing field trip. *Education Week,* 25.

PART / IV

Special Populations

by Joy Lawson Davis

As a nation, we represent more racially and culturally diverse citizens than any other country, worldwide. Our students enter our schools from a wide range of cultural groups, representing families from all of the continents in the world. Additionally, our public schools serve an increasing number of nontraditional families than ever before in our history—families that are multigenerational in one household, families whose first language may not be English, families headed by a single mother or father, and in some cases, single gender couples. Economic conditions have also impacted our school communities and today, 51% of students attending public schools come from low-income families. Taken together, these factors compel us as a field to provide due diligence and pay closer attention to gifted students among these varied and multiple groups to ensure that access is provided to all high-ability and gifted students. Gifted services are generally provided in public schools for students who need academic services above and beyond that provided in the regular classroom. Schools create identification models to identify and provide access to coursework, innovative classroom settings, opportunities for critical thinking, problem solving, and career exploration that aptly fit with their exceptional learning capacities and potential in numerous disciplines, from mathematics to the arts and humanities.

Teaching for High Potential's special populations columns, as well as numerous featured articles over the years, have been used to draw attention to the needs of learners who are culturally and linguistically diverse, are from low-income families or from urban and rural areas, are twice-exceptional, or are members of the LGBTQ community. The articles share how educators can adapt teaching and learning to meet intellectual, affective and academic strengths and needs of special populations. Increasingly, classroom teachers and school administrators are depending upon content area experts in the field to share best practices that they may utilize daily that will help them reach and improve outcomes for *all* gifted learners. We are fortunate in our field that higher education programs are expanding nationwide, creating a larger pool of individuals who can focus attention on how best to reach and teach all gifted learners. As we enter a new era of social movements addressing bias and overt discrimination against people based upon their group membership, we recognize that gifted students from all walks of life will become leaders and members within social justice movements. As such, teachers themselves must examine how they can create curriculum models that teach leadership and nurture the need that some gifted students have to serve their communities.

In sum, *THP* is a true gem to educators who work with gifted children. The teacher-friendly format and emphasis on research-based resources creates an important tool for the field of gifted education. As the standard bearer for all gifted learners, NAGC is committed to sharing resources of the highest caliber and those that are most relevant to the wide range of student populations that we serve across the nation, and *THP* is an excellent tool to help facilitate sharing these resources.

Section I: Cultural Diversity

Chapter 70

Helping Gifted Culturally Diverse Students Cope With Socio-Emotional Concerns

by Chin-Wen Lee

It goes without saying that gifted students have affective needs that are different from those of regular students. Silverman (1993) explained, "cognitive complexity gives rise to emotional depth," and as a result, gifted students "not only *think* differently from their peers, they also *feel* differently" (p. 3). There are several reasons why the socio-emotional development of the gifted needs to be intentionally, purposefully, and proactively nurtured. The most critical reason is that cognitive development and social and emotional development are inseparable. Findings from brain research tell us: (a) emotion has an impact on the learning process, (b) social-emotional functions can facilitate or impede the cognitive processes, and (c) we remember what we have learned better and longer when emotion is a part of our learning process (Clark, 2013). Therefore, both cognitive and social and emotional development should be addressed in any kind of educational delivery.

In this day and age, when developing or implementing an affective curriculum, one cannot overlook the impact of the changing demographics of a population. Cross (2011) stated, "I believe that the changing demographic of people in the United States has had an important impact on gifted education over the past 20 years or so" (p. 219). Although a nationally changing demographic may not reflect a change in gifted education populations, the discussion on promoting gifted, culturally diverse students' social-emotional well-being has not diminished. Ford (2004) delineated the needs of students who are gifted and culturally diverse (Figure 70.1). The importance of ethnic identity toward self-concept can be seen in the *Diverse* circle. For gifted African Americans, ethnic identity has a prominent impact on achievement and attitudes toward school. Moreover, self-concept and cultural identity are also considered as crucial issues in Asian Americans, Native Americans, and Hispanic Americans (Ford & Harris, 1999).

A Socio-Emotional Conceptual Model

Conceptual models are graphical representations of complex ideas that help us visualize and understand key factors of complex relationships. The purpose of developing a conceptual model for helping gifted, culturally diverse students cope with socio-emotional concerns (Figure 70.2) is to help teachers and counselors take into consideration the factors that are involved in the lives of the students that they serve when designing appropriate educational interventions. This model has three components. It begins with five environmental factors— *culture, home, self, school,* and *peers.* These factors influence the *10 things to boost performance,* a list of positive intervention strategies that can be incorporated in the classroom. Finally, the *goals of affective and supportive services* present practical outcomes that serve as a baseline for intervention. It is important to note that although this model provides generalizations that help guide instruction and counseling support, any such model must be modified to take into account the specific needs and cultural differences of the students in the classroom.

A Template for Designing
Learning Opportunities

Prevention Level

Objective: Develop Positive Cultural Identities (applicable to *all* students)
Activity: Read the Biographical Samples: Maya Lin (artist, architectural designer); Jeremy Lin (athlete)

Suggested Learning Opportunities: Teamwork, Intuition and integration, Visual thinking, Creative expression

Description:

- The models provided here are Americans of Chinese descent. One is female and the other is male.
- This activity is expected to be a group project.

1. Provide a template and questions for students to work on this project (adapted from Avery & VanTassel-Baska, 2013, p. 106):
   a. Introduction
      i. Where did he or she grow up and how did his or her upbringing contribute to the direction she or he took in his or her career?
      ii. What achievement launched his or her career and how old was he or she at the time?

   b. What can we learn from him or her?
      i. To what extent did time, place, and circumstances impact his or her ability to succeed?
      ii. In what ways if any has his or her family's Chinese heritage influenced his or her achievement?

   c. What if . . .
      i. Identify one or more barriers that he or she encountered on his or her way to success.
      ii. What if he or she did not overcome these challenges?
      iii. What if he or she had more support at that time?

2. Encourage students to demonstrate their project in both a PowerPoint/video/alternative and oral presentation.
3. Arrange a time for feedback and discussion/evaluation of the presentation.

An Example of Implementation

As previously stated, the convergence of cultural diversity, gifted characteristics, and socio-emotional concerns can be complex. There are several

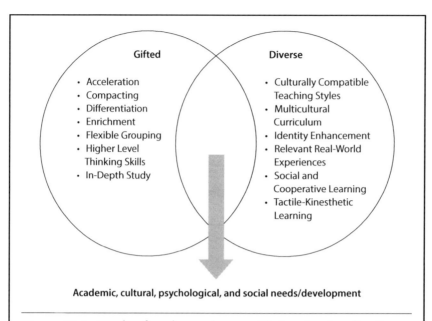

Figure 70.1. Needs of students who are gifted and culturally diverse. Adapted from "Curriculum and Instruction for Culturally Diverse Gifted Learners" by D. Y Ford, in *In Search of the Dream: Designing Schools and Classrooms That Work for High Potential Students From Diverse Cultural Backgrounds* (p. 34), by C. A. Tomlinson, D. Y. Ford, S. M. Reis, C. J. Briggs, and C. A. Strickland, 2004, Washington, DC: National Association for Gifted Children. Copyright 2004 by National Association for Gifted Children. Adapted with permission.

approaches an educator may take to implement the model. Take differentiation as an example. In planning curriculum, teachers could differentiate for:

▶ **Content:** use advanced and complex concepts in discussing cultural identity;

▶ **Process:** use acceleration or compacting in multicultural education;

▶ **Product:** students share their learning of cultural identity with a real audience; and

▶ **Learning environment:** value students' learning styles and have high expectations of them.

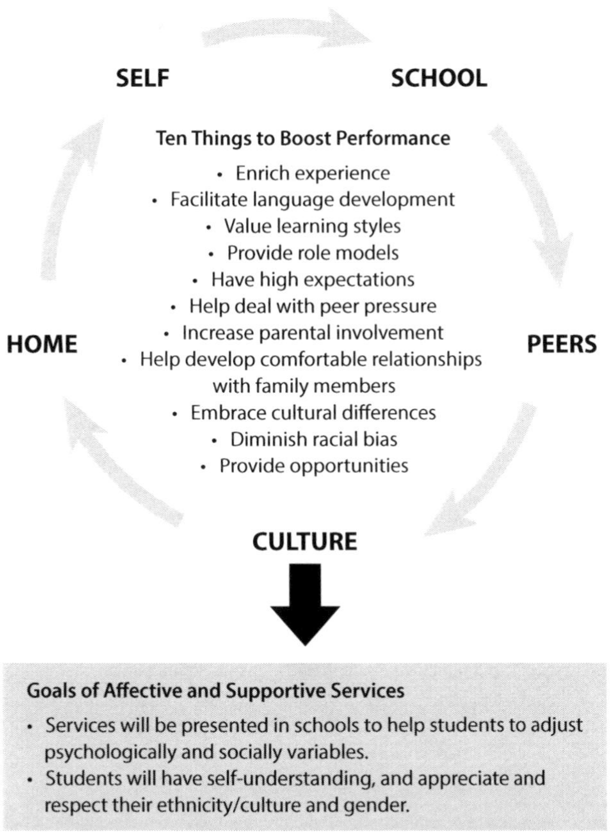

SELF   **SCHOOL**

Ten Things to Boost Performance
- Enrich experience
- Facilitate language development
- Value learning styles
- Provide role models
- Have high expectations
- Help deal with peer pressure
- Increase parental involvement
- Help develop comfortable relationships with family members
- Embrace cultural differences
- Diminish racial bias
- Provide opportunities

HOME   **PEERS**

CULTURE

Goals of Affective and Supportive Services
- Services will be presented in schools to help students to adjust psychologically and socially variables.
- Students will have self-understanding, and appreciate and respect their ethnicity/culture and gender.

Figure 70.2. A conceptual model for helping gifted, culturally diverse students cope with socio-emotional concerns.

Intervention: Dealing With Family Pressures

Activity (I): Identify Different Expectations

Suggested Learning Opportunities: Intuition and integration, Verbal and written expression of feelings

Description:

- Main message: Many family pressures come from family members' expectations. The three activities under this topic, Dealing With Family Pressures, provide opportunities for students and their families to face the potential conflict.
- Students are encouraged to ask their parents for clarification about the parents' expectations for the student's future.
- Directions for students:
  - ▷ Identify your expectations that are different from your parents'.
  - ▷ Depict or deliberate expectations of both sides.
  - ▷ Compare and contrast these expectations.
  - ▷ Think: What if I follow my parents' directions? What if I insist on achieving my goals?

Activity (II): Let's Have a Talk

Suggested Learning Opportunities: Verbal and written expression of feelings

Description:

- Main message: Communication is important!
- Encourage students to present their ideas to their parents and/or other family members and collect feedback from the audience.
- It is extremely important for teachers to bear in mind that there are more indirect interactions within a Chinese family. It is not easy for parents and children to sit down and have a conversation about their expectations. Alternatives must be provided, such as to exchange a conversation log. Also, parents' proficiency in English should be taken into consideration when guiding students to complete this activity.
- Directions for students:
  - ▷ Present your ideas (completed in the previous activity) to your parents and/or other family elders. (Written or spoken in Chinese when necessary.)

    ▷   Ask *Why*: Why do you think this (expectation) is important to me?

    ▷   Write down your audience's answers and feedback and bring this outcome to the discussion group.

Activity (III): So What?

Suggested Learning Opportunities: Verbal and written expression of feelings

Description:

- The use of a discussion group serves as a platform for students to report to their family members' feedback and to share their thoughts on it.
- No judgment or comment should be given by the discussion facilitator.
- Directions for students:
  - ▷ Review *What if* questions in Activity (I). Any new ideas?
  - ▷ Review family members' feedback in Activity (II). Any new ideas?
  - ▷ How can I embrace or gain their support?

Another example involves planning and delivering prevention and intervention activities, where teachers can tailor their lesson plans to target the cultural populations in their classrooms. Prevention activities should be proactive with the purpose of developing positive cultural identity. Conversely, intervention activities are reactive with the objective toward helping students develop strategies to cope with pressures related to home, school, and their peers (Peterson, 2009). The four suggested learning opportunities are examples for a curricular framework template. These examples of prevention intervention activities are targeted toward Asian-American students in a high school setting.

Conclusion

Educators wishing to help gifted, culturally diverse students cope with socio-emotional concerns, can develop academic strategies and affective curricular experiences that support their students. Students exposed to this type of learning will find a path that fulfills their academic, cultural, psychological, and social development. By keeping culturally diverse students' social and emotional needs at the forefront of curricular decisions, educators can find success in providing appropriate, targeted, and comprehensive personalized services.

References

Avery, L. D., & VanTassel-Baska, J. (2013). *Changing tomorrow 3: Leadership curriculum for high-ability high school students*. Waco, TX: Prufrock Press.

Clark, B. (2013). *Growing up gifted: Developing the potential of children at home* (8th ed.). Upper Saddle River, NJ: Pearson.

Cross, T. L. (2011). *On the social and emotional lives of gifted children* (4th ed.). Waco, TX: Prufrock Press.

Ford, D. Y. (2004). Curriculum and instruction for culturally diverse gifted learners. In C. A. Tomlinson, D. Y. Ford, S. M. Reis, C. J. Briggs, & C. A. Strickland (Eds.), *In search of the dream: Designing schools and classrooms that work for high potential students from diverse cultural backgrounds* (pp. 33–45). Washington, DC: National Association for Gifted Children.

Ford, D. Y., & Harris, J. J., III. (1999). *Multicultural gifted education*. New York, NY: Teachers College Press.

Peterson, J. S. (2009). Focusing on where they are: A clinical perspective. In J. L. VanTassel-Baska, T. L. Cross, & F. R. Olenchak (Eds.), *Social-emotional curriculum with gifted and talented students* (pp. 193–226). Waco, TX: Prufrock Press.

Silverman, L. K. (1993). The gifted individual. In L. K. Silverman (Ed.), *Counseling the gifted and talented* (pp. 3–28). Denver, CO: Love.

Chapter 71

Our Powers Combined

Meeting the Needs of Multicultural
Gifted Students Through Collaborative
Teaching and Counseling

by Stacie L. Walker

Teachers and counselors are often viewed as completely separate entities within the school. Both groups of educators impact the lives of students daily by providing services, instruction, and guidance to students within the same building. Gifted children and more specifically, multicultural gifted children, have unique characteristics and challenges that should be addressed by everyone in the school building, school counselors and teachers in particular. What better way to impact students than by combining the expertise of counselors and teachers to best meet the needs of our multicultural gifted students?

Awareness

It is critical that educators be knowledgeable about the challenges faced by multiculturally gifted students. Polish psychologist Kazimierz Dabrowski (1964) described some of these challenges as overexcitabilities, heightened sensitivities that gifted children experience daily to varying degrees through psychomotor, sensual, imaginational, intellectual, and emotional attributes. In order to best serve these students, we must first be aware of the way in which these overexcitabilities work within the child and how they may affect their learning expe-

The Gifted School of Fish--
Where every student is "Fin"tastic in his or her own way!

"Smart Cookies" by Bess Wilson

rience, both positively and negatively (Dabrowski, 1964). Educators also should be concerned with the student's self-concept, perfectionism, and under-achievement. Culturally diverse students can bring additional challenges. It is also critical that educators integrate the ideas of family and community, which vary between cultures, when planning curriculum. It also may be necessary to address additional pressures imposed on the student by their cultural community. The objective of teachers and school counselors should be to meet the needs of multicultural gifted students academically, emotionally, personally, and socially, and to do that, they must work together to become multiculturally competent. To ensure this infusion, it is recommended that they try to incorporate as many of the goals outlined in the text *Multicultural Gifted Education* (Ford & Harris, 1998), which includes multicultural knowledge, cultural pluralism, empowerment, educational equity, equal opportunity, and increased self-awareness.

Advocacy

In addition to becoming aware and multiculturally competent, educators must be advocates for multicultural gifted students. Every student comes to school with a story and a unique personal history. It is important for teachers and counselors to be able to identify gifted students in need, particularly those who experience life with heightened sensitivity and culturally diverse students who may be at various stages in their cultural identity development. School counselors need to be actively involved in gifted education (Holcomb-McCoy, 2007), including serving on committees for the identification of gifted students and for curriculum development. School counselors can also advocate on behalf of their culturally diverse students who are often underrepresented in gifted education, by advocating for "identification policies and criteria that make it more likely that a diverse group of students will be represented in gifted programs" (Holcomb-McCoy, p.111). Advocacy is a crucial catalyst for positive change. Educators should be knowledgeable about ways to give their students a voice even when they are or feel unable to speak for themselves. It is also important to be able to advocate for curriculum changes, access to resources, and policy changes.

Approaches/Activities

The following strategies are based on some of the goals outlined in *Multicultural Gifted Education* (Ford & Harris, 1998) and can be used by school counselors and teachers inside and outside of the classroom.

Bibliotherapy. Encouraging students to explore and learn through books by or about culturally diverse populations can encourage and motivate students with stories of or by successful people who may look like them or have had similar experiences. Counselors can use bibliotherapy for self-esteem development, urging students to draw specific examples and connections from the text. Both the counselor and gifted teacher should work together in choosing books that would best meet the needs of their students and would have an impact on several levels. Students could be asked to create a project based on the story to present to the class or the school. In doing so, not only would all students learn about other cultures, but also the multicultural students would develop a sense of pride and heightened sense of cultural awareness and appreciation, including a deeper sense of self.

Service learning. Designing curricular opportunities that acknowledge the high level of emotional sensitivity that gifted students have can be beneficial in complementing the strong sense of community that many multicultural groups possess. Encourage the students to create and implement a service-learning project that speaks to the needs of their communities or school. This would allow them to use their sensitivity for those in need and also give them the opportunity to do work in their own communities. Students feel empowered in knowing that they have done something on their own for others.

Differentiated instruction. Responding to each child's uniqueness, including different learning styles and strengths and personal and cultural differences, is one of the most important ways to address educational equity. Offering alternate assignments for class projects and counseling using different techniques such as play therapy or expressive arts are good examples. Teachers and counselors can collaborate to ensure that there is a sense of cohesiveness in the instruction and services provided to each student.

Incorporate multicultural figures/books/lessons into the curriculum. Exposing multicultural gifted students to people who share their cultural history or who they can identify with in their curriculum can be beneficial to the learning process. Activities such as culture days where students can share their diverse cultures or research and present on a culture other than their own can increase diversity awareness and appreciation. Exploring a multicultural perspective on field trips to museums and parks can also help in increasing diversity awareness and appreciation in the classroom.

Incorporating family maps and family trees. Offer students the opportunity to learn more about themselves through understanding their family and community. Introspective activities can also build self-understanding and cultural awareness. Teachers and counselors can work collaboratively to connect the material being taught in class with the objects and goals of guidance, counseling, and individual counseling sessions.

Teachers and school counselors can play an integral role in the lives of culturally diverse gifted students. By combining the resources, talents, abilities, and wealth of knowledge that both groups of educators possess, the educational experience and lives of these unique students will be greatly enhanced. Awareness, advocacy, and implementation through programs and activities can help build professional relationships to best serve multicultural gifted students. In the words of one of my favorite childhood cartoons, Captain Planet, "with our powers combined" let's serve our multicultural gifted students through collaboration!

References

Dabrowski, K. (1964). *Positive disintegration*. Boston, MA: Little, Brown.

Ford, D. Y., & Harris III, J. J. (1998). *Multicultural gifted education*. New York, NY: Teachers College Press.

Holcomb-McCoy, C. (2007). *School counseling to close the achievement gap*. Thousand Oaks, CA: Corwin Press.

Chapter / 72

Desegregating Gifted Education for Underrepresented Students

Equity Promotes Equality

by Donna Y. Ford and Robert A. King, Jr.

For decades, teachers have bemoaned the underrepresentation of Black students in gifted education, with rightful attention to both the degree and pervasiveness of their low rates of referrals, identification, and placement. More recently, attention has turned to Hispanic students, who are also underrepresented in gifted education. Unfortunately, in virtually every state and school district (nearly 16,000), Black and Hispanic students are glaringly absent in gifted classrooms. An examination of 2009 and 2011 data from the U.S. Department of Education, Office for Civil Rights Data Collection (CRDC) revealed that underrepresentation exists in all states and in the majority of school districts (see 2009 and 2011; https://ocrdata.ed.gov/SpecialReports). More recently, the CRDC report revealed that Black students comprise 19% of public schools but only 10% of students enrolled in gifted programs; they are underrepresented by 47%. Hispanic students comprise 25% of students in public schools but only 16% of students in gifted education, which equates to 36% underrepresentation. Combined, at least half a million deserving African American and Hispanic students are neither identified nor served as gifted.

This article helps teachers to understand representation barriers using an equity rather than equality lens. Using such a lens, the authors provide an equity-based formula to assist teachers (and decision makers) to be more accountable for racial disparities in gifted education. Philosophically, this article is grounded in the infamous court case *Brown v. Board of Education* (1954), which held that segregation is unconstitutional and, accordingly, schools must desegregate. Simply put, Black and Hispanic students are entitled to enroll in schools and programs with their White classmates, and racial discrimination of any kind has no place in school settings. Nationally, Asian and Native American students are not underrepresented in gifted education programs in the 2009 and 2011 CRDC surveys.

Some 60 years since *Brown*, the mandates of this unprecedented decision have not been fulfilled in most school districts and in gifted education classes and programs. Unfortunately, segregation based on race is often the norm and more prevalent than teachers recognize. This article is a clarion call for educators to become more equity-minded in order to recruit and retain more Black and Hispanic students in gifted education (Ford, 2010, 2011, 2013). Equity refers to the qualities of justness and fairness, while equality refers to equal sharing and proportional representation. In other words, equality represents quantity, and equity refers to quality.

Teachers as Gatekeepers

Because teachers often function as the first line in the screening process, they play a major role in access to gifted education. They play a significant role in whether underrepresented groups will have an opportunity to be formally identified as gifted and placed in such programs. Most studies have reported that teachers underrefer Black students for gifted education screening; in half of the studies, Hispanic students are underreferred (see summary by Ford, Grantham, & Whiting, 2008).

Civil Rights and Access to Gifted Education

Discrimination, whether it is intentional or unintentional, entails acting on beliefs that deny Black and Hispanic students the rights and opportunities to which they are legally entitled. In gifted education, the majority of allegations and investigations of racial discrimination (e.g., underreferral, criteria, instruments, policies, and procedures) involve Black students' underrepresentation (Ford, 2011; Ford & Trotman, 2000).

Two antidiscrimination laws are particularly germane to education. Title IX is a portion of the Education Amendments of 1972. It states,

> No person in the United States shall, on the basis of sex, be excluded from participation in, be denied the benefits of, or be subjected to discrimination under any education program or activity receiving Federal financial assistance.

Further, the Civil Rights Act of 1964 outlawed discrimination against racial, ethnic, national, and religious minorities and women. This act ended racial segregation in schools, workplaces, and facilities that serve the general public. However, our field has yet to take these laws into the work that we do when addressing underrepresentation and to consider the implications for failing to do so, which are described next.

Equity Index for Determining Representation Goals

In contemporary America, there is no place for de jure segregation in gifted programs (or Advanced Placement and other advanced academic classes). In the 2013 court ruling *McFadden v. Board of Education for Illinois School District U-46*, U.S. District Court Judge Robert Gettlemen found segregated gifted programs for Hispanic and White students. The district ran one gifted program in grades 4–6 that was almost 100% White and then one that was 100% Hispanic. These Hispanic students were former ELL students (English language learners) and capable of being instructed in English, with little or no support in Spanish.

Teachers must be aware that debate is plentiful regarding how to determine when underrepresentation is unreasonable or unacceptable and when discrimination or bias is operating. Such questions include but are not limited to: "When is underrepresentation significant?" and "How severe must underrepresentation be before it is discriminatory?" Borrowing from the U.S. Department of Education's Office for Civil Rights's 20% equity threshold rule, Ford (2013) revived and devised an "Equity Index" to guide teachers and decision makers: (a) in determining a target goal for what is the *minimally* accepted level of underrepresentation for each group (i.e., relative to race/culture, gender, income, etc.); and (b) in acknowledging that proportional percentages are ideal and equitable but cannot always be achieved due to how chance and real factors affect individuals and groups (e.g., one group is wealthier than another, one group has less education than another, one group has more resources than another). The important caveat is that, when the percentage of underrepresentation *exceeds* the designated threshold in the Equity Index, it is beyond statistical chance; thus, human error is operating (e.g., attitudes, biased or inappropriate tests and instruments, policies and procedures that are potentially discriminatory against Hispanic and African American students). For more information, see Ford (2013) and the MALDEF website at http://www.maldef.org/news/releases/maldef_u46_discrimination_case.

Although it is essential for teachers to know the percentage of underrepresentation for each group, no underrepresentation formula suffices for determining what is unacceptable, unreasonable, or illegal/discriminatory underrepresentation—nor is the formula specific enough to set goals for improving representation. This is where the Equity Index is needed (see Ford, 2013).

Calculating the Equity Index for African American students is a two-step process. Step 1: (Composition (%) of African American students in general education) x Threshold of 20% = A. This is abbreviated as C x T = A.

Step 2: (Composition (%) of African American students in general education) – A = Equity Index (EI).

The full formula is abbreviated as C – A = EI.

Nationally, African Americans were 19% of students in general education in 2013; thus, the Equity Index using a 20% threshold would be: A is 19% x 20% = 3.8% and EI is 19% – 3.8% = 15.2%. Therefore, African Americans (who represent 19% of general education students) should represent at *minimum* 15.2% of students in gifted education programs and services. Nationally, their representation in gifted education is 10%. It is safe to conclude that underrepresentation is significant and beyond statistical chance. To achieve minimal equity, teachers must increase African American representation nationally from 10% to *at least* 15.2%. (See Table 72.1.)

For Hispanic students nationally, the Equity Index is approximately 20% for 2013. (See Table 72.1.) Given that they represent almost 16% of gifted education rather than the minimal 20% when viewed through an equity perspective, Hispanic students are also underrepresented beyond statistical probability.

These trends present a troubling and longstanding reality—our nation's gifted programs are clearly segregated racially for African American and

TABLE 72.1

Underrepresentation and Equity Index for Black and Hispanic Students in Gifted Education Nationally

	Black Students	**Hispanic Students**
Enrollment School District Enrollment Percentage vs. Gifted Education Enrollment Percentage	19% vs. 10%	25% vs. 16%
Underrepresentation Discrepancy between percentage in school district vs. percentage in gifted education	47%	36%
Equity Index Goal/Allowance *Minimal* percentage in gifted education to be equitable	15.2% (Must increase from 10% to 15.2%)	20% (Must increase from 16% to 20%)

Hispanic students. *Brown v. Board of Education* ruled racial segregation unconstitutional; African American (and all other minority) students have the legal (and moral) right to be educated in classrooms with White students. This principle was reinforced and upheld in *McFadden v. Board of Education for Illinois School District U-46*. However, we are far from fulfilling the mandates of *Brown* for African Americans and Hispanics in gifted education.

A Final Word

Our nation has a long way to go to implement these standards and achieve equity in gifted education to increase access for Black and Hispanic students. Teachers play significant roles—not just as imparters of knowledge but also as advocates for those who often have the least support and whose gifts are frequently misunderstood and go unnoticed. We encourage teachers to seek formal preparation in gifted education *and* formal preparation in multicultural education in order to ensure an end to segregated gifted programs. Our students are depending on us for such support. And teachers can provide it. As the saying goes, "where there's a will, there's a way."

References

Brown v. Board of Education of Topeka, 347 U.S. 483 (1954).

Civil Rights Act of 1964, Pub.L. 88-352, 78 Stat. 241 (1964).

Ford, D. Y. (2010). *Reversing underachievement among gifted Black students* (2nd ed.). Waco, TX: Prufrock Press.

Ford, D. Y. (2011). *Multicultural gifted education* (2nd ed.). Waco, TX: Prufrock Press.

Ford, D. Y. (2013). *Recruiting and retaining culturally different students in gifted education*. Waco, TX: Prufrock Press.

Ford, D. Y., Grantham, T. C., & Whiting, G. W. (2008). Culturally and linguistically diverse students in gifted education: Recruitment and retention issues. *Exceptional Children, 74*, 289–308.

Ford, D. Y., & Trotman, M. F. (2000). The Office for Civil Rights and nondiscriminatory testing, policies, and procedures: Implications for gifted education. *Roeper Review, 23*, 109–112.

McFadden v. Board of Education for Illinois School District U-46. Retrieved from http://www.maldef.org/news/releases/maldef_u46_discrimination_case

Title IX of the Educational Amendments of 1972, 20 U.S.C. § 1681 et seq.

U.S. Department of Education, Office for Civil Rights. (2009). *Civil rights data collection survey*. Retrieved from https://ocrdata.ed.gov/SpecialReports

U.S. Department of Education, Office for Civil Rights. (2011). *Civil rights data collection survey*. Retrieved from https://ocrdata.ed.gov/SpecialReports

Chapter 73

It Begins With Identification

A Focus on Hispanic Immigrant Students

by Jaime A. Castellano

Hispanic immigrant populations continue to impact our schools across the country, representing all 22 Spanish-speaking countries and territories of the world. Increasing numbers of students are coming to live in America from Mexico, El Salvador, Guatemala, Honduras, and other countries, with the greatest growth occurring in young school-aged populations. In response, schools are scrambling to determine how best to meet their needs. However, despite more than 5 million English language learners (ELL) in our schools, the majority of whom are Hispanic, ELLs continue to be overrepresented in special education programs and underrepresented in classrooms serving gifted, advanced, and high-ability learners. Perhaps one way to reverse this trend is to begin looking at the skills and abilities they do have, rather than what they do not have when they arrive in our schools.

The Struggle for Identification

The identification process for Hispanic immigrant students should include a combination of qualitative and quantitative data that embraces a multicriteria philosophy. There is a wealth of research-based identification materials appropriate for ELLs, and other culturally and linguistically diverse gifted learners readily available (see resource listing). Districts that value ELL students' inclusion and make a conscious effort to identify them recognize the multifaceted approach needed. Many believe that these children also bring prior knowledge and a view of the world that enriches the cognitive, academic, social, and emotional environment for their classmates.

Despite this published knowledge of how to identify, many districts continue to struggle to increase access to gifted education programs for ELL students through successful identification. The many reasons for this failure are enough for three columns' worth of material, but I believe that by embracing the cultural differences and family dynamics of Hispanic students, educators and administrators can move one step closer to understanding the needs of ELL students.

Hispanic Immigrant Parents

Parents across all ethnic, cultural, and linguistic groups want their children to do well in school. Obtaining an education prepares children for optimistic futures, making it possible to secure meaningful employment and to contribute to society. Parents commonly share their own stories—often containing personal struggles and barriers—with their children in an effort to motivate and encourage them and in some cases, to prevent the recurring consequences of not seeking a formal education. Parents of gifted ELLs support the school their children attend and want to foster the academic achievement of their sons and daughters, but language barriers and thus poor or misunderstood communication about gifted identification opportunities and procedures often result.

Keeping language barriers in mind, schools and gifted education program leaders should make every effort to ensure that written communication from schools occurs in the heritage language of their students' families. Additionally, onsite translators are critical for informational workshops and meetings addressing availability of services and the referral and identification processes. Speakers presenting to parents and caregivers on gifted and talented issues should also be persons who are knowledgeable and respectful of the Hispanic culture. Addressing language and cultural issues is the first step in forming a bond of understanding that can lead to effective partnership with the families of ELL gifted and high-potential children.

Looking Ahead: Increasing Access for ALL Diverse Populations

Our schools need to revisit the policies, practices, and processes that are preventing not only Hispanic immigrant students, but also other diverse gifted learners from accessing a rigorous and relevant curriculum. The nation's needs dictate that we increase our expectations, support high academic achievement, and identify high achievers as early as possible, putting into place the support systems that help them sustain success. This also means an investment in research and training on giftedness as it relates to diverse student populations. The success of our nation demands that we make fundamental changes in our beliefs, values, and attitudes in how we create access for all of our nation's best and brightest.

Resources

Castellano, J. A. (2003). *Special populations in gifted education: Working with diverse gifted learners.* Boston, MA: Allyn & Bacon.

Castellano, J. A. & Frazier, A. D. (2011). *Special populations in gifted education: Understanding our most able students from diverse backgrounds.* Waco, TX: Prufrock Press.

National Association for Gifted Children. (2011). *Identifying and serving culturally and linguistically diverse learners* [Position statement]. Retrieved from https://www.nagc.org/sites/default/files/Position%20Statement/Identifying%20and%20Serving%20Culturally%20and%20Linguistically.pdf

National Association for Gifted Children. (2012). *NAGC national summit on low-income, high-ability learners.* Retrieved from http://www.nagc.org/sites/default/files/key%20reports/Unlocking%20Emergent%20Talent%20%28final%29.pdf

University of Massachusetts Boston. (2016). *Talented and gifted (TAG) Latino program.* Retrieved from https://www.umb.edu/tag

Chapter 74

Native American Students

Understanding Cultural and Language Diversity

by Jerry Lassos

This school year was amazing for me, a teacher with more than 30 years experience, including time in the regular classroom, in gifted and talented class-rooms, and as a gifted and talented resource consultant. Most recently I have taught middle school Indian Education classes in Denver Public Schools. I feel as if I learned so much about what is important and how schools and school districts need to change in order for more Native American students to be successful.

Teachers who judge culturally and linguistically diverse students only through their own lenses and experiences often fail to connect on a meaning-ful level. This can be damaging to students' self-esteem. By punishing behaviors based on values that conflict with the students' struggle for survival in their own socioeconomic environments, the relationship gap widens and students feel nudged closer toward exiting systems that don't value or understand them.

From my own school experience, which is not that different from that of many of the students I interact with every day, I have found that there are four consistent elements that ensure success when working with any group of stu-dents, especially this population of culturally and linguistically diverse students.

1. Build a strong teacher-student relationship. The teachers who form relationships with their students understand their unique needs and experiences and judge them less harshly than many of their counterparts. Feeling overburdened and stressed from the pressure related to student success on state assessments, many teachers delve immediately into curriculum and content. Without first building trust and relationships, many teachers never see the real student, the real person with whom they work.

2. Focus on student strengths. Engaging students in their strength areas is essential. By focusing on what each student is capable of, teachers can offer praise for success while at the same time working on areas where more effort is needed. Native American students, like many other culturally and linguistically diverse students, often find themselves in remedial "catch up" classes with little opportunity to demonstrate their academic and creative strengths. Beginning with the identification of educational and creative strengths at the start of the year or class can break down the barriers that often hold up the recognition and development of talent.

3. Appeal to the visual-spatial learner. All students benefit from opportunities to receive content in a variety of ways. Close to 80% of Native American students are visual-spatial learners. Our educational system forces teachers to think in a linear-sequential way and the mismatch between the linear-sequential learning styles of teachers and the visual-spatial learning style of students can lead to a lack of understanding and frustration at both ends.

4. Utilize technology. Connecting technology to curriculum can provide a host of opportunities for students. For example, utilizing video editing gives rise to voice through school news broadcasts, interviews, and digital storytelling, which can focus on culture, heritage, and genealogy. Another great technology tool available is podcasts. Teachers can select online episodes to share with the students or offer the opportunity for them to create their own.

Although these four elements are among a host of other successful approaches in classrooms with Native American learners, I always seem to gravitate toward them. They have continually guided me throughout the years. As gifted education teachers, we have the responsibility to identify talent in our students, especially those from culturally and linguistically diverse backgrounds, who are so often denied the opportunity to take part in advanced classes.

Editor's Note: This column has been edited from an article written by Jerry that appeared on the WeAreGifted2 blog maintained by Dr. Joy Lawson Davis, author of *THP*'s Special Populations column and NAGC Board Member.

Chapter 75

Celebrating and Exploring Diversity Through Children's Literature

by Kimberley L. Chandler and Barbara Dullaghan

> Diversity makes for a rich tapestry, and we must understand that all the threads of the tapestry are equal in value no matter what their color.
> —Maya Angelou

Taking a cue from departing columnist Bob Seney, the authors would like to ask, "Why do primary teachers read picture books to their students?" One reason is to show the beautiful illustrations and hear the words gently woven into the stories, but teachers also read them to teach lessons and broaden students' experiences and thoughts.

Although there are now many children's books that teach tolerance and acceptance, many books still approach the subject using "safe characters" such as animals or metaphorically as shapes and colors. To address the needs of culturally and linguistically diverse (CLD) gifted learners, Stambaugh and Chandler (2012) suggest:

> Choose curriculum materials that include characters, examples, and situations related to the cultures of CLD students in the classroom. It is important for students to see themselves reflected in the materials used in the gifted education program. (p. 56)

In their blog, Katherine Rose and Dr. Mandy Stewart (2014), state that: "Every child needs and deserves the mirror experience in literature." The "mirror experience" is described as providing "books that reflect themselves and family but also a window into others' lives." It is as important to represent the population you are teaching as it is to expose students to other cultures and lives outside of their environment.

Here are some wonderful examples of picture books for exploring cultural and linguistically diverse populations in your classroom! Pick up a copy, read it aloud, and then let the discussions follow. It is a great place to start.

One Green Apple by Eve Bunting (2006, Clarion Books)
This book about a young Muslim immigrant provides insight into the challenges
    faced by a child trying to assimilate into a new culture.

Jack and Jim by Kitty Crowther (2000, Disney-Hyperion)
In this book, two birds from different parts of the world become friends.
    Readers learn about the importance of looking beyond external appearance
    to learn what is inside someone's heart.

The Crayon Box That Talked by Shane DeRolf and Michael Letzig (1997,
    Random House)
In the form of a poem, this book features arguing crayons and the message that
    there can be harmony if we embrace diversity.

The Colors of Us by Karen Katz (2002, Square Fish)
This story features Lena, a little girl who wants to paint a picture of herself.
    When she and her mother walk through their neighborhood, Lena learns
    an important lesson about skin color and the diversity in the world.

Here I Am by Patti Kim (2013, Capstone)
This is a story about a young immigrant and his first experiences in a large
    American city. The images paint a strong picture of the fears of the boy
    and the things that comfort him as he learns about his new home.

Take Me Out to the Yakyu by Aaron Meshon (2013, Atheneum)
In this book about a boy and his two grandfathers, baseball is the avenue for
    exploring both American and Japanese cultural traditions. Through his
    comparisons, the author illustrates how very different cultures have some
    commonalities and how human emotions are the same in all people.

The Sandwich Swap by Queen Rania of Jordan Al Abdullah and Kelly
    DiPucchio (2010, Disney-Hyperion)
    In this story, a disagreement about a hummus sandwich causes conflict
between two friends and eventually intolerance within their school. The principal's reaction helps the girls to reconcile and the student body to celebrate
diversity.

The Sneetches and Other Stories by Dr. Seuss (1961, Random House)
This book features four short stories, all which teach messages about diversity
    and the importance of tolerance.

Most children look to their teachers for help in opening doors and exploring ideas in their lives. Try adding more literature to your lessons in order to help
your students celebrate and explore diversity. If you need help, ask a librarian!

References

Rose, K., & Stewart, M. (2014). *Why more diversity in children's literature
    is absolutely necessary* [Web log post]. Retrieved from http://www.
    huffingtonpost.com/katherine-rose/why-more-diversity-in-chi_b_5544
    182.html
Stambaugh, T., & Chandler, K. L. (2012). *Effective curriculum for underserved
    gifted students*. Waco, TX: Prufrock Press.

Chapter / 76

Talking About Race in Middle and High School Classrooms

by Joy Lawson Davis

When discussing the traits of gifted learners, most experts would agree that they usually are very socially conscious individuals who express compassion and deep concern for their fellow human beings. No characteristics chart describing gifted learners is complete without the use of such terms as compassionate, heightened sense of justice, lack of tolerance for hypocrisy, and/or unusually sensitive to the needs of others.

Our nation has just emerged from one of the most socially volatile, emotional, and visible civil protest periods since the 1960s. Last year, communities across the nation rallied behind causes to defend and support the humane treatment of all citizens. One issue that has received a great deal of attention nationwide is the purported racial discrimination and maltreatment of African American males, in particular. As a result of a series of incidents involving the deaths of three young African American males, protests emerged across the nation.

Over the past few years, racism has become one of the most controversial topics discussed across news forums in the nation. For the first time in my adult experience, RACE IS OUT IN THE OPEN! In schools across the nation, students from all different ethnic backgrounds gathered to support some of these causes, asked questions, stated their opinions, and demanded to be heard. Race is not an easy matter to contend with, and racism, like sexism, ageism, and other intolerances worldwide, is intricately interwoven into the fabric of American society.

It is a false assumption to think that we can "hold school as usual" this year without having conversations about race and without allowing our bright, compassionate, deeply sensitive students to express their views. It will be a huge challenge in some communities, but one that we must face head-on. The best classroom setting that we can provide for the gifted is the setting wherein they are allowed to openly discuss issues and develop resolutions to the problems that plague us as a society. The challenge is for educators to be well-prepared, confident, and courageous enough to lead the conversations.

Below are a few resources and ideas that may serve as prompts for teachers, counselors, and gifted education coordinators to begin these conversations. The resources provided should also assist in developing additional ideas that have the goal of creating socially conscious/race-sensitive educational environments in your classrooms.

Activity #1—Define race, racism in context. Provide a definition of race and have students write a brief autobiography sharing their cultural background, and how their race has affected their experiences in three of four environments: at home, school, community/neighborhood, in public settings (e.g., malls, movies, traveling, houses of worship). Ask them to be specific and describe how they felt different or how they witnessed the treatment of others or interactions of others of different races/cultural backgrounds.

Activity #2—Utilize a Socratic discussion with the theme, "the danger of a single story." Use Nigerian novelist Chimamanda Adichie's popular TED Talk as a focal point and set up a Socratic discussion to allow students an opportunity to explore Adichie's premise of a "single story" and how individuals are impressionable and vulnerable in the face of a single story. (*Tip*: For a Socratic discussion framework/directions, go to http://www.socraticmethod. net/morality/page1.htm.)

Activity #3—Examine the role of youth in historic movements. Suggestions include the examination of the Ferguson Movement, USA, the Anti-Apartheid movement in South Africa, and the American Civil Rights Movement. Students could write a comparative essay using at least two youth leaders from historical movements.

Activity #4—Initiate social justice 'Affinity' group sessions at your school. These sessions can be used to allow students to share experiences, review films, read and discuss books, and discuss implications for their own community. The goal is to allow an open, nondefensive setting for conversation that will lead to resolving school and local issues.

Activity #5—Conduct a read and react exercise involving White privilege with the guiding question, "What is it and how does it 'color' our world?" Share Peggy McIntosh's essay (https://nationalseedproject.org/white-privilege-unpacking-the-invisible-knapsack) on White privilege. Discuss the invisible knapsack. Share 8–10 privileges as noted by Dr. McIntosh in her initial essay; ask students to name 5–10 more.

Before you begin any of these lessons, remind yourself to be neutral and unbiased, attempt to read as much historical background materials as you can, and be ready to share your own views. Students will ask what you think and what your position is. Make sure to clear any potentially controversial materials with your administration. If your students are middle school level, you may wish to send home a letter to parents to advise them of the activities that will take place. Finally, get ready to open minds, engage learners, and change outcomes for communities as your students take charge and become social justice leaders of the next generation!

Resources

Blum, L. (2012). *High school, race and America's future: What students can teach us about morality, diversity, and community.* Cambridge, MA: Harvard Education Press.

Cornish, A. (2014). *Young Ferguson Protestor: 'It's bigger than us'* [Interview]. Retrieved from http://www.npr.org/2014/11/25/366620504/young-ferguson-protestor-its-bigger-than-us

Lee, A. (Producer), & Greene, C. (Director). (2014). *I'm not racist . . . am I?* [Motion Picture]. USA: Point Made Films.

McIntosh, P. (1989, July/August). White privilege: Unpacking the invisible knapsack. *Peace and Freedom Magazine,* 10–12. Retrieved from https://nationalseedproject.org/white-privilege-unpacking-the-invisible-knapsack

Chapter 77

The Power of the Personal Narrative

by Joy Lawson Davis

Until the lion tells his side of the story, the tale of the hunt will always glorify the hunter.

—Proverb from Zimbabwe

Everyone has a story, and each is unique. Students in gifted education classrooms originate from a variety of backgrounds, but have so much in common. They share a love of learning and rapid thinking processes, are generally very creative and compassionate, and see the world full of possibilities for change and improvement, all with a futuristic outlook. What makes these students unique is their culture, gender, family background, and community experiences. For teachers who may not share their diverse gifted students' culture, language, community, or racial backgrounds, it is particularly challenging to understand the daily experiences of their students.

Recent research has documented the important role of teachers in raising expectations for all students. In particular, researchers at Johns Hopkins noted that educational prospects of Black boys and girls were doubted more by White teachers than by Black teachers. Typically, most classroom teachers are White, middle class females. This same holds true for teachers of the gifted. As a result, as more efforts are made to provide access to gifted education classrooms for diverse learners, these students will not only face classmates who do not share their culture and experience, they will also face teachers who do not share their ethnic and cultural background.

Teachers who have limited experiences with students of another race have what may be considered a "single story" expectation, based on limited involvement on a personal and professional level with students from varied ethnic or cultural groups. Without a deeper knowledge or relationship with individuals who come from varied experiences, the culture in the classroom can be less than ideal. This is where the power of the personal narrative can help.

Personal Narratives

A personal narrative is an opportunity for gifted students to tell their own stories, providing details of family history, special events that have shaped who they are, and an opportunity to describe their hopes and dreams for the future. The power of the personal narrative cannot be underestimated.

In classrooms from Pre-K to high school, being comfortable telling your story helps all learners feel a sense of belonging, increases their self-esteem, and improves the value that others have for their classmates who may be different. Throughout history, great contributors to society have shared their unique stories as a way of informing others and empowering individuals like themselves. Using the personal narrative in the gifted education classroom can have great benefits for all students (and for teachers), empowering diverse gifted learners and creating classrooms that are more receptive, accepting, and respectful of individual differences.

The personal narrative can mediate the effects of microaggressions, everyday slights, and insults that people use that are offensive. Microaggressions are often very painful and cause problems in school settings if overlooked and ignored. When students are able to openly tell their own stories, the effects of microaggressions from classmates and adults can be mediated. An excellent resource discussing the painful effects of microaggressions is a video titled "Being 12: 'People Think I'm Supposed to Talk Ghetto, Whatever That Is'" (2015) with middle school students of varied backgrounds discussing how they are offended daily. Giving gifted students the opportunity to discuss their experiences via video documentary or written essays can be empowering, enabling students and teachers to discover how painful language affects relationships in classrooms.

Assigning personal narratives gives students the opportunity to tell their story from a "place of power" when they can be open and honest about their feelings of isolation or a lack of belonging, eventually creating settings where all students are comfortable sharing who they are and their intellectual and social-emotional needs. Narratives shared by gifted children of color who have been placed in gifted classrooms away from their social and racial peers provide evidence of the sense of isolation felt by these students.

The personal narrative can enhance the cultural sensitivity of the classroom, where there often exists a cultural or racial mismatch. This mismatch creates a wedge between the teacher and students that can create a less than ideal learning environment. Gender-different students may also feel isolation and lack a sense of belonging in settings where there is no indication of acceptance or when teachers or classmates are unwilling to embrace their nontraditional gender lifestyles.

All schools are responsible for ensuring that *all* students are safe and comfortable in the classroom environment. For gifted learners from backgrounds that are diverse by race, culture, language, gender, and income, it is crucial for teachers to create learning experiences that will improve their socialization and increase their comfort level with their intellectual peers. Personal narratives shared in nondefensive settings empower students to freely express their ideas and constructively create positive responses to instructional challenges. Classrooms that are open to multiple stories stimulate cooperation and collaboration and treat all students as valued members of the intellectual community.

Recommended Resources

Alexie, S. (2009). *The absolutely true diary of a part-time Indian*. Boston, MA: Little Brown.

Angelou, M. (1997). *I know why the caged bird sings*. New York, NY: Random House. (Originally published 1969)

Coates, T. (2015). *Between the world and me*. New York, NY: Spiegel & Grau.

Cisneros, S. (1991). *The house on Mango Street*. New York, NY: Bloomsbury.

Hsu, J. (2015). Being 12: 'People think I'm supposed to talk ghetto, whatever that is.' *WNYC*. Retrieved from http://www.wnyc.org/story/people-sometimes-think-im-supposed-talk-ghetto-whatever-kids-race

Okada, J. (2014). *No-no boy*. Seattle, WA: University of Washington Press.

Tschida, C. M., Ryan, C. L., & Ticknor, A.W. (2014). Building on windows and mirrors: Encouraging the disruption of 'single stories' through children's literature. *Journal of Children's Literature, 40*(1), 30–39.

Website

Teaching Tolerance Blog
http://www.tolerance.org
A place where educators who care about diversity, equity, and justice can find news, suggestions, and conversation and support.

Section II: Students From Low-Income Families

Chapter 78

Curriculum Planning for Low-Income Learners

An Interview With Dr. Tamra Stambaugh

by Jennifer Beasley

I had the pleasure of listening to a keynote address in Arkansas by a wonderful fellow educator, Dr. Tamra Stambaugh. Her message on developing critical thinking and reading skills in students of poverty was not only refreshing, but also much needed. Dr. Stambaugh is a research assistant professor of special education and director of Programs for Talented Youth at Vanderbilt University. Among her publishing credits, she is the coeditor of *Overlooked Gems: A National Perspective on Low-Income Promising Learners* (available on the NAGC website at http://www.nagc.org). As I listened to her address, I couldn't help but think about the connections I need to continue making with many of my students from diverse backgrounds. Dr. Stambaugh graciously answered several questions for this column on making curricular connections with promising students of poverty.

Q: What do you see as important about the connection between *who* we teach and *what* we teach?

TS: As with any population, we must consider *who* we teach. The specific needs and characteristics of our students should drive *how* we teach and the extent to which we delve into the *what*.

469

Research has shown that students of poverty are less likely to be identified and even less likely to be taught by highly qualified teachers. The curriculum provided in high-poverty schools is less likely to focus on higher level skills, questions, and concepts. There are specific characteristics of students of poverty that should be considered when planning instruction. For example, these students are less likely to set long-term goals, more likely to succeed at creative tasks and real-world problems as opposed to more abstract concepts and tasks, more likely to question authority, less likely to do homework, will work harder in class if they like you, and typically have lower self-esteem and efficacy than their wealthier counterparts. How we teach these students is critical to their future trajectory. Keeping these factors in mind, educators should incorporate more hands-on experiences, link concepts to familiar settings, assist students with goal setting, and work to incorporate positive relationships with these students.

Much of my career has been spent working in or with high-poverty schools, including directing two Javits grant projects that focused on curriculum interventions for promising students of poverty as part of the work of Dr. Joyce VanTassel-Baska at William & Mary. In my own research I found that teachers in Title I schools are more skeptical of their students' abilities to perform at high levels. However, when teachers are shown how to scaffold a lesson, students perform at much higher levels.

As teachers trained in gifted education know, scaffolding includes moving students from lower level to higher-level thinking skills, less to more independence, and familiar to less familiar contexts as they work through more complex tasks. The Jacob's Ladder Reading Comprehension Program is a model of this approach. I also have found that students of poverty who participate in accelerated activities beyond the school day need more guidance, encouragement, and mentoring in social situations to be successful.

Lastly, as part of the 2007 National Conference on Promising Students of Poverty, held in conjunction with William & Mary, the Jack Kent Cooke Foundation, and NAGC, I compiled the following generalizable themes and patterns across the research and conference presentations: (1) Early identification and subsequent services matched to their abilities are critical to students' future trajectory and access to gifted programming; (2) students of poverty who are gifted can be successfully identified through alternative identification measures; (3) ongoing mentoring by counselors, teachers, and researchers positively impacts academic success, social skills, and student efficacy; (4) proactive, targeted career and guidance counseling positively impacts rigorous high school course selection and postsecondary application and enrollment at selective universities; (5) family involvement and education matter; (6) deliberately accelerated and enriched afterschool, extracurricular, Saturday, and summer programs positively affect college application, school attendance, and selection of advanced courses; and (7) well-defined accelerated curriculum and enrichment opportunities provided during the school day have demonstrated gains in critical thinking and content acquisition for promising students of poverty.

Q: What is essential for today's gifted teacher to consider in regards to curriculum for this special population?

TS: Curriculum selections are critical to the success of promising students of poverty. The curriculum must be respectful and higher level, while considering students' unique needs. Curricular design must include the following elements: (1) teacher modeling of language and practices of the discipline through explanation of student ideas, both written and verbal; (2) specific graphic organizers that focus on higher level skills; (3) linkages to real-world problems and contexts applicable to students of poverty; (4) scaffolding from lower to higher level skills; (5) involvement and ongoing professional development with educators *and* student families; (6) the use of preassessment as a guide for educational planning (these preassessments involve less writing and more graphic depictions and concrete representations of tasks); and (7) the teaching of concrete to abstract concepts with interest-based components.

Q: Are there specific resources that you might recommend to teachers wishing to learn more about this population?

TS: The resource and research list for promising students of poverty is growing, but is still limited. Specific curriculum with quasi-experimental designs and a positive research base include the following: Mentoring Mathematical Minds and the William & Mary Language Arts Curriculum (both available from Kendall Hunt), The William & Mary Project Clarion Science Curriculum and the Jacob's Ladder Reading Comprehension Program (both available from Prufrock Press), and Project U-STARS~PLUS (available from NAGC and the Council for Exceptional Children). Another successful program to review is the SEM-R project from the University of Connecticut. Also, be sure to check the NAGC *Teaching for High Potential* webpage for an abridged list of resources that may be helpful for educators interested in learning more about this special population.

Chapter 79

Benefits of Providing Enrichment to High-Potential Students From Low-Income Families

by Rachelle Miller and Marcia Gentry

This article, connecting research and practice, is based on Scott Peters and Marcia Gentry's Fall 2010 *Gifted Child Quarterly* article, "Multigroup Construct Validity Evidence of the HOPE Scale: Instrumentation to Identify Low-Income Elementary Students for Gifted Programs" focused on the validity of the HOPE Scale, a 13-item teacher-rating instrument designed to identify academic and social components of giftedness in elementary-aged students.

What happens when a well-established Super Saturday program created for gifted and talented learners provides scholarships to high-potential students from low-income families? Will these students, who are traditionally underrepresented in gifted and talented programs, need additional academic and social support from their families and teachers in order to be successful in this program? Will these students enjoy the rigorous activities and advanced content routinely experienced by students who participate in this program? Let's find out.

The achievement gap continues to widen between students from low-income and those from non-low-income families who score at the highest levels on achievement tests (Plucker, Burroughs, & Song, 2010). All too often, educators use test scores as a single or major criterion for entrance into gifted programs, which results in students from low-income families, who have high potential, being excluded from these opportunities (Worrell, 2007). Furthermore, educators who are concerned solely with achievement scores, unaware of other characteristics of high-ability children, often do not recognize the potential in these students (VanTassel-Baska, Feng, Quek & Struck, 2004). In light of these facts, it is important to note that students from low-income families who achieve at or above the 75th percentile are comparable to other students who achieve at or above the 95th percentile (Wyner, Bridgeland, & DiIulio, 2007). They possess high levels of motivation, enthusiasm, and good grades in school.

In 2008, the Gifted Education Resource Institute (GERI) at Purdue University began Project HOPE (Having Opportunities Promotes Excellence), a 3-year grant project funded from the Jack Kent Cooke Foundation. This project allowed us to provide scholarships to high-potential students from low-income families. We defined these high-potential students as those who qualified for the federal free and reduced meals program. Students who scored at or above the 70th percentile on achievement tests or who were recommended by an educator as having potential were also considered. These students were provided full tuition (including any materials) and transportation to Super Saturday and Super Summer programs.

Scholar Selection

Five Midwestern school districts that had more than 30% of their students from low-income families were invited to participate in Project HOPE. Multiple measures were used throughout the HOPE Scholar recruitment process. First, the contact person in each school district invited students from low-income families who scored at or above the 70th percentile on their achievement tests. Second, each contact person contacted parents through letters, phone calls, and parent meetings in order to help parents understand the *Super Saturday* program and how it could benefit their child. Spanish translations of the courses were provided to families as needed. Third, teachers completed the *HOPE Scale* (Peters & Gentry, 2010) on each of their students.

Super Saturday and Super Summer

Super Saturday is an enrichment program created for gifted and talented students in Pre-K through eighth grade. These classes are offered six consecutive Saturdays during the spring and fall semesters from 9 a.m. to noon. Science, technology, engineering, mathematics, and humanities courses are offered at two or more grade levels above. High-quality teachers are selected to teach these courses, and are required to attend a teacher-training program.

Super Summer occurs for 2 weeks during the summer months. Students can attend two classes per day, one in the morning for 3 hours and another one in the afternoon for 3 hours. Again, all courses include advanced content and are similar to the courses offered in Super Saturday. This program is similar to a "day camp."

Courses are developed by the Super Saturday/Super Summer coordinator, and proposals are also accepted from instructors, teachers, or parents. Instructors who teach these courses are experts in a particular field or have a passion for that content area. For example, for the last 6 years a doctoral student in chemistry taught courses such as Biomedical Engineering, Chemical Engineering, and Forensic Science. In addition, all teachers require students to complete a project by the end of the last day of Super Saturday, and parents are invited to view the presentation of these projects.

An Examination of the HOPE Scholars' Experiences

Researchers examined the experiences of HOPE Scholars in the Super Saturday program. Miller and Gentry (2010) examined the perceptions of HOPE Scholars who attended Super Saturday during their first session of participation. Thirty-three out of 113 HOPE Scholars consented to be observed in their Super Saturday class and/or interviewed during the fourth or fifth Saturday of the program. All Super Saturday participants completed a My Class Activities form (Gentry & Gable, 2001), which assesses the frequency that students perceive the interest, challenge, choice, and enjoyment of their classes. Student evaluations were examined for three groups: HOPE Scholars who consented to be interviewed and/or observed, HOPE Scholars who did not consent to be interviewed and/or observed, and general Super Saturday students

(students who did not receive HOPE scholarships). Findings indicated that HOPE Scholars had positive experiences, learned advanced content, and experienced hands-on learning and social support. Descriptive results showed that all three groups evaluated their courses similarly and favorably, which means that HOPE Scholars perceived their classes no differently then general *Super Saturday* students.

Miller, Yang, and Gentry (2010) examined the perceptions of HOPE Scholars using a larger sample of 274. Findings from both of these studies indicate that high-potential students from low-income families can successfully achieve in an out-of-school enrichment program.

Five Tips for Providing Opportunities at Your School

Based on our experiences in providing out-of-school enrichment programs, we would like to share a few tips if you are interested in creating a similar enrichment program at your school.

1. Create courses that include advanced content outside of the students' curriculum. When planning the first session, you may want to ask students and parents for their suggestions in order to find out what topics would interest the students. Start off small by offering only a few classes to see how students respond to them. These courses can be created by the gifted education coordinator or by a team of teachers who are familiar with creating curriculum for gifted students. Another option is to use commercially prepared units of study such as those available from William & Mary, Science Education for Public Understanding Program, or Boston Museum of Science. It is important that your curricula include various differentiation techniques and support an appropriate environment for gifted learners.

2. Keep cost in mind. Cost is something that you should anticipate when creating a program, but starting small is definitely more cost effective. Following the reflection of your first session, you can then expand or modify as necessary. Your school may have the additional funds to support a program like this, but many times that is not the situation. You may consider charging parents a registration fee for the program. These fees would allow you to pay teachers, unless teachers choose to volunteer for the program, and to purchase supplies. What if your community desperately needs this kind of enrichment but the families at your school cannot afford to pay a registration fee? This presents a perfect opportunity to ask businesses or organizations to sponsor this program or donate supplies.

3. Select interested educators. Are teachers at your school interested in being a part of this program? Do they have the expertise if you are interested in offering classes like Robotics or Intro to Engineering? Do you have parents with expertise in a certain area who could teach a Mini Medical School class or a Vet Med class? Are there any professionals in your community who are interested in volunteering? These are the questions you should ask. Once you have decided who is the best qualified to teach in your program, you can then complete background checks on all instructors and volunteers of your program to ensure the safety of your students.

4. Extend enrichment activities within the program. Would you like to incorporate field trips and guest speakers in your program? Because the Super Saturday program is located on the Purdue campus, our teachers have access to the engineering buildings, biology labs, and the theater. If your school does not have a nearby college, think about places in your community that would be ideal for a field trip that would contribute to authentic learning in the course. Maybe your students can visit a law firm if your class is learning about law or an animal hospital if your class is learning veterinary medicine.

5. Be clear on program eligibility. Who would benefit the most if they participated in this program? Do you have high-potential students from low-income families? If these students have a strong interest in a particular course you are offering, they will probably be successful in your program. Recall that the goal of your program should be to offer students experiences that they would not typically have in their classroom; experiences that could positively affect them academically and socially. Examples of resources that can help you begin your own out-of-school enrichment program can be found on the *Teaching for High Potential* website.

Providing enrichment opportunities for gifted and talented children, especially those who lack opportunities at home, should be at the forefront of education. The creation of a Super Summer or even a Super Saturday program in your area might be all that is needed to increase the numbers of identified students so often gone unnoticed.

References

Gentry, M., & Gable, R. K. (2001). *My class activities: A survey instrument to assess students' perceptions of interest, challenge, choice and enjoyment in their classrooms.* Mansfield Center, CT: Creative Learning Press.

Miller, R., & Gentry, M. (2010). Developing talents among high-potential students from low-income families in an out-of-school enrichment program. *Journal of Advanced Academics, 21,* 594–627.

Miller, R., Yang, Y., & Gentry, M. (November, 2010). *Opportunities leading to successful experiences: Positive perceptions of low-income students in an out-of-school enrichment program.* Paper presented at the annual meeting of National Association for Gifted Children, Atlanta, GA.

Peters, S. J., & Gentry, M. (2010). Multi-group construct validity evidence of the HOPE Scale: Instrumentation to identify low-income elementary students for gifted programs. *Gifted Child Quarterly, 54,* 298–313.

Plucker, J. A., Burroughs, N., & Song, R. (2010). *Mind the (other) gap! The growing excellence gap in K–12 education.* Bloomington, IN: Center for Evaluation and Education Policy, Indiana University. Retrieved from http://ceep.indiana.edu/pdf/The_Growing_Excellence_Gap_K12_Education.pdf

VanTassel-Baska, J., Feng, A., Quek, C., & Struck, J. (2004). A study of educators' and students' perceptions of academic success for underrepresented populations identified for gifted programs. *Psychological Science, 46,* 110–123.

Worrell, F. C. (2007). Identifying and including low-income learners in programs for the gifted and talented: Multiple complexities. In J. VanTassel-Baska & T. Stambaugh (Eds.), *Overlooked gems: A national perspective on low-income promising learners. Conference proceedings from the National Leadership Conference on Low-Income Learners* (pp. 47–51). Washington, DC: National Association for Gifted Children.

Wyner, J. S., Bridgeland, J. M., & DiIulio, J. J., Jr. (2007). *Achievement trap: How America is failing millions of high-achieving students from lower-income families.* Lansdowne, VA: Jack Kent Cooke Foundation. Retrieved from http://www.jkcf.org/assets/1/7/Achievement_Trap.pdf

Authors' Note: This project was supported by a grant from the Jack Kent Cooke Foundation. Special thanks to Jillian Gates, Scott Peters, and Rebecca Mann who assisted with the HOPE Project.

Section III:
Twice-Exceptionality

Chapter 80

Screening and Identifying 2e Students

Best Practices for a Unique Population

by Steve McCallum and Sherry Mee Bell

Students may be characterized as "twice-exceptional" if they meet the criteria typically advanced by state departments of education for giftedness *and* if they also have significant cognitive and related academic deficits that characterize specific learning disabilities (SLD). As we noted in "A Model for Screening Twice-Exceptional Students (Gifted with Learning Disabilities) within a Response to Intervention Paradigm" in the Fall 2013 issue of *GCQ*, students who have an SLD but who also have high potential are identified for gifted education services with less frequency than their peers who are gifted but who do not have an SLD (Trail, 2011). Underidentification of these students occurs in part because gifted students compensate for their weaknesses with salient cognitive strengths and may be missed by curriculum-based measures (CBM) typically employed in Response to Intervention (RtI) models. But, underidentification also occurs because identification models are too insensitive; this is particularly a problem for the RtI model, one of three models codified into federal policy within IDEA (2004) as appropriate for identifying SLD. The other two models include the Ability-Achievement Discrepancy model and other "research-based procedures." Thus we offer some recommendations for screening and identifying students who otherwise may be overlooked by traditional use of any of the three models, but especially by RtI as typically implemented. In addition, we provide recommendations for how the three models of identifying students may inform classroom practice.

Ability-Achievement Discrepancy Model for Identifying Gifted Students Who Have a Learning Disability

For years, educators have used the Ability-Achievement Discrepancy model for identifying students who have SLD. This model requires that a "severe" discrepancy exist between ability (i.e., intelligence) and achievement in one or more of eight academic areas, with ability being greater than achievement. Consequently, the model is presumed to operationalize "unexpected underachievement." This model has been criticized as a "wait to fail" model because struggling young students typically do not show a severe discrepancy, due in part to limited floor on achievement measures at young ages. It also has been criticized for a variety of other reasons, such as students identified under the model often do not respond to interventions differently from students with low achievement who do not have elevated ability. In addition, some argue that the error embedded in making multiple comparisons between an IQ score and numerous achievement measures increases the likelihood of finding discrepancies by chance, and results in overidentification of students who have SLD. As a model for identification of twice-exceptional status, the strongest criticism is related to underidentification: Students with high potential often never show a severe discrepancy, or, if they do, they may be performing within the broad range of average, yet still performing well below their measured aptitude. Despite the frustration of performing well below ability, these students often have strong compensatory mechanisms and thus never get screened or identified for instructional help, including special education services.

Recommendations

For school systems that continue to use the Ability-Achievement Discrepancy model, we recommend use of three modified screening and identification strategies. First, we recommend that teacher and parent recommendations be given particularly strong consideration in the screening stage and that sensitive and culture-reduced rating scales (e.g., Universal Multidimensional

Ability Scale) be used. Second, at the identification stage, we recommend that students not be required to earn achievement standard scores below average to qualify for services. Third, because relative cognitive deficits (e.g., slow processing speed, poor auditory and/or visual processing, limited memory) and cultural/language task demands (e.g., tests that are administered in a second language for ELL students) sometimes mask giftedness at the identification stage, we recommend that examiners choose the operationalization of cognition carefully, as does the National Association for Gifted Children (NAGC, 2010, 2011). For example, NAGC recommends use of the General Ability Index (emphasizing reasoning over processing speed and/or short-term memory) from the Wechsler Intelligence Scales for Children—IV (Wechsler, 2003) as an operationalization of IQ, as opposed to Full Scale IQ or use of either Verbal Comprehension Index or Perceptual Reasoning Index independently as the ability measure in the IQ-achievement discrepancy comparison. This recommendation is a good option for some students whose overall IQs may be depressed by limited low-level cognitive skills. Similarly, the cognitive abilities of some students may be masked by limited exposure to the mainstream culture and language (NAGC, 2011). For these students, examiners should include data from multiple criteria, work samples, interviews, teacher ratings, and valid measures of intelligence.

Response to Intervention (RtI) Model for Identifying Gifted Students Who Have a Learning Disability

Many, if not most, school systems across the country are adopting RtI for identification of students with SLD rather than, or in combination with, either the ability-achievement discrepancy model or another strategy. Because most current RtI models focus on identifying students who are performing well below average compared to their peers in reading and math (typically using brief timed probes emphasizing word reading fluency and math computation only), those performing above traditional RtI cut scores on academic probes will not be selected for additional support. The probes are constructed to reflect grade-level curriculum based on established standards and to conform to accepted guidelines for development of curriculum-based measures (CBM; Shinn, 1998). School systems can determine the cut scores to be used, which may be as low as the 10th percentile or as high as the 25th percentile. Within the RtI model, those who score below the cut scores and who continue to "fail to respond" (often defined as the rate of progress of the child at the 25th percentile), will be tracked into "tiers" and offered additional support in the targeted area(s). Those who earn higher scores will not be targeted for additional support, no matter their potential. School systems that rely only on RtI probes for identifying those who need additional academic services, or that fail to use RtI data in an innovative fashion to help screen and identify individuals who may be twice-exceptional, run the risk of underidentifying students who need help to approach their academic potential.

Recommendations

For school systems using the RtI model, we offer the following three recommendations: First, we recommend that students be screened for reading *and* math deficits as a minimum and, as additional assessment tools become available, written language skills as well. Second, we recommend that screening probes be multidimensional, that they *not* rely solely on oral word fluency for reading and calculation for math, but also assess reading comprehension and math reasoning. Third, we recommend that RtI probe data be used to screen for twice-exceptional status by selecting students who score well above the mean in one area, reading, math, or written language, and who also have a significant discrepancy. The process that we recommend identifies students who are *academic-discrepant*—those whose performance in two major academic areas is highly discrepant, and consequently may have an SLD. In order to identify students with high potential, system personnel may select those in the top 2.5%, 5%, or 16th percentile in a given academic area, and then isolate those who have a significant discrepancy in another academic area. (See details in our article in the Fall 2013 *GCQ*.) This procedure selects those who have unexpected underachievement with data that already exist within the system (i.e., RtI data); these students can be further evaluated to determine whether they meet more stringent criteria for identification for receipt of special education services for gifted/talented.

Alternative Research-Based Procedures Model for Identifying Gifted Students Who Have a Learning Disability

The third and last method for identifying those with SLD allows schools to use "alternative research-based procedures." Several states (e.g., Oregon) are using a research-based approach referred to as the *pattern of strengths and weaknesses* model (PSW) that requires educators to consider students' academic performance in relation to age and grade expectations as well as intellectual development. Further, consistent with the federal definition of SLD and with converging evidence that SLD is a valid construct characterized by intra-individual cognitive and academic variability (Learning Disabilities Roundtable, 2005), PSW models require establishment of a definitive link between one or more academic deficits and cognitive abilities that underlie those deficits, such as processing speed, auditory processing, working and/or long-term memory. For example, a student who has weak basic reading skills (e.g., weak phonetic decoding skills and/or weak sight word recognition) will likely have relatively poor auditory processing, limited working memory, and/or slow processing speed/rapid naming. There is a solid and growing body of research tying specific academic difficulties to related cognitive processing difficulties (APA, 2013; Flanagan, Ortiz, & Alfonso, 2013; Mather & Jaffee, 2002), consistent with implementation of this model. Perhaps most importantly, the model probably operationalizes a learning disability in a manner most consistent with the definition and original conceptualization of SLD.

Recommendations

For those systems that use a PSW model, we offer the following recommendations. First, utility of the model for identification should rely on the relative strengths and weaknesses, not rigidly defined cut scores (e.g., achievement standard scores below 90). Second, because the model requires that a link between cognitive and academic achievement be established, interventions can be based on this knowledge (e.g., see Wendling & Mather, 2009). Third, because this model does not require that certain minimum scores be obtained on CBM (at screening stage) or standardized measures (at identification stage) to establish the deficit cognitive and academic linkages, the burden is on examiners to make a strong case using psychometrically sound instruments and reasoned logical arguments. Gifted students are less likely overlooked within this model because criteria are not set so conservatively that very high-ability students with significant processing and academic gaps are missed.

General Recommendations for Schools

Classroom implications can be drawn from data taken from any of these models. For example, all of the models provide some information about cognitive and academic strengths and weaknesses. Importantly, teachers can use RtI data for more than sorting the lowest performing students. Preliminary data cited in the *GCQ* article indicate that CBMs may have enough ceiling to accurately identify top performing students, though more research is needed to confirm this observation. Top scores can be used to identify individuals with high potential whether or not these scores are used in the manner we describe above. That is, they can be employed as a first step to screen students for giftedness regardless of the procedures implemented afterward. Students performing at the top of their class on CBM measures should be considered for further screening for giftedness and they should benefit from strategies known to be effective with high-achieving and gifted students (e.g., compacting, ability grouping in appropriate subjects/content, inquiry-based instruction). Second, teachers can use CBM data to identify students with *academic* discrepancies (e.g., reading is significantly stronger than math and vice versa). Although uncommon, these students exist, as we demonstrated in the *GCQ* article. Assuming a history of generally effective instruction, these students are likely to exhibit SLD based on further assessment, and are potentially twice-exceptional. In addition to referring for additional assessment, teachers can provide academic support at appropriate challenge levels. Further, for those students whose reading skills are significantly lower than math skills, accommodations such as reading aloud math problems, preteaching math vocabulary, and providing visual prompts may be needed to help students maximize their math potential (see Wendling & Mather, 2009; Vaughn & Bos, 2012). Conversely, students whose math skills are much lower than reading will benefit from use of calculator and conceptual, language-loaded approaches to math instruction.

In conclusion, school districts have the choice of three methods for identifying SLD and all have implications for who is and is not ultimately identified as twice exceptional. Despite the model employed, many districts are embracing universal screening using CBMs as part of the prereferral process. As CBM data increasingly become part of the educational landscape, educators should use the data to make decisions about selection/identification (of 2e and non-2e students) and for differentiating instruction.

References

American Psychiatric Association. (2013). *Diagnostic and statistical manual of mental disorders* (5th ed.). Washington, DC: Author.

Flanagan, D. P., Ortiz, S. O., & Alfonso, V. C. (2013). *Essentials of cross-battery assessment* (3rd ed.) Hoboken, NJ: Wiley & Sons.

Individuals with Disabilities Education Improvement Act, Pub. Law 108-446 (December 3, 2004).

Learning Disabilities Roundtable. (2005). *Comments and recommendations on regulatory issues under the Individuals with Disabilities Education Improvement Act of 2004 (Public Law 108-446).* Washington, DC: Author.

Mather, N., & Jaffe, L. (2002). *Woodcock-Johnson III: Reports, recommendations and strategies.* Hoboken, NJ: John Wiley & Sons.

McCallum, R. S., Bell, S. M., Coles, J. T., Miller, K. C., Hopkins, M. B., Hilton-Prillhart, A. (2013). A model for screening twice-exceptional students (gifted with learning disabilities) within a Response to Intervention (RtI) paradigm. *Gifted Child Quarterly, 57,* 209–222.

National Association for Gifted Children. (2010). *Use of the WISC-IV for gifted identification* [Position statement]. Washington, DC: Author.

National Association for Gifted Children. (2011). *Identifying and serving culturally and linguistically diverse gifted students* [Position statement]. Washington, DC: Author.

Shinn, M. R. (Ed.). (1998). *Advanced applications of curriculum-based measurement.* New York, NY: Guilford.

Trail, B. (2011). *Twice-exceptional gifted children: Understanding, teaching, and counseling gifted students.* Waco, TX: Prufrock Press.

Vaughn, S., & Bos, C. (2012). *Strategies for teaching students with learning and behavior problems* (8th ed.). Boston, MA: Pearson.

Wechsler, D. (2003). *The WISC-IV technical and interpretive manual.* San Antonio, TX: Psychological Corporation.

Wendling, B. J., & Mather, N. (2009). *Essentials of evidence-based based academic interventions.* Hoboken, NJ: Wiley & Sons.

Chapter 81

Uncovering Buried Treasure

Effective Learning Strategies for
Twice-Exceptional Students

by Colleen Willard-Holt and Kristen Morrison

In "Perspectives of Effective Learning Strategies," from the Fall 2013 issue of *Gifted Child Quarterly*, we described a study in which we surveyed and interviewed twice-exceptional students about their school and learning experiences. Our research questions were "What learning strategies have twice-exceptional students used and found most beneficial?" and "Have the school experiences of twice-exceptional students improved over the last 15 years?" The 11 participants who completed both parts of this study ranged in age from 10 to 23 and their coexisting exceptionalities included Asperger's syndrome, learning disabilities, ADD/ADHD, emotional disorders, neurological disorders, and hearing impairment. The major findings are as follows:

- ▸ There has been progress in identifying twice-exceptional students, as shown by the simultaneous identification of giftedness and the coexisting disability in three participants and the identification of giftedness first in four other cases.
- ▸ Ten of 11 participants described their school experiences as failing to help them learn to their potential.
- ▸ Participants desired choice and flexibility in pace, assessment, collaborative work, topic, and learning strategy.
- ▸ Most participants used their strengths in various ways to circumvent their weaknesses.

▶ Accommodations and compensation strategies varied in effectiveness and frequency of use.

▶ An integrated approach to programming, considering strengths and needs simultaneously, is crucial in optimizing learning for twice-exceptional students.

Indicators That a Student May Be Gifted or Twice-Exceptional

1. Disengagement: This could either be a sign of ADD/ADHD or boredom. The key is to observe the child when he or she is interested in something. If the child is able to sustain attention under these conditions, then disengagement is a sign of boredom.
2. Surprising insights or questions from a child that you usually perceive as struggling.
3. Procrastination from children you know are bright. This could mean that they are struggling with how to get their ideas down on paper.
4. Uneven pattern of abilities. Students may display extreme highs and lows, differences between oral language and written expression, and sequential/simultaneous processing differences, which are all keys to identifying twice-exceptional students. Sequential processing is used in activities such as spelling, arithmetic algorithms, counting, and phonics; simultaneous processing is usually associated with creativity, music, art, comprehension of main ideas, and so on.
5. Perception of adult humor from a child with severe challenges.
6. Singular focus and knowledge of a discrete and somewhat arcane topic (such as Victorian doorknobs—no kidding), as is often found in a child with Asperger's syndrome.
7. Negotiation of topics, deadlines, and most anything else.

Realizing that psychoeducational assessments take time, and the student is in your classroom in the meanwhile, there are some behavioral indicators that a student may demonstrate of giftedness and/or coexisting exceptionality(ies). Please remember that in isolation, these indicators may have many underlying causes, but if there seems to be a cluster of them, then you might proceed with a hypothesis of 2e.

So if you do notice that the student of concern (let's call her Sara) is showing these behaviors, a next step might be something we often fail to do: *Ask Sara questions* about her learning. They should provide some direct strategies that you could try, working with her in a partnership to discover ways to make school "work" for her. You might begin by frankly stating to Sara that it seems as if she knows more than she is showing in her schoolwork. The questions below are stated in language that is directed toward a child in grade 2 or 3; feel free to change the language as appropriate.

Questions for Teachers to Ask Twice-Exceptional Students

1. What makes it hard for you to learn? What makes it easy for you to learn?
2. Are there classroom activities that help you do your best learning? Are there classroom activities that make it hard for you to learn?
3. When you are doing an assignment or activity in a group, how do you like to approach the work?
4. What causes you stress, anxiety, or worry at school?
5. What type of choices would you like in your schoolwork?
6. How fast or slow do you like to learn?
7. In what way would you like to show what you know about what we are studying?
8. Are there things I could do to better help you show what you know, on a test for example?
9. Are there ways you use your brain to figure out how to get around roadblocks in your learning?

Armed with this knowledge, now you have some ideas to try, though these will be from Sara's perspective and not be concerned with constraints such as curriculum documents, standards, management issues, accountability and the like. Remember that a definitive diagnosis of giftedness and/or coexisting exceptionalities rests upon the psychoeducational assessment, and that you as a classroom teacher cannot make that diagnosis. What you have is an informed, working hypothesis; your professional knowledge, skills, and instincts as a teacher; and some strategies with which to experiment in an action research type of environment.

Tips for Helping 2e Students Maximize Their Potential

There are numerous strategies to increase the potentiality of 2e students. Here are some of our favorites, which cover a variety of individual learning style differences.

- ▶ Take an integrated approach to meeting educational needs. Don't look at giftedness and the coexisting exceptionality in isolation, as each will impact the other. For example, when involving a 2e student in a high-level conceptual discussion, consider providing the topic in advance to allow the student to work around exceptionalities such as limitations in working memory or oral expression. Or, think about the trade-off between reading selections at the student's conceptual level vs. their reading level. The student may need far more time than you anticipate.
- ▶ Provide *personalized* rather than differentiated programming. The interplay among exceptionalities, as noted above, is a delicate dance. Consider posing ideas for differentiated ("gifted") tasks to the special education teacher, who may be able to suggest tweaking them to meet the student's needs. Or in the case of older, more self-aware 2e students, suggest tasks to the student him- or herself during individual meetings with you or another teacher. There is more information in Tables 3 and 4 of the *GCQ* article.
- ▶ Offer the opportunity for students to submit an academic contract that focuses on personal expectations for skills and classroom work. In this contract the student would propose a project and timelines to fulfill the expectations. As the teacher, you would decide whether the contract is appropriate and set minimum standards for success.
- ▶ For collaborative tasks: Think carefully about the coexisting exceptionalities and their effects on the 2e student within a group setting. Students who have processing or memory issues may need to prepare for the group work by writing things out beforehand. Sensory and

motor disabilities imply other types of accommodations within the group.

- ▷ Allow students opportunities to explain tasks to each other.
- ▷ Discuss with the students whether they prefer to distribute parts of each task among the group, delegate specific parts of the overall project to each group member, or use peers as a sounding board/brainstorming opportunity only, with individual responsibility for completing the task.
- ▷ Assign group members considering how the group could best function for a given task.

- ▸ Differentiate assessment strategies (Baum et al., 2001). Allow students to choose the way in which they demonstrate their learning, and develop evaluation rubrics accordingly. For example, they might create a video, Prezi, or poster instead of a written report. Encourage the use of technology to circumvent the disability. Decrease the number of repetitions required to demonstrate mastery. Provide parameters, guidelines, or rubrics to assist the student in structuring the work.
- ▸ Avoid focusing on weaknesses to the exclusion of strengths, as well as using strengths only to remediate weaknesses. Rather, allow the student to soar in his or her areas of strength and prioritize those weaknesses that get in the way of the gifts. For example, teach students study skills they need to be able to better express their talents.
- ▸ Normalize accommodations. Provide accommodations for all students to best highlight their learning.
- ▸ As Reis et al. (1997) recommended, don't forget the importance of teaching study skills, organization, goal setting, time management, metacognition, and use of technology as assistive devices. Gifted students are often bright enough to succeed without knowing these skills, or teachers overestimate how well they know them. Many of our participants mentioned how helpful these techniques had been.
- ▸ Model acceptance and affirmative behavior toward both exceptionalities (Nicpon et al., 2011).
- ▸ Provide opportunities for students to interact with twice-exceptional peers, or peers sharing at least one exceptionality (Nicpon et al., 2011; Nielsen, 2002; Yssel et al., 2010).
- ▸ Remember the whole child and possible social-emotional concomitants of being 2e. These students are often quite confused or ambivalent about their abilities, and may become quite depressed as a result.

Point out concrete examples of the student's intellectual strengths and stress the coexisting exceptionality as a hurdle to be attacked using problem-solving skills. Finally, work with parents to ensure that they understand that the student is not lazy or simply inattentive (Reis et al., 1997). Until a diagnosis is confirmed, use language revolving around "differences in how she learns."

▸ Support students in becoming advocates for their own learning needs. Helping students to understand what they need in their learning tool-kit in order to be successful is something they can take with them as they continue their academic careers.

We are still learning how to best identify individuals with outstanding gifts who also face significant barriers, but we need look no further than Helen Keller, Temple Grandin, and Carly Fleischmann to know that individuals exist who are twice-exceptional. Like those who helped uncover the genius within those three women, teachers are in a prime position for discovering greatness in their students. However, in order to do so, we must rethink ways in which intelligence is demonstrated in a classroom setting and look for ways to lift the barriers to learning for all of our students.

References

Baum, S. M., Cooper, C. R., & Neu, T. W. (2001). Dual differentiation: An approach for meeting the curricular needs of gifted students with learning disabilities. *Psychology in the Schools, 38,* 477–490.

Nicpon, M. F., Allmon, A., Sieck, B., & Stinson, R. D. (2011). Empirical investigation of twice-exceptionality: Where have we been and where are we going? *Gifted Child Quarterly, 55,* 3–17.

Nielsen, M. E. (2002). Gifted students with learning disabilities: Recommendations for identification and programming. *Exceptionality, 10,* 93–111.

Reis, S. M., Neu, T. W., & McGuire, J. M. (1997). Case studies of high-ability students with learning disabilities who have achieved. *Exceptional Children, 63,* 463–479.

Yssel, N., Prater, M., & Smith, D. (2010). How can such a smart kid not get it? *Gifted Child Today, 33,* 54–61.

Chapter 82

Four Teaching Recommendations That Work for Gifted Youth With ADD

A Student's Perspective

by Amos Gewirtz

Approximately 9% of the K–12 student population has some form of attention deficit. Although some teachers have limited knowledge and negative attitudes toward students with ADD[5], these youth are mentioned ever more frequently in general and gifted education. Throughout my own academic career, there were at least four strategies that my teachers used that were especially effective for high-potential students with ADD like me. This article briefly looks at these methods: organization, individual attention, time management, and creative development.

Organization

A well-known difficulty for gifted students with ADD is organization (Moon, 2002). This problem becomes increasingly challenging as students get

---

5   *Note.* The *Diagnostic and Statistical Manual of Mental Disorders, Third Edition, Revised* (DSM-III-R; American Psychiatric Association, 1987) was the first to introduce the term Attention Deficit/Hyperactivity Disorder (ADHD), eliminating the Attention Deficit Disorder (ADD) diagnosis. The DSM-IV (APA, 1994) and the subsequent revisions through the current DSM-V (APA, 2013) have included three subtypes of ADHD (predominately inattentive, predominately hyperactive/impulsive, and combined).

older. Helpful educators teach organizational strategies—and do so in a structured way, which means not just talking about but actually providing planners, organizers, detailed project descriptions, examples of good notes, and task timelines.

When I was in upper elementary school, my homeroom teacher would end each day with a review of my assignments for the upcoming day so that I would have a detailed plan. She provided me task descriptions, visual guidelines for moving from one task to another, and timelines for accomplishing each task. This fourth-grade educator made a true difference with me. Not only did she provide me with good plans and planning materials, but she also taught me why these plans were effective.

This teacher made my classroom time both pleasant and intellectually stimulating. She stressed organization of work as important as the work itself. My enhanced organization skills allowed me to progress beyond being stuck figuring out what was required to the enjoyable task of creating work that was both personally rewarding and displayed my understanding for the topic presented.

Individualized Attention

There are numerous benefits for gifted students with ADD to receive personal attention from the teacher, especially if these youth are organized (Brand, Dunn, & Greb, 2002). The skills required to plan for short- and long-term assignments, complete work in a timely manner, and create a productive work environment lay the foundation for expressing individuality in the classroom.

Many of my teachers' best methods for individualized attention were also their most creative. For instance, my fifth-grade teacher assigned various parts of the classroom as individual offices for students. During work time, students would go to their offices to work on assignments. The teacher would visit these spaces and provide help as needed. Because students needed differing degrees of attention, this "office" strategy provided students a great deal of individualized attention while allowing the teacher to spend time with each student, responding to his or her specific needs.

Educators who were most effective with me appealed to my visual learning style and to my peers' wide-ranging learning approaches. When my teachers discussed a book, they accompanied a lecture-format explanation with a diagram or "word web." In middle school language arts, one teacher wrote both characters and themes on the board, which the students gradually connected with arrows. This approach, which enabled me to grasp large ideas and small details at a single glance, allowed me to better understand concepts and to further develop my love of both literature and discussion. Gradually, I took my new part-to-whole note-taking approach to social studies and science, improving my comprehension and exam grades in those subjects.

Time Management

No matter how much individualized attention they receive, gifted students with ADD must learn to manage their own time, which often does not come easily. One cornerstone of time planning is allocating time to both work and leisure (Prevatt, Reaser, Proctor, & Petscher, 2007). This balance allows gifted students with ADD to perform at full potential by giving them focused, uninterrupted time to fully work through ideas or simply to complete school tasks (Weaver, 1994). Likewise, it provides opportunities for personal reflection, creativity, or relaxation.

Like many issues surrounding planning, there is a sizable gap between what is said and what is done. Planning something and doing something are two entirely separate things. In order to ensure that the latter is completed in tandem with the former, creating a detailed and itemized plan is imperative. For example, planning a single 4-hour study session for a student with ADHD may seem like a monumental task at first, but planning out four one-hour study sessions across several days, with accompanying lists of what will be covered during each time, aids in minimizing ambiguity and presents a much more structured plan. As a student, my most effective teachers not only help me create plans, but also help me create reasonable ones.

For me, the simple act of managing my time has led to overall success in the classroom. Uninterrupted periods of work time of varying duration offer the chance to complete academic work in a time period that is comfortable and beneficial to me. It also has provided a chance for me to reflect upon, develop, and refine my own efficient learning strategies.

Creative Development

Teaching gifted students with ADD to embrace creative development can help them manage and control their own difficulties with attention (Dunn & Dunn, 1992). Activities such as writing, music, dance, fine arts, and many other creative or artistic hobbies can be therapeutic as well as enjoyable. In many cases, challenges with attention can be reduced or eliminated during an enjoyable and relaxing activity. Over time, the task-related focus developed during creative matters can be transferred to less enjoyable activities, if teachers take the time to point out opportunities for skill generalization. Teaching focusing competencies can provide long-term, transferable strategies that can help to remedy some ADD-associated difficulties (Litner, 2003).

From early elementary through high school, my therapy has been oil painting, in which I could engage during both stressful and relaxing times. Creative production has allowed me to focus more clearly on things that I have trouble doing. Art is my single most powerful tool in combating ADD. Uncovering and developing this skill has been a key factor in my life.

Conclusion

Educational achievement for students with attention challenges is dependent on the development of organization and time-management skills. Educators, in providing individual attention and support in these areas, lay the foundation for success in the classroom and beyond, as students like myself enter college and eventual professional careers. Artistic talent is often overshadowed by the struggles and stress of getting required work completed. Were it not for the encouragement of knowledgeable and caring teachers, I may never have uncovered this hidden talent.

I am hopeful that my story, which is akin to many others in similar situations, encourages educators to assist in the skills development that will, in my view, impact their students' lives forever.

References

American Psychiatric Association. (1987). *Diagnostic and statistical manual of mental disorders* (3rd ed., Revised) Washington, DC: Author.

American Psychiatric Association. (1994). *Diagnostic and statistical manual of mental disorders* (4th ed.). Washington, DC: Author.

American Psychiatric Association. (2013). *Diagnostic and statistical manual of mental disorders* (5th ed.). Washington, DC: Author.

Brand, S., Dunn, R., & Greb, F. (2002). Learning styles of students with Attention Deficit Hyperactivity Disorder: Who are they and how can we teach them? *Clearing House, 75,* 268.

Dunn, R., & Dunn, K. (1992). *Teaching individual students through their individual learning styles: A practical approach.* Boston, MA: Allyn & Bacon.

Litner, B. (2003). Teens with ADHD: The challenge of high school. *Child and Youth Care Forum, 32,* 137–158.

Moon, S. M. (2002). Gifted students with ADHD. In M. Neihart, S. M. Reis, N. M. Robinson, & S. M. Moon, (Eds.), *Social and emotional development of gifted children: What do we know?* Waco, TX: Prufrock Press.

Prevatt, F., Reaser, A., Proctor, B., & Petscher, Y. (2007). The learning/study strategies of college students with ADHD. *ADHD Report, 15*(6), 6–9.

Weaver, C. (1994). Eight tips for teachers with ADHD students. *Instructor, 103*(9), 43.

Chapter 83

Minimizing the Impact of Asperger's Syndrome in the Classroom

Practical Tips for Educators

by Traci McBride

I have known Asperger's syndrome through my child for 21 years now, and, yes, we are survivors. Not only did a well-meaning psychologist describe him as a child with Attention Deficit/Hyperactive Disorder (ADHD) at the age of 4, but he also told me that my child was "acutely" gifted. I did not realize at that time that I had a gifted child with Asperger's syndrome (AS), a twice-exceptional, or 2e, child. It was then that I began a journey of educating teachers and parents alike about effective ways to meet the needs of this special population of gifted children. As an educator and parent of a child with AS, I have learned several tips to make educators' lives easier when dealing with gifted students with AS.

Common Challenges

Students with AS have common challenges that can be dealt with successfully in the classroom if done with some flexibility. Five of these common challenges are lack of social skills, preoccupation with a particular topic or subject, obsessive routines, heightened sensitivity, and selective hearing.

1. Lack of social skills. Students who have AS lack basic social skills. They do not make eye contact, often invade personal space, and do not understand social cues.

My son, Alex, did not have a friend until he was 14 years old. I vividly remember inviting every child in Alex's kindergarten class to his birthday party. Although I had taken him to most of his classmates' parties and knew they were all well attended and very typical with all of the children having fun, only three boys came to Alex's party. Expecting many more children and their parents to attend, I was devastated but tried to make the ones who had come feel welcome. In hindsight the smaller number was actually better because Alex was overstimulated that day and became rather bossy. That day, I realized that I could not make friends for my child but would—so he could gain the skills he was lacking—to help him understand how to be a friend and thereby make friends for himself.

Teacher Tips

▶ Involve the child with AS in small, cooperative groups with assigned roles in order to provide opportunities for AS students to interact with others and vice versa. Although not always a workable, pleasant situation for all parties involved, the student with AS must have exposure to others in order to develop the skills necessary to interact successfully in social situations.

▶ Involve the child with AS in social skills training with the assistance of the school's counselor who can interact with the child through scenarios to train him or her to use the appropriate behaviors for various social settings.

▶ Encourage the child with AS to participate in team sports. Although understanding and flexibility is necessary for the parents, coaches, and other students, it is possible for a child with AS to play team sports. If viewed as a way for the child to learn more about social skills and appropriate social behaviors, the child can gain confidence and self-esteem if he or she becomes an accepted member of the team.

---

2. Preoccupation with a particular subject. Students with AS are often experts on a particular topic. Some are passionate about trains; others, computers; still others, Disney movies.

Even in my earliest memories Alex adored Sonic the Hedgehog and video games. Growing up with technology, Alex had an obsession with "beating the game." He would often slip away from me at Walmart but could always be found in the electronics or book sections, either looking at new games that had just been released or reading up on a "cheats" book so he could break the codes of the game to beat it. Although his fascination/obsession has cost a good deal of money for new game systems and new games, with more stops at GameStop and Electronics Boutique than I could have ever imagined possible, this obsession has been a blessing in many ways. Alex found a place to escape from a world of peers who could not understand him or accept him. He has developed such skill at playing games that he has become an expert and plans to develop his own games in the future and market them to a world full of gamers.

Teacher Tips

- ▸ Recognize the interests of the student with AS and be willing to listen to him discuss his knowledge on the subject.
- ▸ Praise the student with AS for his expertise; however, offer to expand that knowledge into associated academic areas.
- ▸ Suggest related topics for the student with AS to explore by offering books or websites on the topic.
- ▸ Accept that this interest is the student's world, the one thing that makes him feel comfortable and safe. Trying to downplay the interest or disregard it can feel like rejection, not just of the topic but of the child himself.

---

3. Obsessive routines. Some students with AS are ritualistic. They often have difficulties with transitions because of their lack of awareness of time.

Although Alex did not have obsessive routines as some children with AS do, he did have a very difficult time with transitions. Many children do not like to change from one setting to another and are often not ready to stop what they are doing; however, Alex's behavior was rather extreme. Alex could not stop what he was doing when he was told to stop. Our morning and nighttime routines were always difficult. Alex did not want to take a bath; he would not be ready to get into the tub, offering numerous excuses. Once in the bathtub, we would go through the same process of trying to get him out of the tub. Although not a problem when a small child, as he got older, these challenges became more and more difficult.

Teacher Tips

- ▶ Students with AS need time reminders. The internal clock that allows us to sense that 5 minutes or an hour has passed is missing in children with AS. In the classroom, when timed tests are an issue, an egg timer can help the student with AS see time pass. Also, a gentle reminder of how much time has passed either through a verbal or nonverbal cue can help students with AS better grasp the concept of time.
- ▶ Field trips can be difficult for AS students because students are out of their normal routine. A student buddy or paraprofessional can be appointed to stay with the student with AS while away from the school building. Students with AS can be distracted easily and may not realize when it's time to meet the group or be back at the bus.
- ▶ When the school day is not going to run as usual, be proactive and explain to the student with AS what to expect. Additionally, remind him of appropriate behavior for the situation along with any consequences of misbehavior. The more the student is aware of changes in his school day, the greater the chance that the student can successfully deal with them.

---

4. Heightened sensitivity. Students with AS are oversensitive to stimuli in general. Loud noises can create pain in their ears, light seems too bright, and clothes that are too rough can be too irritating to wear.

As a small child, Alex would cry when I put him into the bath water. I did not understand why he was always so upset. I later discovered that his tolerance to hot water was much lower than mine. Similarly, I took Alex with me to basketball games. No sooner would we get settled and situated on the bleachers than he would begin crying at the top of his lungs from noise discomfort. At another time, I took Alex to a Christmas parade so he could enjoy the clowns, the small cars, and see Santa Claus. Even though I had packed up the car, found a parking space, and walked for a couple of blocks to find a good vantage point for Alex to see the parade, he could not tolerate the noise of the fire truck siren, the loud engine sounds of the small cars, nor the loud laughter of the clowns, so we made our way back to the car. His heightened senses sometimes caused additional challenges that could surprise me in a positive way or catch me unaware.

Teacher Tips

- ► Be proactive about fire drills. Loud noises can actually be painful to a student with AS. Removing him from the classroom during a regular drill, offering headphones for him to wear, or simply letting him know ahead of time about the drill can minimize the effects of this familiar school occurrence.
- ► Many students with AS are sensitive to bright light. Recess or P.E. can be difficult for students with light sensitivity. Offer a shady area for them, if possible, or minimize the time outside when this sensitivity is an issue.
- ► If you notice that students with AS become upset when going into the cafeteria or an assembly in the gym, give them options of alternative places to go. The noise level alone may simply be intolerable and could possibly lead to disruptive behavior.

5. Selective listening. Some students with AS may appear to be deaf but often hear everything being said around them. They do not always respond or look at the person talking to them.

Alex was always too busy playing video games, working mazes, and building with blocks to listen to conversations. Calling his name to get his attention rarely prompted any action at all. Alex was seemingly oblivious because of his intensity in another activity. I vividly remember walking in front of him to block the video game or the TV screen to see if I could try to make him listen. Conversely, I would have conversations on the phone away from Alex, but he would comment about them later on. He had been listening the entire time, just not attending.

Teacher Tips

- ▸ Be aware that most students with AS do not purposely try to disregard your verbal commands. Developing a system of giving nonverbal cues may be necessary to get their attention.
- ▸ Be aware that some students with AS can hear conversations across the room due to heightened hearing ability. Even if not attending to the conversation, the student may be listening to every word spoken.
- ▸ Praise students with AS for attending to you when they do so readily. Positive reinforcement can work with students with AS just as it does with other students.

My journey with Alex has been a challenging one from which I have grown both as a parent and educator. Emerson stated, "To be great is to be misunderstood." So often gifted students, especially those with extenuating needs such as AS, are truly misunderstood. Teachers question why students who are so bright cannot follow simple rules. They doubt these students' abilities, for their gifts are often masked by bizarre or inappropriate behaviors. I hope that more educators will use some of these basic strategies to find the greatness and special gifts in students with AS so they can more easily come out from their worlds into ours with respect and dignity.

Chapter 84

Requiem to an Oft Misused Reading Program

by Bob Schultz

In my previous column for *THP*, I introduced readers to the underbelly of the Accelerated Reader (AR) program as it relates to the gifted and talented. That column garnered many comments and personal feedback—both supportive of my contentions, and those questioning my professionalism. In this column, I want to continue the conversation a bit, and add more depth to my arguments against using the AR program with the gifted—and specifically twice-exceptional (also referred to as 2e) learners. A special thanks goes out to Dr. Dan Peters, who shared his family's personal experiences with the AR program as a "case study" for this column and whose story is provided with minor edits herein.

I have three children in elementary school—fourth grade, second grade, and kindergarten. They all are bright, inquisitive, creative, and love to learn. They are also dyslexic—meaning they have difficulty with sound/symbol decoding and processing, along with reading fluency.

AR became a household name—and not a positive one—when our oldest began first grade. Her elementary school uses AR to set the level of books students are allowed to check out from the library, as it is thought to reflect their reading level. No problem here, except the test used to determine reading level is timed.

Dyslexics often read excruciatingly slowly. Our daughter, like many other gifted dyslexic students, is able to understand more of what she reads than one would expect because she has a well-developed visual memory and vivid imagination. However, when timed on how fast she can read and answer questions, the wheels come off and her coping skills and strategies are useless. The result? Banishment from grade-level sections of the library even though she (and other 2e learners like her) fully comprehends material several years above grade level when given time to comprehend and digest it.

There are accommodations to the AR program, but the school has to contact the company and request them. In our case, school personnel have not been in a hurry to address this issue, even though they do offer some resources for dyslexia within the district.

As a psychologist who specializes in twice-exceptional children, I have the wherewithal and experience to know what to do to address the issue. Our family downplays the significance of grades and achievement, emphasizing the importance of effort, persistence, and perseverance. We balance our children's time as much as possible with activities they enjoy and feel competent in. We teach them about their strengths and help them to understand, accept, and compensate for their weaknesses. We read to them often and listen to books on tape to keep their innate passion for reading alive.

Reflection Connection

For the gifted, reading provides a pathway beyond monotony and drudgery of a slow-paced curriculum emphasizing minimum levels of performance. Twice-exceptional children share this joy, even if it takes them longer to process the symbols/sounds.

But schools work on a production line approach. Children are moved along, grade-by-grade, to some finishing point when they are then turned loose on the world. Any discrepancy or deviation from the production schedule (like the need for acceleration or enrichment) means stress and conflict on the system. Add a limiting condition and highlight the misconception that gifted children should be able to learn on their own at a high level and we have a problem.

In Dan's case, his expertise and training became the focal points for addressing the seemingly blind eye of the school. Yet, I am sure many parents and teachers share similar experiences but with fewer positive results.

Ode to Accelerated Reader

AR does provide stressed and overworked teachers with an easily implemented and structured system to promote reading *for grade-level readers*. It is not a comprehensive reading program. It is a supplement only—as noted by the company. And, it lacks research support showing any evidence that it is beneficial for gifted and/or 2e learners.

Children deserve our undivided attention to appropriately support their individual needs, especially when it comes to reading. Our jaunt into the use of the AR program with gifted and 2e learners now comes to a close. Decide for yourselves whether the program will create readers who live happily ever after.

Chapter 85

Teaching Billy

Motivating a High-Potential Student With Emotional and Behavioral Difficulties

by Derek Davis

When I entered the teaching profession 10 years ago, my motivation was to follow in the footsteps of many of my high school teachers and coaches who, whether they know it or not, were very significant role models in my life. I became certified in secondary social sciences and dreamed of a career teaching and coaching in a high school environment similar to the one I attended. When I began to apply for teaching positions, I realized that jobs in my field were not plentiful at the midpoint of the school year, when I finished my teaching program. Eager to begin my career, I accepted a job at a local school serving students with severe emotional and behavioral disabilities (SEBD)[6]. I remember telling one of my new colleagues, "I am only going to work here until I can get a 'real' teaching job."

Ten years later, I am still there, and would never consider teaching anywhere else. Although I entered the teaching profession with a love of social sciences and athletics, I have found that in this setting, I am able to have a significant impact on students' lives. More importantly, I have come to view students from this population in a much different perspective. What I saw as deficits in academic and social functioning, I now see in many cases is untapped gifted poten-

---

6 *Note.* The American Psychiatric Association's *Diagnostic and Statistical Manual of Mental Disorders* (5th ed., 2013) classification is *emotional/behavioral disorders*.

tial. This potential has been hidden beneath layers of prejudice, poverty, abuse, neglect, inappropriate curriculum and instruction, and decades of misconceptions about what constitutes high ability. Here, I describe my experiences in working with Billy, a very bright student with SEBD.

The First Meeting

Billy was a 12-year-old Caucasian sixth grader who was referred to my school due to behavior problems that included being disruptive in class, refusing to follow directions, talking back to teachers, verbally and physically threatening students, using profanity, and making inappropriate sexual comments to teachers. When I met Billy, he appeared to be well-mannered and introduced himself properly by looking me directly in the eye, extending a firm handshake, and displaying a friendly smile. Despite his disheveled hair, tattered clothing, and worn-out sneakers, Billy was a charming and handsome young man.

When I learned that a White student from a rural school system would be arriving in my classroom, I was concerned about how well he would get along with my current students, all of whom were urban African American youngsters. I was afraid they would not accept each other, and frankly, I thought that I would be spending a lot of time breaking up fights. To my surprise, Billy walked into my room and introduced himself to my students in a very different manner from the way he had introduced himself to me, but in a way that gained him immediate acceptance and admiration. Within minutes Billy and my students were laughing and joking with each other, and I quickly surmised that Billy not only had a great sense of humor, but also was very charismatic. I wondered what other surprises Billy had in store for me.

Understanding and Adapting Student Abilities and Learning Styles

Our school psychologist administered reading and math assessments to Billy to determine his ability levels so that we could plan instruction and place him in the appropriate reading and math groups. From Billy's school records, we learned that his overall IQ score was firmly in the average range and we were amazed to see him read on an 11th-grade level and perform math operations and computations on a ninth-grade level. Billy's school records and files made no mention of high ability or gifted potential. Like so many students with behavior problems, his interfering behaviors and conduct infractions seemed to overshadow his strengths.

In my classroom Billy finished assignments in a fraction of the time it took other students. Not used to students with this speed and productivity, I found myself initially unprepared and learned that giving him a greater quantity of work only resulted in boredom and increased the incidence of interfering behaviors. Having been trained in regular and special education, I was not exposed to gifted instruction or programming. I did not know what curriculum compacting was at the time, but I found myself doing just that. I allowed Billy to work at his own pace and skip units in which he was able to prove mastery. This worked great for math where I was able to give Billy a prealgebra book and let him work independently. This strategy not only provided him some much needed confidence and positive recognition, but it also became a motivator for other students who were quite competent in math but had lost interest with what they perceived as dull instruction and boring repetition. When one of my underachieving math students asked, "Why can't I do algebra?" I told him that as soon as he demonstrated competence of the prerequisite skills, he would also be individually accelerated. This motivated many of the students to work harder. When several of my students began to improve assignment completion and accuracy, I planned basic algebra lessons for them.

Despite the fact that several students needed some scaffolding and remediation of the basic computation skills for algebra, they were motivated to work hard at something they felt made them appear successful to their peers. Due to Billy's social acceptance in the class and his high ability, I found him to be both a great motivator and tutor for other students. This provided Billy with another positive outlet for his academic abilities and personality, which had not been made available to him in his regular school.

Compacting Billy's reading instruction was not quite as easy. Due to the remedial nature of the school's academic program, there was no reading class that could accommodate Billy's 11th-grade abilities. We attempted to model the same arrangement we used for math but found that, due to limited staff resources, the direct instruction aspect of our reading program did not lend itself to peer tutoring and/or mentoring, and instead we were forced to place Billy in a reading group. It did not take long for the disruptive behavior to begin. Billy was not challenged and quickly resorted to teasing other students, making fun of their mistakes, and talking back to his teachers. We realized that we needed to do something different.

Developing a Learning Plan

Our treatment team met with Billy to determine what could be done to motivate him to behave appropriately in reading. Our school uses a token reinforcement behavior management system that allows students to purchase secondary reenforcers such as food, drinks, pens, pencils, and toys. This was not working with Billy, as he was not motivated by these types of rewards. We asked Billy to fill out a wish list of things he liked to do and things he would be willing to work for. We learned that he loved to play basketball and play the drums. We drew up a contract for Billy that allowed him to purchase time to do these activities with the positive points he would earn for proper behavior in reading. We also allowed Billy to create his own interest-based reading list. Because Billy was having occasional episodes of impulsive profane language and was becoming argumentative with some of his teachers, we included these behaviors in the contract and allowed Billy to carry sports and music magazines with him to class to serve as reminders of our arrangement.

Response to the Plan

Billy gradually improved his behavior and reduced his profane language. He enjoyed his self-selected reading assignments and became very helpful with the other students. We learned to be patient as Billy endured the challenges that accompanied his progress. There were several occasions where he was unable to participate in his preferred activities due to his poor behavior. When he realized that he was not going to be able to renegotiate the terms of the arrangement, something that he seemed to do with ease in his home school, he quickly improved and became a model student.

Billy's continued success was dependent upon constant monitoring. His academic and behavioral program required frequent modifications. The recognition and acceptance he received by helping other students had given him a tremendous boost in confidence as well as minimized his problem behaviors. We noticed that Billy's altruistic efforts were having a positive effect on other students. Billy needed to continue to be challenged academically on a level we had never experienced in our alternative school. Besides compacting his curriculum and allowing him numerous opportunities for self-selected assignments, we also found it useful to enlist Billy's assistance in everyday classroom tasks such as running errands within the school, photocopying, assisting teachers with bulletin boards, and helping younger children.

Outcomes and Reflections

One of the most rewarding aspects of working in a school like mine is that you get to see students begin to enjoy school again. I enjoyed watching this happen for Billy. He was no longer the class clown or bad kid in the principal's office. He was an important part of my class and our school, and he knew it. He was successful academically, socially, and behaviorally. He had made many new friends and was having positive, appropriate interactions with adults.

Regardless of what a teacher accomplishes in modifying instruction, programming, and curriculum, the impact of a positive, supportive adult relationship can never be underestimated. Billy now has several supportive adults who are fond of him, and he knows it. Billy's academic and behavioral success has been stable and consistent enough that he is now ready to see if he can transfer what he has learned back to his home school, the ultimate goal of our program. Billy is nervous but excited. The transition from our school to his home school will be gradual so that Billy can maintain his important relationships and receive the academic and behavioral support he will need as he attempts to meet the demands of a regular middle school. We are communicating and collaborating with his new teachers so they can be proactive in continuing the modifications that have helped Billy change his behavior and feel good about being in school again.

We are excited and hopeful that Billy is ready to return to his home school, but we are also sad to know that he eventually will be gone from our school. That is the bittersweet irony of teaching in such a setting. We experience the exhilaration of a child's success and happiness, only to have to say goodbye if we are successful. As difficult as it is to say goodbye to this talented student from whom I've learned so much, I eagerly await the next Billy.

For Further Reading

Bianco, M. (2005). The effects of disability labels on special education and general education teachers' referrals for gifted programs. *Learning Disability Quarterly, 28,* 285–293.

Morrison, W. F. (2001). Emotional/behavioral disabilities and gifted and talented behaviors: Paradoxical or semantic differences in characteristics? *Psychology in the Schools, 38,* 425–431.

Winebrenner, S. (1992). *Teaching gifted kids in the regular classroom: Strategies and techniques every teacher can use to meet the academic needs of the gifted and talented.* Minneapolis, MN: Free Spirit.

Reference

American Psychiatric Association. (2013). *Diagnostic and statistical manual of mental disorders* (5th ed.). Washington, DC: Author.

Section IV: GLBTQ

Chapter 86

GLBTQ Curricula Benefit All Students

by Terence P. Friedrichs

For much of the early 60s through the late 80s, I sat in my desk in parquet-floored K–12 schools, cinder-blocked colleges, and chalk-scented graduate classrooms. I learned my basic reading and math, strategies for teaching gifted and special needs youth, research methodologies for discovering what makes for successful educators of exceptional students. But, despite all of these strenuous efforts, I never learned anything about myself. I never learned anything gay.

Admittedly, I also learned little about being gay from home, neighborhood, and church. However, both as a youth and as an adult, my school's failure to teach me was the most disappointing shortcoming. School, I thought, was supposed to be all about learning.

The price I paid for self-ignorance, perpetuated at school and elsewhere, was incalculable. My development was diminished as a son, friend, companion, and student. I never knew, in my teen years, for example, how to address same-sex dates, gay and straight friendships, and team-sport homophobia. I never even learned how to seek out books or other informational sources about people like me.

Since that time, through a valiant 40-year struggle of GLBTQ-supportive parents, teachers, and youth, there have been attempts to make schools better

"Smart Cookies" by Bess Wilson

places. Schools have established legally supported anti-bullying rules and other verbal and bias regulations supporting GLBT youth (Bedell, 2003; Weiner, 2005). Some districts have gone further, actively supporting parents of sexual-minority students, protecting GLBTQ teachers, and mandating community dialogue on sexual-minority issues. The changes have been welcome additions. These students have suffered mightily over the last three decades from verbal and physical harassment, physical violence, substance abuse, and high-risk sexual behaviors (GLSEN, 2015; National Gay and Lesbian Task Force, 1987). At the same time, however, many administrators, counselors, and teachers of GLBTQ youth have also been socialized into silence on these continuing problems. They remain quiet in community atmospheres where townspeople still discuss how GLBTQ educators "prey upon students." In such climates, few teachers have felt confident enough to respond strongly and frequently to anti-GLBTQ insults.

However, in spite of positive school responses, most efforts have fallen short of truly recognizing the holistic needs of gifted GLBTQ youth, particularly those intellectual, academic, creative, arts, and leadership needs related to giftedness (Friedrichs, 2012; Whittenburg & Treat, 2008). High-potential sexual-minority youth need to be supported, not just in hallways and locker rooms, but during the whole school day. That is, these students need support throughout the classroom experiences during which they will develop those intellectual, academic, creative, artistic, and leadership strengths that will help them to begin making their marks on the world. Quite simply, as suggested by NAGC (2001) many years ago, these pupils need to have access to GLBTQ curricula.

GLBTQ-focused curricula can take many forms, and can be very effective with both sexual-minority and straight youth (GLSEN, 2017). Intellectually stimulating academic curricula assist both gifted sexual-minority and gifted straight youth. GLBTQ-infused History (Jennings, 1994) can teach about persecuted sexual-minority youth and adults, as well as about those brave, youthful Stonewall Rebellion participants who fought back in 1969 against anti-GLBTQ oppressions for the first time in American history. Health education (Flunker, Nezhad, & Salisbury, 2014) could focus on how to avoid HIV/

AIDS infections and tobacco and alcohol abuses that sometimes dispropor-tionately affect sexual-minority youth. And civics can teach about how GLBTQ people have organized in some states—and can further organize in other states and in Congress—for various nondiscrimination laws (National LGBTQ Task Force, 2013, 2014). Straight youth can learn a great deal from this education (Lipkin, 2000). Through generalization, they can learn helpful approaches on the following: fighting back against injustices that may apply to their own mar-ginalized age, racial, and ability groups; protecting themselves against the prev-alent diseases and addictions that apply to GLBTQ students and them; and organizing across supportive groups for important political goals that will affect our country's future. In the process, straight youth can learn respect for their sexual-minority classmates, neighbors, and (sometimes) parents and siblings. Straight students will eventually need to stand equally, side-by-side, with all of these individuals for America's future.

GLBTQ-sensitive creative and artistic curricula can provide sexual-minority and straight youth with opportunities to explore the joys, oppressions, and thinking of sexual-minority people. These curricula may include classroom English explorations of GLBTQ playwrights, poets, painters, and potters, as well as internships with—and mentorships from—sexual-minority-supportive experts (NAGC, 2001). Interviews with gifted GLBTQ youth have shown that such curricula have especially increased their creative and artistic knowledge and appreciation of sexual-minority arts and people, as well as their insights on how to pursue artistic careers (Friedrichs, 2005). GLBTQ-related leadership curricula may involve school or community involvement projects and intern-ships related to safe school programming and gay-straight alliances (GSAs).

Thus, through studying wide-ranging, sexual-minority-supportive curric-ula, gifted GLBTQ and gifted straight students can expand their knowledge, skills, perspectives, and aspirations. They can also learn to feel more comfort-able with, and enthused by, the emerging pro-GLBTQ world that their peers, friends, and families may well be a part of. These students can certainly move well beyond the sometimes isolated, ill-informed, and lonely world, which so many of us sexual-minority-supportive people experienced just a few years ago. They can move instead, as so many high-potential children long for, to a place of modern knowledge—and vital self-knowledge.

References

Bedell, J. (2003). Personal liability of school officials who ignore peer harassment of these students. *University of Illinois Law Review, 3,* 829–861.

Flunker, D., Nezhad, S. & Salisbury, J. (2014). *Voices of health: A survey of LGBTQ health in Minnesota.* Minneapolis, MN: Rainbow Health Initiative.

Friedrichs, T. P. (2005). *Contextual social and emotional needs, and preferred instructional approaches, for gifted gay and bi-sexual male adolescents.* Ann Arbor, MI: UMI.

Friedrichs, T. P. (2012). Counseling gifted GLBT students along paths to freedom. In T. L. Cross & J. R. Cross (Eds.), *Handbook for counselors of students with gifts and talents* (pp. 153–178). Waco, TX: Prufrock Press.

GLSEN. (2015). *2015 national school climate survey.* New York, NY: Author. Retrieved from https://www.glsen.org/article/2015-national-school-climate-survey

GLSEN. (2017). *Inclusion and respect: GLSEN resources for educators.* Retrieved from https://www.glsen.org/educate/resources

Jennings, K. (1994). *Becoming visible: A reader in gay and lesbian history for high school and college students.* Boston, MA: Alyson.

Lipkin, A. (2000). *Understanding homosexuality, changing schools: A text for teachers, counselors, and administrators.* Boulder, CO: Westview.

National Association for Gifted Children. (2001). *Appropriate education for gifted GLBT students* [Position statement]. Washington, DC: Author.

National Gay and Lesbian Task Force. (1987). *Statistics on hate crimes and secondary school harassment.* Washington, DC: Author.

National LGBTQ Task Force. (2013). *Hate crimes laws map.* Retrieved from http://www.thetaskforce.org/hate-crimes-laws-map

National LGBTQ Task Force. (2014). *Nondiscrimination laws map.* Retrieved from http://www.thetaskforce.org/nondiscrimination-laws-map

Weiner, C. (2005). Sex education: Recognizing anti-gay harassment as sex discrimination under Title VII and Title IX. *Columbia Human Rights Law Review, 37,* 189–234.

Whittenburg, B., & Treat, A. R. (2008). Shared characteristics of gifted and sexually diverse youth. In N. L. Hafenstein & J. A. Castellano (Eds.), *Perspectives in gifted education: Diverse gifted learners* (Vol. 4, 140–176). Denver, CO: University of Denver.

Chapter 87

Gifted LGBTQ Social-Emotional Issues

by Alena R. Treat

Many were shocked by the mass shooting at Orlando's Pulse, an LGBTQ (lesbian, gay, bisexual, transgender, questioning/queer) nightclub. This tragedy had a devastating effect on gifted LGBTQ (G/LGBTQ) students. Long considered a nonissue in K–12 education, these youth have become visible enough that gifted educators must now consider implications of having them in their classrooms. There are six issues that may create a need for intense, personalized social-emotional support, and additional protections (Whittenburg & Treat, 2009; see Figure 87.1).

1. Violence, harassment, and/or discrimination. Violence against LGBTQ individuals is a source of heightened concern and fear. Numerous homeless teens (20%–40%) are LGBTQ (Center for American Progress, 2010), many of whom left home to escape violence or discrimination directly linked to sexual orientation or gender identity. LGBTQ students are harassed at school—both verbally and physically—at twice the rate of non-LGBTQ youth (Southern Poverty Law Center, 2013). They are often harassed near classes, barely out of direct sight of teachers, usually in hallways and bathrooms. Physical harassment most often happens at off-campus events or on the way to and from school. Sometimes harassment prompts suicide. Alarmingly, about one third of all teen suicides are committed by LGBTQ students (Whittenburg & Treat, 2009).

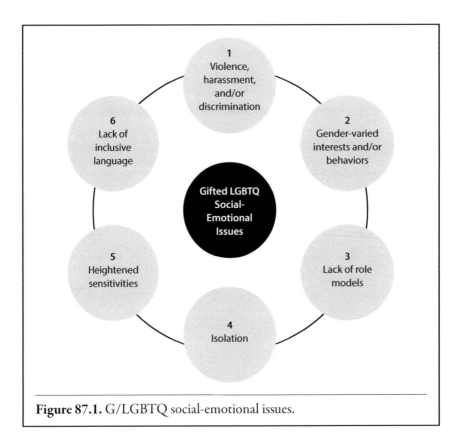

Figure 87.1. G/LGBTQ social-emotional issues.

2. Gender-varied interests and/or behaviors. Many gifted children tend to be androgynous, exhibiting characteristics and interests of both genders. The value of a traditional heterosexual gender role identity is implanted in early childhood by parents and community and is further reinforced in school, but at the cost of stifling creativity and achievement. Western society and gifted education have moved toward accepting and even promoting girls' interests in math, science, and technology—fields seen as traditionally male. Society, however, lacks support with the same enthusiasm for boys in nontraditional domains.

3. Lack of role models. G/LGBTQ students may experience psychological distress, such as trauma or depression that stems from isolation, fear, or unhealthy perfectionism. Both gifted and general education curricula neglect identifying eminent individuals by sexual orientation or gender identity.

4. Isolation. Assumptions made related to intelligence and sexual orientation (assumed heterosexuality) are among the leading causes of invisibility, and therefore, isolation. Whereas many minorities are visible because of race or ethnicity, G/LGBTQ youth may only appear different when they resemble

LGBTQ stereotypes. Some fit those stereotypes, but many do not. G/LGBTQ youth also can be vulnerable to *impostor syndrome*. In gifted populations, the syndrome is driven by fear that being gifted is a *lie*; in LGBTQ populations, fear that the *truth* (sexual orientation and/or gender identity) will become known. G/LGBTQ individuals may cultivate unhealthy perfectionism or under-achievement, experience depression, or may self-isolate in order to avoid being physically or psychologically hurt.

5. Heightened sensitivities. Heightened sensitivities are common to gifted students. The additional stressor of being LGBTQ can intensify those sensitivities due to effects of isolation, alienation, and bullying. Highly gifted/creative individuals, especially writers and visual artists, may also be at high risk for emotional and social disorders.

6. Lack of inclusive language. School communications commonly use terminology that assumes heterosexuality and traditional family configurations. This tends to alienate LGBTQ students as well as those with LGBTQ individuals in their families.

With awareness comes change, and when teachers and administrators are conscious of the needs of G/LGBTQ students they can work to create a safe and welcoming environment where all students feel respected, understood, and nurtured.

A Response to the Six Social-Emotional Issues for G/LGBTQ Students

P. J. Sedillo

Here are suggestions of what teachers can do to help address the six social-emotional issues for gifted LGBTQ (G/LGBTQ) students (Check first to see what's allowable in your particular school/district):

1. Post a "Safe Space" or "Safe Zone" placard/sticker, equality symbol, or rainbow flag in a prominent location. Review non-discrimination policies with students, specifically addressing LGBTQ issues, and display contact information for your school's anti-bullying coordinator. Publicly praise those who actively promote an inclusive environment. Identify "hot spots" (common language in public education; restrooms and other places out of sight of teachers, etc.) where bullying often

occurs and take steps to eliminate them, such as assigning students or asking staff to monitor these locations.

2. Ensure that nontraditional gender roles are included and honored in curricula and general discussions.

3. Ensure that G/LGBTQ role models are included in curricula, job shadowing/internships, guest speakers, mentors, etc.

4. Make LGBTQ issues a natural part of conversations. Help develop self-advocacy abilities in G/LGBTQ students and for those with LGBTQ family members.

5. Include a focus on overexcitabilities/sensitivities when planning curricula. Partner with counselors/experts to meet G/LGBTQ students' needs.

6. Use gender-neutral language in forms and communications (i.e., parent/guardian rather than mother/father). Provide opportunities—not requirements—for students to communicate gender identities. Ensure students are addressed by preferred pronouns.

Suggested Readings

Cohn, S. J. (2003). The gay gifted learner: Facing the challenge of homophobia and antihomosexual bias in schools. In J. A. Castellano (Ed.), *Special populations in gifted education: Working with diverse gifted learners* (pp. 123–149). Boston, MA: Allyn & Bacon.

Cowan, T. (1997). *Gay men and women who enriched the world.* New Canaan, CT: Mulvey Books.

Katz, J. (1992). *Gay American history: Lesbians and gay men in the USA: A documentary history.* New York, NY: Plume.

National Association for Gifted Children. (2015). *Supporting gifted students with diverse sexual orientations and gender identities* [Position Statement]. Retrieved from http://www.nagc.org/sites/default/files/Position%20Statement/GLBTQ%20%28sept%202015%29.pdf

Southern Poverty Law Center. (2013). *Best practices: Creating an LGBT-inclusive school climate, a teaching tolerance guide for school leaders.* Montgomery, AL: Author. Retrieved from http://www.tolerance.org/sites/default/files/general/LGBT%20Best%20Practices_0.pdf

References

Center for American Progress. (2010, June). *On the streets: The federal response to gay and transgender homeless youth.* Retrieved from https://www.americanprogress.org/issues/lgbt/news/2010/06/21/7980/gay-and-transgender-youth-homelessness-by-the-numbers

Southern Poverty Law Center. (2013). *Best practices: Creating an LGBT-inclusive school climate, a teaching tolerance guide for school leaders.* Montgomery, AL: Author. Retrieved from http://www.tolerance.org/sites/default/files/general/LGBT%20Best%20Practices_0.pdf

Whittenburg, B., & Treat, A. R. (2009). Shared characteristics of gifted and sexually diverse youth. In N. L. Hafenstein & J. A. Castellano (Eds.), *Perspectives in gifted education, volume 5: Diverse gifted learners.* Denver, CO: University of Denver.

About the Editors

Jeff Danielian is currently the director of the La Salle Scholars Program in Providence, RI. He received his master's degree in educational psychology from the University of Connecticut and currently holds the position of Teacher Resource Specialist for the National Association for Gifted Children.

C. Matthew Fugate, Ph.D., is Assistant Professor of Educational Psychology in the Urban Education Department at the University of Houston-Downtown. He earned his doctorate in Gifted, Creative, and Talented Studies at Purdue University. Matthew's primary research focus is on twice-exceptional learners, specifically those students who are gifted with ADHD.

Elizabeth Fogarty, Ph.D., studies gifted readers and practices for effective teaching, including differentiation and coteaching. She earned her doctorate in educational psychology at the University of Connecticut in 2006. She is a lecturer in literacy education at the University of Minnesota and lives in Minnesota with her husband and two children.

About the Authors

Cheryll M. Adams, Ph.D., is Director Emerita of the Center for Gifted Studies and Talent Development at Ball State University and teaches graduate courses in gifted education. She has authored or coauthored numerous publications in professional journals, as well as several books and book chapters. She has served on the Board of Directors of the National Association for Gifted Children and the Florida Association for the Gifted, and has been president of the Indiana Association for the Gifted and of The Association for the Gifted, Council for Exceptional Children.

Corinne J. Alfeld, Ph.D., is interested in research on supportive educational environments for young people, particularly those in gifted and talented and career and technical education programs. She oversees grants in these and other research areas as a program officer in the National Center for Education Research, Institute of Education Sciences, U.S. Department of Education.

Lori Andersen, Ph.D., is an assistant professor of science education at Kansas State University.

Jennifer Beasley, Ed.D., has more than 25 years of experience in education as an elementary school teacher, gifted facilitator, and university professor. She is currently the Director of Teacher Education at the University of Arkansas.

Sherry Mee Bell, Ph.D., is a Professor of Special Education and Department Head of Theory and Practice in Teacher Education at the University of Tennessee. A former special educator and school psychologist, her education also includes elementary education and library information science. Her research interests include effective assessment and instructional practices, giftedness and learning disabilities, teacher education, and attribution theory. Author of numerous scholarly articles, she is also coauthor of *Handbook of Reading Assessment* (2nd ed., Routledge) and the *Assessment of Reading Instructional Knowledge-Adults*.

Kevin D. Besnoy, Ph.D., is the associate director of K–12 programming and director of ACCESS Virtual at The University of Alabama. He earned his Ph.D. in curriculum, instruction, and special education with an emphasis in gifted and talented education and instructional technology from The University of Southern Mississippi in 2006.

Paul Bierman, Ph.D., is professor of geology and natural resources at the University of Vermont, where he works with students of all ages. His research focuses on the interaction of humans and the landscape, including storms, floods, and erosion. He has spent his career attempting to integrate teaching and research.

Diane J. Bresson is the principal at Yargo Elementary School in Winder, GA. She earned her Specialist in Education degree from the University of Georgia.

Katherine B. Brown, Ph.D., is the gifted and advanced specialist for the Clarke County School District, where she leads her district in innovative programing, including the International Baccalaureate Programme and the Schoolwide Enrichment Model. She also serves as an adjunct professor at the University of Georgia in the Department of Educational Psychology.

Chris A. Caram, Ph.D., is a retired educator. Dr. Caram served as the Deputy State Superintendent of Education for the State of Oklahoma, Director of Education at the Arkansas Educational Television Network, and Associate Professor in the Department of Educational Leadership and Foundations at Western Carolina University. She has served as associate professor of educational leadership at the University of Arkansas at Little Rock and has been a teacher, principal, director of elementary education, assistant superintendent, and deputy superintendent over instructional programs.

Richard M. Cash, Ed.D., is an internationally recognized education expert and author who has spent 30 years in K–12 gifted education. He has held positions as a classroom teacher, curriculum coordinator and district administrator. He was the 2011 recipient of NAGC's Early Leader Award.

Anna Cassalia, M.Ed., has more than 17 years of experience in education. She holds a Master's in Education degree from the University of North Dakota, and a gifted endorsement from the University of Virginia. During the past 3 years she has been working as a gifted teacher and differentiation coach in Williamson County Public Schools.

Jaime A. Castellano, Ph.D., is a nationally recognized and award-winning principal; an award-winning author, scholar, and researcher; and a published author with four books in the field of gifted education, including dozens of articles and chapters written for multiple publications. His 2011 book, *Special Populations in Gifted Education: Understanding Our Most Able Students From Diverse Backgrounds* was awarded the Legacy Award for Outstanding Scholarly Publication in Gifted Education. Published in March of 2014, his latest book is titled *Talent Development for English Language Learners: Identifying and Developing Potential.*

Scott A. Chamberlin, Ph.D., is a professor at the University of Wyoming. He has research interests in mathematical problem solving, affect, creativity, and giftedness. He prepares preservice teachers and graduate students in mathematics education.

Kimberley L. Chandler, Ph.D., is the Curriculum Director at the Center for Gifted Education at William & Mary. Kimberley has served as the editor and contributing author of numerous curriculum materials from the Center for Gifted Education. She coauthored the book *Effective Curriculum for Underserved Gifted Students* and is the coeditor of the book *Effective Program Models for Gifted Students From Underserved Populations.*

Alicia Cotabish, Ed.D., is an Associate Professor of Teaching and Learning at the University of Central Arkansas. She has authored and coauthored a number of books and journal articles related to STEM and gifted education.

Steve V. Coxon, Ph.D., is associate professor and director of programs in gifted education at Maryville University, including the gifted education graduate programs; the STEM Education Certificate program; the Maryville Young Scholars Program to increase gifted program diversity; the CREST-M math and robotics curricula project; STEM Sprouts for ages 3–5; C3 to engage middle school girls in coding; App Dev. Camp for inner-city secondary students; and the Maryville Science and Robotics Program.

Debbie Dailey, Ed.D., is an assistant professor of teaching and learning at the University of Central Arkansas, where she is the coordinator for the gifted and talented program. Dr. Dailey has authored and coauthored multiple journal articles, books, book chapters, and products focused on K–12 STEM and gifted education. Prior to moving to higher education, she was a high school science teacher and gifted education teacher for 20 years.

Derek Davis, Ph.D., was a special education teacher for more than 12 years. He received his doctorate degree in Gifted and Creative Education at the University of Georgia.

Joy Lawson Davis, Ph.D., is a scholar, author, and gifted education consultant, currently serving as Associate Professor and Chair of the Department of Teacher Education at Virginia Union University. She is a vocal advocate for equity and excellence in education. Her published books include *Bright, Talented, and Black: A Guide for Families of African American Gifted Learners* and *Gifted Children of Color Around the World*.

Patsy B. Davis served as the Director of Academically Gifted Programs in Gaston County (NC) Schools. Her many accolades include nomination for North Carolina Gifted Administrator of 2005. She received her graduate degree in gifted education from Belmont Abbey College.

Alyssa Del Campo graduated from Florida Gulf Coast University with a bachelor's degree in elementary education. Currently, she is pursuing a second bachelor's degree in psychology from Florida International University. She plans to attend graduate school after to conduct research in the field of psychology.

Felicia A. Dixon, Ph.D., is Professor Emerita in the Department of Educational Psychology at Ball State University and an educational consultant focusing on high-ability students at the secondary level. She has authored many journal articles and two major books, *The Handbook of Secondary Gifted Education* (2nd ed., 2015) and *Programs and Services for Gifted Secondary Students* (2008).

Barbara Dullaghan, M.Ed., recently retired as a gifted and talented coordinator after 40 years in gifted education. She is coauthor of the Smart Start series for ages 3–5 (published by Prufrock Press, 2015) and a columnist for *THP*. She also served as Chair of NAGC's Early Childhood Network.

Rebecca D. Eckert, Ph.D., is an associate clinical professor in Teacher Education at the Neag School of Education at the University of Connecticut, where she works with preservice teachers as they navigate the joys and challenges of their first classroom experiences. In her former role as the Gifted Resource Specialist for NAGC, Dr. Eckert helped redesign the NAGC website and develop practical resources for educators and advocates of gifted students— including the inaugural edition of *Teaching for High Potential*. She is a former middle school teacher with experience in geography, history, and theater arts.

Elizabeth C. Fairweather, Ph.D., is a veteran educator with more than 20 years of teaching experience in K–12 public schools and is also an adjunct instructor at the University of Georgia and the University of South Florida. Her research interests include creative process and nurturing children's creativity.

James Fetterly, Ph.D., is an assistant professor in the Mathematics Department at the University of Central Arkansas. He is interested in creativity and problem posing in mathematics.

Kathryn Fishman-Weaver, Ph.D., serves as the Director of Academic Affairs and Engagement for Mizzou K–12. In her faculty appointment in the College of Education, she leads a dynamic instructional team that supports more than 6,000 students globally. Her research interests include school leadership, alternative service delivery models, and affective education.

Donna Y. Ford, Ph.D., is Professor of Education and Human Development at Vanderbilt University. Professor Ford conducts research primarily in gifted education and multicultural/urban education. She consults with school districts, and educational and legal organizations on such topics as gifted education underrepresentation and Advanced Placement, multicultural/urban education and counseling, and closing the achievement gap.

Jennifer A. Fredricks, Ph.D., is a professor in Human Development at Connecticut College, where she also directs the Holleran Center for Community Action and Public Policy. Her research interests include school engagement, motivation, out-of-school activity participation, and gender socialization.

Terry P. Friedrichs, Ph.D., has served gifted gay, lesbian, bisexual, transgender, and questioning (LBGTQ) students for 40 years as a student, teacher, professor, researcher, and legislative advocate. He is the author of 15 articles on these youth, as well as a new NAGC book, *Gifted GLBTQ Students: Educational Needs and Approaches* (Friedrichs, Manzella, & Seney, 2017).

Marcia Gentry, Ph.D., is Professor of Educational Studies and she directs the Gifted Education Resource Institute at Purdue University. She has received multiple grants worth several million dollars in support of her work with programming practices and underrepresented populations in gifted education.

Amos Gewirtz, from Mendota Heights, MN, is a student at the University of Chicago, with a prospective major in history or political science. He currently writes for *The Chicago Maroon* and paints in oil colors. He displays his art in Saint Paul/Mendota Heights coffee shops.

Thomas S. Greenspon, Ph.D., is a recently retired psychologist and marriage and family therapist and a former copresident (with his wife, Barbara) of the Minnesota Council for the Gifted and Talented. He is currently an author and a faculty member at the Minnesota Institute for Contemporary Psychotherapy and Psychoanalysis.

Keri M. Guilbault, Ed.D., is an assistant professor of Gifted Education at Johns Hopkins University. Dr. Guilbault has worked as a district supervisor of gifted and talented programs and as a teacher of the gifted. She currently serves as the Parent Representative on the National Association for Gifted Children Board of Directors.

Mary E. Haas is a professor of social studies education K–12 at West Virginia University. Her specialization is the development of inquiry teaching and instructional strategies in civics education.

Thomas P. Hébert, Ph.D., is Professor of Gifted and Talented Education in the College of Education at the University of South Carolina. He has more than a decade of K–12 classroom experience working with gifted students and 20 years in higher education training graduate students and educators in gifted education. He is the author of the award-winning text *Understanding the Social and Emotional Lives of Gifted Students.*

Suzanna E. Henshon, Ph.D., teaches full-time at Florida Gulf Coast University. She is the author of 350 publications, including several books. Most recently, Sue published *Andy Lightfoot and the Time Warp* (2014) on Amazon Kindle.

Gail N. Herman, Ph.D., a former G/T enrichment teacher, is a creative arts consultant and storyteller who teaches at Confratute and for schools and colleges in the New England and Mid-Atlantic Region. She has written stories and articles for anthologies and educational periodicals, as well as books on storytelling and visual arts appreciation using creative movement and sound. She taught and performed on four continents and in 40 states. Her website is http://gailherman.net.

Jennifer Hoffman teaches in an enrichment and gifted program at J. A. Traphagen School in Waldwick, NJ. She is the 2011 recipient of the Teacher of the Year Award there.

Brian C. Housand, Ph.D., is an Associate Professor, coordinator of the Academically and Intellectually Gifted Program at East Carolina University. Dr. Housand earned a Ph.D. in educational psychology at the University of Connecticut with an emphasis in both gifted education and instructional technology. He researches ways in which technology can enhance the learning environment and is striving to define creative productive giftedness in a digital age. For more information, visit http://brianhousand.com.

Scott Hunsaker, Ph.D., is a Distinguished Associate Professor of Honors Education at Utah State University. He also serves as the Director of Undergraduate Teacher Preparation for USU's School of Teacher Education and Leadership. Scott's long service to gifted education includes terms as a member of the Board of Directors of the National Association for Gifted Children and as President of the Utah Association for Gifted Children.

Todd Jeffrey is the former president of the Oregon Association for Talented and Gifted. He holds MS degrees in Administration from Pepperdine University and Educational Psychology from Purdue University. Todd currently lives in Austin, TX, where he is an administrator and parenting consultant.

Sandra N. Kaplan, Ph.D., is involved in the development of differentiated curriculum and instruction for gifted learners. Currently, she is investigating a nontraditional approach to the identification and teaching/learning of young gifted learners in preschool to second grade.

Barbara A. Kerr, Ph.D., is director of the Counseling Laboratory for the Exploration of Optimal States (CLEOS), a counseling center for creative adolescents, as well as the author of the Smart Girls series of books, coauthor of *Smart Boys*, and many articles on the counseling and guidance of gifted and creative children.

Robert A. King, Jr., received his degree at Vanderbilt University, with a major in psychology and a minor in corporate strategy. He is the founder of Project I Am—an organization aimed at easing the transition of students of color into Vanderbilt University.

Rebecca N. Landis is a doctoral student in School Psychology at the University of Georgia. She received her M.A. in gifted education and is conducting research on the reasons gifted students drop out of high school.

Jerry Lassos is a member of the Tongva tribe, indigenous to Los Angeles. In a career that spans more than 30 years, he was a teacher, gifted and talented teacher, and GT resource consultant in Colorado's largest school district. Most recently a GT resource consultant and an American Indian Resource Specialist in Denver Public Schools, he passionately advocated for Native American students and families.

Chin-Wen "Jean" Lee studies special education at the University of Northern Colorado. She is interested in twice-exceptionality, teacher preparation, professional development, and program evaluation.

Rachel Levinson received her master's degree in educational psychology with an emphasis on talent development from the University of Connecticut. Mrs. Levinson has been teaching at Brookside Elementary School in Monroe Township, NJ, for 12 years. She proposed, piloted, and now helps to implement the very successful cluster grouping model for grades 3–5.

Timothy Lintner, Ph.D., is Professor of Social Studies Education at the University of South Carolina Aiken. His research focuses on the intersection between social studies and exceptional learners.

Bronwyn MacFarlane, Ph.D., is Professor of Gifted Education at the University of Arkansas at Little Rock. She earned her doctorate in Educational Leadership, Policy, and Planning from William & Mary, and her research interests focus upon talent development and assessing programs and curricula interventions to increase talent development among learners. Follow Dr. Bronwyn on Twitter @DrBMacFarlane.

Eric L. Mann, Ph.D., is an assistant professor of mathematics education at Hope College in Holland, MI, where he works with preservice elementary teachers. Previously a K–8 teacher, Dr. Mann studied gifted education at the University of Connecticut. His research interests include pedagogical content knowledge in K–8 mathematics and creativity and talent development in the STEM disciplines.

Traci McBride, Ed.D., is an Academic Dean at Lanier Christian Academy. She also earned a master's degree in English education from the University of Georgia and an Ed.D. in curriculum and instruction from Liberty University. Dr. McBride worked for 30 years as an English teacher and administrator in the district prior to her retirement in 2012.

Steve McCallum, Ph.D., is Professor of School Psychology in the Department of Educational Psychology and Counseling at the University of Tennessee. He has served the field as a practicing school psychologist, faculty member/administrator in higher education, and as author/coauthor of books, book chapters, journal articles, tests, and national/international conference presentations.

Jason S. McIntosh, Ph.D., is an executive board member for the Arizona Association for Gifted and Talented and serves as the gifted specialist for the Littleton Elementary School District. He received his doctorate in gifted, talented, and creative studies from Purdue University in 2015. Prior to his doctoral studies, he served as a gifted pull-out teacher, program coordinator, and regular classroom teacher for a combined total of 14 years.

Michael H. Miller teaches English at the Thomas Jefferson High School for Science and Technology in Alexandria, VA. He is a former Content Review Committee member for Virginia's EOC English Writing Test. E-mail him at michael.miller2@fcps.edu.

Rachelle Miller, Ph.D., received her Ph.D. in educational psychology and is currently an Assistant Professor in the Department of Teaching and Learning at the University of Central Arkansas. She works in the Gifted and Talented Education Program, teaching affective strategies for the gifted and talented. Her research interests include supporting the academic needs of low-income gifted students, integrating the arts into the general and gifted curriculum, and examining teacher perceptions of arts integration.

Kristen Morrison earned her master's degree at Wilfrid Laurier University, where she also earned her Bachelor of Music and Bachelor of Education degrees. Kristen is a music and special education teacher with the Waterloo Region District School Board.

Elinda R. Nedreberg is an English teacher in the Davis School District.

Sara Newell received a Master of Arts in Gifted Education from Converse College. She teaches highly gifted fifth graders in Greenville, SC. She also teaches graduate classes in gifted education. She works to combine sound educational theory with engaging student experiences.

Paula Olszewski-Kubilius, Ph.D., is the director of the Center for Talent Development and a professor in the School of Education and Social Policy at Northwestern University. She has worked for 33 years in gifted education, conducting research and developing programs for diverse groups of gifted learners.

Chea Parton is a doctoral student in English Education at Purdue University. Her research interests include the usage of art in the English classroom and adolescence as a social construct.

Scott J. Peters, Ph.D., is an Assistant Professor of Educational Foundations at the University of Wisconsin–Whitewater, where he teaches courses related to educational measurement and assessment. He received his Ph.D. from Purdue University in 2009, specializing in gifted and talented education, with secondary areas in Applied Research Methodology and English Education.

Jean S. Peterson, Ph.D., has done extensive clinical work and research with gifted youth, often exploring their development in longitudinal, qualitative studies. She received 12 awards for teaching, research, or service at Purdue, as well as numerous national awards, and has authored 120 books, journal articles, and invited chapters in her second career.

Arlene Puryear has more than 30 years of Gifted and Talented experience in public schools. She currently serves as the Director of Field Experiences and Gifted and Talented Coordinator at the University of South Carolina Aiken.

Joseph S. Renzulli, Ed.D., is a Distinguished Professor of Educational Psychology at the University of Connecticut and director of the Renzulli Center for Creativity, Gifted Education, and Talent Development. The American Psychological Association named him among the 25 most influential psychologists in the world, and Dr. Renzulli received the Harold W. McGraw, Jr. Award for Innovation in Education.

Susannah Richards, Ph.D., is an associate professor of education at Eastern Connecticut State University, where she teaches courses in English language arts and children's and young adult literature. She is active in the world of books for youth and served on the 2013 John Newbery and 2017 Geisel Award Committees. She completed her doctorate at the University of Connecticut, where she focused on studying talented readers.

Jennifer Ritchotte, Ph.D., is an assistant professor of Special Education with an emphasis in Gifted and Talented Education at the University of Northern Colorado. Through publications, conference presentations, and workshops, she advocates for the needs of all high-potential learners.

Ed Robson received his master's degree in Gifted and Talented Education from Purdue University. He currently teaches U.S. History (regular and AP) plus AP World History at Benton Central in Oxford, IN, and is a co-GT coordinator for the school system.

Christen C. Rose received her master's degree in education from the University of Utah. She is an Honors English teacher in Davis School District with endorsements in ESL, reading, and gifted and talented. Christen has presented at the conferences of the National Association for Gifted Children, the Utah Council for Teachers of English, and the Utah Association for Gifted Children.

Michelle Sands, Ed.D., is an enrichment specialist in the North Salem Central School District in North Salem, NY, where she coordinates the elementary program for the gifted and talented. She is the author and coauthor of publications related to the Schoolwide Enrichment Model, differentiation and enrichment in mathematics, and social capital. She has also presented at national conferences on the topic of gifted education and Makerspaces, most recently the National Association for Gifted Children convention in 2016.

Robert A. Schultz, Ph.D., is Professor of Gifted Education and Curriculum Studies at the University of Toledo. He is the past chair of the Conceptual Foundations Network of the National Association for Gifted Children (NAGC) and serves as a Young Scholars Specialist for the Davidson Institute. Dr. Schultz serves as a Board Member for the Roeper Institute as well as a Contributing Editor to *Roeper Review, Gifted Child Today* and the *Journal of Educational Research*.

Paul James (PJ) Sedillo, Ph.D., was recently published in *Gifted Child Today* with his article entitled "Gay Gifted Adolescent Suicide and Suicidal Ideation Literature: Research Barriers and Limitations" and another article in *Teaching for High Potential* about best practices for Gifted GLBTQ students. He is currently President for the NM Association for the Gifted and Chair-Elect for the GLBTQ Network for the National Association of the Gifted (NAGC) and working on the Diversity Special Interest Group designing a Diversity Toolbox.

Robert W. (Bob) Seney, Ed.D., is Professor Emeritus, Mississippi University for Women. In retirement, he continues to be actively involved in gifted education through educational consulting, teacher and parent workshops, and presenting at various conferences. Often called "the Book Guy" because of his interest in and work with gifted readers, his "What's New in Young Adult Literature" presentation has been a regular session in the Middle Grades Network for many years.

LaVonda Senn, Ed.D., has been teaching for 16 years and also possesses a master's degree in gifted education, a master's degree in elementary education, and a master's degree in leadership. She currently holds a doctorate in curriculum and instruction with a specialization in teacher education. Married for 27 years with two adult children, she currently enjoys the rewards of being a "Gigi."

Joanna Simpson, Ed.D., was a public school teacher and gifted facilitator for 8 years before moving into higher education. Now she works with aspiring teachers and current teachers to find ways to serve marginalized students. Her areas of expertise are in gifted education, curriculum, and underserved populations.

Kenneth J. Smith, Ph.D., has completed a book series entitled *Challenging Units for Gifted Learners: Teaching the Way Gifted Students Think*. One of the units in the series—A Freudian Approach for Literary Analysis—won the 2012 Curriculum Design Award from NAGC. His most recent book is entitled *Engaging Gifted Readers and Writers: 35 Ideas for Integrating Common Core Into Your Language Arts Classroom*. He was a keynote speaker at the Mississippi Association for Gifted Children's state conference in 2015 and became the first classroom teacher to join the board of *Gifted Child Today*.

Meg Strnat is the High Ability Coordinator for Hamilton Southeastern Schools in Fishers, IN. She taught fourth-grade high-ability students for 10 years and holds a master's degree in education from Indiana University, a BS in Economics from the University of Dayton, and a MBA from Bellarmine.

Rena F. Subotnik, Ph.D., is Director of the Center for Psychology in Schools and Education at the American Psychological Association. One of the Center's central missions is to generate public awareness, advocacy, clinical applications, and cutting-edge research ideas that enhance the achievement and performance of children and adolescents with gifts and talents in all domains.

Juliana Tay is a doctoral candidate in Gifted, Creative, and Talented Studies at Purdue University. Prior to Purdue, she worked as an art teacher in Singapore for more than 10 years. Her research interests are identification and serving gifted art students, as well as program evaluation. She holds an MS from Purdue University.

Alena R. Treat, Ph.D., serves as Chair of the NAGC Diversity and Equity Committee and had served on the NAGC Gifted GLBT Task Force (a.k.a. Workgroup on Gifted Sexually Diverse Populations) for more than 10 years. Her interests include gifted education equity issues related to race, culture, language, socioeconomic status, ability, and sexual orientation.

Thomas N. Turner, Ed.D., coordinates the doctoral program in the education department at the University of Tennessee and teaches a variety of graduate courses, including courses in creative teaching, drama and storytelling in teaching, social science education, and trends and issues in education. His writing and research have reflected his interest in creative teaching, the use of drama in education, and problem-solving activities with students.

Stacie L. Walker has an M.Ed. in School Counseling from the University of Georgia, Athens, GA. She is a member of the Georgia School Counselors Association.

James T. Webb is a clinical psychologist and founder of SENG (Supporting the Emotional Needs of the Gifted). He is a former member of the NAGC Board of Directors and is currently president of Great Potential Press.

Willard L. White, Ph.D., has an extensive background in education, having served as teacher and administrator in Birmingham, MI, schools before accepting the position of Coordinator of Gifted Education with Palm Beach County, FL, schools. He continues as a teacher trainer at Florida Atlantic University and is the author of *America's First Gifted Program: Hollingworth and the Speyer School Experiment.*

Colleen Willard-Holt, Ph.D., is Dean of the Faculty of Education at Wilfrid Laurier University in Waterloo, Ontario, Canada. She is a former teacher of students with special education needs and also of gifted students, and has a long-term interest in twice-exceptional learners.

Hope (Bess) E. Wilson, Ph.D., is an associate professor of education at the University of North Florida where she teaches graduate and undergraduate courses in assessment and educational psychology. She graduated with a Ph.D. in Gifted Education from the University of Connecticut. She is the coauthor of the book *Letting Go of Perfect: Overcoming Perfectionism in Kids* (Prufrock Press, 2009), and her research has been published in *Gifted Child Quarterly, Journal of Advanced Academics, Journal for the Education of the Gifted*, and *Roeper Review.*

Betty Wood, Ph.D., recently retired after 15 years at the University of Arkansas at Little Rock. She and her husband moved to Indiana, where some of the grandchildren live. She now works as an adjunct for Indiana University–Purdue University Indianapolis and UALR.

Susannah M. Wood, Ph.D., is currently an associate professor at the University of Iowa where she teaches both doctoral students and master's students in the school counseling program. Her research interests encompass preparing school counselors for their practice with a focus on serving the gifted population in collaboration with other educators and professionals.

Frank C. Worrell, Ph.D., is a Professor of School Psychology at the University of California, Berkeley, where he also holds an affiliate appointment in the Personality and Social Psychology program. His areas of expertise include talent development/gifted education, at-risk youth, cultural identities, scale development and validation, teacher effectiveness, and the translation of psychological research findings into practice. A current Member-at-Large of the Board of Directors of the American Psychological Association, Dr. Worrell is a Fellow of the Association for Psychological Science, the American Educational Research Association, and five divisions of the APA, a former Editor of Review of *Educational Research*, and a 2013 recipient of the Distinguished Scholar Award from the National Association for Gifted Children.

Robin Young is currently a fifth-grade teacher in Fishers, IN. She has been a K–5 teacher for 25 years. Besides teaching, one of her passions is working with students as a part of Destination Imagination. She received her BS in Elementary Education from Eastern Kentucky University and an M.Ed. in Mathematics and Science Education from the University of Central Florida.

List of Article
Publication Dates

"A Guide to Teaching the Gifted: What We Need to Know . . . and Why We Need to Know It" originally appeared in the Fall 2010 issue of *Teaching for High Potential*. Copyright 2010 by National Association for Gifted Children.

"Building on the Best of Gifted Education with Programming for Talent Development" originally appeared in the Fall 2012 issue of *Teaching for High Potential*. Copyright 2012 by National Association for Gifted Children.

"Three Reasons to Plan an Advocacy Field Trip" was originally published in the Winter 2015 issue of *Teaching for High Potential*. Copyright 2015 by National Association for Gifted Children.

"Making a Makerspace" was originally published in the Winter 2016 issue of *Teaching for High Potential*. Copyright 2016 by National Association for Gifted Children.

"The Enrichment Seminar: A Middle/Secondary Course for Gifted Learners" originally appeared in the Summer 2014 issue of *Teaching for High Potential*. Copyright 2014 by National Association for Gifted Children.

"Extreme ESP: Meaningful Thematic Activities for High-Ability Middle School Students" originally appeared in the Fall 2011 issue of *Teaching for High Potential*. Copyright 2011 by National Association for Gifted Children.

"Principles and Practices of Socratic Circles in Middle Level Classrooms: A Socratic Conversation" originally appeared in the Fall 2015 issue of

"Teaching Current Events as a Feature of a Differentiated Curriculum" originally appeared in the Spring 2012 issue of *Teaching for High Potential*. Copyright 2012 by National Association for Gifted Children.

"Knowing Is a Process, Not a Product: The Curriculum Connection" originally appeared in the Spring 2008 issue of *Teaching for High Potential*. Copyright 2008 by National Association for Gifted Children.

"Curriculum Compacting: How and Why to Differentiate Beyond Proficiency" originally appeared in the Fall 2008 issue of *Teaching for High Potential*. Copyright 2008 by National Association for Gifted Children.

"Self-Assessment: Are You Including the Best Practices for Teaching Gifted and Advanced Learners" originally appeared in the Spring 2011 issue of *Teaching for High Potential*. Copyright 2011 by National Association for Gifted Children.

"Readers for a Lifetime" originally appeared in the Summer 2015 issue of *Teaching for High Potential*. Copyright 2015 by National Association for Gifted Children.

"Promoting Citizenship Development Through Biographies" originally appeared in the Summer 2015 issue of *Teaching for High Potential*. Copyright 2015 by National Association for Gifted Children.

"Vocabulary Instruction in the Common Core State Standards Era" originally appeared in the Fall 2012 issue of *Teaching for High Potential*. Copyright 2012 by National Association for Gifted Children.

"Exploring Between the Pages" was originally published in the Winter 2015 issue of *Teaching for High Potential*. Copyright 2015 by National Association for Gifted Children.

"Differentiation in the English Literature Classroom through Highly Moral Literature" originally appeared in the Winter 2008 issue of *Teaching for High Potential*. Copyright 2008 by National Association for Gifted Children.

"Seney's Top 10" originally appeared in the Summer 2012 issue of *Teaching for High Potential*. Copyright 2012 by National Association for Gifted Children.

"Thinking Like a Mathematician" originally appeared in the Winter 2009 issue of *Teaching for High Potential*. Copyright 2009 by National Association for Gifted Children.

"Nurturing Mathematical Minds: Differentiation Strategies and Curriculum That Promote Growth" originally appeared in the Summer 2012 issue of *Teaching for High Potential*. Copyright 2012 by National Association for Gifted Children.